The
Village & House
in the
Middle Ages

The
Village & House
in the
Middle Ages

Jean Chapelot Robert Fossier

Translated by Henry Cleere

B. T. Batsford Ltd London

© Jean Chapelot, Robert Fossier 1980, 1985
First published 1980 by Hachette, France
First published in Great Britain by Batsford Ltd, 1985

ISBN 0 7134 3322 1 (cased)

Phototypeset by Tradespools Ltd, Frome, Somerset
and printed in Great Britain
by R.J. Acford Ltd, Chichester, Sussex

for the publishers
B. T. Batsford Ltd., 4 Fitzhardinge Street, London W1H 0AH

Contents

Contents

This book, the result of cooperation between a historian and an archaeologist, was conceived as a collaboration that would be as close as possible; this has sometimes led one or other of the authors to revise his approach so as to respond more effectively to the other's intentions. Against this background, and in accordance with this mode of working, each has taken special responsibility for the preparation of certain sections. Jean Chapelot was responsible for pp 41–71 of Chapter II, the whole of Chapter III, pages 180–246 of Chapter V, the whole of Chapter VI, and the captions to illustrations, which were selected jointly. Robert Fossier was responsible for Chapter I, pages 27–41 of Chapter II, the whole of Chapter IV, and pages 167–8 of Chapter V.

Foreword

In the study of cultures and civilizations, the house appears as an isolated document. Naturally, it provides evidence of the history of technology, of living standards, and of everyday life, but if it survives intact it is rarely typical, nor is it explicit when ruined. Its contribution to research is thus a qualitative one, and it is for want of anything better that what can be learned in this way about the life of a handful of people may sometimes be extended to a whole group. The village, on the other hand, provides quantitative data: it is a document of social history since its site, its structure and its activity provide a global picture of such a group – the powerful and the humble, the dead and the living. It provides the pre-eminent evidence of an entire material culture. If, in addition, as in the civilization of medieval western Europe, rural life absorbs the essence of human activity, and if the overall framework of life is based on the rural landscape, then the study of peasant houses and villages must logically dominate the study of the period in that region of the world. The fact that this is far from the situation at the present time demands an explanation.

The fault does not lie with the documentation. It will be seen later on that, whether written or not, what is available is of great value in those fields considered to be the best known – working the soil, for example, or the 'art' of war. It is no less obscure so far as the traditional antitheses are concerned – between landscapes based on large villages and the *bocages* of small fields and woodlands, or between Roman and Germanic countries – they provide information that may influence explanations but not mutilate them. Better still, these original sources necessitate research into constant factors that appear initially to be hidden. On the other hand, two obstacles have discouraged researchers, and this book will have achieved its objective if it succeeds in overcoming these. In countries with an ancient agrarian civilization, such as in western Europe, the concept of the stability of the rural world, of the 'immutable order of the fields', of the weight of peasant tradition, is firmly established. When he leaves the tumult of the towns, where his attention is drawn by a thousand different activities, all of them striking and original, the often hard-pressed historian looks forward to finding, in the silent tilling of the fields, evidence for the suspension of time, even though in the present age land distribution, men, and landscape are manifestly vibrant with an intense dynamism. As a consequence, his attention quickly tires of scanning this slow, ill-defined, and multi-faceted world, which he is unable to clothe with life, and changes in which may seem to him to come about almost in geological time.

The other obstacle is probably more methodological than intellectual and, as a result, it can be observed to weaken as time passes. Countryside, villages and houses remained, until beyond the 1950s, the closely related but not interacting fields of study for archaeologists and social historians. Archaeologists, being more concerned with analysis and synthesis, observed, described and compared: their objective was typology and their raw materials were concrete evidence. Historians sought to attain general explanations by means of the examination and interpretation of written sources. The difficulties cannot be concealed, since they arise from the meanings of words. The 'village' is for the historian a socio-economic structure, whereas for archaeologists 'villages' constitute a category of settlement and a material reality. Similarly, ancient civilizations seem, until recently, to have been capable merely of allowing one group to offer observations and suggestions to the other. The impetus of medieval archaeology and the vigorous progress of historical studies in the last few decades, however, particularly in the field of material culture, lead one to hope that enormous benefit will result, here again, from the coming together of two methodological approaches. However, this will not happen until a minimum of definitions have been established.

The history of the village and of the family underlies the whole of western history. For a century or more, the majority of the population in France and elsewhere has, of course, lived in towns. But it was only a few generations ago that most people were born and raised in a village community, and so we are still familiar with this setting. Moreover, how many urban families still have at least one grandparent living in the country? How many others still have country connections, which result in visits and holidays there? In addition, rises in living standards over the past decade or two, combined with the deterioration of living conditions in towns, have resulted in an increase in the number of second homes. Reversing the age-old process of migration from the countryside, this return of town dwellers to the countryside, although admittedly sporadic and superficial, and sometimes even destructive of ancient ways of life or the natural environment, has had the effect of reviving hamlets and villages which would otherwise be condemned to extinction following a long, slow decline. Even more recently the village has come to represent an ideal way of life: increasing density of habitation and changes in living conditions in towns have led dwellers in the big cities to interest themselves in and aspire towards an alternative form of environment. Elsewhere great efforts have been made to preserve what remains of a certain way of life. In both cases an 'archaizing' image has been created, that of the 'village'.

It is, however, desirable to analyse this ideal concept of the 'village'. This study is all the more necessary in that living in villages does not occur in all societies. Even in western Europe, and especially in France, it can be asserted that this is a relatively recent phenomenon in historical terms – one which first appeared in the earlier Middle Ages and became stabilized in the tenth to twelfth centuries. As a basic component of life over a millennium, it is important, for the foregoing reasons, that the genesis, the antecedents, and the history of the village should be studied. Although the great prosperity of peasant society dates from a period at least three centuries after the end of the Middle Ages, it is to the Middle Ages that it owes its origins, and for this reason it represents an essential stage in the history of western Europe.

A survey among modern town dwellers would depict the village in an idealized form, as a clearly defined section of cultivated countryside inhabited by an essentially peasant population. The better informed or the older town dwellers will certainly point to the presence of a substantial group of craftsmen – smiths, joiners, carpenters, wheelwrights – and to a cluster of dwellings that, properly speaking, make up the 'village'. A larger proportion will doubtless describe houses built in stone and will cite, alongside wooden furniture, a vast fireplace in one wall. Others will point out that the castle or the manor houses were, until the nineteenth century, an invariable element of the village landscape, as so many French place names testify. In sum, a picture emerges of a built and organized ensemble, occupying the centre of a countryside that has been managed for a long period, which is dominated by a network of roads and tracks of varying degrees of importance, and which on occasion includes a market or a fair, and always a village festival.

It is easy to demonstrate that this picture in no way corresponds with the reality of the Middle Ages. It was undeniably the Middle Ages which cleared the landscape and which gave it boundaries and, up to a point, its skeleton of roads. But these early beginnings, this distribution of land, this end-product, are themselves late phenomena, dating from the tenth to twelfth centuries in the majority of cases. What, then, appear to be the most characteristic elements? The church – but was it not that rural agglomerations were not provided with a church until that time? The castle or the manor house: these were not common, with certain rare and early exceptions, before the eleventh century. Building materials, especially stone: until the end of the twelfth century, or even the thirteenth century, rural houses were built in most parts of Europe only in wood and unfired clay, with vegetable materials for roofing. Stone appeared widely only later, and even then it was sometimes not used, in a number of regions of France and England, until very recently. It would be easy to multiply such contrasts and criticisms. Everything contributes to the support of our original assertion: the village as we see it today and as we conceptualize it is a recent creation, closely associated with the flowering in the eighteenth and nineteenth centuries of a village society that had only crystallized out five or six centuries earlier. This ultimate settlement form was born out of structures and modes of population whose foundations lie in the Middle Ages. The object of this book is to demonstrate this thesis.

The skeletons of Roman towns and roads, and the numerous coin hoards or amphora debris give succour to the tenacious picture of an ancient economy that was both urban and monetary. However, at any rate in the western world, there was also a fundamental and numerically preponderant peasantry – the Bretons, the Gauls, the Iberians, and many Italian peoples – who provided the life blood of the Empire. And we should not forget the Germans prowling the regions beyond the Rhine and the Danube. This becomes apparent when the urban façade of Rome breaks down. As in so many other fields, the concept of the 'clean break' resulting from the invasions of the fifth century must here again be rejected. No one believes any longer in the picture of an ethnic flood, even one that was slow and insidious; the interpenetration of cultures, and in this instance of peasant cultures, is now preferred. It is therefore proper to examine the problem from its origins – i.e. from the end of the third century. From this point onwards, for 500 or 600 years, the western world was shaken by multiple shocks, from which only the seventh century seems to have been spared. This period certainly has its own unity which will need to be explored in this study. Like the archaeologist, but perhaps more decisively, the historian identifies a profound break between 900 and 950: at this time all the outlines of the ancient world finally disappeared. The historian will therefore consider this transition alone before regaining a measure of agreement with the results of excavation in the twelfth to fifteenth centuries, and even beyond. Such disagreements are more reassuring than otherwise, since they are evidence of the need for joint research.

Whilst the village is the basic component of French society in the Middle Ages, the same is true of a large part of Europe. For that reason at least, it would be absurd to restrict ourselves to France alone. We shall therefore extend our study to other European countries, the more so because a measure of backwardness in French research at the present time makes us dependent on archaeological work that has been carried out in Great Britain, the Netherlands, Germany and elsewhere. Far from being a tiresome constraint, this represents a desirable and fundamental amplification. So vast a problem, and one of such importance for the history of France, can only be appreciated over a long time-scale of some thousand years – the Middle Ages – and on a very broad geographical canvas – the whole of western Europe.

Glossary

This glossary does not cover terms which are dealt with adequately when first referred to in the text. Words in italic refer to other glossary entries. D = Dutch, F = French, G = German, I = Italian, L = Latin.

Ager (L)   Open arable field (Roman period)

Amphora   Large two-handled storage jar, with narrow mouth, used for oil, wine, etc. (Roman period)

Assarting   Clearance of woodland for agriculture, especially arable farming

Aula (L)   Reception hall, used for dispensing justice, in palace or public building

Bailey   Defended area lying outside *motte*, enclosing domestic buildings and stores

Bay   Constructional element in timber-framed building, consisting of a 'box' defined by four load-bearing *corner posts*, two *wall plates*, and two *trusses*. Houses were usually built in two or three bays, occasionally more

Black house   House in the Hebrides and western Scottish Highlands with low stone or turf walls and thatched roofs, sheltering human beings and livestock under the same roof

Bocage (F)   Landscape of small cultivated fields enclosed by boundaries of thick hedges or trees, often raised on banks, and interspersed with small patches of woodland

Bovate   Medieval land-holding unit, defined as the amount of land that could be ploughed with a single ox in a year: varies between 7 and 16 ha (17–40 acres)

Cadastration   Public registration of the quantity, value, and ownership of land (France)

Calvary   Crucifix in the open air, usually on raised ground

Cashel   Small circular enclosure with stone defensive works (first millennium AD, Ireland) – see also *rath*

Celtic fields   Small squarish blocks of arable land *c*.0.2 ha in area, defined by *lynchets* on their upper and lower edges and by low ridges on the remaining sites (largely Late Bronze Age, Iron Age, and Roman); found in Britain, Scandinavia, and the Netherlands

Centuriation   Regular land division around a Roman *colonia* by roads and other boundaries into blocks 710 m (776 yd) square – see *limitatio*

Civitas (L)   Roman provincial administrative unit, initially under the control of native ruler

Cob   Clay mixed with vegetable matter (straw, dung, etc.) used for wall construction – see pp. 255–7

Collar   Horizontal timber used in roof construction to tie a pair of *principal rafters* below the apex (usually about one-third of the overall length of the rafter) or a pair of *crucks*

Colonia (L)   Town in Roman province, founded to settle retired legionaries, who were granted land and civic rights in return for military service in times of emergency

Common rafters   Closely spaced rafters of equal size resting on *purlins* to support roof covering

Corner posts   Main load-bearing upright timbers at each corner of a box-frame building or of a *bay*

Croft   Small piece of enclosed arable land attached to a house and *toft*

Crown post   Vertical timber in roof structure linking the *collar* with the centre of the *tie beam* – see Fig. 107c for an example

Cruck   Pair of curved timbers serving as principals in roof structure, set in or on the ground (base crucks) or in the walls (raised crucks) and joined at their apex – see Fig. 103

Demesne   Seigneurial land belonging to an overlord and distributed around his residence

Drystone   Method of wall construction using selected stones laid on top of one another without any form of bonding (mortar, clay, etc.)

False tie beam   Horizontal structural timber joining a pair of *wall posts* below the level of the *wall plates* – see Fig. 106c

Fanum (L)   Shrine or oratory, often set in fields

Ferté (F)   A stronghold, later extended to cover the lands directly attributed to that stronghold (cp *demesne*)

Gabled roof   Roof structure in which the *ridge beam* or *purlin* extends the whole length of the building, giving a vertical triangular end wall section from eaves to apex

Ganghaus (G)   See *passage house*

Genecium, gynaecea (L)   Building reserved for women's occupations (spinning, weaving)

Headland   The area between the furrows of *open fields* where strips and *ridge and furrow* ended, used to allow ploughs and plough teams to turn and to provide access to strips

Hipped roof   Roof with projecting inclined edge at each end, extending from the ridge to the eaves: this means that the *ridge beam* is shorter than the overall length of the building – see Fig. 99

Hospitalitas (L)   An obligation to provide food and lodging for travellers

Imbrex (L)   Half-cylindrical hollow tile used on roofs of Roman buildings, covering the raised flanges on contiguous *tegulae*

Incastellamento (I)   The fortification of a settlement with a defensive wall and, usually, a castle or fortress

Infield   Intensively cultivated and manured permanent arable land, associated with larger, intermittently cropped areas (*outfield*) in the infield-outfield system

King post   Vertical timber in roof structure linking the *ridge beam* with the centre of the *tie beam* – see Fig. 107a, e, f for examples

Glossary

Laeti (L) Barbarian groups settled in Roman frontier districts with obligation of military service in the Roman army

Latifundia (L) Vast estates in late Roman Italy and Gaul, based primarily on stock raising

Limes (L) The frontier zone of the Roman Empire

Limitatio (L) See *centuriation*

Loess (G) Wind-borne rock dust laid down as a thick stratum in regions adjoining ice sheets, providing a fertile, easily worked soil

Loomweights Clay or stone weights used to tension the warp threads in vertical looms

Lynchet Low banks marking the boundaries of ancient fields on sloping ground, formed by soil movement downhill as a result of repeated ploughing

Métayage (F) System of payment of rent in kind, the landowner supplying tenants with seed and receiving a proportion of the crop (= share cropping)

Montagne (F) Primary uncleared woodland

Motte Flat-topped conical earth mound surrounded by a ditch, supporting a wooden watch-tower or, later, a stone keep, associated with a palisaded enclosure or *bailey*

Mould board Curved piece of wood fixed behind the share of a plough which turns over the sod lifted by the share

Open fields Large areas of arable land without hedges or ditches, divided into strips (lands) in individual ownership or tenancy

Oppidum (L) Large Late Iron-Age hillfort settled permanently with a considerable degree of internal organization, representing a form of proto-town

Padstone Flat stone lying on or embedded in the ground surface which serves as the base for an upright timber element in a building

Palatium (L) A royal, ducal, or episcopal residence

Passage house House layout permitting internal access from one range of rooms to another (*Ganghaus*)

Polder Area of low-lying land reclaimed from the sea and enclosed by dykes

Polyptych (Fr. polyptyque) Originally a writing table composed of a number of leaves; later a register of the holdings, goods, tenants, debtors etc. of a religious establishment (diocese, abbey etc.)

Principal rafters Main load-bearing timbers at the ends of *bays*, rising from *tie beams* to *ridge beams* or *king posts*

Purlins Horizontal timbers in roof structures running the length of the roof, resting on the *principal rafters* and supporting the *common rafters*

Quern Apparatus for grinding corn: a saddle quern consists of a dished stone base with a separate stone rubber; a rotary quern has a fixed round base and an upper stone on a shaft which can be rotated by hand

Rath Small circular enclosure with earthen ramparts (first millennium AD, Ireland) – see also *cashel*

Ridge and furrow Name given to earthworks resulting from the *open field* system. Strips were usually ploughed clockwise, causing them to be ridged up in the centre, leaving flat sides sloping down from ridge to furrow. The resulting regular pattern is very common in the midland counties of England

Ridge beam Horizontal timber running the length of the apex of a roof and supported at each end by a *wall post*

Ridge purlin Horizontal timber running the length of the apex of a roof which connects rafters but does not support them

Saltus (L) Primary woodland used for grazing livestock (Roman period)

Scissors posts Pairs of obliquely mounted posts meeting at the apex of a building and crossing so as to receive a *ridge beam* (German Pfostenscheren) – see p. 289

Sill beam Horizontal wooden beam used as the foundation for a wall, set either directly on the ground surface or in a shallow trench (syn. sleeper beam)

Souterrain (F) Man-made underground chamber, used for residence, storage, or refuge

Stabbau (G) Form of building construction using vertical plank walling – see pp. 261–73

Ständerbau (G) Form of building construction utilizing *sill beams* as wall bases

Tegula (L) Flat roof tile with raised flanges on sides used in Roman buildings – see also *imbrex*

Terpen (D) Artificial mounds in the low-lying northern coastal plains of Holland and Germany, built to elevate settlements above flooding levels (German *Wurten*)

Terra sigillata (L) Fine table ware in red fabric with self slip: plain forms were wheel-made and relief-decorated forms were made in stamped moulds. First made in Italy in the first century BC (Arretine ware), then successively in southern, central, and eastern Gaul (Samian ware): production ceased in the late third century AD

Terrier Register of landed property, including lists of vassals and tenants, with details of their holdings, services, and rents

Thatch Roof covering of vegetable material, usually corn straw or reeds

Tie beam Horizontal structural timber joining a pair of *wall plates* or *crucks*

Tithe barn Barn used for storing agricultural produce (corn, hay, fruit, etc.) paid over in support of a parish priest or religious establishment (tithes)

Toft A house plot

Transhumance Form of agrarian economy involving seasonal displacement of livestock to regions of differing climate or vegetation

Truss Rigid vertical triangular element of roof structure, composed of a pair of *rafters* connected by a *tie beam* – see pp. 308–10

Vallus (L) A mechanical harvesting machine of the Roman period

Vicus (L) A small Roman settlement, either isolated or associated with a military establishment

Wattle and daub Method of wall filling consisting of vertical thin wooden stakes, interlaced with twigs or withies in a basket-weave pattern and coated on both sides with clay or *cob*

Wall plate Longitudinal horizontal timber joining *wall posts* or *corner posts* at their summits

Wall posts Upright timbers forming a framework of walls. They are joined at their summits by *wall plates* and may rest on *sill beams*

Wurten (G) See *terpen*

Chapter One: The dominant factors of the early Middle Ages

The researcher into the obscurity of the early Middle Ages runs one primary risk from the start: that of taking the exceptional for the normal, of applying over an entire region information about a princely economy that has survived by chance, or of generalizing the data deriving from a single excavation in respect of an entire period. This danger becomes greater when these contrasts lead him on to study on a broad canvas the similarities that exist in a western Europe already given over almost entirely to the circumscribed way of life of small groups of people. Unfortunately, the light thrown on the subject by written records is very faint. Does it not therefore appear an unattainable, even ridiculous, aim, to isolate the dominant aspects of the settlement of the land over a period of seven centuries? An attempt to define the fundamentals is nonetheless necessary.

I AN INADEQUATE DEMOGRAPHIC AND TECHNOLOGICAL LEVEL

A small population

Without any doubt, populations were small almost everywhere. There is certainly no reliable quantitative evidence available before the time of Charlemagne, when the rolls of Bavarian donations and the polyptychs of northern and eastern Gaul, those inventories of goods and rents of the opening years of the ninth century, reveal a miserable society which at best subsisted at a density of two to five inhabitants per square kilometre in Germany and England and at perhaps twice that in France. It is not difficult, however, to bring together documentary references and the evidence from cemeteries. The ravages of epidemics, helped by malnutrition, promiscuity, and lack of hygiene – which it will be seen later were encouraged immeasurably by living conditions – carried off people in their thousands. Although plagues, the shattering ravages of which in the seventh and eighth centuries have recently been studied by Le Goff and Biraben, affected the towns more savagely, the lack of adequate food everywhere deprived men and women of any serious resistance to the recurring famines which the economic anarchy of the period often caused. Michel Rouche has recently given the lie, even for the richest members of society, to the high levels of food and the richness in terms of calories apparently indicated by written sources: a surfeit of starchy foods and alcoholic drinks, swollen bellies, bad digestions, chronic vitamin deficiency, and – he dared to assert – a society that suffered continual discomfort, extending from those with empty bellies, incapable of effort, to obese hypochondriacs, given over to violence and injustice. In this respect, the proportion of young children buried in the tenth-century Hungarian cemeteries, and the decalcification of adult skeletons in graveyards in Normandy (Hérouvillette) or Lorraine (Pompey and Villey-Saint-Etienne) amply prove human vulnerability. Hagiographic texts bristle with evidence of the emptiness of the countryside – the moors and forests that St Colomban passed over without finding any souls to save, countrymen who travelled for two whole days to hear St Malo preach, or isolated villages that it took St Riquier several hours of walking to reach.

Some measure of gradation is, of course, necessary. It is becoming increasingly clear that, between the population decline of the third century, which facilitated or even provoked the earliest Germanic penetration into the weakened Mediterranean region, and the stagnation into mediocrity of Carolingian Europe, there was – on the Germanic and Celtic fringes of the continent at least – a vigorous population growth, perhaps between 650 and 750, which favoured the pluvial regions of Europe and heralded the permanent decline of the societies of the south. The proliferation of place names from this period, whether new creations or renamings, is evidence for the historian of a strong movement to occupy settled places. We shall return in due course to the fact that these places, whose names have elements such as *curtis* (large-scale exploitation: -*court*), *villare* (small-scale exploitation: -*villers*, -*willer*), *mansionile* (dividing up of a *curtis*: -*mesnil*) or endings in -*dorf* or -*rod*, may equally well date from the sixth or the tenth centuries, need be no more than hamlets rather than villages, and may provide evidence of warrior activity rather than economic exploitation, all of which are relevant questions. However, it is the overall volume of these place names which is striking, rather than any consideration of them in detail. If one considers the subsequent extent of agricultural development in northern Gaul, or the role of the military and landed aristocracy which drew both profit and power from it, the question will not appear to be a negligible one.

Communal settlement

So far as the present discussion is concerned, size of population is of less importance than what follows: the degree of fusion between ethnic groups that were slowly pushed together throughout this phase of European history. Whether it is a matter of infiltration by small groups into a majority indigenous population (central Gaul, Spain, central Italy in the sixth century), of a more vigorous incursion which significantly modifies the structure of society (northern Gaul in the fifth century, sixth-century Lombardy), or of a true process of eviction and replacement (some parts of the British Isles in the fifth and sixth centuries), the noteworthy feature of this 'Germanic' phase is the overwhelming pressure of the intrusive group, even when it was in a minority. This is not to be observed again – at least, not so clearly – until the 'Scandinavian' or Moslem expansion of the ninth and tenth centuries. It becomes necessary, therefore, to assess the effects of a juxtaposition, whether peaceful or otherwise, of groups which at the outset differ by virtue of their economic practices rather than their level of 'civilization', or, perhaps, their technology and forms of expression: camps of *laeti* (auxiliary troops) and barbarian soldiers; warrior groups settled on expropriated land in the middle of ancient *villa* estates; foreign peasants installed on the common lands of an estate or, at a later period, groups of Danish pirates converted into peaceful farmers; Gaulish emigrants returning to Armorica, or monastic colonists sent out into the forests of Germany. All we know about this phenomenon – which is slight, since it is based on legal prescriptions and therefore theoretical in nature – is the rule of *hospitalitas* (an obligation to provide lodging) that was imposed in the west after 418 on major landowners, who were thereby compelled to cede a portion of their goods to the Germans. For the Burgundians and the Visigoths, this amounted to two-thirds of their lands, one-third of their slaves, and half their forests, but it was less for the Ostrogoths in Italy. Many questions are raised by these texts. Do they refer to land that was being cultivated or that which had already been abandoned, to physical occupation or merely division of revenues, apportioning of the whole estate or only that part which had lately been leased to 'Roman' colonists? A leader would often speak on behalf of the entire group, or perhaps the whole clan, and Sidonius Apollinarius, the Bishop of Clermont, who had to suffer the Burgundians, has described them for us, invading the kitchen from daybreak and stinking of butter and onions. Was it at this moment or later that these people who had come from elsewhere began to mingle with the village and its inhabitants? Were their fields far removed from those of the 'Romans'? Did they settle new sites or did they build their shanties on the outskirts of ancient settlements to which they had been refused entry? Did the original inhabitants abandon ruins to them which they renamed, and resettle themselves elsewhere? These are basic but almost unanswerable questions. Documentary sources seem to imply an enduring partition, particularly in Italy, Spain, and perhaps in Britain as well, but rather for religious reasons. Further north, the partition was less apparent, and had almost disappeared after a few generations. Even in the latter case, are we to understand that the two groups lived side by side in two more or less contiguous settlements? Skeletons quickly mingled with one another in the cemeteries: in towns, such as Trier or Lyons, but for the most part in the countryside – in the north at Hérouvillette (Calvados) and in the south at Pélissane (Bouches-du-Rhône) – the dead could only be distinguished from one another by the opulence of the goods that accompanied them into the other world. In those places where, from the sixth century onwards, one group remained separate, isolated from the rest of the dead, one has the feeling that this was exceptional, indicating an ethnic group that was very alien to those who mingled in the settlement of the living. The problems become almost insoluble when the inevitable inter-racial breeding make it impossible any longer to read the messages conveyed by the bones. This is perhaps the only solution to the puzzles posed for archaeologists and historians by uncompleted and disturbing excavations such as those at Brébières, near Douai, where it was the masters, the Franks, who squatted in the depths of their narrow shacks whilst the Gallo-Romans took their ease in the nearby ruins of the large *villa* – almost a palace – of Vitry-en-Artois. It is easy to imagine that the difficulties arising from this communal settlement were not confined to the hamlet or the cemetery, and that it will be necessary to analyse the structure of the countryside settlement soon in order to obtain a more complete picture.

One final comment is necessary: the composition of families, so far as it can be delineated in the semi-obscurity of the Carolingian period, gives a feeling of groups that are strongly coherent but also very densely distributed. Figures of 25 to 40 adults per square kilometre can be put forward with some degree of certainty, 32 or 34 around St Bertin, and the same figure for the Ile-de-France on the estates of St Germain-des-Prés. In consequence, it is only possible to reconcile this impression of human pressure and that of the emptiness of the countryside with the hypothesis of settlement in 'patches', with woods and scrublands left between them. The economies of such groupings would therefore not have been able to rise above the level of subsistence production, and the effects are very evident in the pattern of settlement: poor hamlets scattered around a defensive nucleus.

A scarcity of iron

This rural poverty, which the brilliance of the urban façades or the opulence of some abbatial villa often disguise, also doubtless results from a chronic shortage of material equipment. Without going into the general problems of the agrarian economy of this period, it is necessary to identify those aspects which serve to illustrate this assertion. It goes without saying that the quality and performance of agricultural implements come to mind first. We are unhappily all too aware of the inaccuracy of the terminology used by a pedantic scribe, for whom 'plough' is rendered in Latin as *aratrum*, and everything else follows on accordingly – nothing more specific in relation to the method of harnessing or the ploughs pulled by eight or less oxen that Deléage observed from Kent to Burgundy. What can be said about yields, which provide incontrovertible evidence of peasant skill? So far as sowing and manuring are concerned, the sparse details provided by written sources, such as the specimen inventory known as the *Brevium exempla* which relates to Annappes and its environs, near Lille, are a source of consternation and scepticism, since they lead to crop levels that are barely adequate for seed corn for the following year, the wages of the threshers, and the master's table. How can we know whether this is attributable to an exceptional case or to a scribal error?

It would thus be wiser to confine oneself to the hard facts of archaeology. Long ago the *vallus*, the harvesting machine described by Palladius and depicted on the bas-reliefs of Buzénol-Montauban, Arlon, and the Rheims gate, excited the imagination of economic historians: sadly, we have sought material remains of it in vain. Will other implements be found? Around 850 at Corbie, Abbot Adalard recommended that *ferralia* (iron objects) should be counted and recounted after use, an indication of their rarity. Moreover, the inventory at Annappes, although rural in origin, after enumerating a very small quantity of hafted blades for a 5000ha estate, concluded that everything else was made of wood and left it at that, which obviously restricts hopes of their being recovered. This pessimism is further confirmed by grave goods: a rich harvest of weapons and even, at Hérouvillette, blacksmith's tools, but hardly any ploughshares, sickles, or horseshoes. This obvious scarcity of metal tends to lend support to all the literature, which ranks the man who works iron with fire as a sorcerer.

It therefore becomes difficult to believe in any substantial measure of progress, whether Germanic or not in origin, which introduced a perfected ploughing implement around this time into northern Gaul and the Rhine valley, as an entrenched Franco-German historiographic tradition would have us believe. Pliny had undeniably already written of four- or six-oxen teams in Rhaetia or among the Belgae which drew an implement that was not a swing plough (see Figure 1). Much later, an edict of Rothari in 643 in Lombardy used the term *plum* to describe it, which may reflect the Germanic and Saxon *Pflug* or *plough*. In fact, however, this terminological problem can totally mask technological realities. At the least it suggests, for lack of material evidence, that in northern Europe there was long-lasting competition between two equally inefficient implements because neither could replace the other. In fact, the fossil 'Merovingian fields' studied in the Netherlands demonstrate furrow cultivation: one group from the third century at Camperdium incontrovertibly resulted from the use of a swing plough, whilst on the others at Haamstede, Santpoort, and elsewhere in the second and seventh centuries, the occasional use of a mould-board plough may be conceded. One final counter-argument: in those regions where the spread of countryside under cultivation was widest from 1100 onwards, such as the Auvergne or Picardy, for example, this was at the expense of heavy clay sites, of high pedological value, but which had been neglected up to that time because of the heavy work involved when using the primitive light implements of the early Middle Ages. Counter examples that may be cited, as in the case of Franconia, where the heavy soils were almost the first to be settled from the ninth century onwards, probably relate to the cleared fringes which enclosed the Carolingian world (cf. Figure 12).

Fig. 1. *Cultivation with the swing plough at the beginning of the ninth century*

This pen drawing, made between 817 and 834 at the monastery of Hautvillers (Marne), shows one of the three classic types of swing plough, the stilt sole type, where the stilt and sole are made from a single piece of wood. The beam on the right passes through the stilt-sole and is fixed to a horn yoke. In addition to its realism, this drawing is of interest in that it establishes the use of these types of harnessing and ploughing implement which, by the seventeenth century and doubtless before that date, had disappeared from this region and had become confined to southern France.

(*Utrecht Psalter*, University Library, Utrecht; MS. 32, folio 62 verso)

Low-grade and ill-bred livestock

What we know about livestock increases the notion of poverty (see Figure 2). The number of animals sometimes seems high at first glance. At Annappes, for example, 100 horses were recorded, along with an equal number of cattle and 300 sheep, whilst at Saint-Julien de Brioude, Saint-Rémy de Reims and Stafelsee, several thousand animals were recorded in the mid ninth century. Barbarian legislation in the sixth and seventh centuries (Burgundian, Ripuarian Frankish and Alemannic laws), the ninth-century Royal Capitulary known as *de villis*, and the statutes promulgated by Adalard at Corbie, as well as the lives of the saints, teem with references to horses and their rearing. But this

Fig. 2. *Stock-raising as evidenced by osteological data*

Excavation of rural sites often produces very large quantities of animal bones: at the Frisian site of Feddersen Wierde, occupied from the first century BC to the fifth century AD, 42,754 animal bones were recorded, admittedly from an exceptionally large excavation.

Excavation of the Anglo-Saxon site of Maxey (Northamptonshire), occupied from 650 to 850, made it possible to assess the relative significance of various animal species on the basis of the number of bones of each species and the likely weight of meat that each species would yield:

	No. of bones (as %)	Weight of edible meat (as %)
Cattle	36.5	58
Goat/sheep	36	11
Pig	11.1	5
Horse	7.9	21
Bird (incl. domestic poultry)	8.5	0.05

Estimates of this kind are always relatively imprecise, largely because of our ignorance of feeding habits (cuts that were eaten), butchery techniques (which can nevertheless be derived from the study of the condition of the bones) and, above all, the meat yield of animal species. Moreover, attention should be paid to the fact that all the animal bones may not always be related to human food – horses, for example.

Study of the ages of animals at slaughter is an important factor in obtaining basic data on stock raising, such as the possibilities of storing fodder. Whether good or bad, they lead in due course, in the latter case, to large-scale slaughter at the start of winter, with direct significant consequences in relation to the buildings needed or useless for the storage of food reserves and for sheltering livestock during the period of winter stalling or, on the other hand, for preserving the resulting food.

At Feddersen Wierde, determination of the age at slaughter of cattle and horses was, for the reasons mentioned above, of special interest (figures are percentages of cattle):

0–3 months	4–6 months	6–12 months	Total less than 12 months	12–24 months	24–36 months	More than 36 months	Total over 12 months
13.3	3.7	3.0	20	6.1	12.6	61.3	80

These data do not correspond with natural mortality rates. The high proportion of young animals (less than one or two years) in particular indicates a heavy consumption of meat from young cattle, which is understandable in the light of the large number of heads of livestock sheltered on the farms of this site (cf. Figure 30). The very large proportion of animals of over 36 months poses a very interesting question; at the present time, after fattening the average age of slaughter is five years. If fattening was not practised and if a number of animals exceeded a certain age, around eight years, it is possible to conclude that the meat produced in this way was certainly inferior and that these cattle in fact played an essential role more in the production of milk and its derivatives than as sources of meat, which would have been exported from the settlement itself.

The age at slaughter of horses at Feddersen Wierde also supplies important data on the place of this animal in this settlement (figures are percentages):

Less than 9 months	9–12 months	12–24 months	24–36 months	36–48 months	About 48 months	More than 48 months
28.15	12.4	7.4	1.7	1.7	5.8	43

It will be seen that around 40 per cent of the horses were slaughtered at less than 12 months and nearly half by 36 months. At Maxey only 11 per cent of the horses were slaughtered before 30 months. It is possible to conclude, therefore, that at Feddersen Wierde the consumption of horse meat, known among Germanic peoples from contemporary documents, was certainly practised. However, it is clear that a considerable number of horses were also used for agricultural work, since nearly half exceeded the age of 36 months.

(From P. V. Addyman, A Dark Age Settlement at Maxey, Northants, *Medieval Archaeology*, 8 (1964), 20–73, and H. Jankuhn, *Archäologie und Geschichte I: Beitrage zu Siedlungsarchäologischen Forschung*, 1976).

abundance is deceptive: it seems to play no role in improving food supply nor in development of the use of animal power. One need only offer in support of this view the chronic deficiency in animal proteins, meat and dairy products in the diets quoted above, or the deficiency in calcium salts shown by bones from cemeteries. And what can be said of the regular practice of harnessing four, six, or even eight oxen to draw a length of timber through the soil? Here again, the abundance of theoretical forces and the low quality of the results achieved can be attributed to a complete lack of zoological experimentation: the reproduction of species seems to have been inconsistent, the optimum sex ratios disregarded, and the numbers of juveniles in relation to adult animals left to the hazards of parasitic diseases. Animal bones were of wild species, whilst the ratio between domestic species confirm this anarchic situation: up to the tenth century, 11–20 per cent of the bones were of wild species, whilst the ration between domestic species varied completely at random – from 500 to 900 the proportion of pigs varied between 10 per cent and 32 per cent and that of sheep between 16 per cent and 24 per cent.

Man is surrounded by animals. He must provide a shelter for them – an enclosure, as at West Stow (Suffolk), or part of the house itself, as in the 'mixed houses' combining human habitation and animal accommodation on the continent – and some space for them to graze on, but he seems to have been incapable of recovering from them as a rule anything more than a little bacon, some leather, a few tufts of wool and some thin milk.

All these observations, drawn from sources that are diverse yet in agreement, have already sketched in a preliminary outline of human settlement – a light and uneven distribution, dense in places and non-existent elsewhere, perhaps still not properly anchored and liable to be displaced to suit the needs of extensive agriculture, still in part itinerant, and voracious of land which becomes exhausted because it is not properly mastered. Thus, very varied types of settlement may be expected, from the seasonal hamlet built in light materials which is occupied for fishing or when livestock move into the woodland edges, through the temporary village that is abandoned after a few years, to the permanent centre established round the house of a holy man or a lay overlord. Enormous deserted areas would surround or, better perhaps, isolate these inhabited points and cultivation would move around with the animals. Moreover, it is possible that it had long been the practice when a move was made to redistribute the holdings of each member of the clan, a flexible community system which astonished Tacitus among the first-century Germans, accustomed as he was to the system around the Mediterranean of individual land-holding that was long-established, or at any rate definitive, in those poor and exhausted soils.

The need to produce food was probably the major constraint on specialization. The only manifestation of an organized settlement was probably the dwelling of the lord, with its workshop for metals – in short, the dominant exploitation of the cultural clearing, the ancient rich man's *villa*, the monastic house, the palace (cf. Figure 41). Even there one should not deceive oneself over the level that was reached when one contemplates the abbots, the emperors, the princes or the counts moving about ceaselessly from one of these granaries to another, and emptying them at a single stroke with their clans and the noisy, hungry crowds who followed them.

II A SHRUNKEN AND DEFENSIVE SOCIETY

Broad groupings

A broadly-based type of social structure is apparent in various ways – the family, tribe, community. This extended sense of community, whether the cause or the result of economic anaemia, has a profound effect on settlement and landscape. Furthermore, the gradations that may result from variations in the quality of building materials or relative skills in tilling the soil will produce further distinctions. Roman law or 'barbarian' codes each in their own way reflect the same image of the 'group'.

The striking example of place names, with the large number of new creations in the sixth and seventh centuries, has already been shown to be a significant indication of this process. Gallo-Roman or Germanic collective suffixes abound, linked with the name of the head of a group or some tribal totem, as we have seen. However, place-name formations which might provide more evidence of a truly collective settlement – for example, -*dorf* or -*hof* endings from the seventh century – seem not to have existed beyond the Rhine before this relatively late period, as though only imitations of Roman usages were in use. How, then, can we know whether these were in fact new creations, whether a village as such existed from the start, or whether the appellation extended any further than the lord's *sala* (meeting hall and its associated rooms)? It is therefore advisable not to lean too heavily on information from place names.

Another aspect of human groupings is, however, all too often overlooked by scholars and is worthy of study. During the slow Christianization of the Saxon, Gallo-Roman or Germanic countryside, the tide of conversion, which began in the towns and monasteries and was taken up in defended settlements and great estates, spread in concentric circles, often respecting the obstacles constituted by uninhabited regions and following land or water routes taken by soldiers, solitary merchants, or the trains escorting a great man. In addition to the interest for the social historian afforded by this contact between hitherto isolated patches of settlement, it is observable that Christianization frequently took the form of the popularization of local cults, the name of a patron saint being adopted by several villages that were united in a common act of devotion. The study of attributions such as John the Baptist, the protomartyr Stephen, evangelists such as St Martin or even St Peter during the spread of Benedictine monasticism, or the proliferation of names associated with the success of a powerful monastery or an episcopal see reputed to be 'apostolic', would without doubt throw more light on the Christian 'mists' of the countryside of western Europe. The establishment of a religious cult building provides an anchor for the settlement and a fixed point for both living and dead: a baptismal font or an *atrium* (cemetery) would generally win men over. The peasants would then feel obliged to dispose their maze of land holdings around the churches devoted to their patron saints. A study of the framework of settlements linked in this way would doubtless show that they were the earliest to break away from a pattern of itinerant agriculture and a pre-occupation with the present.

In addition to family groups and congregations of believers, there were also economic groups around wells and grain stores. In this respect, the field of study that would be most fruitful would be that of intrusive groups, such as the *laeti* of the later Empire, the Lombard or Frankish *fara* (tribal groups) of later periods, or the subsequent Viking or Saracen encampments. Although there is no doubt as to the military origin of these settlements, the exploitation of surrounding fields, provisioning, or communal settlement pose certain problems – not so much in relation to segregation between living or dead communities, but rather in relation to differing agricultural practices (as perhaps in the Caux region) or levels of technological development. Some multi-nucleated villages may well owe their complex structures to a subsequent fusion of groups that were originally distinct.

An uncertain economy

A society that is contracted into more or less dense groups by a sense of community, derived as much from fear and hunger as from blood relationships, obviously acquires a very hierarchical structure whose topmost element assumes the role of protector in the event of danger. From this it naturally follows that a chief will choose a site that, by virtue of its natural position, is defensible or guards an enforced communication route: if this does not result in the site itself being settled by a human community, it at least favours the creation of permanent settlements nearby. The problem of early medieval fortification is not, properly speaking, within the scope of this study, but its essential role cannot be overlooked.

However, the study of the mechanisms of land exploitation does not lie outside the bounds of the present work. Whether this relates to an ancient structure that was conceived as such from the outset, or the effect of gradual abandonment of an investment enterprise based on slavery, the 'estate' that we hear about from written sources and at various stages of development over the whole of western Europe consists of two elements. The first is parcelled out into holdings of varying sizes, the second being exploited directly by means of domestic manpower and by the services provided by the people settled on the parcels. Such a 'system' implies, in principle, that the parcels must not be situated too distant from the land that has to be worked or, at the least, as in the Germanic *villicatio* (an organizational principle that is loose in terms of space), that the elements scattered over a wide area as a result of sparse population are none the less organized as a coherent group. The structure of the settled landscape is based on this fundamental prerequisite: either all the land belongs to a single man and western Europe is merely a juxtaposition of 'great estates', or there were many small private land holdings, as a result of which the land can only be seen as a confused mosaic. This is a fundamental problem, and we are increasingly moving towards the second explanation, which results in the 'domainal system' being considered as totally inadequate in terms of agrarian profitability. No one believes that the Gallo-Roman or Carolingian *villa* was profitable: based on slavery, it took five centuries to disintegrate by reason of its wastefulness, a fact which effectively demonstrates the economic weakness of the times. We shall have to return to a consideration of the image that it has left on the ground. But this picture of land tenure is of less interest than the fate of the men who inhabited it. Where did these peasants live? Perhaps each on his own plot of land, which would mean that settlement was dispersed. Perhaps in the lord's house, the *villa*, the *casa*, the *curtis*, the palace – but their shacks would then be mixed up with those of the domestic slaves. Perhaps in an independent communal settlement more or less close at hand, leaving the *villa* to relatives and dependants – more likely, but what then would be the role of the church, of the well, or of the smithy? Whatever the circumstances, every Carolingian polyptych reveals the discontinuities in the overall picture – legal ones arising from inequalities in degrees of freedom; economic ones due to the rents or the forced labour that were demanded; moral ones based on origins or prestige. We must therefore expect to encounter wide divergences in buildings, in the use of space, and in material equipment.

If it is borne in mind that the 'anchor points' of a settlement mode that was still impermanent, inconsistent and lacking a secure basis – i.e. the church, the strongpoint, the nearby forest that was an abundant provider, or sources of water or iron – can also contribute an additional element in the differentiation between villages as well as houses, it becomes advisable to picture the countryside of western Europe between the third and eleventh centuries as ill-defined, full of shadows and contrasts – isolated and unorganized islands of cultivation, patches of uncertain authority, scattered family groupings round a patriarch, a chieftain, or a rich man. It is a landscape still in a state of anarchy – in short, the picture of a world that man seemed unable to control or dominate.

Chapter Two: Early medieval landscapes and settlements

I EVOLUTION OF THE SETTLED LANDSCAPE

A Incomplete occupation of the land

1 Saltus *or* ager

A layout of great expanses of unpeopled land alongside dense settlement concentrations gives a preliminary impression of agricultural clearings that were more or less regularly under cultivation – the Roman *ager* (open field) or the infield of later periods, enclosed by a penumbra of wastelands, scrub and brushwood, and the *saltus* (primary woodland) or outfield. In places such as the Auvergne, these terms inherited from antiquity carry an additional psychological meaning: the *saltus* remains the *montagne* – that forested region dominated by wild animals and by fear – whilst the *ager* betokens the low-lying land and safety. Unfortunately there is virtually no way of estimating the relative distribution of the two before the eleventh century. Nor is there any chance of knowing whether the cultivated area expanded or contracted: the uncertainties of place-name studies have already been described. In those regions such as the Belgian and French Ardennes where it has been possible, pollen analysis has permitted some quantification, but only on a localized scale. References to new lands are not lacking in written sources, to be sure, and these excite the partisans of the Carolingian period, but these would appear to relate in reality more to the reclamations of areas that nature had been allowed to take over temporarily rather than to expansion in the true sense. It has long been maintained that such an expansion took place in the ninth century – for example in western Gaul (around Redon), in eastern Gaul (Montier-en-Der), in central Germany (Fulda, Werden, Salzburg), as well as Septimania and the Auvergne. Place names ending in *-rod* or *-rieth* abound on the slopes of the Bavarian Alps or the Black Forest and may well date from that period. Royal ordinances (Aix 801, 813; Pitres 864) encourage the search for new lands, but this should perhaps be seen as a relaxation of economic constraints and not as conquest. How could it otherwise have been possible, given the condition of the labour force and the technology of the period?

However, we are not entirely without research tools. Thanks to its polyptychs, the Carolingian period enables us to attempt the reconstitution of some land-tenure systems – usually belonging to the church, though this is of no significance. Thus it has been possible with some degree of certainty to trace the boundaries of the *villae* in northern Gaul, Picardy, Brabant and the Ardennes, as well as in the Toulouse region, Languedoc and Provence in the south. These holdings of 2000 to 5000ha appear to have belonged to a single landowner. It is even possible to go so far as to say that, whether they belong to the State or not, several could be contiguous, like the 16 *villae* of Sta Melania in Sicily in late antiquity, which thus constituted a wide area of continuous economic control – often more suitable, admittedly, for large-scale stock raising than for arable culture. Unfortunately, since this type of estate seems to have been exceptional, it would be rash to extrapolate information derived from land deeds to the whole of the landscape.

Attempts have also been made to discover fossil landscapes, disregarding the type of agriculture that they may have supported, from archaeological observation alone. The task is an arduous one and the resulting theories are open to criticism: as an example, let us consider the circular land-allotment systems in which France and southern England are so rich. Do these date from later prehistory, five millennia or more ago, since they supply water, flint and wide treeless areas at a reasonable altitude, as Jacqueline Soyer suggests, or are they merely early medieval, as Roger Agache maintains? Do they result from slow coalescence, like settlement capsules that long remained without external contacts, or do they on the contrary represent a collective seizure, even if at the outset they were only selected as grazing lands by pastoral peoples? For their part, the enclosed parcels of land known as 'Celtic' fields in Kent or Cornwall, and those associated with the highland refuge settlements of the upper Vosges or Savoy, may equally represent tribal clearance zones, insulated from one another by unpopulated areas but with their own internal organization.

Wherever the study of a landscape moulded by certain defined topographical elements is coordinated with the study of ancient itineraries and is further illuminated by excavation, remarkable continuity can be observed in an individual region of clearance. It is true that evidence of later prehistoric and even Roman settlement, without any continuity into the Middle Ages, is abundantly distributed throughout latter-day woodland, and equally true that by an agricultural clearance area is understood a wide region that may contain several separate units of human landscape. Account has to be taken of the fact that there was no absolute link between cultivation and settlement at this period, and so any generalization must be rejected in favour of the following modest statement. In very many cases, and bearing in mind not only the mobility of the built area but also of the fields themselves resulting from the constraints imposed by the technology or the needs of the period, landscapes that are compact in structure and orientated on a radiating network of rural linking roads were occupied from later prehistory to the tenth century and beyond. We are considering here light soils that are easy of access, for the most part stripped of tree cover, where the human group encountered no significant physical obstacles in siting their houses and fields. In some places, where building in stone arrived early or where a permanent religious centre was quickly established, they would soon become static, but elsewhere occupation would remain scattered over several centres and with little or no coherent structure. However, going beyond these somewhat diversified physical appearances, it is possible to assert that there is a relationship between the random settlement of the less inhabited regions (the colder areas such as Wales or Brittany), and the denser but none the less anarchic settlement in upper Provence or Latium.

2   Three structures

The disposition of individual holdings within this great clearance zone was most assuredly dependent upon the conditions of exploitation – technological considerations, of course, as for example when the use of an underground water table or a wood, or the requirements of a particular animal species, led to the establishment of a settlement or a building that was specially adapted to this purpose. The development of *latifundia* (vast areas of pasture) in the Late Roman Empire, when men and cereals were banished from Italy to make room for flocks and herds, is well known, as is the establishment of Provençal villages at the interface between two monocultures, vines and corn, as at Pélissane. Leaving aside these special cases, it is possible to identify three types of organized landscape at this period.

The first, extolled by Varro, Cato and Columella, was long considered to be the best adapted to the needs of relatively small groups. In fact, it was more suitable for soils that did not impose serious demands in personnel or care: light soils on the southern flank of Europe, where communities became settled early on and the level of population was modest. According to this 'rational model', the centre of the landscape was a *villa*, as much a residence as an economic organism, established on the best soil and well enough provided with slaves to be self-sufficient. It made no call on the services of neighbouring peasant colonists, who were themselves almost lords of their own very extensive landholdings. It is not surprising that these portions of great estates have been identified from the mid thirteenth century – by Charles Higounet at Rouergue, for example. This type of settlement thus has a 'planetary' appearance: the *villa, cella* (smaller-scale establishment), or large *casale* (defended residence) of the lord surrounded at some distance by the satellite *casae* (houses) of the colonists.

In those regions where permanent settlement arrived later, the distribution of land was more anarchic and fragmented. For this reason, the establishment of the coordinating element was rather more artificial: the links between the demesne of the very rich lord and the houses of the poor were much stronger. In a landscape of this type, the peasant settlement, in close proximity to the centre of power, which in fact formed a part of it, more quickly assumed an appearance that was collective, compact and dominated a more effective communications network. The supremacy of this type of land settlement derived in reality from the quality of the soil. On the other hand, it became established more slowly, and so was less profitable, in the countrysides of northern Gaul or Germany, where it was more favoured. The main problem confronting historians of the seventh to ninth centuries in studying this second type of settled landscape is that of the stability of the land. Certain historians, such as F. L. Ganshof and A. Verhulst in Belgium, without returning to the nineteenth-century German historians' theory of the redistribution and movement of land allotments in a communal or collectively expropriated landscape, deny the existence before 600 or 650 of regular units of cultivation, known as *manses* in Gaul, (Germanic *hufe*, Saxon *hides*), which were coherent groups of plots that could be worked by a single family. More precisely, they only acknowledge these in new lands, such as Saint-Bertin in coastal Flanders, or following the violent Anglo-Saxon occupation of regions such as Lincoln-shire or Berkshire, where land holdings were carved out of a ravaged countryside. Opinion is now coming down more and more in favour of the co-existence of both types of land allotment in this northern zone. One part remained split up into small square fields, traditionally known as 'Celtic', and in fact probably dating from late prehistory like the homesteads of Wiltshire and elsewhere in England, alongside a more highly organized part, based round a lordly *villa*, as illustrated by the fossilized land-allotment system at Cappy-sur-Somme, which is formed of contiguous rectangular strips. How-ever, in both cases the main characteristic of the exploitation, where this can be discerned from ninth-century written sources, is the scattering of the separate parcels of land which make up the holding of each individual involved in working the land, and even probably the mixing up of assigned holdings with free land or common land (*alleutières*). This was an uncoordinated, and in some measure less solid, structure than that further south, which obviously favoured its early spread.

This survey of types of organized landscape would not be complete without a description of a third, and most original, structure. It is a commonplace that those who occupy new lands will seek to settle them for their own purposes whilst respecting the characteristics of the site. The establishment of military camps or 'colonies' in sandy or heath regions needs no further comment. However, official imposition of an artificial geometrical land-holding scheme on an area which has its own boundaries and methods of working is a creative act arising from a combination of political design and economic interest. The stages and principles of Roman centuriation (division into equal-sized holdings) are beginning to become understood. Aerial survey has multiplied evidence of its extent, not only in northern Italy, where it still forms the basis of much contemporary land allotment, but also near Givors in Languedoc, to the east of Amiens, and near Corbie, to cite several regions where it has been studied.

It is to the great credit of Raymond Chevallier that he has shown to what extent this artificial structure is capable of surviving as the basis of all later changes, even though it will not, in the first instance, have worked in the interests of the native populations expelled from their lands for the benefit of State colonists or former legionaries. We still do not know, of course, whether this system was confined to the vicinity of *civitas* capitals or *coloniae* nor what its economic yield was, especially where the topography made its application most problematical. The rapid disappearance of centuriation in central and northern Gaul and in Britain in the Middle Ages may be due as much to its relative rarity in those regions as to systematic rejection by the local peasantry, which retained or resumed its own agricultural traditions. Nevertheless, these great rectangles with sides of more than 700m (765yd), which both determine and rely upon the road system, each perhaps containing the house of the plot holder, assuredly helped to consolidate on the southern flank of Europe the type of compact land allotment system that has just been discussed, beneficial at the outset but an inconvenience at the time of the agricultural upheaval of the eleventh and twelfth centuries that we shall refer to later.

B Enclosed fields or open countryside?

It is possible that the temporary fields of late prehistory were enclosed, but enclosure was not necessary. It is undeniable that modern land holdings have boundaries, but boundaries need not be hedges. There is no doubt that there were Iberian and Gaulish enclosed fields, which can still be made out from the air, but an isolated enclosure does not constitute a *bocage* landscape of enclosed fields and woodland. Written documents throw little light on these questions. The barbarian legal codes are full of references to enclosures, but these relate to temporary protection of a wood used for hunting or a field that has been sown. Caesar's commentaries and the lives of the saints talk of bushes, but legionaries and holy bishops travelled the roads, not across country. The polyptychs mention annual deliveries of stakes for vines and enclosures, but a hedged countryside is not re-made every year. Even the concept of 'hedge' remains ambiguous: was it brushwood for hunting, an enclosed woodland, even a ditch, or a true interlace of branches? The magnitude of the problem is such that, with the aid of archaeology, we must collect together our meagre harvest.

The first question that must be tackled is that of the appearance and stabilization of land boundaries and the main outlines of holdings and, in particular, their orientation. The second concerns the presence of permanent material boundaries around the periphery of cultivated holdings: ditches, banks, green hedges, headland ridges. The third and final question relates to the quantification of the preceding phenomenon: how many individual holdings in a given land allotment system possess permanent boundaries (banks and hedges in particular) and to what extent, for which regions, and from what date is it legitimate to talk of a true enclosed landscape?

Although these three questions are intimately linked, they cannot be posed and answered in the same way. For the first and second, direct observations using archaeological and other survey methods from the air and on the ground can provide very important qualitative insights. However, in the third case, an overall analysis of a land tenure system, leading to appreciation of the collective role of individual holdings, is more difficult to acquire from archaeological data alone, although in certain cases more thorough investigations may be contemplated and are to some extent in progress.

These three problems, as we shall see, are not necessarily contemporaneous, especially the third, which represents a later phase of research, and do not have the same documentary difficulties, especially in relation to written sources.

1 *Did cultural landscapes have boundaries?*

Careful analysis of later parish boundaries, especially those of the eighteenth and nineteenth centuries, shows that in France and certain parts of England these were often based on datable physical elements such as Roman roads. It is widely accepted that Roman roads have defined land-tenure boundaries since the early Middle Ages, as witnessed in a number of cases by descriptions in documentary sources. Various other archaeological elements indirectly confirm this dating, at least in certain European regions characterized by dense and early settlement.

In Saxon England, between the fifth and eighth centuries, a number of linear fortifications were constructed, some of them tens of kilometres in length, the exact function of which often remains uncertain, but which have nevertheless been interpreted as frontiers of settlement, defining Celtic or Saxon territories. In contrast to what was said about Roman roads in the same regions, such as Somerset, it can be seen that these linear works, which constitute prominent topographical features and at the same time settlement frontiers, were, with only rare exceptions, not utilized subsequently as land-holding boundaries. This indirectly confirms the early date of these boundaries, well before the construction of the linear fortifications.

One further argument can be adduced to confirm these observations. Structural analysis of the spatial distribution of settlement in a defined region at a specific period – e.g. Roman Britain or the early medieval Rhineland (see Figure 3) – shows that the distances between settlement nuclei are not the result of chance, but follow certain rules which are themselves functions of the land and sub-soil. In a given region, settlement tends to be regularly distributed, so that each village has a comparable area of land attributed to it, comprising as far as possible the same types of soil and vegetation: cultivable land and woodland, for example.

Leaving aside regions of ancient land allotment, where this remains a determining factor in organization, at least for the broad lines of land division, it is possible to cite various English, German and Dutch areas of settlement where the stabilization of the main outlines of the land-tenure system is of very early date.

At Wharram Percy (Yorkshire), which will be dealt with in more detail later,

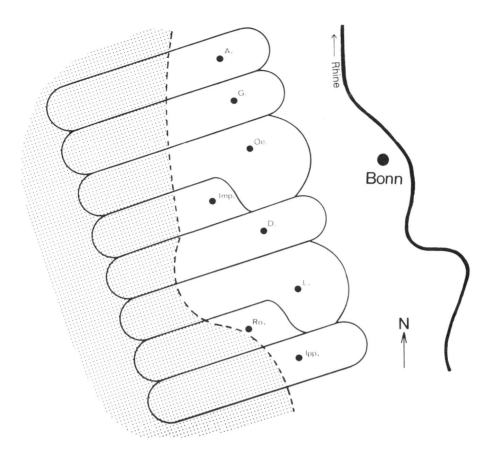

Fig. 3. *Formation of land-holding boundaries in the Rhineland Vorgebirge, west of Bonn*

In this hilly region on the west bank of the Rhine, the Merovingian and Carolingian settlements were established, as determined from the present-day boundaries, according to a very regular system (shown here in simplified form). This reveals several factors: equality of plan and surface area, with two exceptions which may result from the dismemberment of older parishes (they seem to have been carved out of two units that were larger than the others), and comparable siting of settlement centres, in relation to the river and the wooded region, on the slopes and crests of the hills to the west of the settlement centres.

(W. Janssen, *Studien zur Wüstungsfrage im fränkischen Altsiedelland zwischen Rhein, Mosel und Eifelnordrand*, Bonn (1975), fig. 20, p. 132)

---

there was extensive agricultural occupation, in the form of four distinct establishments, in the first and second centuries. The inhabitants were dispersed after the end of the Roman period and it was not until the seventh century that human settlement reappeared. Although consisting of a completely different population group, this new settlement none the less followed the boundaries of the Romano-British land holdings, especially in respect of their major orientations. Excavation of the ditches has proved that those which were in use in the Middle Ages sometimes go back to Romano-British times.

In the Netherlands village of Odoorn (see Figure 4), occupied from the fifth to tenth centuries, the buildings of the settlement are scattered within large enclosures which later, after the settlement had been abandoned, served as the axes and boundaries of the tenurial units up to the time the cadastral survey was made in 1831.

The same phenomenon – the very early origin of the axes and main boundaries of modern layouts of villages that overlie the sites of abandoned settlements and land-holding systems dating from the early Middle Ages – has been observed elsewhere in the Netherlands – at Wijster and Kootwijk, for example.

Archaeology or written sources often give an indication of the ancient origins of these Romano-British or Merovingian settlements. In some examples, particularly from Germany and England, it can be observed that the creation of intermediate settlement centres leads to the dismemberment of ancient settlement systems and the establishment of new boundaries – at Chalton, for example, which was certainly broken up in the seventh to eighth centuries, or several German instances from the same period. This proves indirectly that the establishment of a settlement in the Roman period or the early Middle Ages leads to the stabilization of tenurial boundaries, even though the 'full' cultivated landscape does not yet conform with them: it was to develop gradually within the boundaries, respecting this general framework while proceeding to completion.

Ancient documents, such as the Domesday Book, dating from the end of the eleventh century, confirm the early date for the stabilization of territorial boundaries. It has long been recognized that land boundaries are never defined precisely in this document, except in the case of recent divisions of estates, which clearly shows that by the time the survey was made they had been in existence so long that everyone knew and tacitly accepted them.

Thus it becomes possible to consider that over a large part of Europe land-holding boundaries were defined and stabilized in the Roman period or the early Middle Ages. This does not mean that there was no subsequent variation in settlement forms and locations: on the contrary, these often changed very markedly. But it is certain that the development of settlement modes took place within recognized boundaries in the early Middle Ages and in those parts of western Europe that had been densely settled at an early period.

2 Cultivated plots with stable boundaries?

Research into the origins of land boundaries assumes the careful excavation of ditches, banks and hedgerows – in effect, detailed analysis of an entire settled landscape. Until such time as the results of work on these lines in progress become available, examples such as Wharram Percy and some settlements in the Netherlands can be used. They lead to the view that many nineteenth-century boundaries date back a long way, to the Roman period or the early Middle Ages. However, archaeology is not the only approach available. English historians and archaeologists have put forward the hypothesis that

ODOORN

1831

0   100 m

Fig. 4. *Medieval origins of the land allotment system at Odoorn (Netherlands)*

There are obvious relationships between the modern layout, as shown in the cadastral survey of 1831, and the orientation, if not the precise outline, of the house enclosures of the early Middle Ages. After the abandonment of this settlement in the tenth century, its outline was preserved in that of the fields which replaced it.

(H. T. Waterbolk, Odoorn im frühen Mittelalter, *Neue Ausgrabungen und Forschungen in Niedersachsen*, 8 (1973); fig. 3, p. 42 and fig. 33, p. 86)

0   20 m

35

identification and counting of tree species present in a living hedgerow can provide data on its age. Experimental work on hedgerows in Otford (Kent) shows agreement between the relatively large number of tree species present in certain hedgerows (as high as eight to thirteen) and very old boundaries, referred to as early as 822. According to this work, one new species appears in a hedgerow roughly every century (see Figure 55).

Headland ridges can perhaps be tackled in the same way. Banks gradually build up from the action of the plough and the consequent regular, albeit minute, movement of the ploughed soil, and so their dimensions should be proportional to their age. Observations in Alsace, and more recently in Beauce, reveal the general validity of this observation. However, the practical, and in particular the chronological, difficulties inherent in the use of this technique are great. Nevertheless, some careful surveys, such as that at Josnes (Loir-et-Cher) carried out meticulously by English geographers (see Figure 5), have shown that some plot boundaries may date back to Roman or early medieval times.

However, this does not, unfortunately, provide an answer to our third question: were these agricultural boundaries, denoted on the ground by a ditch, a bank, a hedgerow or a ploughing ridge, systematically laid out around every part and, if so, when? In particular, when was the enclosed landscape established?

Without disregarding the contribution of archaeology, which is essentially qualitative but nevertheless decisive, at least in chronological terms, it is necessary in this case to turn to traditional historical sources, primarily archives, the more so since this third aspect of the problem – the appearance of the enclosed landscape – is a purely medieval phenomenon which occurs sufficiently late for archival data to be available. This is a question that has interested historians for several decades. Since it is a late medieval phenomenon, we shall see below how it can be studied, using primarily archival, archaeological and botanical data derived from modern analytical techniques.

It seems clear that in regions of relatively early settlement, dating from the early Middle Ages, settlement boundaries were sufficiently well-defined on the land itself, in one way or another, to have survived almost unchanged to the present day. Furthermore, despite the general expansion of cultivation throughout the Middle Ages and particularly in the tenth to thirteenth centuries, it appears that the outlines of certain individual holdings or groups of holdings perpetuated boundaries of great antiquity, dating back to the early Middle Ages or even the Roman period, until the nineteenth century.

3   Land management boundaries

The installation of a system of crop rotation, dividing the land into equal parts for the rotation of crops and for winter and spring ploughing, is related more to the prevailing economic system than to land allotment. However, since most authors persist in maintaining that it was in existence as early as the eleventh century – and on a three-year cycle – it cannot be overlooked. It will be obvious

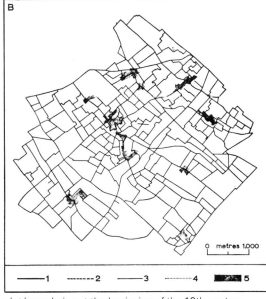

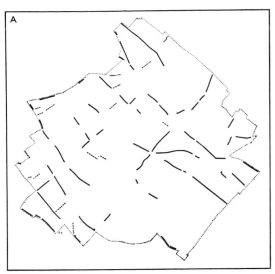

Headland ridges visible today

plot boundaries at the beginning of the 19th century

1. Existing headland ridges corresponding to access ways at the beginning of the 19th century

2. Existing headland ridges that do not correspond with 19th century access ways

3. Plot boundaries at the beginning of the 19th century

4. Commune boundary

5. Settlement

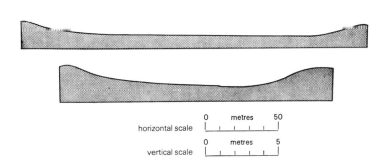

Fig. 5. *Headland ridges in the commune of Josnes (Loir-et-Cher)*

Comparison of the two figures shows that almost all (80 per cent) of the ridges still visible today are, in fact, on the sites of access ways that were already in existence by the beginning of the nineteenth century, according to the cadastral survey. All of them correspond with the boundaries of groups of holdings of that period. These were, therefore, relatively old and of significance at that time. It is difficult to say when they first appeared, but it may be observed first that the difference in level between the fields and the tops of the headland ridges is generally 1–2m (3ft 3in.–6ft 6in.) which implies earth movement over a long period, and secondly, that recent observations have shown that in places Roman sites were overlain by these ridges. An origin during the Middle Ages, without being more precise, may thus be considered.

(A. H. R. Baker, Neglected Field Form: the Headland Ridge, *The Agricultural History Review*, (1973); fig. 1, p. 49 and fig. 2, p. 50)

37

that, if such a system is to be profitable, there has to be some 'rational' redistribution of holdings: an incontrovertible token of progress. There must be agreement on the terminology. Crop rotation only exists if three conditions are met: a—division of cultivation into two or three parts of equal size, which may be spread over several plots; b—regular annual rotation of sowings or fallow in each part; and c—integration of the entire cultivated area into this system. Without this there would only be occasional spring ploughing or double cropping at random over the entire cultivated area or at best seigneurial cultivation. Pliny and Columella knew about spring sowing; seventh-century documents relating to Le Mans and a 771 reference to Lorsch, the polyptychs of Saint-Germain-des-Prés, Saint-Rémy de Reims and Saint-Bertin, and a score of other ninth-century texts prove the existence of spring 'corn' (blés – the generic word in these texts for all cereals). None of them is referring to anything other than sowings or harvests made at one season or another. There is no comparison of crop volumes other than the *Brevium exempla*, which records different cereal species, nor any indication of the succession from one year to another, from one crop to another, on the same plot. There is, moreover, no reference to any identical procedure other than on the seigneurial lands. It is difficult to see how it would have been possible at this time to achieve, even on princely lands, the technological level of the Ile-de-France, Picardy, or the area north of London, which written sources show was not attained until 1240 at the earliest.

It would seem necessary, finally, to determine whether the communications network underlies the land allotment, thereby providing the framework of the landscape and controlling its exploitation. Reconstruction of an ancient road system poses some difficult problems, especially in the rural environment. If there are strong presumptions of antiquity in respect of a road which serves as the line of a parish boundary, which links two settlements with Celtic names, or which originates at a *fanum* (type of oratory often located in the middle of a field system) or at a *vicus* (the name given to pre-medieval villages), these are still not adequate to decide whether a field system was based on the road or vice versa, which is the fundamental question.

Only a system of centuriation can provide an incontrovertible link between holdings and tracks, but the artificial, and at times opportunistic, nature of this type of system has already been touched upon. This means that this question must be left unanswered, the creation of a true road system being considered later rather than earlier. One last factor must be evoked to support this latter view. The criteria for Roman roads are for the most part well known: they disregard *fana, casae* and *villae*, and relate only to *vici* established at crossroads or posting stations. Occasional side roads which leave the highway to reach nearby villas, as at Estrées-sur-Noye, are very rare indeed: roads connect towns. Thus, whether it was a road network established without regard for pre-Roman trade movements or whether – as was doubtless often the case – it represented the re-use of older routes, the negative role of Roman roads in the countryside is apparent. They left country districts isolated, and this factor is so important that we have left it until last, before turning to the village proper.

II WHAT DO WE KNOW ABOUT THE EARLY MEDIEVAL VILLAGE?

A What roles could it play?

1 *Religion and justice*

Without borrowing models from ancient forms of agriculture that can still occasionally be observed today, it may be accepted that, for an expanding society whose agricultural or pastoral practices demand continuous movement, the pre-eminent need is to identify and locate sacred ritual sites for gods who guard the land and for ancestor worship. The sacrificial cult sites of the Celts and the Germans without doubt acted as anchor points for the semi-nomadic settlers of late antiquity, like the great sacred enclosures of the Greeks and Romans earlier, and just as permanently. The classical establishments probably encouraged the development in the 'Romanized' zone of Europe of an original type of sacred settlement, as at Nommée (Marne) centred on a temple or a well, priests' dwellings, food stores, tombs or funerary mounds. The large Gallo-Roman sanctuaries deep in the countryside, such as those of Ribémont or Estrées-sur-Noye in Picardy, may even have been established on the sites of older holy places – caves, springs, or sacred trees – with the intention of stabilizing a local population that was not yet wholly subjected. These 'pre-urban nuclei', as Roger Agache described them, thus unified religious tradition and political will. They were built in the first or second century with other permanent elements such as baths, theatres and basilicas, but as far as we can judge, they never led to the creation of true villages or towns, at least in northern Gaul or Britain. On the other hand, in Auvergne or Poitou, many early medieval *vici* had their origins in this religious function.

It should also be emphasized that written sources and air photographs often reveal, in the middle of a cultivated region, at the summit of a low eminence or alongside a spring, an isolated *fanum* (there are more than 30 in Picardy) or a *xenodochium* (a chapel for sheltering pilgrims), where offerings could be made and a hermit would welcome travellers and pilgrims. At this stage there is no question of a village. However, there is no reason to exclude from these attempts to stabilize rural settlement the powerful monastic expansion of the early Middle Ages. It is said that the monks 'quartered' the barbarian north and north-west of Europe, a striking expression which suggests a wish to dominate ill-defined and scattered groups of peoples, and not just through the care of their souls. In this respect, monasteries acted as nuclei for later villages and towns.

The occasion of a festival, a pilgrimage, or one of those Gaulish *conciliabula* that Caesar so much feared, and the resulting crowds, may have justified the creation of great ditched enclosures, varying in size from the 5ha at Allans (Cher), near Bourges, to the 130ha at Vendeuil (Somme), to the south of Amiens. A political function would then be added to the original religious function. What we know of the 'palaces' of Roman governors or barbarian kings leads us to the belief that the role of dispensing justice was added to their economic roles (to be discussed later), the courts being transported from the declining town into the heart of the countryside. Doubtless this could lead to the creation of a new town, but the original nucleus of towns such as Aix, Goslar or St Albans was the combination of spring, funerary chapel and *aula* (princely justice chamber).

2 Defence

The defensive function inspires a good deal more hesitation. Fear is naturally an important factor in creating groupings, and in troubled times peasants would seek to group themselves round a strong point. However, it would seem that in almost every case at this period, in both northern and southern Europe, a defended site did not result in permanent settlement. The defended promontories of the Belgae, the Breton ring-forts of Cornouailles, and the lofty fortresses of Provence, Languedoc, Greece or Sicily were occupied in times of stress, to be abandoned and then reoccupied, but there was no permanent settlement – only eight or ten houses and occasionally a cemetery. The hesitant appearance in the seventh and eighth centuries of hilltop settlements – sometimes temporary, as in Tuscany or Latium, sometimes more solid, as in the Auvergne – were precise indications of the early beginnings of a capital town, an aspect that will be discussed again in the appropriate place.

3 Community of the living and the dead

The legal establishment of a group on land which would thereafter be appropriated to them also has a role to play. In fact the taking over of land for food production is difficult to observe, especially outside the Romanized zone, where collective expropriation – that Germanic process whose role we have already mentioned – could become established. It can be accepted without any doubt, on the basis of Roman and barbarian legal codes, that the principle of private appropriation by individuals or families had, by the fifth century, long been adopted by the Romans: the structure of the *villa* or palace attests to this fact.

However, the constraints imposed by obligations of collective or mutual responsibility, which weighed heavily on settler groups, indicate another conception of the relationships between men and the land. Throughout the fourth century (in 357, 367 and 371), the renewal of ordinances designed to deny to *consortes* (members of rural societies) the right to sell their land freely or to quit the land, is evidence not so much of a concern to stabilize settlement (which as we have just seen remained very mobile), but rather to tie the group to the land. Fiscal considerations – preventing the flight of sources of tax revenue – certainly provide the broad explanation, but it must be assumed that in the Germanic world, where this public constraint did not apply, the need for collective links would have been equally great, or at least rapidly became so, as evidenced by what we have said above about collective expropriation.

It is permissible to postulate that the basis of this attachment to the land was not economic, military or political, but religious. By this we do not mean a cult link with a divinity and the manifestations of his power, but rather that of a sacred area inherited by a group, independently of any economic possibilities. This suggestion is founded upon the importance accorded in villages to the dead and to cemeteries. The considerable homogeneity of material from graves and from dwellings might well be evidence of the absence of any discontinuity between the worlds of the living and the dead. It is undeniable that the place made available for the dead, the guardians of the land, does not always occupy an identical position relative to the village of the living, but this is perhaps because the latter could move about the sacred zone, whilst the dead were unable to do so. At Hérouvillette (Calvados) the earliest cemetery is 2km (1 mile) from the village near an ancient sanctuary which had been abandoned or become superseded. A similar survival could doubtless be observed in many other examples from the Neolithic up to the seventh century. But all cemeteries belong to one period or another. The abandonment of this custom and the regrouping of all subsequent interments around the church, or even within it, is an indication of much more than the victory of Christianity: it signifies the breaking of the religious link between the land belonging to the dead and that of the living.

It is thus possible to say that these three primary factors, the three most powerful forces in bringing men together – religion, justice and defence – additionally give rise to isolated compact structures, the remains of which are still visible and known today, and that the village that grew up round a monastery or an administrative palace, or within a girdle of walls, belongs to another period. Cultivation of the soil obviously played the decisive role in stabilizing the group, and so the primary function of this process of agglomeration was economic. However, this raises certain difficulties: settlement may have been determined by soil quality, contact between two different types of cultivation, the proximity of water, or the crossing of two routes, and these have already been considered above. But this did not operate in a mandatory way, and there are many sites which are ostensibly absurd. It would seem advisable therefore to proceed to a simple descriptive exercise.

B   Types of rural settlement

Detailed analysis of settlement types in Europe over the period from the second to third centuries to the ninth to tenth centuries is essential. It is based mainly on archaeological data which, having been studied unevenly over the geographical region that forms the subject of this book, cannot therefore respond everywhere with the same degree of detail or accuracy to the

Fig. 6. *Ancient settlement in the Somme plain in the first to third centuries, from aerial photography*

The structures shown on this map, with exception of the alignments of Roman roads, the town plan of Amiens (*Samarobriva*), and that of the Vendeuil-Caply group, were discovered by R. Agache by aerial reconnaissance. They are probably not all contemporaneous. However, most of the settlements and sanctuaries shown seem to have been destroyed and for the most part abandoned in the second half of the third century. This is, therefore, a map showing the main settlement structures in this region in the first to third centuries. The extent of settlement in large villas, which are much more numerous than the existing settlement centres, is clearly apparent.

Legend

1 Gallo-Roman villa. The orientation of the symbol corresponds to that of the structure itself. The site of the main building, the owner's house, is shown by a short line (cf. Figure 7)

2 Gallo-Roman villa over 250m (273yd) in length (same as 1 above)

3 Ordered group of Gallo-Roman buildings of uncertain type or villa whose exact layout is not known

4 Sanctuary

5 Theatre: the exact orientation is shown by the position of the symbol

6 Legionary camp

7 Gallo-Roman foundations of indeterminate nature

8 Site of a former settlement marked by dark patches and of unknown date, although probably Gallo-Roman

9 Presumed sites of localities mentioned in the *Antonine Itinerary* or the *Peutinger Table* or sites of other localities or *vici*

10 Hypothetical structures

11 Principal Roman roads

(R. Agache, La campagne à l'époque romaine dans les grandes plaines du Nord de la France, *Aufstieg und Niedergang der römischen Welt* (1975); fig. 12, pp. 708–9)

---

questions we wish to be able to solve.

For various reasons it would seem necessary to distinguish in this region of Europe three distinct zones, characterized by their degree of Romanization. There are the Mediterranean lands of Europe, which early fell under Roman influence and were strongly affected by an apparently systematic cadastration (land survey and registration for tax purposes) and the early and substantial development of urbanization. Then there is free Germany, to the east of the Rhine, often massively denuded of its inhabitants after the fifth century, but in any case not affected at all by Romanization before that date. Between these two zones lies the zone of graduations between the two extremes that they represent, in particular the situation over most of France, Great Britain, Belgium and the southern Netherlands.

In trying to define the types of rural settlement in early medieval Europe, we must therefore identify three distinct cases: *a*—early, substantial Romanization; *b*—later and less systematic Romanization and *c*—no Romanization. In order to emphasize the dimensions of this problem, we shall begin with an

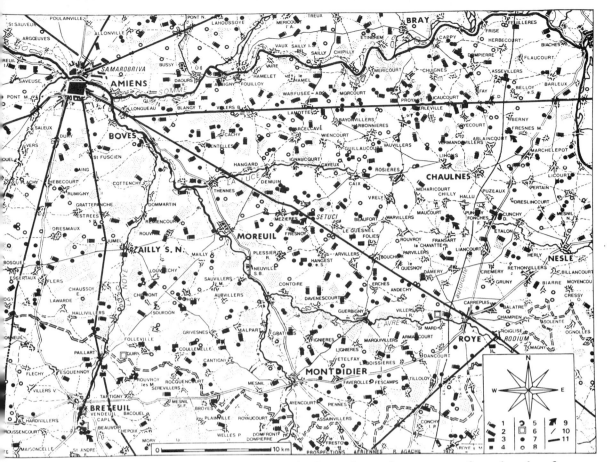

intermediate region (Picardy), which has the advantages of a level of Romanization that is well-defined but less than that in southern France, together with serious in-depth research into its Roman settlement.

1 A moderately Romanized region: Picardy

Conditions of study

Aerial research of ancient settlement by Roger Agache since 1960, based on the present-day Somme *département* (surface area 6277 sq. km [2423 sq. miles], 835 *communes*), has been of exceptional importance (see Figure 6). Systematic intensive aerial survey in varying conditions of weather, humidity, cultivation etc, associated with conditions in the region which favour air survey, makes it possible to say that, at least so far as knowledge of Roman settlements in stone or with stone foundations is concerned, Picardy provides very representative data, little distorted by conditions that are not comprehensible to the historian.

Leaving aside the coastal region and the valley bottoms, where the soil is different and less favourable to air survey, the Somme *département* is essentially composed of a single terrain – chalk plateaux that are today largely, if not entirely, deforested and entirely given over to large-scale agriculture with deep ploughing. There are no meadows or wooded areas which elsewhere very often mask a considerable portion of the land surface. What is even more

43

remarkable is the fact that there is, in the region, a very nucleated type of settlement surrounded by small gardens, with very infrequent intermediate settlements. These are all conditions which, in conjunction with those quoted earlier, make by far the greater portion of the land surface available for observation and also, thanks to the form of cultivation practised, in a uniform condition for archaeological work. It should, however, be noted that the soil of the Somme *département*, unlike those in, for example, the Rhineland, is not well suited to the observation of insubstantial remains: it offers nothing to compare with the large Bronze Age house plans which can sometimes be seen from the air in the Aisne, marked by the complete outline of their post-holes.

Villas: a common settlement type

In Picardy, as elsewhere in the Roman Empire, at least on the better soils, the most common method of agricultural exploitation – at least, that most visible from the air – was that of the villa. This was an isolated domanial operation, varying in length from 80–180m (87–197yd) average to as much as 300m (328yd) for the largest. Within a single enclosure (usually rectangular), the villa brought together the dwelling houses of the owner, his steward, and the subordinate workforce who worked the estate lands.

Exceptional aerial prospection conditions have enabled Roger Agache to locate more than 500 villas. This is, of course, a minimum figure, since the whole of Picardy has not yet been surveyed uniformly. Nevertheless, it is a substantial figure when compared with the number of modern communes (835 in the Somme *département*), and in relation to the estimated overall population growth in France between the peace and high prosperity of the second century, when it was a few million, and the beginning of the fourteenth century, when it reached some 18 million. It is likely that these villas, which seem for the most part to have been built in the first and second centuries and were mostly abandoned in the second half of the third century, housed the majority of the population in a very dispersed form of settlement. This view is reinforced by looking, for example, at the region round Warfusée-Abancourt (Somme), on the major Roman road from Amiens to Trier, where there are no fewer than five Gallo-Roman villas, several of very large size.

We are, therefore, dealing here, as in most of the Roman Empire, with the very rapid establishment over about two centuries of a type of rural settlement which is distinguished from its Iron Age predecessor, not so much by its dispersed nature (already common in the Iron Age) as by its regular and standardized layout and by the use of stone, at least for the owner's dwelling or the more important buildings in their entirety, and always for building foundations. However, although these settlements present a hierarchical structure very much in keeping with the contemporary society, with one part for the master and another for the subordinate workforce, they are none the less settlements of a type no longer found in these regions, but reflections of which can doubtless still be found in the exploitation of new lands in America or Africa. A villa may well have borne the name of a man, the owner of the estate (*fundus*) on which it was built, but it still sheltered several hundred workers of varying status, relatives and dependants. What has been observed round many monasteries or bishops' palaces in the succeeding era, at Saint-Riquier or Annappes, for example, shows that this is an economic structure that can adapt itself to a form that is either religious or military in origin.

Villas: types and development

Naturally, the forms of these 'villages' themselves vary according to both time and space. Around the Mediterranean, following Italian practice, greater importance was accorded to the residential villa (the *villa urbana*) than to the agricultural villa (the *villa rustica*), as at Chiragan or Montmaurin in southern Gaul. In some places these were combined in a single large block: this was the case in Sicily and Tuscany, also occasionally in northern Gaul (Haccourt) and Belgium (L'Hostée). However, the general rule in central and northern Gaul was for the villa to spread its buildings over an area of as much as 5 or 6ha; the striking discoveries made by Roger Agache from the air at Warfusée (see Figure 7), Le Mesge, Grivesnes, Cappy and elsewhere, confirm the evidence from the large 'village' at Anthée in Belgium.

These differences certainly derive from divergences in economic practice. At one villa, a higher priority will have been given to extensive stock rearing and free-range pasturage, while elsewhere there would have been more emphasis on arable farming and services, with provision for the stalling of animals. However, the origin of these differences may also be attributable to the survival of pre-Roman forms of settlement: Greeks or Iberians around the Mediterranean, no doubt, but what happened further north, where Rome was not able to convert the local aristocracies to its practices? One may study the archetypes of the villas of Belgium, Brittany and Picardy: were they Celtic La Tène structures or *aedificia* which brought together, in one more or less oval enclosure at one time, livestock, the chief's house, and a few dozen lesser houses, as at Chysauster (Cornwall) or Glastonbury (Somerset), or were they less tangible groupings of Germanic holdings, echoes of which are preserved in certain Saxon or Danish settlements?

Particularly at the end of the third century, the large artificial villas, set in isolation on the best hillsides, following the precepts of ancient agronomy, seem to have been abandoned, either before or after destruction, and replaced by more concentrated building complexes, generally located either close to a village settlement of different and probably earlier origin or alongside water or woodland, as though the contraction of the economy had driven men together to seek refuge much closer to natural resources. This development may have been encouraged in the fourth and fifth centuries by the custom of *hospitalitas*, which led to the villa acquiring a new dependent settlement which gradually absorbed the human component of the original enterprise. It may also have been that the working buildings and the peasant shacks became detached from the *villa urbana* to form a new grouping – the *curtis*, the *hof* or the *villare*.

This may explain the flowering of place names ending in -*court* and -*hof*

45

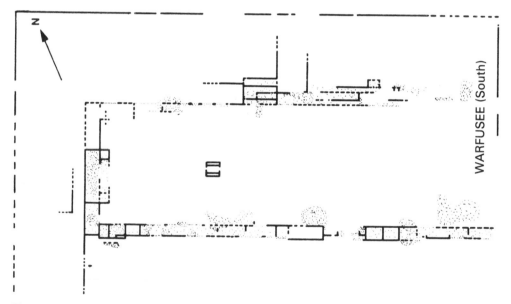

Fig. 7. *A large Gallo-Roman villa at Warfusée (Somme)*

These enormous regular complexes were, for the most part, established in the first or second centuries and usually abandoned in the second half of the third century. The general layout is always the same: a long rectangular courtyard spreads out in front of the main building used as a residence by the owner (here on the west side). The many subsidiary buildings lie on either side of the courtyard. Followed the precepts of ancient agronomy, all these buildings were disposed regularly on a slope, the main residence being above and orientated to face the rising sun.

(R. Agache, La campagne à l'époque romaine dans les grandes plaines du Nord de la France, *Aufstieg und Niedergang der römischen Welt* (1975); fig. 8, p. 68 and photograph by R. Agache)

46

dating from the sixth or eighth centuries some half-kilometre from the remains of third-century villas, by contrast with the first- and second-century villas, which are often isolated from any later settlements. We even know of successive transplantations, as at the Fontaine-Valmont villa in Belgium, which was deserted and ploughed up in the fifth century when a new centre was established some distance away, to be demolished and rebuilt elsewhere in its turn when the lands were ceded to the abbey of Lobbes in 743.

So far as this study is concerned, it cannot be denied that we obviously have no example of continuity from the first century to the present day. The evolution of social and economic systems has, of course, made such a situation rarer than has long been claimed, but can we be sure of this? One important link is missing in the history of this settlement type: the location and structure of the villas and palaces reported in Carolingian documents, which are sparing of details. They are generally viewed as being fairly close to the large Roman complexes of northern Gaul: an *aula* or reception hall, a basilica, a chapel, workshops and humble dwellings. The description of the fisc or public domain at Annappes, or what Roger Agache believes he has been able to identify of the Merovingian villa of Quierzy-sur-Oise, fit well into this schema. However, continuity has not been established with the ancient models, since excavations on the land at Annappes which is not built over at the present time have produced Gallo-Roman remains without any material that can be ascribed to the ninth century. This leads to the possibility that it was the villa of Charlemagne which became the present-day village of Annappes, 1–2km (½–1 mile) from the Gallo-Roman remains. At least where documents and finds on the ground are in agreement, as in the Auvergne or between the Tarn and the Garonne, the *casa* or owner's house, whether built on the site of an establishment from antiquity or constructed a few hundred metres away from it, seems to have been surrounded by a number of *appendicia* or dependencies, where the slaves and smallholders lived. This thus represents a pre-village nucleus, the first clumsy sketch of the future village.

The study of villas, whether 'classical' or otherwise, is not, however, enough. It is apparent that, even before the barbarian period, another form of settlement was possible. Does this perhaps constitute one of the factors that contribute to the gradual formation of a permanent group settlement? The systematic survey work in Picardy by Roger Agache has revealed the existence of both villas and Gallo-Roman sites of a different type.

To appreciate the importance of these observations, we should start from better-known ground: the medieval rural settlement. We know that in this region, as in many others, there was some settlement abandonment in the thirteenth–fifteenth centuries. Abandoned medieval settlements are, however, difficult to observe from the air. There are two reasons for this: in general they were not built in stone, and the fact that they were not laid out on the regular lines of villas means they are more difficult to pick out. However, there may be more profound reasons to account for the absence of a deserted medieval settlement: as Agache has commented, the small number of such settlements that have been located blend well with the land-allotment pattern and are perfectly integrated with the network of ancient roads and fields that surround and conform with them. Why should this be? Because they were established within a land pattern that was based upon the settlements themselves. By contrast, all the Roman villas in the Somme *département* and elsewhere, with certain exceptions to which we shall return, are not associated with the visible agricultural landscape. They probably do not underlie modern settlements, since their large size would mean that they would often be visible. And, more remarkable still, they do not conform with the modern secondary land-holding pattern or network of tracks, and so they must predate the latter and are systematically disregarded by them.

This admirably confirms our earlier observation: between the abandonment of these villas and the formation of the modern landscape – effectively the eighth to ninth centuries – there was a long period of some five centuries that was of great significance. This was the period when the land-holding pattern was restructured and when a new form of settlement, still visible today, or a settlement of the same type, was established.

Does this mean that the foundation of these villages coincides with the destruction of the villas? Exclusive reliance on this explanation would seem to be impossible for various reasons. We know that the third to eighth centuries were marked by various events, of which the migrations of people were only the most spectacular manifestations which, at the level of the whole of western Europe, resulted in the movement of settlements, particularly in the third and fourth centuries and again from the end of the seventh to the early years of the ninth century. However, these events also took place in a period which – at least up to the eighth century and perhaps even into the ninth century – is characterized by a substantial fall in population. It is consequently impossible that all the villages of today could have been founded at that time: this is amply borne out by the history of later periods. On the other hand, it is inconceivable that, both here and elsewhere, there were no new settlements in the third to fourth and seventh to ninth centuries, or that there was no abandonment of this type of settlement later, leaving deserted sites to be located.

Sparse settlement?

In these circumstances, another explanation is needed to account for the chronological and typological hiatus between villas and modern villages. All archaeological experience in western Europe shows that it is usually very difficult to locate early medieval rural settlements; in most cases those that have been or are being excavated were found by chance when earth-moving work, especially drainage or pipeline laying, was being carried out. As we shall see later, the villages were crudely built in perishable materials and so they leave few traces, at least so far as aerial survey is concerned. Apart from chance discoveries, some of these sites have been identified by detailed surface prospection, which has revealed first the existence and in due course the extent and boundaries of a settlement rather than its precise form or the outlines of its buildings. Only in exceptional soil conditions (on gravels in particular, as in the Thames Valley), as, for example, at Mucking, which will be discussed in greater detail later, or in the Aisne Valley at Maizy-sur-Aisne, have the foundations of huts or relatively large buildings been visible (cf. Figure 37). These examples are very rare, however, and occur on soils that do not exist in the Somme Valley. In such circumstances – for this problem as for any other – negative evidence is not admissible. The complete absence on air photographs of any traces of rural settlement, between the very visible villas and modern inhabited villages, can in no case be interpreted as evidence of a direct transition between the early Roman Empire and the early Middle Ages from one mode of settlement to another, without any break in chronological continuity or possible intermediate forms.

This becomes all the more relevant when it is considered that, whilst aerial survey in the Somme *département* has shown that there were many villas and other monuments built in stone such as rural temples or *fana*, aerial photographs have also revealed a large number of archaeological anomalies that are indistinct and show little organization or planned layout, but which investigation on the ground has shown to be Gallo-Roman. In this area surveyed by Roger Agache, 6000 anomalies of this type have been recorded alongside more than 550 villas – which is all the more important since they are difficult to identify.

Vici *and small villages*

What do these traces mean? The first explanation that comes to mind, at least for many of these anomalies, is that they must be what Roman and early medieval documents call *vici*, i.e. villages. Ancient written sources regularly refer to the presence of rural settlements of varying size alongside villas, located on roads and sometimes, when they bring together a number of craftsmen and traders, attaining the status of non-agricultural townships.

In this context, many place names ending in *-y*, *-ac*, *-heim*, *-ing* etc may generally be considered to be totemic or clan names, having been transferred from the villa to the nearby village. The study of the history of such villages was largely directed towards what are called, *faute de mieux*, small towns (*bourgs*), i.e. complexes that were relatively large, usually equipped with a church and sometimes a strong point, whose role seems by the early Middle Ages to have become very diversified – religious, political, military, commercial.

The origins of such agglomerations present no problems. Continuity from a Roman (or sometimes pre-Roman) micro-urban structure is very common: they may be based on centres of craftsmen alongside major roads, with some large houses whose owners adopted urban attitudes, and a chapel. In his detailed study of the Auvergne, Gabriel Fournier was able to trace the histories of Brioude, Lezoux and Issoire, and also of tenth century fortified small towns, such as Artonne or Gannat, back to the third century. There are similar examples in Picardy such as Airaines or Poix. In Alsace, the determining factor seems to have been a crossroads or, in these threatened regions, a defended locality from the fourth century onwards, such as Ehl, at a ford over the Rhine, or Illzach, north of Mulhouse. A place of pagan pilgrimage converted into a Christian sanctuary would ensure continuity from classical times, as at Marteville, at the base of the *oppidum* at Vermand, or at Fismes-Saint-Macre on the river Vesle.

Less often than we should like, we find references in these documents to purely agricultural *vici*, in many cases no doubt more peasant hamlets dependent upon the operations of a large estate, working lands assigned to them by the large landowner, than settlements of independent peasants, though this point is of little relevance in this context.

Some *vici* of this type have been excavated, but it is difficult to assess their role or their numbers in relation to villas in the agrarian economy of the first to third centuries, and still less their fate after that period and during the early Middle Ages.

Examples where detailed field survey, followed by multiple excavations, have made it possible to understand the course and form of settlement during the first millennium AD are rare. Chalton (Hampshire) is a priceless exception in this respect (see Figure 8).

Over a period of ten years, under the direction of Barry Cunliffe, all disturbances to the soil within this landscape, covering some 30 sq. km (11 sq. miles), and all fields, whether cultivated or not, were monitored. Aerial photographs were taken and a number of excavations were carried out. As a result, 120 distinct archaeological sites, from the Mesolithic (7000 BC) to the early Middle Ages, are now known and the settlement history can be recreated with a measure of accuracy.

In the Iron Age, the basic unit of settlement was the small family agricultural unit, the numbers of which increased gradually during the first millennium BC, reaching a total of 14 distinct sites by its end. Irregular four-sided fields, easily seen on air photographs and belonging to the class known as 'Celtic fields', were associated with the settlement of this period.

The Romano-British period, like the preceding Iron Age, was one of popular growth: new fields appear, now in the form of strips, connected with the bringing of new lands under the plough. The numerous settlement units of the Iron Age survived, some of them perhaps through to the sixth to seventh centuries. However, in this Romanized region, where settlement in stone-built villas appeared on the scene, a trend towards concentration of settlement began. Although no structure of this type has been located in the Chalton study area, this is purely by chance: they have been found in the surrounding areas. A characteristic of this region, and indeed of many comparably Romanized regions in southern Britain and Gaul, is the indisputable trend towards concentration of settlement in the third to fourth centuries on three sites which doubtless owe their origins to the first century. In the sixth century, these three settlements were in their turn abandoned in favour of a settlement agglomeration, founded on the top of a ridge that had been used for pasture in the Romano-British period: this was the Anglo-Saxon settlement known as

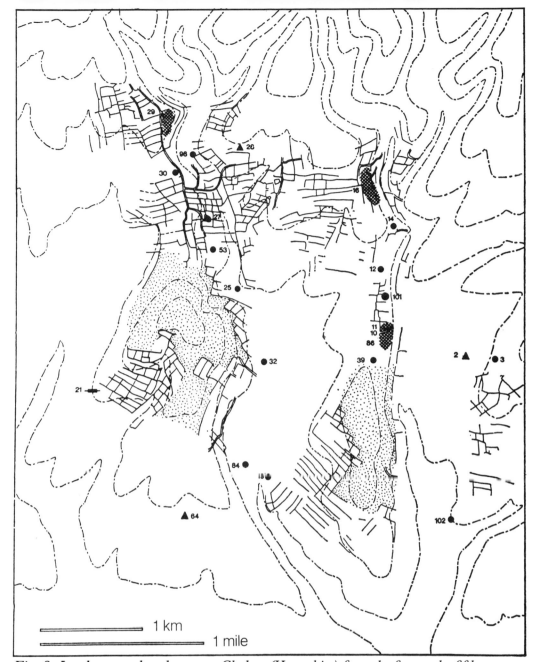

Fig. 8. *Landscape and settlement at Chalton (Hampshire) from the first to the fifth century*

Field survey and aerial reconnaissance have made it possible to reconstitute part of the agrarian landscape – that part which has not been too severely disturbed by later agricultural activities – around several settlement centres, usually very small in size. The cultivated fields that have been located, square or rectangular in shape, belong to the class of 'Celtic fields', which are characteristic of southern England between 600 BC and *c.*AD 200. They are separated by more or less well-marked banks.

- ● Settlement
- ▲ Stone construction
- ▦ Concentration of buildings ('village'?)

- ⌐ Fields
- ░ Pasture
- ▬ Cemetery

(B. W. Cunliffe, Chalton, Hants, *The Antiquaries Journal*, 50 (1972); fig. 6, p. 186)

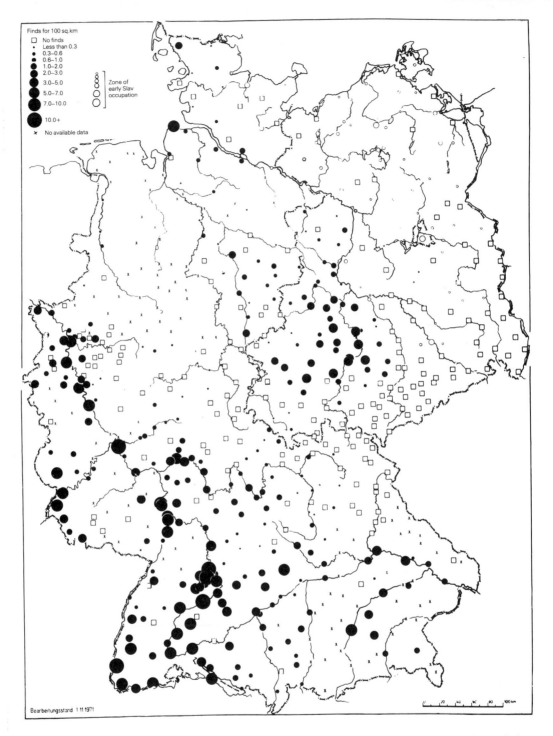

Bearbeitungsstand 1.11.1971

Church Down, which we shall discuss later when studying the results of the
excavations there since 1971.

It is, naturally, difficult to say to what extent the settlement history of the
Chalton landscape is representative of other regions of western Europe.
However, in our present state of knowledge, and taking into account other
work which is comparable, if not so detailed, we can at least draw two or three

Fig. 9. *Settlement in Germany in the fifth to seventh centuries*

This map is based on a survey of all the archaeological finds (cemeteries, villages, various objects) quoted in the bibliography. The number of finds in each group is represented by a symbol, whose area is proportional to the total surface area of each. It may be assumed that the number of discoveries is a reflection of the intensity of settlement. Three main settlement zones become apparent: the valley of the Rhine and its tributaries from the Netherlands frontier to Switzerland; to a lesser extent the Danube valley; and a strip running roughly WNW–ESE from Friesland to the Harz and Thuringia. Outside these three zones the significant absence of finds can be observed, such as the area to the east of the Harz and along the Baltic where there are traces of the earliest Slav inhabitants who, at that time, began to occupy the spaces left empty by the Germans.

(E. Gringmuth-Dallmer, Zur Kulturlandschaftentwicklung in frühgeschichtlicher Zeit im germanischen Gebiet, *Zeitschrift für Archäologie*, 6 (1972); 1, pp. 63–90)

---

conclusions of very general application. The first is the existence of scattered settlement by family units in the pre-Roman period. Then in Roman times there was a general trend towards concentration of population, the best illustrations of which are the large stone villas, which introduced a double discontinuity by concentrating the local inhabitants and, at the same time, being constructed on a regular plan using stone materials and lime mortar. Finally this special form of rural settlement was abandoned, along with the building materials and techniques associated with it, apparently accompanied at the same time by massive desertion at a more or less early date of the settlement sites of the Roman period in favour of new sites. Here less substantial materials of construction were used, although the trend towards concentration of population in one, two or three centres in each area of land was nevertheless continued.

The result was the restoration of arable farming and the complete restructuring, not only of the modes of settlement, but even more so of the agricultural exploitation of the area. The local inhabitants regrouped themselves into a smaller number of settlements. Gradually, over the course of several abandonments and transplantations, leading to an expansionist phase which began in Picardy around 550, these new settlement centres developed in the early Middle Ages into villages which correspond with the majority of those of today.

Picardy and Chalton are not isolated phenomena. All the studies carried out in regions which are comparable in terms of their degree of Romanization, in France, Germany or Britain, demonstrate the simultaneous general abandonment of the villa system after the fourth century, and the emergence from even earlier than that date, and the exclusive existence thereafter, of a very different form of rural settlement. What forms did this type of small- or medium-scale rural settlement (which for various reasons does not yet merit the appellation of 'village') take and how did they evolve? To explore this problem, the best area of study is undoubtedly Germany.

2   The case of Germany

Conditions of study

Germany is an excellent region for studying the forms and development of rural settlement during the early Middle Ages because of the scale and quality of the work carried out there on sites of this period.

One of the largest migrations of Germanic peoples towards north-western Europe, France and the British Isles took place at the beginning of the fifth century. This migration had two results – the depopulation of certain northern and eastern regions of Germany, in places very complete and long-lasting, and the consequent concentration of a relatively large German population in the western and southern regions of Germany, hitherto the most Romanized. A map showing the Germanic settlement zones of the fifth to seventh centuries clearly reveals the distinction between the two sectors (see Figure 9).

This contrast manifests itself in various other ways, notably from pollen analysis data which show the marked decline in cereal cultivation in eastern Germany over a period lasting from the fifth century to, in certain extreme cases, the tenth century (see Figure 10).

This therefore leads us, using accurate data provided by historians and archaeologists, to distinguish these two cases in studying the two ultimately different types of settlement in early medieval Germany.

The Romanized areas of Germany

Study of the Romanized areas of Germany, such as the Trier region, reveals examples and forms of settlement development that are doubtless very close to those of Picardy or other comparable regions of France, Belgium or Great Britain.

If the bases chosen for settlement studies of the Trier region are the cemeteries, the period of use of which can be established with accuracy thanks to the archaeological material found in graves of up to about 700, and the known settlement sites, it becomes apparent that, alongside a continuity of landscape from Roman foundations, there are various phases of new settlement creation in regions that had been under cultivation in classical times. A map of settlement sites, like a cereal pollen diagram, demonstrates some decrease in farming in the fourth to fifth centuries, followed by a very marked upturn.

New settlements came into being from the first decade of the fifth century and regularly thereafter, without the number of abandonments being high; indeed, abandonments may be considered as exceptional, since all the settlements founded before 600 were still in occupation around 700. Out of 53 settlements known to have been already in existence or founded in the sixth century, only four were abandoned before 700. Kurt Böhner has gone further:

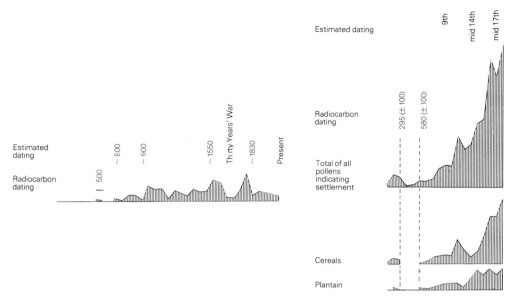

Fig. 10. *Cereal pollen diagrams for two German sites*

In the Thuringian forest, the cereal pollen diagram highlights the major events of German history: the migrations of the Germanic peoples and the resulting depopulation of the seventh to eighth centuries; the growth of the agrosystem after the tenth century, with the start of a period of population growth and expansion of cultivated lands; the agrarian crisis of the fourteenth to fifteenth centuries, and especially that of the Thirty Years' War in the seventeenth century. The same phenomena have produced comparable results at Zwillbrocker Venn, although here the curve for plantain (*plantago*) makes it possible to describe the development of the exploitation of the agrosystem with more accuracy. The sudden increase in this species in the fourteenth to fifteenth centuries, at a time when cereals were decreasing, is due to a classic phenomenon of that period: an increase in pasture at the expense of arable land.

(E. Gringmuth-Dallmer, Zur Kulturlandschaftentwicklung in frühgeschichtlicher Zeit im germanischen Gebiet, *Zeitschrift für Archäologie*, 6 (1972); fig. 3, p. 69 and fig. 5, p. 74)

---

he estimates that more than two-thirds of the settlements founded in the Frankish period are still in existence today. These data, demonstrating as they do a fairly rapid resumption of agriculture on the cultivated lands of antiquity, early continuous phases of new settlement creation, and the continuity of these settlements, indicate that this was a relatively well Romanized region. Such data are valid for other comparable regions, and especially the middle Rhineland, where the same phenomena can be observed.

Study of these two German regions – Trier and the middle Rhineland – makes it possible to go beyond the identification of early settlement foundations and their permanence. It is in fact possible to establish the major chronological phases of settlement.

A very marked wave of settlement took place in the seventh century. In the Trier region, 20 new settlements appeared between 450 and 525, 28 between 525 and 600, and 67 between 600 and 700. In the Rhineland around Cologne 28 settlements have been identified as having been in existence in the sixth century and there were 67 in the seventh century. Careful study of more accurate data allows us to refine these raw data and to show that this expansion in the number of settlements was based on a growth in population (doubtless reinforced by the arrival of migrant Germanic peoples) and better development of the land.

Böhner draws attention to the increase in the number of interments in the cemeteries between the sixth and seventh centuries, symptomatic of a growth in the population of the corresponding settlements. Palaeodemography has confirmed this empirical observation and makes it possible to assert that the population grew substantially between the sixth and seventh centuries, at least in those regions under consideration here which had clearly progressed beyond the stage of German provinces (see Figure 11).

Fig. 11. *Population development in the sixth to seventh centuries in the German region on the basis of palaeodemographic data*

Many early medieval cemeteries have been excavated since last century, essentially because of the amount and quality of the archaeological material they contain. Meticulous analysis of this material allows the date of burial to be determined, which in turn makes it possible to divide the total interments — often several hundred graves — into two or three successive chronological phases. The most suitable periods for this type of analysis are the sixth and seventh centuries, when the grave goods were especially abundant in Germanic burials. This tends to change after about 700, which limits the potential for palaeodemography to those cases where burials can be assigned to chronological phases on the basis of stratigraphic data alone, a more difficult procedure than the use of dated grave goods.

Using these chronological phases in the case of a cemetery, certain authors, mainly Hungarian, such as Acsadi and Nemeskeri, have developed a method for evaluating the probable living population in the contemporary settlement from which the dead came. This method is based on knowledge of the total number of burials in a cemetery (excavation must be as complete as possible or, if the cemetery is a large one, must permit its total population to be evaluated), the length of use of the cemetery, and the life expectancy of a new-born child. This last factor is established partly on the basis of observed data and partly on mortality tables for contemporary populations believed to be similar to those of the Middle Ages. This factor can only be an estimate because, for various reasons (principally associated with preservation), skeletons of new-born infants or foetuses are only rarely detectable in cemetery excavations.

Using this method it is possible to estimate either the average population of the settlement corresponding with a cemetery, for the whole period the latter was in use (column 3), or the population during each of the phases of use of the cemetery (columns 4 and 5). In the latter case, a true demographic study can be undertaken (column 6). Despite its relative uncertainties, this technique is an essential one in that it is the only one which makes it possible to study fluctuations in population in periods for which no written records often exist, such as the early Middle Ages.

	Total no. of burials observed	Probable duration of use of cemetery	Average population	Estimated average population		Rate of growth (6th century = base 1)	Estimated average no. of agricultural units in whole settlement	
				6th century	7th century		6th cent.	7th cent.
	1	*2*	*3*	*4*	*5*	*6*	*7*	*8*
Hailfingen	1074	200	163	47	278	5.9	2	11
Junkersdorf	921	200	141	133	151	1.1	5	6
Herten	598	200	92	47	138	3.0	2	6
Bulach	542	200	84	28	125	4.5	1	5
		(150?)	(111)					
	233	200	36	28	48	1.6	1	2
Köln-Mungersdorf								
Pulling	156	100	48	–	45	–	–	3
Eisenach	147	100	45	–	44	–	–	2
Beggingen-Löbern	142	100	44	–	44	–	–	2
Lörrach-Stetten	78	75	32	–	32	–	–	1
		(100?)	(34)		(24)			
Basle	69	100	21	–	21	–	–	1

In addition to demographic estimates, studies of this kind help in interpretation of the excavated settlement. Direct examination of skeletons reveals the presence of older individuals, and thus the normal existence in early medieval German settlements of three generations, comprising 6–8 adults and 9–12 children. Thus one may conceive of a population made up of extended families of 15–20 people. The data in columns 7 and 8 above relate to settlements generally made up of one to three such units — weak human groupings — as well as to the archaeologically observed tally of buildings themselves.

(P. Donat and H. Ulrich, Einwohnerzalhen und Siedlungsgrösse der Merowingerzeit: Ein methodischer Beitrag zur demographischen Rekonstruktion frühgeschichtlicher Bevölkerungen, *Zeitschrift für Archäologie*, 5 (1971), pp. 234–65)

Owing to their general nature, pollen diagrams, which give an idea of the overall progress of agricultural exploitation in a given region, particularly when it is possible to establish a cereal pollen curve, make it possible to confirm this expansion and to pinpoint its beginings to the sixth or seventh century in different cases.

Whilst these regions demonstrate an early development of rural settlement and a measure of stability, it should be added that this is associated with some migration of sites. Detailed study of the Rhineland has shown that settlements were located near rivers on alluvial clay soils in the late fourth and early fifth centuries. In the next phase, from 450 to 625, a trend towards the establishment of new settlements on the slightly higher river terraces, on different soils, can be observed. Finally, in the seventh century, it was more the clay and loess soils nearer rivers which attracted new settlements. Generally speaking, when compared with settlement in the Roman period, it is the restriction of settlement to sites close to rivers rather than this mobility of sites that is more striking – that is to say, a change which is based on topography as well as being qualitative in nature, in so far as it marks the appearance of 'village' settlement. However, what best characterizes one mode of transition from classical to medieval settlement in many extensively Romanized regions is gradual expansion of the cultivated landscape and growth of population, with the continuous creation of relatively static 'villages'.

Non-Romanized areas

If we now move to central Germany – the provinces of Franconia, the Main region, or Schleswig-Holstein – we find ourselves in regions that were less thickly populated in the Roman period than those we have just been discussing. The subsequent migration of the major part of their populations into the more westerly regions of Europe only served to accentuate this lack of settlement, by creating zones that were almost devoid of human occupation (cf. Figure 9). Let us take the case of that part of Schleswig-Holstein that has been studied by Herbert Jankuhn. During the Roman period there was a distinct increase in settlements, which remained relatively numerous in the third and fourth centuries, as revealed by examination of habitation sites and cemeteries. However, there is an almost total dearth of archaeological finds from the ensuing two or three centuries. It is difficult not to relate this situation to the departure of the Saxon inhabitants to the British Isles, and the resulting desert depicted by contemporary Anglo-Saxon chroniclers such as Bcde. This abandonment of the land – or at least the marked drop in population – so well documented by Jankuhn, affected all the regions from which the Saxons left en masse and not just Schleswig-Holstein. Thus in the region lying between the mouths of the Elbe and the Weser, which is being studied at the present time, one may observe the same massive decline in settlement, with sometimes a consequential semi-disappearance of archaeological finds. Excavation of the cemetery at Mahndorf, near Bremen, has shown that the population of the corresponding settlement numbered about 80 over the period 250–500, and dropped to only some 15 to 20 in the period 500–750, to rise again to 75 between 750 and 950.

After the centuries of abandonment referred to above, archaeological material from Schleswig-Holstein becomes relatively abundant again after 830. But it was not until the tenth century that fresh colonization of these deserted areas became a firm reality, with the arrival of peoples from further north – Danes, or even perhaps Swedes. Place-name data from the appearance of a welter of Scandinavian names in the tenth to eleventh centuries, together with the rise in the cereal pollen curve at the same time, confirm the indications from archaeological excavations. The numerous settlements clearly to be seen in the third to fifth centuries disappeared in the sixth to eighth centuries, and did not reappear properly until the tenth century, or even as late as the thirteenth to fourteenth centuries, a period of deforestation in this region.

Although it has not been so well explored, the settlement history of other German regions that did not lie within the Roman Empire is not much different in various respects from the situation in the Rhineland or the province of Trier.

In central Germany, rural settlement, apart from a lower density than that of the Romanized parts of Germany, is characterized principally in the period 450–700 by a high level of fluidity. Before 600, a relatively large number of settlements were founded – more than 60, or 5.2 new sites in each ten-year period – whilst between 600 and 700 there were no more than 3.2 per decade. Furthermore, almost all the older settlements had been abandoned by the seventh century. These two factors – considerable foundation of settlements before 600, widespread abandonment in the seventh century of the settlements formerly occupied – contrast with what has been observed in the Trier region or the Rhineland.

This instability of settlement in central Germany before 700 is encountered in other regions such as central Franconia or the Main-Tauber region.

Conclusion: Settlement evolution in early medieval Germany

To summarize the situation in Germany in terms of phases of creation and abandonment of settlements, one may make use of the results of the synthesis made by Walter Janssen, based on information from both excavation of rural sites and written sources. He distinguishes five major phases in the history of rural sites:

1 Foundations of the late La Tène or early Roman periods, abandoned in the second or third centuries;

2 a new phase of foundation in the second and third centuries, followed by abandonment in the fourth to fifth centuries: e.g. Wijster (Netherlands);

3 settlements founded in the early Empire and abandoned in the fifth to sixth centuries: e.g. Feddersen Wierde;

4 settlements deserted in the eighth to ninth centuries after a short existence of about 150 years: e.g. Warendorf, Oberbillig, Haldern;

5 finally, settlements established in the ninth and early tenth centuries which either survive to the present day or were abandoned after an existence of four or five centuries. Settlements founded in this phase depended for their survival on a phase of massive abandonment which, in Germany as elsewhere, manifested itself in the early thirteenth century and was stepped up in the fourteenth and fifteenth centuries, although appearing in certain regions as early as the eleventh to twelfth centuries (cf. Figure 52).

Janssen concludes that there were several phases of abandonment. Thus in the Eifel, where archaeology and written sources testify to the desertion of 450 villages between the eleventh and nineteenth centuries, an earlier phase can be postulated which began as early as the seventh century, continuing until the eleventh century; the paucity of source material available prevents the precise evaluation of its magnitude. Before that period, according to Jankuhn and the data given earlier, it is possible to assign to this region, as in northern Germany, a phase of settlement desertion in the fourth and fifth centuries, whilst in eastern Germany this occurs in the sixth and seventh centuries, before the arrival of the Slavs in the eighth century.

A third phase of abandonment began in the Eifel in the twelfth century, becoming very severe in the later fifteenth and early sixteenth centuries, so far as the Middle Ages are concerned.

In fact, if we move on from the specific problem of settlement abandonment to the wider aspect of settlement on the land, we see that Germany affords a distinct opposition between two periods, before and after the eleventh century.

If account is taken of the number of settlements created, the general rise in population, and average settlement life, an initial period of relatively long duration becomes apparent. This begins in the early first century AD and is divided into two successive phases. First, the settlements are not only small but also unstable, and often short-lived. Then, in the second phase, from the sixth to the tenth century, population grows and new settlements are founded, whilst those already in existence become larger. There is certainly a positive balance between new and deserted settlements in the sixth to tenth centuries. We should talk of settlement mobility within more or less circumscribed blocks of cultivated land rather than abandonment, as Chalton has demonstrated.

In the second period, which starts in the tenth century, this balance becomes a negative one, at least after the tenth to thirteenth centuries. But the essential factor in this period – a general rule which applies in Great Britain as well as in France – is the concentration of population in larger centres than hitherto, true villages in effect, and the greater stability of these settlements, which often become permanent. Some of these were doubtless earlier foundations, and it is difficult to say how many of the villages in existence in the twelfth to thirteenth centuries were recent creations and how many were earlier in origin. However, this aspect is relatively unimportant by comparison with the two factors emphasized above: stability and increase in size. The desertions in the last two centuries of the Middle Ages were different in character from those before the tenth century. They took place against a background of falling population, which was not the case before the eleventh century. However – and this is a new and important factor – these desertions only affected settlements that were of secondary importance in population terms, often recent creations, and marginal or at risk in relation to the main settlement centres or the areas of superior soils. These abandonments were thus different in character from those in the early Middle Ages: the latter were linked with an unstable form of settlement in small groups, in landscapes that were only sketchily organized and partly empty, and in which occupied sites could move about or change their nature. Desertion of whole settled landscapes was rare at that time, apart from in certain regions, such as that following the migration of the Germanic people, for example. Late medieval desertions came about in conditions that were diametrically opposite to those just described: the final balance was a negative one and entire landscapes were abandoned. This must be borne in mind when assessing the specific character of the evolution of early medieval rural settlement.

Continuing at this general level, it is interesting to observe that settlement mobility of the early Middle Ages is related to changes in the nature of cultivated soils: this fits in well with the picture of settlements wandering within landscapes that are partly empty, or at least available or little exploited. In central Germany, most settlements were located between 450 and the eleventh century on medium soils – more than two-thirds of the known sites.

However, between the fifth and sixth centuries, when light soils played a significant role in some 80 per cent of the known examples, and the eighth to eleventh centuries, when by contrast it was the heavy soils that reached this level (light soils continued to be used, but to a lesser extent), there was a very marked development. It is difficult to determine whether this was due to climatic reasons or improvements in farming techniques, or a combination of the two, but transfers from one type of soil to another are a feature over long periods of settlement (see Figure 12).

Settlement history during the Roman and early medieval periods in Germany provides a general schema which is of relevance to other parts of Europe, although it would be wrong to overlook significant regional variations, whether or not these are based on Roman settlement traditions in different areas.

Data from various sources seem to indicate that population increased between the sixth and seventh centuries and subsequently, partly owing to the settlement of migrant groups around existing centres of population and also as a result of some absolute growth of population. The examples to be discussed later suggest that there was often a progression from the original colonization by a single farm to the embryo of a rural agglomeration, resulting from the regrouping or juxtaposition of several farms.

This phenomenon becomes apparent in the first to the fifth centuries. The example of the village of Wijster (Netherlands), beyond the Roman frontier, is very illuminating in this respect. This settlement, extensively excavated by W. van Es, is made up of a number of agricultural units represented by small buildings of various types grouped round a larger house. In the first period of occupation (c.150–255), there were four large houses and three smaller ones. In the intermediate phase between periods I and II, there were five large houses, and in period II proper (c.255–325), the number had grown to 19 large and seven small buildings. Finally in period III (c.325–430), before abandonment, there were altogether 35 large and 14 small buildings. Thus there was a progression from several isolated farms, made up of seven buildings at the outset, to a true 'village' comprising over 40 buildings. This growth is linked with the evolution of the overall layout, from a complex of a few farms to an organized plan, with regular blocks defined by a network of roads aligned east-west and north-south.

This phenomenon of growth in settlement size, which was often sharply

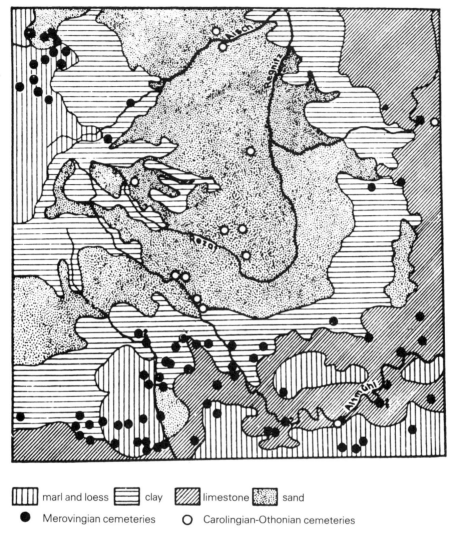

|||| marl and loess   ≡ clay   ▨ limestone   ▨ sand

● Merovingian cemeteries   ○ Carolingian-Othonian cemeteries

Merovingian, Carolingian and Othonian cemeteries in relation to soil types in central Franconia.

Fig. 12. *Settlement and soil quality in Germany*

It is often accepted that improvements in domestic animal species, the appearance of heavier and more powerful ploughs, an increase in the numbers of draught animals on farms, and the spread of the harness collar represent progress towards the cultivation of heavy soils. This would seem to be borne out by analysis of the types of soil in the German Democratic Republic upon which known settlements datable to the fifth to eleventh centuries were established:

	No. of known datable sites	Light soils	Medium soils	Heavy soils
Second half of 5th century 6th century	254	18.1%	79.1%	2.8%
7th century	53	1.9%	84.9%	13.2%
8th–11th centuries	65	15.4%	66.2%	18.4%

The increase in the proportion of settlements established on heavy soils between the fifth and eleventh centuries is significant.

However, hasty generalizations should be avoided. In central Franconia, the development appears to have gone the other way. The location of sixth- to eleventh-century cemeteries – if it is accepted that cemeteries are sited in the middle of cultivated landscapes – indicates that settlement took place on sandy soils, in contrast with the new areas opened up in the Carolingian and Othonian periods, i.e. after the ninth century.

(E. Gringmuth-Dallmer, Zur Kulturlandschaftentwicklung in frühgeschichtlicher Zeit im germanischen Gebiet, *Zeitschrift für Archäologie*, 6 (1972); 1, pp. 63–90; and H. Jankuhn, *Archäologie und Geschichte*, I (1976); fig. 10, p. 257.)

---

interrupted by the incursion of Germanic emigrants who had abandoned their original homelands, or which was at the very least disturbed by the socio-economic and political impact of the migration period, appears to have begun again in Germany in the sixth century, at least in the more advanced areas.

There were differences from region to region, and these were no doubt very pronounced. In certain regions, the almost total exodus of the population resulted after the fifth century in a hiatus in settlement that lasted several centuries. In such cases, resettlement could be relatively early, starting in the sixth century, or much later – in the ninth to tenth centuries in Schleswig-Holstein. However, it was always a gradual process, from a single isolated farm to an agglomeration of varying size, from a settlement in a cleared area to much more extensive deforestation, leading to complete removal of the woodland cover and the opening up of the entire landscape. In fact, the differences between one region and another are essentially chronological, with varying degrees of delay in the process. Similarly, the mobility of settlement between the sixth and ninth to tenth centuries is typical of certain regions of Germany, as we have seen, but it doubtless applied equally in parts of the British Isles or France. Recent work has thrown more light on this phenomenon, particularly in Great Britain.

This process of settlement in the northern half of Europe in the early Middle Ages, with its varying modes and chronological stages, took place everywhere in comparable ways within an equivalent socio-economic context. One may seek to see the same major phenomena everywhere: mobility of settlement site rather than true abandonment phases; the resumption of

63

cultivation of deserted landscapes more or less rapidly, rather than the opening up of new lands; initial localized and small-scale settlement, becoming more concentrated and substantial everywhere.

3 The Anglo-Saxon and Irish lands

One of the classic characteristics of early medieval settlement in Germany is its mobility, and the numerous abandonments that typify this period. The same applies to Great Britain: recent research has amply demonstrated the 'Middle Saxon shuffle', that lack of fixity in settlement which characterizes the seventh to eighth centuries there, even though the precise reasons for the desertion of the primary Anglo-Saxon sites are, as in Germany, hard to ascertain. However, so far as other factors are concerned, some prudence must be exercised in extending all the observations made on the Continent to the British Isles.

Regions persisted where no gradual coalescence took place or where it was incomplete in early medieval Europe up to the eleventh century: these can be seen in England, in Germany and, to a lesser extent, in Scandinavia. Ireland is a typical example of this type of region. In that country there was no settlement in true villages similar in form and function to those of medieval England in some southern and eastern parts until the eighteenth to nineteenth centuries. However, there were late foundations in Ireland, the work of the Anglo-Norman invaders of the twelfth to thirteenth centuries.

The most obvious form of pre-Norman settlement in the modern country-side consists of enclosures of earthen, or more rarely stone, banks, some dozen metres in diameter. These are known as 'ringworks' in England and southern Ireland, and in northern Ireland as 'raths', when the ramparts are earthen, and 'cashels' when they are stone-built. This terminology will be adopted here.

Some 30,000 raths are known in Ireland, generally dating from the first millennium AD. They average 30m (68ft) in diameter and the later examples were in use up to the twelfth century, as protection for a handful of farm buildings. About 60 of them have been excavated over the last 40 years. The houses that have been discovered had an average floor area of 18 sq. m (194 sq. ft), at best suitable for a small family group. Alongside these round or rectangular houses lie the traditional ancillary buildings: barns, stores, granaries etc. Archaeological discoveries have shown that this was an economy based on agriculture but above all else on stock-rearing: cattle were most common, constituting 70 per cent of the livestock.

It is interesting to note that these raths often contain evidence of ironworking. Metal tools were still relatively common. In at least two cases, the production of metal objects exceeded the needs of the farm, according to the archaeological evidence. As so often in early medieval sites, bronze continued to play an important role alongside iron, and it, too, was worked in some of these raths. The working of wood, bone (greatly used), ivory etc is also attested in a number of these establishments. Finds of sherds of continental early medieval pottery from France – probably the Saintonge – testify to the maintenance of at least indirect economic relations with the continent during

64

this time, possibly based on the wine and salt trade.

These raths and cashels represent an original form of scattered settlement, very similar to that in Scandinavia, here characterized by the presence of a circular enclosure round a farming unit. These enclosures would have housed free rural peoples, who were superior in rank to the rest of contemporary society (less well understood owing to a lack of excavation) and who lived in small groups of a few unfortified farms, to be found in varying concentrations in the same regions as the raths and cashels. The study of certain regions of Ireland, such as County Down, has shown that raths and these small aggregations, known as bailes, occupy mutually exclusive areas and so are contemporaneous, but doubtless represent differences in status or other socio-economic phenomena.

Thus Ireland provides a seeming predominance throughout the Middle Ages, irrespective of building types, of a particular type of rural settlement based on single farming units or small groups of such units, sometimes fortified. In this region we do not find the phenomenon of growth in size of rural settlements which is to be observed on the continent or in Great Britain at the same time over the first millennium, and particularly towards its end. This is thus a special type of rural settlement, perhaps close to that in certain parts of Scandinavia or Brittany. We know little about settlement in Brittany in the early Middle Ages, but there is no doubt that scattered settlement was the rule there, and recent excavations have suggested that a form of settlement similar to that of early medieval Ireland may have been common. An excavation directed by P.-R. Giot on the island of Guennoc in the *commune* of Landea (Finistère) has revealed, in a stone-built enclosure some 40m (44yd) in diameter, four rectangular stone houses ranging in date from the Middle Ages to the seventeenth to eighteenth centuries and constituting a settlement very similar to an Irish cashel (see Figure 13).

4   The Mediterranean lands

The problem becomes much more complex in southern France and, wider still, the Mediterranean world, where Roman civilization had made a much greater impression.

It is easy to see that there the converse of the situation in Picardy, for example, applies. Roman land-allotment systems are very often not only visible but still in use: for example, around Cesena (Italy) the countryside is divided up regularly into 710m (776yd) squares – Roman *limitatio* or centuriation, the square units of which measure 2400 Roman feet (*c.*720m [787yd]). This centuriation, which profoundly influences the present-day Italian countryside, notably in the plain of the Po, is also to be found far from Italy: very clear traces are still to be seen today around Arles and Béziers.

In southern France the survival of the Roman system, at least in the more important areas, can doubtless be explained by exploitation of the land in the Roman period in so profound a way in material terms that early medieval cultivation had no effect on its form. Even though the dimensions of this

Fig. 13. *Aerial view of the island of Guennoc, Landea (Finistère)*

This island has been inhabited since the Neolithic period. Most of the visible structures lying outside the circular enclosure are from later prehistoric times. The medieval circular enclosure provides protection for several buildings of the period, along with a post-medieval house with a wall round its small courtyard, the best preserved of the structures visible within the enclosure. The well-preserved rectangular structure towards the bottom of the photograph, lying outside the enclosure, is a modern sheep shelter.

(Photograph kindly provided by the excavator, P.-R. Giot)

---

phenomenon of continuity remain as yet unquantified, it is none the less very important to take it into account. Should we conclude from this that the different process in northern France has nothing to do with the peoples and settlements of classical times in southern France and Italy?

Unfortunately we suffer from an almost total lack of synthetic studies of this problem and, what is more, of excavations of early medieval sites, as Gabrielle d'Archimbaud has remarked with regard to Provence earlier than the twelfth century. Some exceptions from Italy will be dealt with later. In these Mediterranean regions, the possibilities for aerial photography are restricted by reason of the steep or tortuous relief, the small field patterns, the landscape which is wooded or planted with shrubs, vines, or olive trees, etc. Only systematic planned field survey and excavation can yield results. Unfortunately this is the area of Europe where archaeological research is least well developed, despite some remarkable experiments and fieldwork, particularly in

Provence and certain regions of Italy.

We must, therefore, make do with what we have, and in these circumstances the results, despite general similarities, seem to be somewhat different from those observed further north.

It appears that in this region, as elsewhere, the villa system crumbled in the fourth and fifth centuries. By the end of that period, and in every case by the fifth century, the villas seem to have been abandoned. As in the more northern regions, there are traces of peripheral and more or less temporary reoccupation of ruins or a few rooms of villa buildings, but this cannot be counted as continuity. Nevertheless, some examples of continuity of use, particularly in Italy and lasting several centuries, cannot be totally ignored.

Very early on – from the end of the fourth century – a classic phenomenon of the Mediterranean region makes its appearance: the building of hilltop settlements. This phenomenon recurs around 1000.

The way in which these hilltop settlements were established is very clear, especially in Italy. At the same time, fortified settlements of regrouped people were set up in the plains – the *castra*. Here, as in northern Europe, this regrouping of the population went hand in hand with the dissolution of the classical landscape and its mode of agriculture. The transition to nucleated hilltop settlements, which marked a clear break (as in the medieval settlement of Picardy and elsewhere) with the Roman system of dispersed settlement, established a link with the earlier traditions of the Italic peoples or the Celtic tribes of Gaul – the *oppidum* or elevated fortress. In some cases it is possible to assert that earlier sites were re-occupied.

An example may be given from Provence, in the lands of the commune of Rougiers (Var). During the Roman period the settlement, comprising several villas, was down on the plain. These were abandoned at the end of the Roman period and the displaced population relocated themselves 300m (328yd) above the plain, on a La Tène II defended promontory site (cf. Figure 57). A small rectangular fortlet was built there, the inhabitants living in huts. It is remarkable, and perhaps typical of this type of settlement, that this occupation was short-lived, the inhabitants moving on to a new site, the location of which is still unknown but which was probably a *castrum* (strong point) at high level, known only through documents recording its destruction in the twelfth century.

In some cases, it is possible to observe that settlement took place on new hilltop sites but using techniques and styles that derive directly from the Iron Age *oppida*.

An example is the site at Lombren (Venejean, Gard). The village (see Figure 14), which commands the left bank of the Rhône, not far from Orange, is built on a well-defined limestone platform that is difficult to approach, and thus easy to defend, or at any rate protect. A rampart bars access from the west and north, the other sides being protected by cliffs. Like the buildings on the site, the rampart is of drystone construction, without mortar. The houses, each consisting of a single rectangular room measuring some 12 sq. m (14 sq. yd),

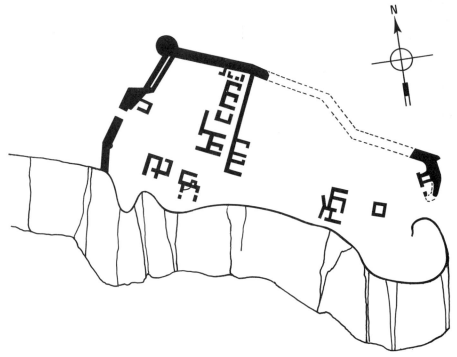

Fig. 14. *The oppidum of Lombren (Gard), dated to the late fourth to fifth century: area excavated up to 1970*

(J. Charmasson, Un *oppidum* du Bas-Empire, Lombren, *Archéologia*, No. 36 (1970), p. 56)

are regularly laid out within the enclosure.

One interesting fact, which distinguishes these from sites of the same period in northern France, is the continued use of the Roman roofing system, with *tegulae* and *imbrices*. However, the oil lamps mass-produced in specialized workshops and abundantly characteristic of the Roman period become very rare: only three from 23 excavated houses. The interesting factor is the presence of craftsmen: metal and pottery production, iron and leather working, spinning and weaving were all being practised. Finally, evidence of trade is furnished by finds of coins, high-quality pottery from the surviving large specialized workshops, bronze artefacts and amphorae.

Although it is very close in type, construction techniques and form to some of the large Celtic *oppida* not far away, such as Entremont or Ensérune, Lombren was built and laid out to a fairly regular plan and quite quickly, in the late fourth century. Again worthy of comment is the fact that it was only briefly occupied, probably until the late fifth century. What sort of site replaced it? We do not know, but the amount of labour involved in setting it up and its degree of deliberate planning seem to indicate that it was the work of an organized group of some size (at least 23 houses have been excavated), coupled with the unstable nature of settlement at this period, especially following the crisis and the great upheavals in the late fourth and fifth centuries.

We can find further proof in southern France of the rapid movements of populations desperate for refuge in the late fourth and the entire fifth centuries, and also of the frequent short-term use of places of refuge: this is provided by the cave settlements which the relief of southern France so often furnishes.

A good example is the prehistoric cave at l'Hortus in the commune of Velflaunès (Hérault). This was occupied several times during the fourth and fifth centuries, directly on top of the Mousterian occupation levels. The first occupation, in the later fourth century, was slight and discarded material is rare, but by contrast the second occupation (at the end of the fourth century) and the third (early fifth century) were fairly intensive, with much waste material. This cave continued to be used sporadically throughout the first half of the fifth century. What is interesting in this example, in addition to the nature of the site itself and the concern for protection that it implies, is the contrast between the rich, often luxury, material from the later fourth century, including objects in the Roman tradition of high quality, and the much poorer material from the fifth century occupation. This is very significant evidence of the diminished availability of luxury goods, along with a general impoverishment of the population and, even more, of a profound change in material culture. Another interesting observation is that, whilst wild animal bones are very abundant in the fourth-century occupation, evidence of a pronounced recourse to hunting, in the fifth century domestic species preponderate mainly sheep, then goats, and finally pigs and cattle, in all making up three-quarters of the bones found. Pollen analysis, which testifies to considerable deforestation between the two periods, gives the same picture of greater importance being assigned to domestic animals for food. After a difficult phase in the fourth century, the land was brought under cultivation again and stock-raising increased. All this evidence points to a rapid return to a more stable and less exceptional form of settlement, as demonstrated by the short and sporadic occupation of this cave.

III CONCLUSIONS

The diversity of situations in early medieval Europe naturally restricts generalization. Nevertheless, it is possible to distinguish broad outlines for part of the continent.

In the Romanized area, a form of scattered settlement based on the stone-built villas was established in the first and second centuries and survived more or less intact until the third to fourth centuries. This form of settlement was very dense in the southern part of Europe, but more patchy in northern France and in Britain. It overlay settlement by small family agrarian units, of a type that had long been established all over Europe, which continued to characterize the 'barbarian' regions lying beyond the Imperial *limes*, especially in Germany, Scandinavia and the Celtic areas during the Roman period.

From the third century onwards, however, in many Romanized areas of northern France and Britain, there was a trend towards the abandonment of villas and resettlement in rural agglomerations that were completely different in concept. It is very difficult to trace the origins of these new communal settlements or of their numbers or density. What is certain is that this was a general movement that arose in the Romanized areas at the same time as the decline of the Roman agrarian system.

This development took place in a complex period, characterized by important phenomena that had profound repercussions on modes of settlement: population movements, which began as early as the second century, and became very substantial in the fifth century, affecting the whole of western Europe, and radical socio-economic changes in farming methods.

These migrations of peoples emptied entire regions, especially in northern and eastern Germany. However, the main problem was neither the desertion of these regions nor the pressure, which was ultimately checked, of Germanic peoples on the areas that had long been Romanized. The most significant aspects were the contemporary phenomena which affected rural settlement between the fifth and eleventh centuries.

The trend towards rural resettlement on sites which, unlike the villas, were constructed of perishable materials (wood, foliage and baked clay) affected the whole of Europe, though the phenomenon was less pronounced in the south than in the north. It was characterized in various ways, primarily by some degree of settlement mobility and instability. The timescales and intensities varied, but it appears that in the best studied areas – Germany, the Netherlands, Great Britain – rural settlements of the fifth to eleventh centuries were often short-lived, of the order of no more than two or three centuries.

This instability of settlement was probably due either to a fall in population or to the insecurity of the period. Where archaeological and historical research has provided adequate data, certain phenomena become apparent which run counter to the interpretation of this abandonment of settlements on the basis of population decline, as was the case in the fourteenth and fifteenth centuries.

In fact, two phenomena – instability and a gradual increase in size of rural settlements – influenced the entire period up to the eleventh century, although there were divergences or discontinuities at various times or in different areas. Settlements which had grown from two to several dozen buildings abruptly disappeared, sometimes because their inhabitants had emigrated to the British Isles, sometimes for other reasons which are unfortunately often not understood. On the other hand, there is no doubt that this phenomenon of concentration of settlement did not apply in certain peripheral regions of Europe such as Scandinavia, or the Celtic lands such as Ireland, by contrast with the rest of Europe at this period. The traditional form of settlement remained the farm or isolated building until well after the early Middle Ages.

However, leaving aside these special cases or single events, it can be said that the same phenomenon of transition took place, from scattered rural settlement to one that became gradually more concentrated. This occurred in different stages, according to whether it was happening in the highly Romanized areas of the Mediterranean, the less Romanized regions such as northern France or Britain, or the deserted zones of eastern and northern Germany.

Towards the end of the period, in the eighth to tenth centuries, large rural settlements were in existence, in some of which parish churches had already been erected. It is only at this stage, when a number of socio-economic criteria begin to exercise an influence, that it becomes possible to talk of the 'village'. What is certain is that the early medieval period, for all its fluctuations and uncertainties, witnessed the birth of this type of rural settlement which was to characterize all the succeeding centuries. Detailed analysis, using archaeological methods, of some examples of excavated rural settlements will illustrate this important phenomenon from another angle.

Chapter Three: The house and its ancillaries in early medieval rural settlement

From the third century up to the tenth to eleventh centuries, agglomerated settlements gradually defined and established themselves. Through various phases of desertion and creation, this mode of settlement came to encompass clearly defined contiguous areas of cultivated landscape, and assumed the stable forms that persisted to the early years of the present century. Over this period, too, medieval house types also slowly evolved and spread. We shall attempt to describe early medieval rural settlements and the buildings of which they were composed, using a number of examples.

I THE VARIETIES OF RURAL BUILDINGS

Germany is the region of Europe that, by virtue of the volume and quality of the research that has been carried out, is the best on which to base this survey. To assist the study of early medieval settlement in that country, we have at our disposal the results of a large number of excellent excavations, as well as documentary data. One of the most important of these excavations, at Warendorf, provides the introduction to this problem.

A The Continental Germans

As in the case of most of the sites that will be referred to in this study, we do not know the original name given by its inhabitants to the site that was excavated. It will therefore be referred to, following the custom of the archaeological literature, under the name of the district in which it is located: Warendorf (Westphalia, Federal Republic of Germany).

1 *Warendorf (Westphalia)*

Four successive and continuous occupation levels were found on this site, dating from the second half of the seventh century to the end of the eighth century. Warendorf bears witness to the advance of the Saxons, who took advantage of the departure westwards of the Franks towards the Roman Empire to fill their place in the territory they had vacated. It was no doubt the Frankish reconquest towards the end of the eighth century – more accurately

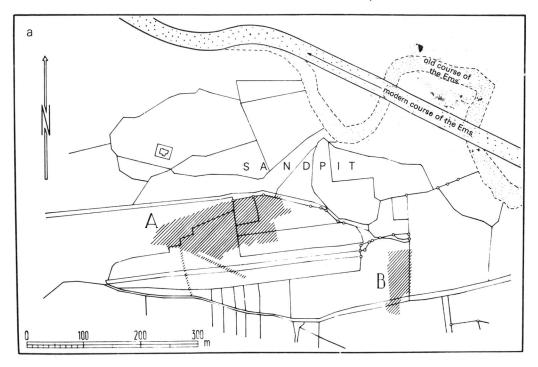

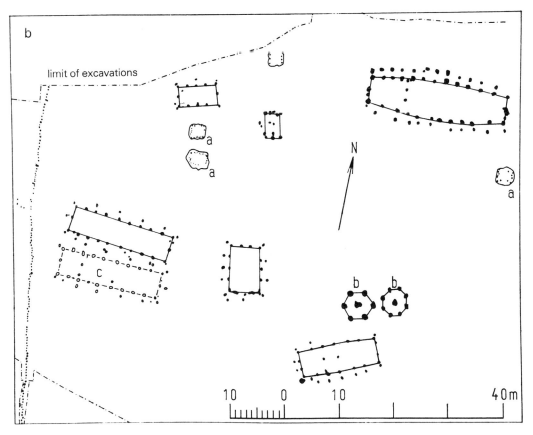

Fig. 15. *The seventh- to eighth-century settlement at Warendorf (Westphalia)*
a Location of the two areas excavated, the larger to the west
b Simplified partial plan, showing a group of contemporaneous buildings which form a true single farming unit: a large house, boat-shaped in plan; four sunken huts; various ancillary buildings of different sizes, for dwellings or storage; and two hexagonal granaries. These 12–13 buildings, occupying an area of *c.*70 × 50 m (76 × 55 yd) (one third of a hectare), represent the traditional agricultural exploitation of the site.

(W. Winkelmann, Die Ausgrabungen in der frühmittelalterlichen Siedlung bei Warendorf, Westfalen, *Neue Ausgrabungen in Deutschland*, (1958), p. 435; W. Sage, *Die frankische Siedlung bei Gladbach, Kr. Neuwied* (1969))

---

the great campaigns of that period – and the expulsion of the Saxons which led to the abandonment of the site.

Excavations between 1951 and 1958 over an area of some 2.6ha revealed a total of 186 buildings, differing greatly in layout, size, methods of building and function (see Figure 15). One group of above-ground buildings can be distinguished which were used as dwellings or annexes to them: 25 large buildings measuring 14–29m (46–95ft) long by 4.5–7m (15–23ft) wide, 40 smaller ones measuring 4–11m (13–36ft) by 3–3.5m (10–11ft) and 20 small ancillary buildings. A second group of buildings with sunken floors numbered 20 in all: these were roughly rectangular depressions with areas of several square metres and some tens of centimetres deep. Finally there were various buildings raised up on posts – 25 hexagonal in shape, three octagonal, and three roughly circular or semi-circular – which are the remains of raised granaries or posts to support roofs protecting stacks of cereals or hay (see Figures 16 and 17).

A group of 15 such varied buildings around a single large house constitute a single farming unit, covering an area of about 70m × 50m (76 × 55yd), on a fairly rudimentarily organized layout.

The large buildings constituted the basic element which was present in every group, and so the study of the site will commence with them.

The larger buildings are usually orientated on an east-west axis. At Warendorf they are of two types: rectangular in the earlier phase of the site, and with curved sides in the later phase – boat-shaped houses.

What is of interest here is the difference in plan between these two house types. This difference seems to be associated with certain distinctive characteristics, such as the number of postholes on the short sides (see Figure 16a). The rectangular houses have an even number of postholes (four), all of the same size, whilst the boat-shaped houses have only three, the centre one being very substantial. This difference, which may appear unimportant, means in fact that in the former case, where there is no central support, the roof was certainly hipped (see Figure 16d), whilst in the latter, by contrast, the

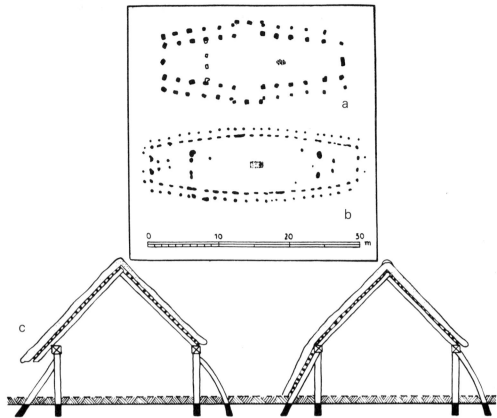

Fig. 16. *The boat-shaped house in northern Europe*

Excavations at Warendorf (**a**) or the Danish fortress of Trelleborg (**b**) have produced large buildings, usually measuring between 14 m (15 yd) and 30 m (33 yd) or even more in length, with long rounded sides, taking up the general shape of a boat. Buildings of this type from the fifth to the tenth centuries are also known from Scandinavia, Denmark, northern Germany, the Netherlands (e.g. Kootwijk – cf. Figure 18 – and Dorestad) and England (e.g. Catholme – Figure 22 – and Hamwih, the early medieval port which preceded Southampton).

The frames of these buildings are kept in place by lines of external angled buttresses, a technique found in association with buildings of other forms (cf. Figure 102), especially the rectangular houses at Warendorf. With the aid of various factors, especially graphical representations, it is possible to reconstruct the general appearance of this type of building (**e**): evidence is supplied by, for example, the chest from the cathedral at Cammin, Pomerania (now Kamień Pomorski), made of wood covered with bone plates secured by lead framing and dated to around 1000 (**f**), a coin from the Swedish port of Birka (**g**), and other similar objects. Both the examples illustrated show heads of monsters or gargoyles mounted at the ends of the ridge beam, which is curved in section.

(*a, b, d*: R. Cramp, Beowulf and Archaeology, *Medieval Archaeology*, 1 (1957); figs. 16a, 16b
c: B. Trier, *Das Haus im Nordwesten der Germania Libera*, IV, Veröffentlichungen der Altertumskommission im Provinzialinstitut für westfälische Landes- und Volkskunde, Aschendorffsche Verlagsbuchhandlung, Münster/Westfalen (1969), Tafel 17a
e, f: L'art scandinave, Editions Zodiaque, I (1969), fig. 34, p. 163 and fig. 38, p. 172
g: H. Schmidt, The Trelleborg House reconsidered, *Medieval Archaeology*, 17 (1973), fig. 24, p. 63)

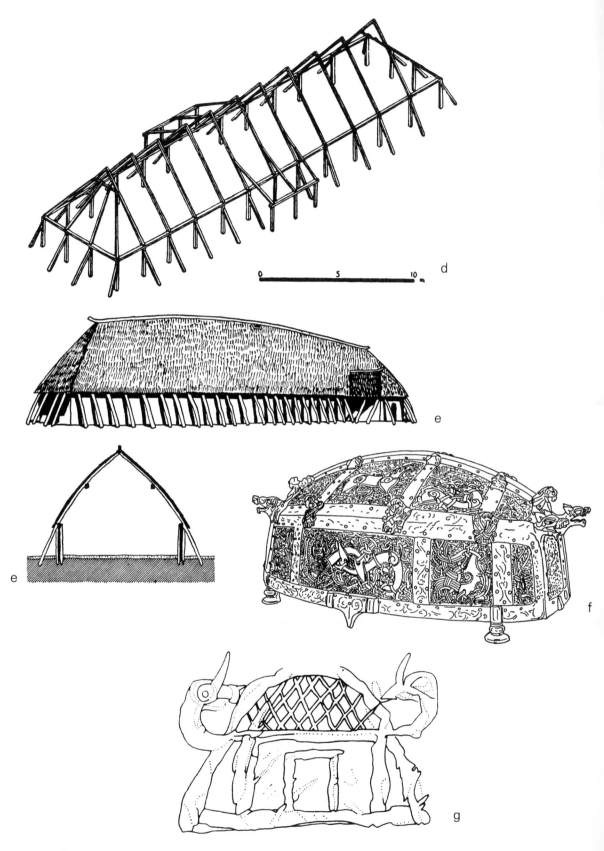

d

e

e

f

g

reinforced central support means that the roof was gabled, the ridge beam directly supported by the post in the centre of the short sides (see Figure 16a).

Alongside this structural difference, there is another distinction, partly resulting from the former. In both types of construction, the frame is directly supported by principal rafters, each of which is linked by tie-beams to a line of vertical posts, identified by a series of postholes surviving around the perimeter of the building. Each of these upright posts, which formed the wall, was braced externally by an additional angled post which served as a buttress (see Figure 16c). The existence of these bracing posts explains the double line of postholes which encircles the living space, the outer ring being the remains of the angled supports. The angled orientation of the latter was easily confirmed by excavating vertical sections of the postholes, which showed that the supports were inserted in the ground at an angle of 70° to the horizontal.

Although both types of building had these external bracing posts, only the rectangular houses used them to take the thrust from the shorter sides. This is illustrated by the fact that in this case the roof is hipped, which produces oblique external thrusts on the axis of the building (see Figure 16b, d, e). By contrast, in the boat-shaped houses, with upright gable ends, there is no need to take the thrust on the short walls.

These structural differences, significant in themselves, do not produce important differences in the utilization of the living area. In both cases there were two entrances, located opposite one another at the centre of the two long sides. A single hearth was situated in one half of the building, as defined by the two doors, on the long axis of the building. This similarity in the use of the interior is of interest because it confirms that, although there are two distinct types of building, they were basically used in the same way.

As on many other sites, there were other smaller buildings of similar construction alongside the large houses. When these have hearths they can be interpreted as dwellings, but otherwise they were probably barns (see Figure 17b). Overall they are slightly more numerous than the large houses, which themselves in some cases have no hearths (see Figure 17a).

At Warendorf, as on so many other sites of this period, there are almost as many sunken huts as there are ground-level buildings: 70 of the former as compared with 85 of the latter (see Figure 17a). This poses a problem, that of what these sunken huts were used for, to which we shall return later. The excavator was tempted to see them as merely workshops, especially for weaving.

Alongside these dwellings, stores and workshops, there are also various other structures basically intended for the protection of cereal stacks. These are small structures consisting of a roof carried on upright posts, rectangular in plan (see Figure 17e), or, like those still in use in the Netherlands and northern Germany, simple octagonal or hexagonal roofs mounted on posts, and capable of being raised and lowered vertically as the sheaves accumulate or are withdrawn (see Figure 17f). Finally, it may be assumed there were also simple grids of wooden beams mounted on low uprights, intended solely to

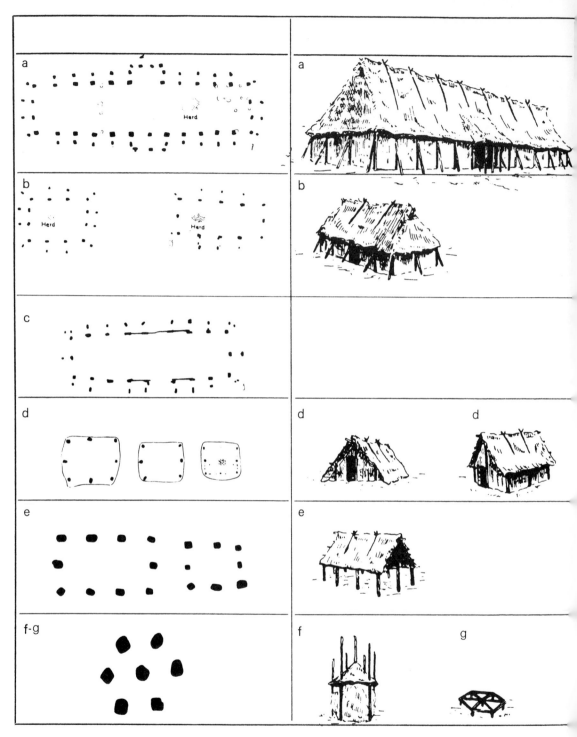

Fig. 17. *The buildings at Warendorf (7th–8th centuries) and their functions*

Five types of structure, all constructed in perishable materials, the conjunction of which constituted a farming unit (cf. Figure 15b), existed on the site:

1 Large buildings, rectangular (cf. Figure 16d) or boat-shaped (cf. Figure 16a)

2 Rectangular buildings constructed in the same manner as 1 but smaller. These two

Allemans	Bavarians	Salian Franks	Ripuarian Franks	Saxons	Anglo-Saxons
domus lib. casa } hus sala	– domus lib. – casa dom. – seli, casa, hus	– domus lib. – casa } hus – salina	– domus – hus – casa	– domus – casa	– hus – aern } domus – healle – seli
scuria lib. u.a. armenta equarum et vaccarum granicia cellaria domus servi	– scuria lib. conclusa parietibus et pessulis cum clave munita – domus servi	– scuria cum animalibus – sutes cum porcis – cellarium	 – sotes paricus	 – stabulum – horreum	– scipena – bern (horreum) – styllan = stallbauen – fald – lochyrdl = Hürdebauen
genicia stuba spicaria servi, ovile pocaricia	– coquina – balnearius – pistoria – mita – mita minoria = scopar	– genicium – screona	– ovile – appearius	– screona (alvearium)	– cylne
spicaria dom. scuria servi	– scuria absque parietibus = scof	– spicarium aut horreum cum tecto		– spyker	
—	– granarium = parc – fenile	– machalum = horreum sine tecto fenile		– granarium	– hreac = machalum

types of building may or may not have hearths: the former would be dwelling houses and the latter ancillary to the dwellings

3 Sunken huts

4 Improvised structures made up of a roof supported on posts and with no partitions

5 Hexagonal structures which can be reconstructed either as simple frames to raise

harvested crops above ground level, or as moveable roofs used for a similar purpose and analogous with structures in common use in northern Germany and the Netherlands to the present day

Analysis of contemporary documents, particularly the various legal codes of the Germanic peoples, confirm that the rural settlements of these peoples were composed of farming units consisting of several buildings with specialized functions (dwelling, workshop, protection of crops and livestock), which makes it possible to attribute likely functions to the Warendorf buildings.

(W. Winkelmann, Eine westfälische Siedlung des 8. Jahrhunderts bei Warendorf, Kr. Warendorf, *Germania,* 32 (1954), and H. Dölling, *Haus und Hof in Westgermanischen Volksrechten*, Aschendorffsche Verlagsbuchhandlung, Münster/Westfalen (1958), p. 91)

---

insulate the sheaves from damp by raising them slightly off the ground. All these forms of protection for harvested crops, which are to be found elsewhere in north-western Europe in various forms, as at Wijster, Bennekom (cf. Figure 21), or Kootwijk (cf. Figure 18), are of great interest. They attest to the magnitude of cereal or hay production and at the same time to the quasi-impossibility of using one half of the large houses for grain or hay storage. Differentiation in this way between types of structure and the very advanced fragmentation of function in buildings, separating the places for living, work and storage, may be surprising. In fact, these two factors agree perfectly with what is known of the settlements of Germanic people from contemporary written sources.

As the surviving documents make abundantly plain, these were not egalitarian societies. Broadly speaking they were divided into three very distinct groups. The uppermost group consisted of nobles, chiefs, sometimes kings (*herses* and *jarls* in Norway, *godhi* in Iceland, *ethelings* among the continental Saxons, *eorls* in Anglo-Saxon England etc). Then came the more numerous group of free peasants, whose status was somewhat variable and who were sometimes themselves graduated; this group, known as *bondi* in Scandinavian societies, *friling* among the continental Saxons, *ceorls* in Anglo-Saxon England, formed the basis of society. Finally, there were the slaves, and in some places freedmen, the latter forming a special group intermediate between the free peasants and slaves. This division leads to the view that there are marked differences to be observed, in the majority of cases at least, between various types of dwelling house. In practice there were probably only two categories, free peasants and slaves. In so far as this applied generally in Germanic societies, with a greater fragmentation in terms of building in the rural context, a very pronounced specialization becomes apparent in building types. All the barbarian legal codes are unanimous and specific on this point (see Figure 17). These laws enumerate various elements when referring to 'villages' described as such (most often using the term *villa*). There is the farm proper (usually *curtis*, sometimes *hof*) and the group of buildings which seem in fact, according to both written sources and excavations, to have existed in villages. Then there is the dwelling house proper (*domus*, *casa* and *sala* were the terms most frequently used), variable in size and number of inhabitants; the workshops, essentially reserved for the women and usually devoted to spinning and weaving (*screona*, *genicium*); the various sheds for livestock and barns (*scuria cum animalibus*, *sutes cum porcis*, *stabulum* etc), structures for storage (*spicarium*, *cellarium*, *horreum*, *horreum sine tecto*, *granarium*, *machalo* etc); and the defensive enclosure.

The Germanic peoples were agrarian societies, practising mixed stock-raising and agriculture. In their rural settlements they usually built a series of structures of distinct forms, very variable in size and complexity, and with four very specific functions: the housing of men (whether free or enslaved), the housing of livestock, the protection of harvested crops and food reserves, and the protection of livestock and the village itself. Written documents always refer not only to the livestock enclosure, but also in particular to the palisade which surrounds the settlement and its farming units (*sepis* in most documents).

If the example of Warendorf seems to be an extreme one, by virtue of the size of each of its farming units, covering an area of some 70m × 50m (76 × 55yd) and with a group around each large house consisting of about a dozen buildings of various kinds (eight to ten built at ground level, whether as dwellings or not, two roofed structures for stacks of sheaves, and three or four sunken huts), it is in no way to be distinguished from other contemporaneous sites (cf. Figure 15b). This, moreover, holds good for a very wide region, which recent excavation has shown to embrace the Netherlands, Denmark, Scandinavia, a large part of Germany, and even England.

A good example of the comparability of continental farming units of this period is afforded by a site in the Netherlands at Kootwijk, a little later in date than that at Warendorf.

2 Kootwijk (Gelderland, Netherlands)

The Kootwijk site, in the Kootwijk district of the province of Gelderland, was discovered in 1964, some 1.5km (1 mile) to the east of the modern village from which it takes its name. The excavations were carried out by the Institute for Prehistory and Protohistory of the University of Amsterdam between 1971 and 1974. A rectangular area of about 300m × 150m (328 × 164yd) was excavated: this gives some idea of the large areas that have to be excavated in order to obtain data on rural sites of these early periods.

In all 45 houses, 177 sunken huts, 14 barns, and three post granaries were discovered (see Figure 18), together with data on the environment, to which we shall return. In fact the excavated area represented only a portion of the original settlement, the total extent of which was probably about 7ha. The remains that were brought to light belong to an occupation which must have lasted from the late seventh/early eighth century to about 1000.

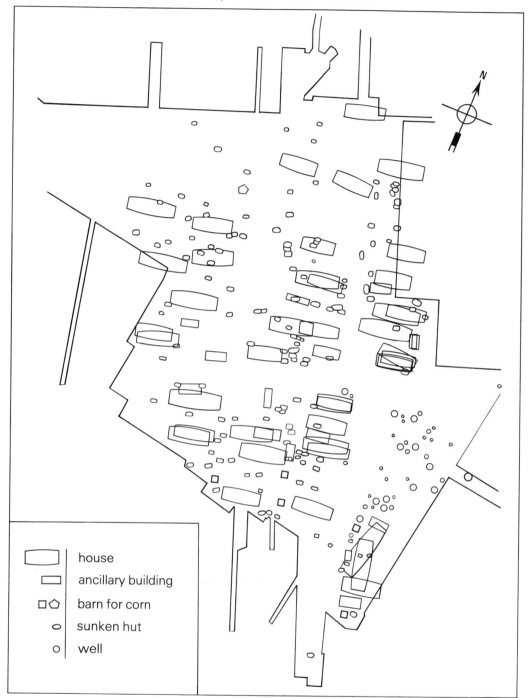

Fig. 18. *Plan of the late seventh- to late tenth-century settlement at Kootwijk (Netherlands)*
This plan has all the occupation phases superimposed, and it is possible to distinguish streets and various built structures. The overall impression is very reminiscent of Warendorf (cf. Figures 15, 16, 17)

(H. A. Heidinga, *Verdwenen dorpen in het Kootwijkerzand* (1976); fig. 6, p. 16)

This settlement was originally founded on a fairly fertile Pleistocene sand. There was at that time a small lake lying to the east of the site chosen by the original settlers, who must have been an organized group, judging by the regular alignment of the houses and the rectangular grid of streets.

It is difficult to obtain an accurate idea of the population of this settlement, but at the height of its activity it probably consisted of 15 large houses with the requisite specialized buildings around them.

Here one can recognize the characteristics of the early medieval settlement described above. The houses were 12–23.5m (39–77ft) long and the maximum breadth, in the centre of the structure, was 6–8m (20–26ft). The two ends were smaller, since these houses were boat-shaped (cf. Figure 16).

The interior was usually divided into two or three rooms. Only the largest, situated in the middle of the house, had a hearth, at ground level in the centre of the room. This large central room, the hall or room for meetings or meals, played an essential role in settlements of this period, at least in the Germanic region, which we know most about at the present time. The extremities of the house, usually occupied by one or two rooms that were smaller than the hall, also had a special role, although this is difficult to reconstruct on the basis of these excavations. However, it can be postulated from other excavations and sources that one would have served as a sleeping chamber and the other possibly as a livestock shed, men and animals being housed under the same roof, as at Warendorf.

These were not the only buildings on the site. The group of buildings that comprised farming units included these and other types of structure.

It may be estimated that each farm group, based on a large house, had in addition three or four sunken huts.

In addition to the houses and sunken huts, rectangular buildings were found, identified as barns and less numerous than either of the preceding two groups. Fourteen in all were found on the site, 8–10m (26–33ft) in length.

To complete the picture of agricultural buildings, there were at Kootwijk granaries raised on posts, similar to those from the same period found on other sites such as Bennekom (cf. Figure 21).

The Kootwijk site was considerably disturbed owing to the rebuilding of various structures during the life of the settlement, and also as a result of its subsequent history. However, this did not prevent the discovery of palisades consisting of lines of posts in shallow trenches which delimited the groups of buildings making up the farming units, which were comparable with those found at Warendorf (cf. Figure 15) or Catholme (cf. Figure 22), to cite only two examples.

Alongside these farming units, which differed only in the sizes of their principal buildings and the presence or absence of barns and granaries (which is worthy of notice in itself), many wells were found in the village.

The small lake that existed when the settlement was founded in the late seventh or early eighth century, dried up gradually over the ninth to tenth centuries. A layer of impermeable ferruginous sand or iron pan that underlay the site trapped the surface water and led to the formation of a water table that could be reached at a depth of 1.5m (5ft). Some 40 wells were discovered on the site of the lake, which must mean that several would have been in use at any given time – perhaps, even, by analogy with other sites, one for each house, since there are as many wells as houses. Two types of well were recorded: one type was made out of the two halves of a split trunk of oak, hollowed out with fire by the method used elsewhere for dugout canoes (the most common type on the site), and the other lined with wooden planks and square in plan.

The circumstances of the abandonment of the site throw light on the cultivation methods and the fields used by the inhabitants. Throughout the tenth century the soil conditions deteriorated, no doubt as a result of deforestation, and the settlement began to be threatened by encroaching sand dunes. The banks which delineated the fields at that time certainly served to protect them for a time. However, the situation steadily grew worse and little by little the fields and the settlement itself were covered with sand. By the end of the tenth century there was probably only one inhabited farm left, and this, too, was abandoned around 1000.

The gradual engulfment of the countryside by sand somewhat fossilized the fields, so that they retained their shape and even their furrows, which provides interesting data on methods of cultivation (see Figure 19); data which can be amplified by pollen analysis. The latter shows that rye was the main crop, alongside barley, wheat and oats, especially in the latest phase of the history of the village. These data on the relative use of various cereals can usefully be compared with those from another site of the same period from the Netherlands, Dorestad (see Figure 20).

Study of the animal bones enables us to state that the villagers practised animal husbandry, notably cattle and pigs, with some sheep and goats. They also had horses: it may have been a village of arable and animal farmers, but it was not an inward-looking rural community. Study of the pottery, that priceless aid of archaeologists concerned with problems of social and economic history, shows that although the bulk of the pottery used on the site is local in origin, hand-made and belonging to the characteristic regional category of globular pots (German *Kugeltopfen*), significant quantities of imported Rhenish pottery were found: some 30 per cent of the pottery from the site comes from workshops in villages between Cologne and Bonn, along the Rhine (Badorf and Pingsdorf), and from the Eifel. This was a well-fired and well-thrown ware, high in quality by comparison with all the local pottery of the time, which we know to have been exported, often far afield, in late Merovingian and Carolingian times, thanks to the river trade along the Rhine.

Kootwijk is only a village and so such a high proportion of imported pottery is noteworthy. At Dorestad, which was an important commercial centre on the Rhine, analysis of the late eighth- and ninth-century pottery from the recent excavations by W. van Es has shown that hand-made pottery, similar to that from Kootwijk, constituted only 10 per cent of the total, the other 90 per cent being imported from the Badorf, Pingsdorf and Eifel kilns. However, in a

Fig. 19. *Fossilized plough marks at Kootwijk (Netherlands), post-tenth-century*

The cultivated area at Kootwijk was gradually and inexorably invaded by sand throughout the tenth century, thereby fossilizing the plough furrows. Meticulous excavation made it possible to discover their orientation and form. The archaeology of fields, and more particularly observation of evidence of cultivation, has been developed best in those parts of Europe where the sub-soil best preserves such traces and where, as at Kootwijk, fields have been covered with sand (e.g. Denmark). These observations have great importance in helping to assess the power of ploughing implements, the existence of a mould-board, the technique of ploughing (cross-ploughing, for example), field shapes (square or strip) and sizes, etc., all of which are excellent indicators of medieval farming potentialities but about which traditional sources, especially documents, are reticent.

(H. A. Heidinga, *Verdwenen dorpen in het Kootwijkerzand* (1976), p. 35)

contemporary Carolingian palace at Paderborn, it was the ordinary local pottery which predominated. More interesting still, in a Netherlands village that was almost contemporaneous with Kootwijk, Odoorn (Drenthe), there was no imported pottery.

The history of the Kootwijk site did not come to an end with the abandonment of its houses and the departure of its inhabitants. As with many cases of settlement desertion, the fields continued in cultivation, at least for a time, because the advance of the sand did not let up. In order to permit cultivation, layers of humus were laid over the sand in the tenth and eleventh

85

Fig. 20. *Cereal grains from Dorestad (Netherlands) – late eighth- to ninth-century*

This site has produced grain that has been perfectly preserved by fire and so is identifiable. The photographs show barley (1), oats (2), rye (3), and wheat (4). The finds from the site demonstrate that these four cereals were grown in decreasing order, that of the photographs above. It is likely that, as is known to have been the case elsewhere in medieval and post-medieval Europe, the same field was sown with two different cereals: here it would have been barley and oats, in the ratio of 5:1.

It is also known that among the four cereals whose relative place is usually difficult to determine, in the Scandinavian lands in the ninth and tenth centuries at least, rye became the most common. The same was true of another region – Kootwijk (Netherlands), in the latter part of the occupation of the site, in the tenth century. The growing importance of rye, an autumn-sown crop, by contrast with barley and oats, which in northern European latitudes are usually (though not exclusively) spring-sown, may be an indication of the increasing trend towards autumn sowing.

(W. van Zeist, Agriculture in Early-Medieval Dorestad, A Preliminary Report, *Berichten van de Rijksdienst voor het Oudheidkundig Bodemonderzock*, 19 (1969); pp. 209–12, pl. XXI–XXIV)

centuries. This is very remarkable: although the area that had previously been a settlement gradually came under the plough, the general layout was preserved, since the same tracks continued to be used. This continuity in early medieval settlements that were subsequently replaced by cultivated fields, can be observed on other sites. We have seen one example at Odoorn (cf. Figure 4). However, the sand finally prevailed, and the whole cultivated area was abandoned, probably in the eleventh to twelfth centuries, and certainly before the thirteenth century.

It would be very helpful to know with greater accuracy the period of use and the extent of this type of rural settlement, characterized at Warendorf and Kootwijk by the existence side-by-side of farming units made up of several structures of differing type around a large house, often accompanied by a well and almost always surrounded by a palisade. Recent excavations have shown that these occur early and are fairly common in the Netherlands, even on a 'pre-urban' site such as the great port of Dorestad (ninth to eleventh centuries). In addition to Wijster (150–425), one may cite Dalfsen, Ede and, in particular, Bennekom, all occupied between the second century and 400 (see Figure 21).

The only difference between these Roman-period sites and those dating to after the fifth century is the architectural change that the main houses undergo: they were three-aisled in the older examples but were often built without internal posts in the later period, as at Warendorf or Kootwijk. This problem will be explored further. Over a number of years, excavations in Great Britain seem to reveal, on some sites at any rate, a similar organization of rural settlements: a recent example is Catholme (Staffordshire) (see Figure 22).

B   The Anglo-Saxons

Catholme (Staffordshire)

Excavation from 1973 to 1976 laid bare more than 2ha of this site (see Figure 22): 58 houses built above-ground in three different styles, and six sunken huts made up the most important finds, along with numerous traces of palisades. In the centre of the excavated area an enclosure of some 2500 sq. m (2990 sq. yd) (i.e. comparable with the farming unit enclosures at Warendorf and Bennekom) contained several different buildings with, in the centre, a large boat-shaped building. Excavation revealed that this enclosure had been rebuilt four times, and that access was gained to it through a gate opening to the north-east on to a road flanked by two parallel palisades some 3.8m (12ft) apart. There were other similar enclosures around this one, each containing one farming unit.

Certain of the ground-level structures were outbuildings. Traces of spinning and weaving were discovered in several of the sunken huts, as is

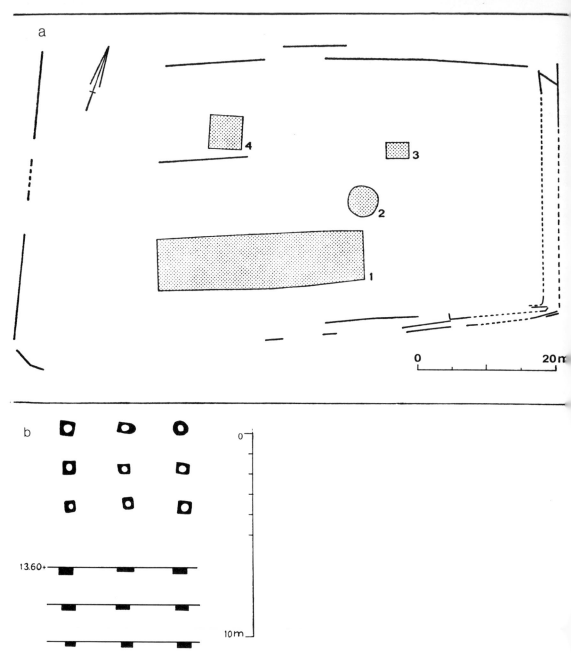

Fig. 21. *The second- to fourth-century settlement at Bennekom (Netherlands)*

Some 1.6ha of this site was excavated. As in numerous other contemporary or neighbouring sites such as Warendorf (Figure 15), Kootwijk (Figure 18), and Catholme (Figure 22), farming units were formed side-by-side, composed of several buildings with specialized functions enclosed within a rectangular palisade, with a rough grid layout of roads (1). Each enclosure contained a granary raised up on posts, as in other contemporaneous sites such as Feddersen Wierde (cf. Figure 28), the custom in medieval northern Europe.

(W. A. van Es, Roman-period Settlement, *Berichten van de Rijksdienst voor het Oudheidkundig Bodemonderzoek*, 23 (1973); fig. 6, p. 278, and fig. 5, p. 277)

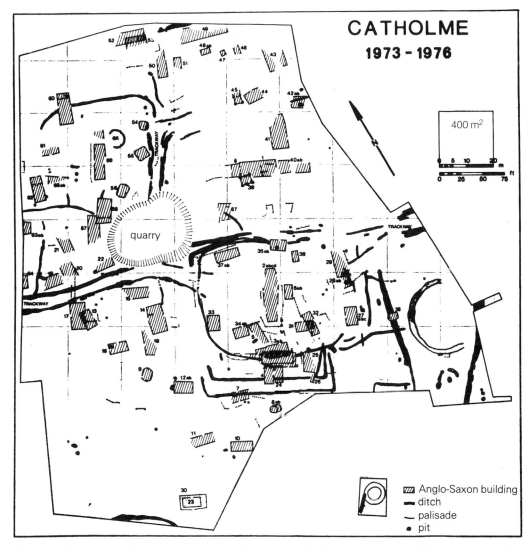

Fig. 22. *The Anglo-Saxon settlement at Catholme (Staffordshire) – late fifth-/early sixth-century to early tenth-century. Excavated area at 1976*

In addition to a large central enclosure of about 2500 sq. m (2990 sq. yd), there seem to be six others, more or less complete. The plan of this settlement is strongly reminiscent of those of Warendorf (Figure 15), Kootwijk (Figure 18), and Odoorn (Figure 4).

(Catholme, *Medieval Archaeology*, 21 (1977); fig. 72, p. 213)

usually the case in this type of building.

Subsequently, as is so often the case with many rural settlements after abandonment, Catholme was overlain by cultivated fields. The ditches delimiting 13 7.5m (24ft 6in) wide open-field strips covered the whole site and were very pronounced even before excavation began.

Taking account of all the various rebuilding phases that followed one another on this site during the time it was occupied, from the late fifth or early sixth century to the first half of the tenth century, it can be said that it was composed of a series of farms, each probably enclosed by a palisade and, like the continental examples, including various subsidiary structures – sunken huts, raised granaries, and rectangular ancillary buildings – around a large building used as a dwelling house. All the structures exposed so far seem to point to there having been seven different farms over the four centuries of occupation.

However, it would be wrong to conclude from this that there was general and complete uniformity in this type of rural settlement at this period. On the contrary, without going outside the relatively restricted but best studied area comprising Scandinavia, Germany, the Netherlands, Great Britain, Iceland and Greenland, significant variations in various forms can be detected. They relate to the size of the farming unit, the number and nature of the structures which compose it, the functions of the large rectangular house (which is in every case the main building), the construction, techniques, and materials used, the types of house framework – all elements which can vary considerably. In studying these diverse problems we shall see regional and chronological variations begin to appear that are of considerable relative significance, and this should allow us to consider the socio-economic problems underlying these regional variations.

C Size variations in farming units: some examples

1 *Germany*

In a site such as Gladbach (sixth to seventh centuries), excavated before World War II and unfortunately not fully published, there were very distinct groups of rectangular buildings and sunken huts more or less enclosed by palisades, as at Warendorf and Kootwijk (cf. Figure 32). There were two 12.5m × 9m (41 × 30ft) houses, three 4m × 7m (13 × 23ft), and three smaller ones; there were fewer of these than there were of sunken huts, which totalled 57: 13 were of the type in which the roof is supported on two posts, each set in the centre of one of the short sides, and 44 of the classic type with six postholes, one at each corner and one in the centre of each short side. Even more than at Kootwijk, what is striking at Gladbach is the large number of sunken huts in relation to ground-level buildings. However, what limits the value of this site somewhat is the fact that the general layout of buildings is difficult to understand, apart from the northern part of the site, where a number of sunken huts can be observed grouped around a large house. However, this should be borne in mind as an example of relatively small houses as compared with Warendorf or Kootwijk.

Some further German examples, from further south, give fuller information about other groupings of buildings and sizes of main houses.

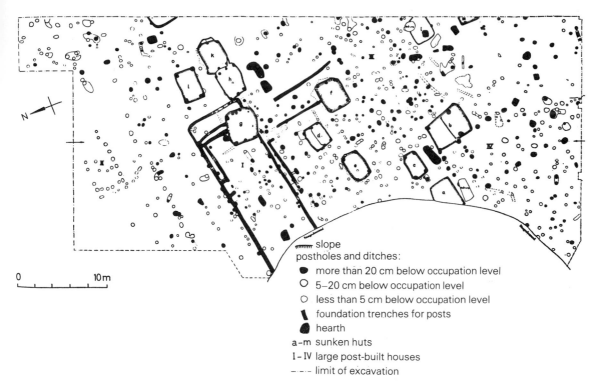

slope
postholes and ditches:
- ● more than 20 cm below occupation level
- ○ 5–20 cm below occupation level
- ○ less than 5 cm below occupation level
- ▮ foundation trenches for posts
- ◗ hearth
- a–m sunken huts
- I–IV large post-built houses
- – · – limit of excavation

Fig. 23. *The seventh- to early ninth-century settlement at Burgheim, Federal Republic of Germany*

The plan shows all the archaeological structures that were found. Three elements can be seen: a large rectangular structure in the centre, aligned east-west and consisting of walls made of upright wooden posts, no doubt supported on a sill-beam sunk in a trench (the multiple parallel trenches are due to rebuilding or modifications); smaller buildings, recognizable by the wall foundation trenches, of varying lengths (one lies parallel to the large building and to the south of it; two others are at right angles to it, also to the south); several sunken huts and many post-holes. The relatively small area excavated (1375 sq. m [1644 sq. yd]) prevents general conclusions being drawn.

(G. Fehring, Zur archäologischen Erforschung . . . , *Zeitschrift für Agrargeschichte und Agrarsoziologie*, 1 (1973), DLG-Verlags GmbH, Frankfurt; fig. 2, pp. 16–17)

At Wülfingen-am-Kocher (Forchtenberg, Kr. Ohringen), the presence of both ground-level buildings and sunken huts on a relatively large sixth- to twelfth-century site also suggests the presence of adjacent farming units, each made up of houses and huts. However, subsequent modifications to this site make it difficult to establish how they related one with another. Excavation of 6000 sq. m (7176 sq. yd) of the site produced 1500 postholes! The only certain fact is that the houses were small in size. However, the elements making up a farming unit appeared very clearly on another site, Burgheim (Kr. Neuberg-an-der-Donau), illustrated in Figure 23.

In fact, these different examples are in agreement with contemporary written sources in showing what could have been early medieval farming in the continental Germanic territories. Warendorf and Burgheim represent the two extremes of a wide spectrum of other examples from Germany that are too numerous to list here. On the one hand there is the large establishment, consisting of 15 built units covering some 3000 sq. m (3588 sq. yd), and on the other between one and seven ancillary sunken-floored buildings, not all necessarily contemporaneous, round a large house and occupying a much smaller area (cf. Figures 15, 21–23, 32).

We must now look at the geographical distribution of this type of rural settlement which certainly existed in Germany and the Netherlands. It is very difficult, for lack of archaeological information, to comment so far as France and the Mediterranean lands are concerned, but the Scandinavian countries, Germany and the British Isles are worthy of close scrutiny.

2   *Scandinavia*

It may be appropriate to recall that, unlike the more southerly regions of Europe, the Scandinavian countries remained faithful to a dispersed mode of settlement for most of the Middle Ages, although there was not absolute uniformity in this respect.

When, from the ninth century onwards, and in some places earlier, Scandinavian (particularly Norwegian) peoples undertook the colonization of the small islands to the north of the British Isles (Shetland, Faroes), or in the Irish Sea (Isle of Man), and later that of Iceland and Greenland, it was this form of settlement that they took with them. However, this difference between Scandinavia and, say, Germany, which was perhaps less marked in the early Middle Ages than later, in that dispersed settlement was the more common mode among most of the Germanic peoples, does not hide the fact that the large, long rectangular house was the main element of Scandinavian rural settlement (cf. Figure 31). It constituted the bulk of the settlement, in fact, since ancillary buildings were much less common.

Despite the examples of a few sites such as eleventh-century Lindholme Høje (Denmark), or Gårdlösa (Sweden), which lasted from the Roman period to the Viking Age, and where 25 and 52 sunken huts respectively were found alongside various ground-level buildings, rural settlement in Scandinavia made little use of this type of structure. Nevertheless, combinations of different types of building similar to those in Germany are encountered from time to time.

Vallhagar (Sweden)

Vallhagar, on the island of Gotland, almost constitutes a true 'village', with its 25 stone houses, each built inside an enclosure defined by walls made of stones cleared from the fields (see Figure 24).

These rather large enclosures are more like fields, unlike the previous examples we have seen. Another difference is the absence of ancillary buildings. However, the explanation may be a simple one: the climatic conditions here were such that livestock could be outdoors for almost the whole winter season and, as a result, the large rectangular house, which was intended, as we have seen on many sites, to shelter both humans and animals,

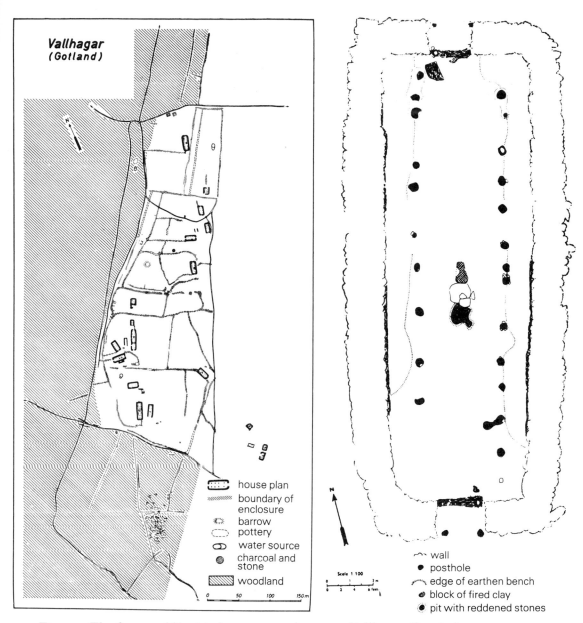

Fig. 24. *The first- to fifth-/sixth-century settlement at Vallhagar (Sweden)*

In its use of solely large rectangular houses without ancillary buildings, set in a stone enclosure, this settlement differs somewhat from contemporaneous settlements such as Warendorf, Kootwijk or Catholme. The existence of installations for collective use is an interesting feature. (**H. Jankuhn**, *Archäologie und Geschichte*, I (1976); fig. 11, p. 284)

Fig. 25. *House from the first- to fifth-/sixth-century settlement at Vallhagar (Sweden)*

This house is typical of the buildings on this site: stone walls, roof carried on two parallel rows of closely set, somewhat slender, posts, doors in the centre of the short sides. As in many Scandinavian houses, especially in Iceland and Greenland, there is a firepit on the long axis in the centre of the building, and there are benches round the sides. Closely spaced upright posts serve to revet the earth packing of these benches.

(Based on M. Stenberger and O. Klindt-Jensen, *Vallhagar* (1953); fig. 42)

93

did not need to be so long (see Figure 25). The inhabitants of this settlement, located in a poor agricultural area, lived mainly on livestock raising; however, they did grow cereals, a fairly large amount of which was found in one half of one of the houses, which clearly shows that harvested crops had to be stored in the houses themselves, without special constructions of their own.

A settlement such as Vallhagar, occupied from the first to the fifth or sixth century, was probably one of a mixed farming group characterized by only slight differences in wealth. There were no craftsmen or significant evidence of trading contacts – in short, there was no evidence of social differentiation or stratification. Two communal installations – an oven for drying corn and another for baking bread – along with a site for pottery making suggest that there was a minimal degree of collective organization and interdependence. The complete absence of sunken huts is worthy of note.

Vallhagar illustrates the process of rural settlement growth in the early Middle Ages, which has already been noted in Germany. In Norway and Sweden and the islands of Gotland and Öland, the normal mode of settlement up to the Migration Period (fifth century) was the isolated farm or group of farms. This was particularly the case in the northern and mountainous regions of Norway and Sweden. From this time onwards, however, we begin to find more stable agglomerations of six to ten farms. Vallhagar belongs to this latter group, which at this period were sometimes defended by a rampart and could reach ten to 20 farms, which means 30 to 50 buildings, by the seventh century. The village of Eketorp (Öland, Sweden) was typical in this respect in its earliest phase, between 450 and 750: a circular stone enclosure some 80m in diameter contained at least 31 stone-built houses.

D Conclusions

We are thus led to the conclusion that, in Germany and the Scandinavian lands, the normal form of settlement in the early Middle Ages consisted of a rectangular house, varying in size but often long – between 10m (33ft) and 30m (98ft), sometimes more – surrounded with ancillary buildings, each with its specific function. Sunken huts are common, though not invariably present. Smaller dwelling houses may have existed, doubtless for lower social grades, along with various buildings for storage of food and grain or housing animals. It is possible, so far as animals are concerned, that climatic variations may explain differences in the size or number of such structures. The trend towards agglomeration of the population should also be taken into consideration as a factor: this is barely perceptible in Scandinavia but more evident elsewhere, notably in Britain, Germany and the Netherlands over these centuries. The most striking feature in these rural settlements is the juxtaposition of farming units composed of built features separated one from another. Although they may vary in size or number, this juxtaposition is always present, leading in due course to 'villages', or more often to hamlets, very irregular in form, even though Kootwijk, and to a lesser extent Warendorf, show a certain measure of organization in layout by reason of the regular alignment of the houses. We are, of course, still far from the nucleated, sometimes deliberately planned, villages that come after the tenth century. This is perhaps the most significant feature of rural settlement of the early Middle Ages, at least in north-western Europe.

Overall, we can thus affirm that general rural settlement at this time seems to have been based on the juxtaposition of farming units, usually few in number, but steadily increasing on any given site as the tenth to eleventh centuries become closer, often laid out irregularly, though in some cases aligned on a rectangular grid of roads. However, although a general structure for rural settlements seems to be emerging, in north-western Europe at least, the same does not hold good for the composition and nature of the component farming units.

Two particular problems need to be considered. The first relates to the uses to which the dwelling house is put: is it reserved exclusively for human occupation or does it provide shelter for both people and livestock? These two possibilities produce two different situations, which almost constitute two distinct types of dwelling house. The second problem is that of the ancillary buildings, and especially their character and number. This applies to all types of ancillary building – raised granaries as well as sunken huts or barns. Once again, as in the previous case, the solution of this problem is linked with knowledge of the type of agrarian economy on the site under investigation: the presence of livestock within the dwelling house is a function of the role animals play in the economy of a single family or of an entire settlement at a given moment in time. The nature and number of ancillary buildings pose problems whose solutions are comparable, but which are related more to the size of the population of a farm, the importance of livestock – both aspects which affect storage – or the relative role of arable farming and animal husbandry, i.e. the quantity of corn or fodder which has to be stocked. Thus the second point links up to some extent with the first: it is necessary to study, as a function of the probable type of agrarian economy, the buildings that serve as dwellings along with the various buildings that surround them – to study a complete farming operation and not single buildings. In addition, other problems arise in connection with buildings other than those used for living in: certain ancillary activities are more or less indispensable for farming and so it is important to study the traces they leave in the archaeological record. For example, there are the indications of where slaves or domestic servants were housed, where tools and implements were stored, where work was carried out, especially the domestic tasks performed by women, such as spinning and weaving. This brings us to the problem of the sunken huts, because these were usually devoted to such tasks. Thus it is essential to consider their presence or absence around dwelling houses, the number used in any farming operation, and indications as to their use derived from archaeological data.

In order, therefore, to define our knowledge of early medieval rural settlement more precisely, we shall study these two architectural aspects of the farming unit in turn: the size, and more particularly the exact function, of the dwelling house (whether for humans alone or jointly with livestock), the nature and number of ancillary buildings surrounding the dwelling house and, in particular, the typology and functions of sunken huts in early medieval rural settlement.

II THE DWELLING HOUSE

The long rectangular house, which occurs on almost all the early medieval settlements in northern and north-western Europe that constitute the basic element in the exploitation of the countryside, poses a major problem: what were its functions? We shall study this question by reference to two examples: Chalton (Hampshire, England), a sixth- to seventh-century Anglo-Saxon settlement, and Feddersen Wierde (Federal German Republic), a settlement occupied from the first century BC until the fifth century AD. These two sites, many of whose features are fairly typical of settlements of this period, represent the two extreme solutions: a dwelling house for human habitation alone at Chalton and a very large building used for housing both men and animals at Feddersen Wierde.

A Two alternative solutions: Anglo-Saxon England and Frisia

For the period we are concerned with, the number of English excavations, still small by comparison with those in Germany, and the very recent nature of certain basic studies means that we do not have sufficient confirmed data available to enable a detailed picture to be constructed. For the most part, an area of at least one hectare, if not more, needs to be excavated, because only large-area excavations can produce convincing data.

Work on this scale is rare, however, since the excavation of one hectare of an early medieval settlement demands very strict working conditions. It is necessary to find an available site that has not undergone subsequent changes, to command considerable material and human resources, and to be able to carry out work over several seasons: all goals that are not easy to achieve, especially in countries without a tradition of large-scale scientific archaeology like France. The enormous growth in research into early medieval settlement in recent years in the British Isles is very noteworthy.

This spectacular development is beginning to produce results, in so far as they agree or disagree with continental results, to justify the preliminary theories being advanced by British scholars, and above all to make it possible to put forward some general propositions, something that would have been difficult to envisage some eight or ten years ago.

1   Chalton (Hampshire)

The Anglo-Saxon site at Chalton (Hampshire), excavated every year since 1971, has been shown by fieldwalking to cover some 6ha; by 1976 1.8ha (30 per cent of the estimated total area) had been excavated.

It was clearly only occupied in the sixth to seventh centuries, and was established on the crest of a fairly pronounced hill, orientated north-south (cf. Figure 8). Analysis of several thousand excavated postholes has revealed more than 52 buildings and two surviving enclosure systems (see Figures 26 and 27). A general east-west orientation of the settlement has emerged quite clearly, as at Kootwijk.

Some conclusions can be put forward, bearing in mind that only part of the site has been excavated. The main feature is that the buildings at Chalton are, as on many other sites, rectangular structures made up of a framework of wooden beams.

As elsewhere, these buildings vary in size, seemingly according to the presence or absence of hearths. This leads one to believe that the differences in size must be related to differences in function. Of the 24 buildings found in 1971 and 1972, eight large ones were dwelling houses in the strict sense, those of medium size (also eight) had some indeterminate function, and the eight smaller buildings would have been ancillary buildings, serving some domestic purpose. The large houses, which varied in length between 7.8m (25ft) and 13.8m (45ft) (average 11m [36ft]) and in breadth between 4.7m (15ft) and 6.7m (22ft) are smaller than those in certain continental 'villages' such as Kootwijk or Warendorf, though this difference is not very pronounced. Other Anglo-Saxon 'villages', such as Thetford and West Stow, have produced a number of buildings that are comparable in size as well as in arrangement and function.

We find at Chalton, as on the German sites, the classic association between large structures used for living in and smaller buildings used either as dwellings or for ancillary purposes, along with two sunken huts (cf. Figures 34 and 105). The very small number of these huts need not be counted as a major feature, since, first, only part of the site – a significant part, unquestionably, but none the less a small part – has so far been excavated and so there may be more sunken huts, and secondly – and more importantly – they do not occur as consistent features of settlements of this period, as we shall see.

At least two very distinct groups of structures appeared during the 1972 excavations: a dwelling house was built up against a palisaded enclosure, larger than the former, measuring at least 23m (75ft) in breadth and more than 30m (98ft) long (it was not completely excavated in this direction). The latter enclosure, which contained at least two ancillary buildings, communicated directly with the dwelling house through one of the latter's three doorways. Although differing somewhat from the continental examples, this exhibits once again the general layout of all the rural settlements of this period: a relatively organized plan, with a preferential axis of alignment for the buildings, and a group of farming units consisting of a fairly large rectangular dwelling house,

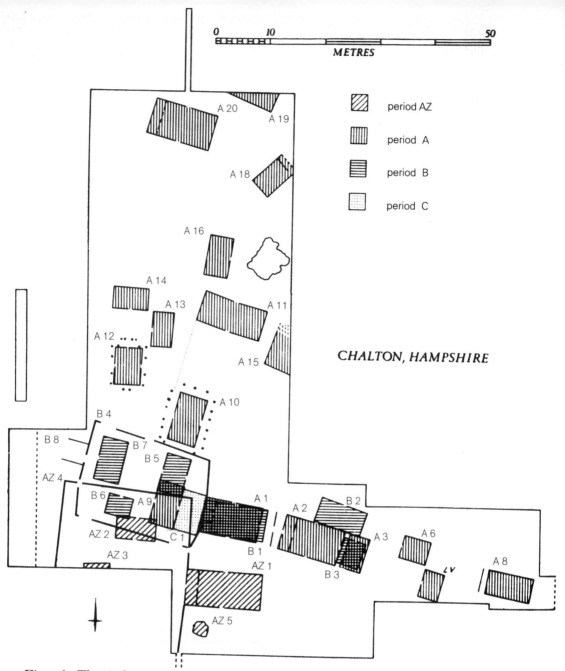

Fig. 26. *The sixth- to seventh-century Anglo-Saxon settlement on Church Down, Chalton (Hampshire): results of excavations up to 1972*

The buildings belonging to four successive periods of occupation of the site are shown superimposed on this plan. The two wholly or partly excavated enclosures in the northern part of the site, and the associated buildings either adjacent to or inside the enclosures, are especially worthy of note. The excavated area has been considerably extended since 1972. After it was abandoned, the population of this Anglo-Saxon settlement was dispersed over a number of smaller hamlets, one of which was the origin of the modern village of Chalton (cf. Figure 8).

(P. V. Addyman and D. Leigh, The Anglo-Saxon Village at Chalton, *Medieval Archaeology*, 17 (1973); fig. 3, p. 5)

Fig. 27. *Aerial view of the sixth- to seventh-century Anglo-Saxon settlement on Church Down, Chalton (Hampshire)*

This oblique air photograph, taken looking south, shows the excavation at an earlier stage than that shown in Figure 26. The existence of various methods of construction for the house walls (cf. Figure 80) explains the different appearance of the visible buildings – both lines of postholes and trenches. Towards the centre of the photograph, a building with walls indicated by continuous trenches has in addition a line of external postholes which must be for angled supporting beams.

(P. V. Addyman and D. Leigh, The Anglo-Saxon Village at Chalton, Hampshire, *Medieval Archaeology*, 17 (1973); pl. 1)

over 10m in length, surrounded by a varying number of ancillary buildings of different types, the whole enclosed or palisaded. A slight difference lies in the small number of ancillary buildings and, in particular, their relative lack of variety: they are basically ground-level structures with very few sunken huts and no raised granaries. The rather small number of dwelling houses, fairly typical of many Anglo-Saxon rural sites, is also a noteworthy individual feature of this settlement, at least when it is compared with those at Warendorf. However, there is no such contrast with other German examples, such as Gladbach or Wülfingen.

2 *Feddersen Wierde*

Feddersen Wierde produced a completely different type of house (see Figure 28). This is a settlement established in a rather special situation, on the shore of the North Sea in the coastal strip running from the Zuider Zee in the Netherlands to Denmark: the Dutch *terpen* and German *Wurten* or *Wirten*. These are gradual accumulations of land, usually established in a cultivated area or the site of earlier occupation, which are steadily raised in height by the action of men who strive to remove their settlements from the risk of flooding in those regions that were not yet protected by dykes. A series of sites of this type have been excavated, of which Feddersen Wierde is one of the classic examples.

The houses, which are rectangular and for the most part fairly long, are ranged parallel to these roads, within enclosures which also contain a type of granary raised on three rows of three posts, and measuring about 3m (10ft) by 4.4m (14ft) at the base, as at Bennekom (cf. Figure 21).

The houses vary in size, but all the larger ones are divided in two by two doorways in or near the centres of the two long sides (cf. Figure 79a).

In certain of the enclosures, there are one or several smaller dwellings of the same type alongside a large house. It is noteworthy that such an enclosure would nevertheless contain a single raised granary, located alongside the main house. Evidence of craft activities such as leather or bone working are to be found in certain areas of the village. The ancillary houses in the enclosures with raised granaries are substantially smaller than the usual houses in the settlement, largely because the portion of the building divided up into stalls at right-angles to the two longer walls is less spacious than usual. The regular presence of dung in those parts of the houses indicate with certainty that these were reserved for animals. Thus we have houses occupied by craftsmen who were engaged in both arable farming (the granary) and animal husbandry (the stalls in one part of the building), though to a lesser extent than the inhabitants of the large houses, which are the most numerous on the site.

The connection, so clearly visible at Feddersen Wierde, between one section of the houses and the stalling of animals, leads to another series of observations. Towards the end of the history of the site, the relative size of the sections of houses reserved for animals tends to diminish, which doubtless indicates a reduction in stock raising. At the time when this activity was at its

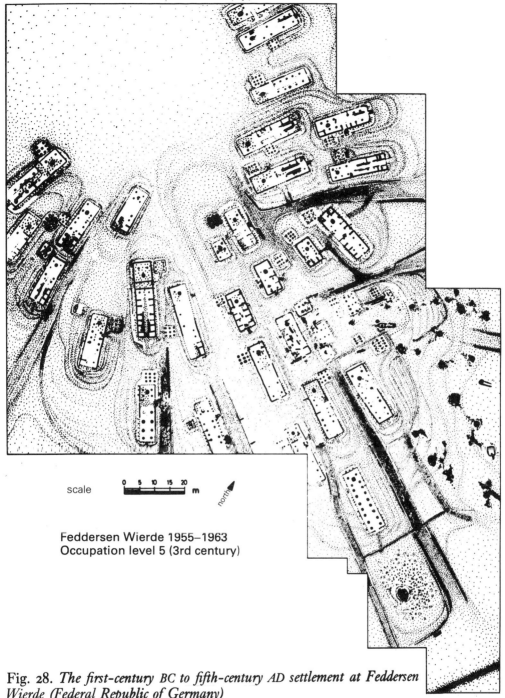

scale 0 5 10 15 20 m

north

Feddersen Wierde 1955–1963
Occupation level 5 (3rd century)

Fig. 28. *The first-century BC to fifth-century AD settlement at Feddersen Wierde (Federal Republic of Germany)*

This settlement was established on an artificial mound that was not liable to flooding and which was built up gradually. It is characterized by the use of large rectangular houses (cf. Figure 79a) and a degree of general organization in its layout: all the houses seem to radiate from the centre of the mound. This has been only partially excavated, over some two-thirds of its total area. Square or rectangular granaries, usually raised on three rows of three posts, can also be seen.

(H. Jankuhn, *Archäologie und Geschichte*, I (1976); fig. 15, p. 290)

height on the site, some of the buildings could house up to 32 animals, on the basis of the number of stalls (cf. Figure 30). In this situation a change in the way of life or the farming practices of the inhabitants has directly influenced the size of the later houses. Feddersen Wierde is in a cold area, considerably colder than the island of Gotland, and it is certain that such climatic conditions can directly affect settlement modes. It should not be overlooked that in certain regions a proportion of animal flocks remain outdoors throughout the entire year: at the moment 24 per cent in Norfolk and 14 per cent in Suffolk.

At the same time as animal husbandry declined at Feddersen Wierde, the role of the craftsman seems to have grown. During the last two (fourth to fifth) centuries of the settlement's history, the number of sunken huts increased. They seem to have formed an organized craftsmen's area of the type seen at Midlum in the same region and at the Haselhörn settlement at Flögeln. However, whilst house size decreased at Feddersen Wierde when craftsmen began to play a larger role in the economy of the village, the precise opposite can be observed on other sites which are otherwise very similar in cultural and geographical terms. Careful analysis of animal bones from Feddersen Wierde or other contemporary or slightly later sites emphasizes the role of animal husbandry through the period of occupation (cf. Figures 2 and 30).

The high age of animals at slaughter, in particular that of sheep, is a constant feature at all the *Wurten* and many Anglo-Saxon sites of the same period. From this it can be deduced that wool was more important than meat, which led to a growth in flocks of sheep that was incompatible with serious selection in favour of good-quality animals. The same observations can be made at Haselhörn in particular.

The fundamental role played by dairy products in diet is obvious: more than 60 per cent of the cattle were over three years old, and only 17 per cent of veal can be identified in the beef that was consumed (cf. Figure 2). If cattle and sheep played an essential role in the economy, this did not have the same consequences in archaeological terms. Cattle (in particular the cows) were shut up in byres for the winter, which explains the size of these portions of the buildings. The sheep would have remained in the meadows throughout the year, where arrangements would have been made to provide them with shelter in the winter. Their significance to the economy can only be gauged from the bones that have survived. Bones complete the picture that we are able to draw of the diet of the inhabitants, showing the very small contribution of hunting and fishing, a classic feature of the early Middle Ages. By contrast, the substantial consumption of horse meat, which confirms the attraction this type of meat had for the Germanic peoples, is shown by the fact that 41 per cent of horses were slaughtered before they were one year old. Slaughter of more than 50 per cent of pigs at three years old or above indicates the contribution of this animal to the meat component of the diet (cf. Figure 2).

However, the main interest of an excavation such as that at Feddersen Wierde is the way in which it enables us to obtain an impression of the evolution of settlement mode and size.

Feddersen Wierde began in the first century BC as a small group of a few farms built at natural soil level. The comparable site of Ezinge in the Netherlands began at exactly the same time in the form of a small hamlet. Around the beginning of the first century AD a rise in water level compelled the inhabitants of Feddersen Wierde to undertake the construction of an artificial mound for their protection. The number of farming units grew substantially at this time, from five in the first century BC to 12 at the end of the first century AD, if it is accepted that the eight farms so far excavated represent only two-thirds of the entire settlement. This rapid growth in population inspires the thought that in fact the site was inhabited at that time, not by a group that grew naturally, but with the addition of groups who had abandoned other settlement sites to join the inhabitants of Feddersen Wierde in building the artificial mound.

Between the first and third centuries AD the number of farms rose from 12 to 39 (calculated on the basis of the 22 found in the excavated area). Growth of this size also occurred, as we have seen, in other regions of Germany, especially in the sixth to seventh centuries.

An analysis of the population of seven other *Wurten*, comparable with first-century Feddersen Wierde, on the basis of surface area and excavation data, reveals the same phenomenon of growth over the whole region of some 23 sq. km (9 miles) on the right bank of the Weser estuary. Another question is posed by Feddersen Wierde, independent of this population problem: the status of the inhabitants.

Archaeological observation of the late second-century occupation level gives rise to a number of speculations. The site of this period that was excavated, representing two-thirds of the original area (one-third underlies the modern village and so could not be excavated), comprised 22 settlement units, 19 of them based on farming (four with large, 12 with medium-sized, and three with small houses) and three on craft activities, grouped as we have already seen. In addition there was a further building, three-aisled like the others, but without the section reserved for animals. It was enclosed within a strong palisade, reinforced by a ditch, and accompanied by three granaries, whereas the other farms, even the largest, had no palisades. This enclosure also contained traces of bronze casting and perhaps of blacksmithing. Other crafts were in evidence elsewhere in the village, but it was only this house and its enclosure that contained evidence of metal working at this period. It is not only the palisade, which made it into a kind of defended farm, that distinguished this building from the others, but also the absence of the quarters reserved for animals within the house, the evidence of metal working, and the presence of *terra sigillata* in the house and enclosure, evidence of direct or indirect contacts with the Roman world.

It is naturally very difficult to say what the status of those who lived in this house was or what their relationship was to the other villages. In calling this establishment the *Herrenhof* (lord's farm), Werner Haarnagel underlines – and with justification – the pre-eminent status of its occupants. However, it is difficult to go beyond this observation, based on broad and accurate archaeological data, into the realm of social relationships.

The most noteworthy feature of this excavation, so typical of the region lying between the mouths of the Weser and the Elbe, is the transition from small hamlet to complex rural communal settlement as early as the second century. It should be noted that settlement evolution is related more to population movement, the abandonment of peripheral sites and their regrouping, than to natural population growth. Like Ezinge or Wijster, Feddersen Wierde confirms the trend that we have already seen in Great Britain, Germany, and the Netherlands, more particularly in the sixth to eighth centuries.

Another typical aspect of Feddersen Wierde is the almost exclusive presence on this site of large rectangular dwellings, housing humans and animals under the same roof.

B Conclusions

The unequal development of excavation on rural sites of these periods in the various European countries, especially France and the Mediterranean lands, stands between us and an exact understanding of rural settlement and houses in the first 12 centuries AD. We are thus compelled to base our arguments on north-western Europe – the British Isles, the Netherlands, Germany, and Scandinavia.

Taking these regions as a whole, a zone where there was almost exclusive use of one type of house, with a double function, becomes clearly apparent from the beginning of the first millennium AD (see Figure 29).

First, there are the regions of Scandinavian settlement: the south-western coasts of Norway, the Swedish islands in the Baltic, southern Sweden, and the western half of the Danish peninsula. In the later period, when the colonization of the islands to the north of Great Britain and then of Iceland and Greenland began, a comparable form of house was used, even though the function of shelter for animals was, as we shall see, often removed from the house itself and transferred to ancillary buildings (see Figure 31).

On the Continent it may be said that the large house used by humans and a fairly large number of animals is to be found along the whole coastline of the North Sea and the Danish peninsula up to the mouths of the Rhine and the Meuse, during the first ten or twelve centuries of the Christian era, and only in the region where this type of construction was already in existence in the Iron Age. The *Terpen-Wurten*, in particular, systematically demonstrate this form of construction. The number of animals that they could accommodate – in some cases more than 30 – is striking (see Figure 30), and it is this which gives them their name – byre-house.

However, when we go outside this clearly defined and essentially coastal or insular region, it can be seen that large areas of north-western Europe which

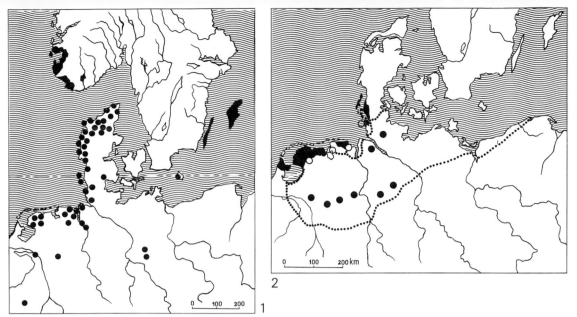

Fig. 29. *The byre-house in the first to fifteenth centuries AD*

From the Iron Age to the early Middle Ages, the large byre-house was characteristic of the coastal region of Germany and the Netherlands, and exclusive to this region (1). At that period it does not occur further south in Germany, outside this coastal strip. During the thirteenth century, however, this type of house occurs outside the coastal region (2), in lower Germany, which gives its name to medieval and post-medieval examples – the *Niederdeutsche Halle* (cf. Figure 79). This was not an extension southwards of influences coming from Frisia but rather the regional expression of a characteristic phenomenon of Europe at this time, the greater importance accorded to domestic animals in rural buildings. The mixed house, which occurs in central Germany, France, and the British Isles from the same period, is a parallel manifestation of the same phenomenon.

(H. Hinz, Zur Geschichte der niederdeutsche Halle, *Zeitschrift für Volkskunde*, 60 (1964); figs. 3 and 9)

---

are well-known from numerous scientific excavations, show no evidence of this type of building during the same period, i.e. up to the thirteenth century: central and southern Germany, for example, or the British Isles. Nothing comparable is found at sites such as Gladbach in central Germany or Wülfingen and Kirchheim further south. The most southerly site characterized by buildings of this type in Germany before the thirteenth century is Warendorf.

It is even clearer that the large byre-house was unknown in the British Isles since, with the exception of Catholme, buildings were rarely more than 15m (49ft) in length and no traces of stalls for animals have been found. As in the Scandinavian settlement sites, large buildings are to be found in certain cases in the British Isles, but these seem to have been used as reception or dwelling halls and not as byre-houses. This is an architectural form that is to be found in particular on the islands settled by Scandinavians, or at certain Anglo-Saxon palaces such as Sulgrave, Cheddar or Yeavering. The general plan and the

Fig. 30. *Herds of cattle at Feddersen Wierde (first century BC – fifth century AD)*

Phases	No. of farms excavated	Estimated total no. of animals	Average herd per farm
Ia Ist cent. BC	5	98	20
Ib Beginning of Ist cent. AD	8	176	22
Ic Ist cent. AD	8	196	24
2 *c.* AD 100	14	298	21
3 2nd cent. AD	17	297	17.5
4 *c.* AD 200	19	377	20
5 3rd cent. AD	23	443	19
6 *c.* AD 300	23	307	13

The average figures are valid only for the coastal region, where buildings equivalent to those at Feddersen Wierde are to be found (cf. Figures 29, 79, 96). With herds of 20–24 animals and an average age at slaughter of two years (cf. Figure 2), the annual yield must have been of the order of 500–600 kg (1102–1323 lb) of meat and 6000 kg (13,228 lb) of milk. This level of production suggests either that three generations normally lived together on these farms, perhaps some 20 people, or that the nutritional level was high, especially since, as has already been shown, horsemeat, pork and mutton were also being consumed, hunting and fishing were practised, and there was a contribution that is difficult to calculate from agriculture, or even that there were considerable outlets for export of products – but in which direction, for whom, and how was the material preserved? These are new socio-economic problems that are becoming apparent.

(P. Donat, Stallgrosse und Viehbesitz nach Befunden germanischer Wohnstall-häuser, *Archäologie als Geschichtswissenschaft*, Berlin (1977); pp. 251–63)

architectural type of the Frisian house have apparently been transposed, but no longer as byre-houses or even, in the case of the Anglo-Saxon sites referred to above, as rural buildings in the strict sense of the term.

On the other hand, there is no lack of smaller buildings, some 12m (39ft) long on average, as at West Stow (Figure 34d) or Gladbach (Figures 32, 33, 99). Nothing in the interior fittings or the archaeological finds reveals the presence of animals. In fact, their absence is a distinguishing criterion of greater importance than size of building: these are buildings solely for the use of human beings. There were indeed domestic animals, especially cattle, in these villages, as shown by the Anglo-Saxon site of Maxey (cf. Figure 98), where the houses were the same size as those at Chalton (cf. Figure 105). In villages of this type, which are the most numerous, it must be accepted either that the animals were left out in the open throughout the year (which is feasible in certain regions of north-western Europe, especially the southern half of

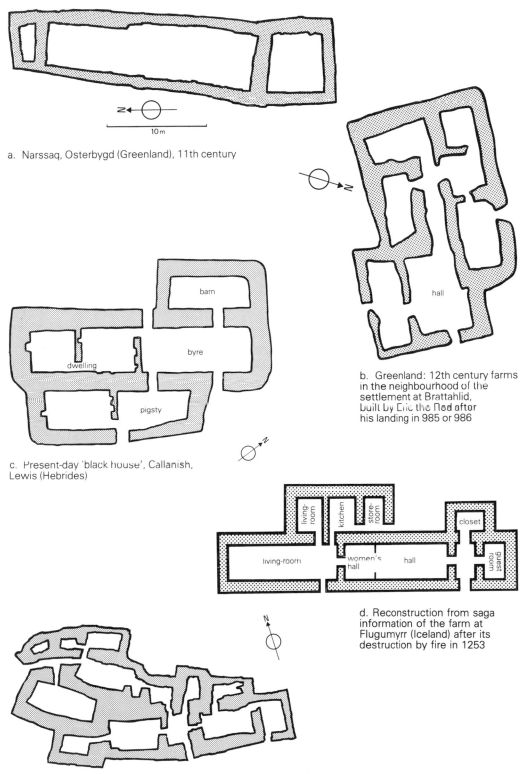

a. Narssaq, Osterbygd (Greenland), 11th century

b. Greenland: 12th century farms in the neighbourhood of the settlement at Brattahlid, built by Eric the Red after his landing in 985 or 986

c. Present-day 'black house', Callanish, Lewis (Hebrides)

d. Reconstruction from saga information of the farm at Flugumyrr (Iceland) after its destruction by fire in 1253

e. Austmannadel, Vesterbygd (Greenland), 13th century

107

Fig. 31. *Development of houses in Scandinavian settlement sites in northern Europe (tenth to fourteenth century AD)*

At the time of their colonization of part of Great Britain, followed by the islands in the North Sea and the Atlantic, the Scandinavians first constructed elongated rectangular buildings, following the traditional models of their homeland such as Vallhagar (Figure 24). Buildings of this type are to be found in particular in the tenth- and eleventh-century settlements in Iceland and Greenland (a). However, these buildings rapidly changed, to take account of local conditions in terms of the materials available and local climatic conditions. A new type of house appeared in the course of the twelfth century in the Norse colonies in Iceland and Greenland.

It is characterized by the addition, to a building of traditional form, of one or two structures that are parallel to and integral with it; they were smaller and communicated on one side with the main building, which generally remained the main hall, the adjoining buildings being used for various domestic purposes (b). The facility for passing from one part of this building complex to another from room to room explains the name naturally given to it: the passage house (German *Ganghaus*). Buildings of this type also existed in the Hebrides where, under the name of 'black houses', they remained the traditional house type until well after the Middle Ages (c). As well as being economical in building materials, by having common walls, houses of this type brought together the various farm buildings (which had hitherto been dispersed) and made them more or less easily accessible in winter in these regions of severe climates. Protection against cold and wind, especially of the hall, located right in the middle of the complex, was strengthened by the compact nature of the buildings. Contemporary texts from the twelfth century onwards (principally the Sagas), describe the Icelandic houses, which were in fact *Ganghäuser*. They often give detailed information about the internal furnishings of these houses, and the uses of different sections: for example, the farm at Flugumyrr, described in the *Islendinga Saga* at the time of its destruction by fire in 1253 (d).

Evolution of the Scandinavian house in these northern regions did not stop here. During the thirteenth century, an even more complex type of building came into use: the centralized house (*Zentralhaus*). This shows not only a proliferation of annexed ancillary buildings, particularly barns and byres, but also greater complexity in the overall plan and an increase in the built surface area. Many excavations in Iceland and Greenland since before World War II have made it possible to follow this development, which shows the gradual establishment over three or four centuries of a specific rural architecture.

(*a, b, e:* M. Müller-Wille, Zur mittelalterlichen Besiedlungs und Wirtschaftsgeschichte Grönlands, *Jahrbuch des Römisch-Germanische Zentral Museum Mainz*, 19 (1972); pp. 169–71
c: J. G. Hurst & M. W. Beresford, *Deserted Medieval Villages* (1971); fig. 33, p. 239
d: P. G. Foote & D. M. Wilson, *The Viking Achievement* (1973); fig. 11, p. 155)

England), or that there were fewer animals, especially cattle, than in Frisia. This tends to be the view of Britain at this period. Two factors can throw light on this problem: subsequent development from the thirteenth century onwards, to which we shall return, and the exceptional nature of the byre-

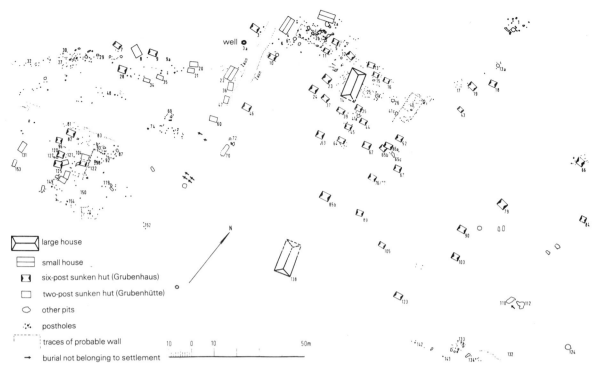

well

large house

small house

six-post sunken hut (Grubenhaus)

two-post sunken hut (Grubenhütte)

other pits

postholes

traces of probable wall

burial not belonging to settlement

N

10 0 10   50m

Fig. 32. *The settlement at Gladbach (Federal Republic of Germany): seventh to eighth centuries*

This shows farming units composed of 5 medium-sized or small houses built at ground level and 57 two- or six-posthole sunken huts (44 six-post, 13 two-post).

(W. Sage, *Die fränkische Siedlung bei Gladbach, Kr. Neuwied* (1969); p.19)

---

houses of Frisia and its surrounding region. A herd of several dozen cattle must have been rare at this period, and for this reason alone it must be accepted that the byre-house, although a very homogenous and distinct type, was very restricted in its distribution.

It has to be recognized that this distinction between two types of building is in the last analysis an artificial one. It is only the large byre-house that can be precisely defined and identified; on the sites where it is found, it is effectively exclusive. By contrast, the other building under consideration cannot properly be reduced to a homogenous type. It is difficult in normal archaeological terms to demonstrate the absence of animals in such cases: we shall see this later in respect of more recent examples. This is well illustrated by the hall house, the existence of which cannot always be discerned archaeologically but which is confirmed by documentary sources. It is characteristic of the seigneurial settlement from the Anglo-Saxon period in Britain, to take an example. As we have seen, an architectural form was adopted for Anglo-Saxon palaces that is close to that of the large byre-houses. In another region and at a lower social level, the hall house sheltering the family of the lord, his immediate entourage, and his guests where appropriate, in a large building which in particular made it possible to hold communal meals, is characteristic of Scandinavian colonial settlement, which is well known from the Icelandic sagas.

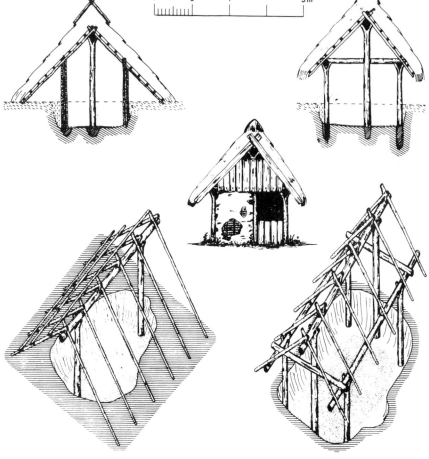

Fig. 33. *Types of sunken hut at Gladbach (Federal Republic of Germany): seventh to eighth centuries*

The reconstructions proposed here for the two main types of sunken hut with two and six postholes are valid for all examples of these types.

(W. Sage, *Die frankische Siedlung bei Gladbach, Kr. Neuwied*, (1969); fig. 16)

The existence of this architectural tradition, confirmed by several sites and many sagas, and its historical development, which is perpetuated in the large seigneurial halls that are so characteristic of feudal houses, is worth emphasizing. However, it must be recognized that it results more from various sources than from an archaeological reality that can be demonstrated by material remains alone.

III ANCILLARIES TO THE HOUSE

In early medieval settlements, the main buildings constructed at ground level had clustered round them, in order to serve the various functions needed in farming, other structures that were more simple in form but none the less interesting. These were, in particular, facilities for storing grain and sunken huts.

A Grain storage

In a number of rural sites in northern Germany, such as Feddersen Wierde or Kootwijk (cf. Figures 18, 28), to quote only two, or in Saxon England, such as Catholme (cf. Figure 22), it is common to find, near the buildings constructed at ground level, groups of posts, often three rows of three: these are the supports for granaries (cf. Figure 21). It would appear that, at least in the first millennium AD, this type of structure was never to be found in central or southern Germany.

In southern European sites, until well after the first millennium AD, the normal structure for grain storage was a pit dug into the ground, variable in size: the underground granary or silo. The use by the Saxons of the word *spicarium*, derived from *spica* (an ear of corn), in various German texts, or its germanized form, *Spyker*, to denote a place for grain storage confirms this practice, if any confirmation is needed. In later times the German word *Speicher* came to denote a granary in a more general form. This usage is obviously associated with late harvests, in September or October, of corn which was left to dry before being threshed. By contrast, the use of underground storage is connected in the Mediterranean world with threshing immediately after reaping, and thus of corn storage in the form of grain. It is likely that various climatic reasons, and also perhaps constraints deriving from the nature of the cereals being used, may explain these divergent customs, which need more serious study.

B Sunken huts

It is usual to find sunken huts around ground-level buildings on almost all first millennium AD sites. These small, simply constructed structures pose complex problems of interpretation.

1 *Types and forms of construction*

Generally these are structures partially dug into the soil to a depth of 0.25–1.00m (9in–3ft 3in), with a surface area of 5–10 sq. m (16–33 sq. ft), rarely larger. In the overwhelming majority of cases they are rectangular, though some oval examples are known.

The method of construction is relatively consistent: the pit is dug out, and then, at the bottom, on the eventual occupation floor, vertical elements are set up in postholes to form the main skeleton of the walls and to support the roof. Two very common, almost mutually exclusive, types can be distinguished, according to the number of posts. In the simpler case, two posts, each at the centre of one of the shorter sides, are adequate; in the other, in addition to these two elements, which are fundamental in that they support the ridge beam, there are four more uprights, one at each corner.

From a study of all the known sites in Europe, it would seem impossible to

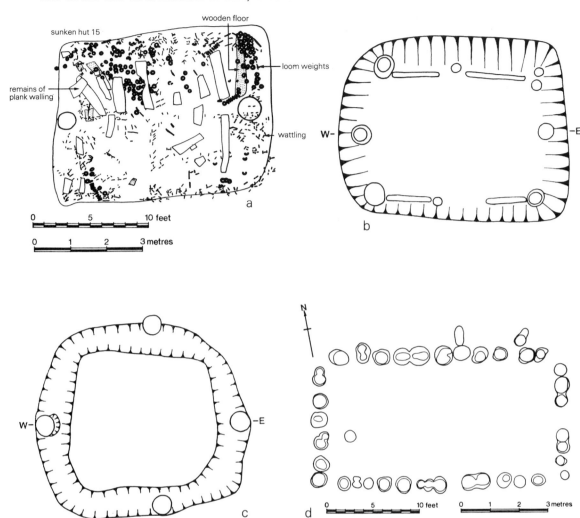

Fig. 34. *Sunken huts at the Anglo-Saxon settlement of West Stow (fifth to sixth centuries)*

Most of the West Stow sunken huts belonged to the two-posthole type (**a**). One of these, where the fittings were remarkably well preserved as the result of a fire, made it possible not only to identify the likely function of the building (from the presence of about 100 loomweights), but also to demonstrate the use of plank walls and the existence of a wooden floor covering the base of the pit (**a**). One of the sunken huts also revealed traces of wooden walls in the form of small foundation slots (**b**). Another had a foundation trench containing four posts which must have been the base for a turf wall (**c**). In addition to sunken huts, West Stow produced medium-sized rectangular houses (**d**) comparable with those from more or less contemporary sites such as Chalton and Thetford, and quite similar – in size and function at any rate – with those from Gladbach. Certain of the West Stow houses had, beneath their floors, cellars strongly reminiscent of sunken huts (Figure 36).

(S. E. West, The Anglo-Saxon Village of West Stow, *Medieval Archaeology*, 13 (1969); figs. 3, 4, 5, 7)

consider that the distinction between these two types has any special chronological or practical significance. Nor would it appear that one type is more common than the other. However, on a single site one or the other may clearly predominate. Thus at Wijster (Netherlands), a site occupied between 150 and 425, there are 118 six-posthole sunken huts and only 16 two-posthole examples. By contrast, at Mucking (England), occupied from the start of the fifth century to the start of the eighth century, of the 112 sunken huts discovered by 1975, a handful appeared to have no postholes at all, one was of the six-post type, and all the rest were two-post structures.

This was usually a very simple form of construction and the materials used were similar to those used for ground-level buildings, that is to say, wattle, daub, turfs, and foliage, which do not leave readily identifiable traces. However, in some cases the walls, which had to be built from the base of the pit to the ground level at least, may leave some direct or indirect indications – for example, holes left in the soil by the upright supports for the wattling (cf. Figure 44).

Foundation trenches at the base of the structure may, as at West Stow (see Figure 34) or various sites around the North Sea, correspond to turf walls. In other cases, especially in central and southern Germany, stone walls are found – for example, at Osterfingen (Switzerland), eighth- to twelfth-century Zimmern (Federal Republic of Germany), or Tilleda (German Democratic Republic) (see Figure 35). Similar examples are known from the French Alps – at Brandes, for example, still in course of excavation. In certain rare cases, planking walls have been observed and, in the sunken hut at Wijster, a wooden floor.

Access to these structures, given their sunken nature, must have required certain fittings, which are in fact rarely observed. One of the sunken huts at Gladbach, however, has a door-sill of small horizontal trunks.

It should be pointed out that not only the traces of constructional materials are usually difficult to detect but also those of the interior layout and fittings. In these cases it is often not easy to understand the functions of these structures.

2 Functions

By reason of the inadequate archaeological data, it is very difficult in many cases to reach any conclusions. Moreover, it is impossible to study this question without relating the functions of sunken huts to those of surrounding and adjacent structures. To confront this problem with any certainty assumes that a number of conditions are met, which is not always the case, at least until recently in a number of European regions, such as France. These are the excavation of a large area of the site, which makes it possible to clear a significant number of archaeological structures, and from this to distinguish their organization, and the careful clearing and meticulous analysis not only of the fillings of sunken huts but also of their immediate surroundings.

The latter point would seem to be self-evident, but it will be shown that certain examples of apparently classic 'sunken huts' were in fact nothing more

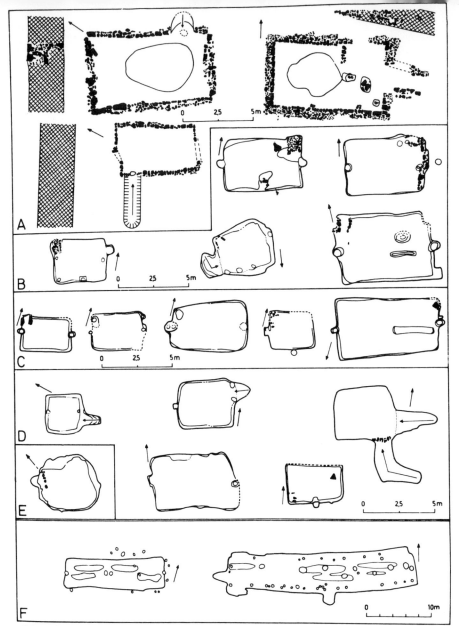

Fig. 35. *Use of sunken huts in the lower courtyard of the palace at Tilleda, ninth- to twelfth-century* (cf. Figures 41, 42)

A Stone buildings: guard houses. These are the stone-walled lower floors of houses rather than sunken huts
Sunken huts
B With ovens: dwellings
C With hearths: dwellings
D Without provision for fire: domestic outbuildings
E Used for iron working
F Used for weaving: the small postholes inside the huts, especially the larger, are the remains of the frames of vertical looms

(P. Grimm, The Royal Palace at Tilleda, *Medieval Archaeology*, 12 (1968); fig. 24, p. 98.)

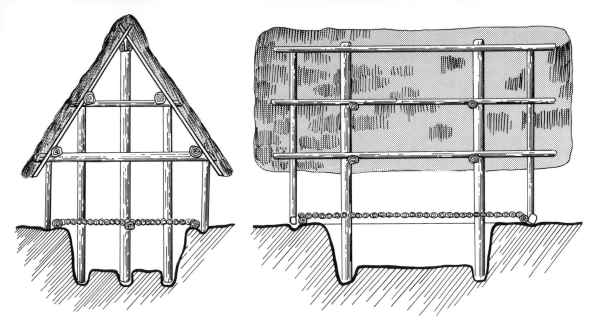

Fig. 36. *House with cellar in the Anglo-Saxon settlement of West Stow (fifth to seventh centuries)*

(Experiment and the Anglo-Saxon Environment, *Anglo-Saxon Settlement, British Archaeological Reports* 6 (1974); fig. 11, p. 80)

---

than cellars of a sort, dug into the floors of ground-level buildings. Careful excavation would produce evidence of this larger building: this was recently the case at West Stow, occupied in the fifth to seventh centuries AD (see Figure 36), and at Thetford, another Anglo-Saxon site, whilst Tilleda (Figure 35) and Midlum have shown the same on the Continent.

These are examples revealed by good excavation techniques, but they are probably more common than might be thought. It should not be overlooked that a high proportion of early medieval settlements have been revealed in a rescue context, under working conditions which sometimes restrict the quality of excavation and the subtlety of archaeological observation.

When consideration is restricted to true sunken huts (i.e. structures that are partially underground and not covered by a floor), it must be admitted that identification of function is often difficult. In addition to those already mentioned, there is a further reason which is more generally valid: these structures, set up as ancillaries to ground-level buildings, may have not one but several functions that change over time and are therefore not always detectable by excavation. In addition, some of these usages leave very slight archaeological traces.

In approaching this problem, when the area examined and the quality of excavation are such as to make the observations reliable, it is necessary to distinguish two separate cases. On the one hand, there are those sites where the sunken huts are associated with ground-level buildings, which appears to be the most common situation, and on the other, those sites where sunken huts are the only structures to be found.

Over a decade large-area excavations (1ha and more) have multiplied on

Some major excavations of first millennium AD rural sites

Site	Period of occupation (centuries)	No. of buildings	No. of sunken huts	Area excavated (ha)
Wijster (Netherlands)	2nd half 2nd–early 5th	86	140	3.5
Flögeln (Germany)	2nd–5th	40	40	1.5
Mucking (UK)	5th/6th–early 8th	10	190	?
West Stow (UK)	5th–8th	6	68	?
Odoorn (Netherlands)	5th–9th/10th	72	69	1.9
Chalton (UK)	5th–7th	50	2	1.8
Catholme (UK)	6th–10th	58	6	2
Gladbach (Germany)	7th–8th	5	57	3
Warendorf (Germany)	2nd half 7th–late 8th	65	70	2.6
Kootwijk (Netherlands)	late 7th–early 11th	45	177	4.5

early medieval rural settlements in Germany, the Netherlands and Great Britain. In the majority of cases the sunken huts seem to have been associated, in differing proportions, with ground-level buildings of various types.

Between these ten sites, numbered among the largest excavations of early medieval rural settlements carried out so far, which span the whole of the first millennium AD, very substantial variations in the absolute numbers of sunken huts and in their ratio to ground-level buildings become apparent. In some cases, such as Mucking or West Stow, one may almost consider sunken huts to be the only structures really represented on the site.

This leads naturally on to a consideration of those sites where ground-level buildings are absent and where only sunken huts have been observed. For a number of years, from the start of excavations in 1965, the Mucking site produced nothing but sunken huts. Ground-level buildings only came to light in the later years of the excavations. In these circumstances, the problem of the functions of sunken huts is quickly posed, on the basis of sound archaeological data: why so many sunken huts and so few houses?

Mucking was without doubt one of the first landfalls in the British Isles for Germanic people – in this case Anglo-Saxons (see Figure 37). It is probable that, from AD 400 onwards, they were installed here under the direction of the surviving Roman authorities, and that later, when the Imperial organization had disappeared, groups who were originally no more than armed auxiliaries became settlers, like those other Germanic peoples who followed them after AD 450. This early origin for the Mucking settlement is important in relation to the number of sunken huts found on the site. A very similar situation has been observed in contemporary sites on the North Sea coast, in Dutch Friesland, the departure region for these same Anglo-Saxons. This applies especially to Ezinge (Netherlands).

This site, occupied from the late La Tène period until the early fifth century, is similar to that at Feddersen Wierde: it is near the sea, in an area

Fig. 37. *Aerial view of the Anglo-Saxon settlement at Mucking, Essex (fifth to early eighth centuries), before excavation*

In the middle of late Iron Age circles and Romano-British ditches, Anglo-Saxon sunken huts show up as large numbers of small dark marks. The rescue excavation of this site, from 1965 to 1981, was probably the largest early medieval excavation in the British Isles: by 1975 10,000 postholes and pits, 7 km (4 miles) of ditches, and 121 sunken huts had been discovered. The excavation revealed the existence of two distinct but contemporary Anglo-Saxon settlements and two cemeteries, with more than 800 inhumations and cremations.

(Photograph by Professor J.K.S. St Joseph, Cambridge University Collection, 161/673803, 12 June 1961)

---

liable to flooding, and is built on an artificial earth mound. Throughout its earlier phase it was a settlement composed of ground-level houses, with a few rare sunken huts. After a widespread fire, it was occupied by an Anglo-Saxon group in the fourth to fifth centuries, doubtless in their progress westwards from the lower part of the Danish peninsula to the British Isles. The settlement from this period was entirely composed of sunken huts. This is all the more surprising when it is considered that the earlier settlements of these Saxon peoples, further to the east, were characterized, in the traditional manner, by the juxtaposition of ground-level houses and sunken huts. It would, therefore, seem right to interpret this final settlement phase at Ezinge, and the Mucking settlement as well, as being linked to a temporary mode of settlement for migrant peoples – Ezinge being the point of departure for Mucking, the location of which, on the north side of the Thames estuary, made it an easy landfall for the boats of the immigrant Anglo-Saxons.

Thus, in studying the functions of sunken huts, it is possible to identify one special case, that of settlements composed exclusively (or almost so) of sunken huts, such as Mucking or West Stow, which is also a very early Anglo-Saxon settlement. In these cases the sunken hut is a true dwelling – a house whose simplicity and speed of erection is ideally suited to migrant or relatively unstable groups.

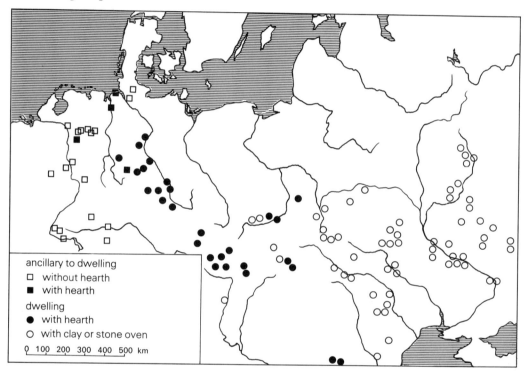

Fig. 38. *Functions of sunken huts from excavations of Germanic and Slav rural sites*

Excavations on III sites of the sixth to tenth centuries AD, in a region extending from the Federal Republic of Germany in the west to the Ukraine in the east, have produced sunken huts. If these are divided into those with hearths and those without hearths but associated with true houses built at ground level, two distinct groupings become apparent:

– *Geophysical:* All sites lying to the west of the Weser have sunken huts alongside ground-level buildings. By contrast, to the east of the Weser, in the Slav region, sunken huts are the only structures to be observed, and there are no ground-level buildings, so the former must be true dwellings.

– *Internal features:* All the sunken huts in the Slav region contain hearths or ovens, whilst provisions for heating or cooking are very rare indeed to the west of the Weser in the Germanic region.

(From P. Donat, Zur Nordausbreitung der slawischen Grubenhäuser, *Zeitschrift für Archäologie*, 4 (1970))

This explanation becomes even more satisfactory when account is taken of the fact that other contemporary peoples, especially the Slavs, used nothing but sunken huts as dwellings, at least throughout the entire first millennium AD. In a geographical area extending from the Rhine to the Dnieper and from the North Sea to the Danube, a study of more than 100 rural sites from this period shows very clearly that sunken huts were used exclusively as dwellings (see Figure 38). This is therefore connected with another settlement tradition which continued until relatively recently – up to the nineteenth century in Romania, for example – using rural houses that were partly below ground.

In the most common case (at least in western Europe) of sunken huts associated with ground-level buildings, studying the function of sunken huts is more tricky, especially in the absence of any trace of internal fittings or layout.

For certain sunken huts, objects discovered in the filling, and especially in the occupation layers, make it possible to put forward some precise ideas concerning their usage. The discovery of spindle whorls, and especially of loomweights, illustrates one of the most common and specific examples. Several scores of these objects were found in the occupation layer of one of the West Stow sunken huts (cf. Figure 34a). Documentary sources tell us that spinning and weaving were very common domestic occupations for women in the early Middle Ages. In addition, two other factors, one technological and the other documentary, made it possible to assert that in a proportion of cases that is unfortunately not easy to quantify, sunken huts were the working places for women – spinning and weaving workshops.

The classic horizontal loom began to spread and came into general use from the thirteenth century onwards. Before that date there are various indications that the loom in use had a vertical frame. The warp threads hung down vertically, and, to maintain tension in them and to allow the system to function properly, they had weights attached to them. This type of loom is in twofold accordance with archaeological observations: it explains the proliferation of weights, a great number of which were needed, even if the looms were relatively narrow, and it explains the presence in sunken huts of postholes without any architectural function, closely spaced and usually located up against a wall. These postholes served as supports for the main vertical elements of the loom frame. This hypothesis is demonstrated by the sunken huts from Tilleda (cf. Figure 35f).

Documentary sources confirm and reinforce the archaeological information. In early medieval texts, and particularly in the various Germanic Laws, frequent reference is made to meeting places for women to carry out spinning and weaving (see Figure 39). These buildings are usually designated by the Latin term *genecium* or by *screona*. Carolingian texts and other more recent ones, up to the fourteenth and even the sixteenth to eighteenth centuries in regions such as Champagne and Burgundy, continue to refer to spinning and weaving workshops reserved for women, using either the Latin term or gallicized forms of the Germanic terms, such as *écraigne*, *escregne*, *escriene* etc. These provide sufficient information to identify these as sunken huts. Other

Fig. 39. *Spinning and weaving in the ninth century*

This manuscript, embellished with pen drawings between 817 and 834 in a monastery on the Marne, shows a group of women in a setting which may evoke a sunken hut, or at least one of those *gynaecea* where they carried out spinning and weaving. The vertical loom is easily identifiable with its two upright beams buried in the soil and its narrow width.

(*Utrecht Psalter*, University Library, Utrecht, MS.32, folio 84 recto)

---

texts are even more precise. Pliny in his *Natural History* reports that in Germany the women work in underground huts. Nearer our own time, various seventeenth- to nineteenth-century texts report the survival in Champagne of huts sunk into the ground and covered with turfs, where the women met in the evenings to spin and weave.

All these elements, both documentary and archaeological, combine perfectly to indicate that in many cases sunken huts would have served for both these activities. A technological explanation can also be adduced: the cool and humid atmosphere of such a building would have prevented the thread from breaking. It is for this reason that in more recent times in various regions, such as the Cambrésis, woollen weavers, like the embroideresses of Valenciennes, worked in cellars.

In most cases, spinning and weaving will probably have left no traces in the sunken huts that have been excavated. However, in view of the obvious importance of these activities, of their fundamental character, and of their wide distribution over the entire rural world, it may be assumed that many sunken huts must have been built for this purpose or used in this way at some time or another.

In addition to spinning and weaving, there is another activity which requires the temperature and humidity conditions consistent with the characteristics of a semi-underground building: cheese making and, more generally, the storage of milk. In various regions of France, especially in the mountains, cheese making was carried out until recently in structures similar to sunkens huts. In some cases, as at Morken (Figure 40), it is reasonable to assume that the

Fig. 40. *Sunken huts at the Morken settlement (Federal Republic of Germany): Carolingian period*

Eight pits, hemispherical or nearly so, were intended to receive large pottery vessels. Vessels of this type were made in the region in the period. The various observations suggest that this sunken hut may have served as a dairy.

(H. Hinz, Morken, *Kirche und Burg* (1962); p.169)

---

sunken hut was built for this purpose. However, this is clearly a use which will leave no trace at all.

The use of sunken huts for temporary storage alongside a dwelling house would also leave no evidence. Their use as workshops, on the other hand, should be easier to detect.

A number of excavations, such as those at Sutton Courtenay, West Stow, or Tilleda, have shown that sunken huts could be used as workshops, especially for craftsmen employing fire. On the Stow sites there are usually one or more hearths or ovens in sunken huts, and so they could be either dwellings or, in later periods, detached kitchens. At Tilleda (see Figures 41 and 42) sunken huts in the 'industrial' area of the site, some distance from the dwelling houses, have produced evidence of iron smelting and working, bronze working, leather working, pottery manufacture, working of goat horns and even of hippopota-

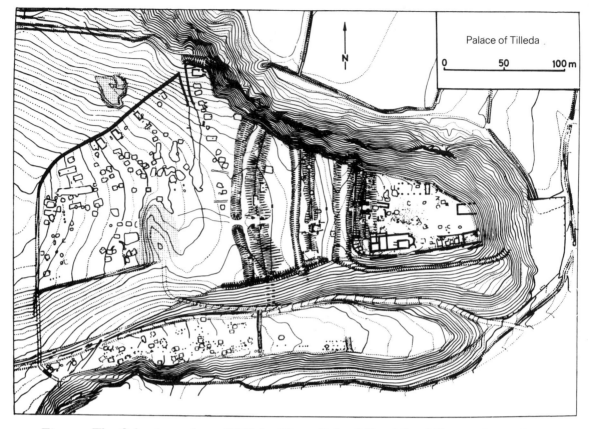

Fig. 41. *The Othonian palace of Tilleda (Harz, Federal Republic of Germany): ninth- to twelfth-century. Excavation plan in early 1975* (cf. Figure 35)

At this site, lying on the promontory of a plateau, the following may be distinguished from east to west: the palace proper, defended by three ditches and banks; the bailey sheltering many dwelling houses and workshops, itself defended by a stone wall to the west; at the foot of the plateau and to the south, various other ancillary structures.

(P. Grimm, Die Königspfalz Tilleda, *Ausgrabungen und Funde*, 21 (1976); fig. 1, p. 141)

---

mus ivory, and weaving. Two pottery kilns were found among these sunken huts, one of which contained a stone window lintel in the process of being made, attesting stone working as well. In the Belgian site at Huy, a number of seventh-century sunken hearths have been discovered associated with various craft activities such as bone working, pottery and bronze working.

The functions of sunken huts are complex and call for varying explanations (though their conditions of survival, as Figure 43 shows, often make interpretation very difficult). In the Germano-Slav cultural area, they correspond in particular with migrant peoples whose settlements are unstable or temporary. However, in most first millennium AD sites, they are associated

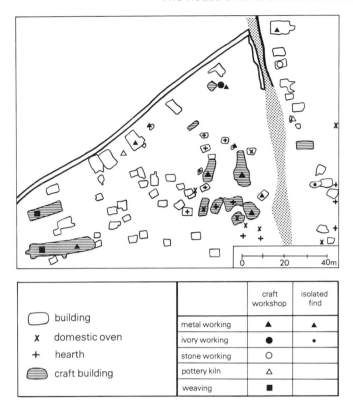

building		craft workshop	isolated find
x domestic oven	metal working	▲	▲
+ hearth	ivory working	●	•
craft building	stone working	O	
	pottery kiln	Δ	
	weaving	■	

Fig. 42. *Craft activities in the bailey of the palace of Tilleda   tenth to twelfth century* (P. Grimm, Beiträge zu Handwerk und Handel in der Vorburg der Pfalz Tilleda, *Zeitschrift für Archäologie* (1972); fig. 29, p. 143)

with ground-level buildings. In such cases they can serve several purposes. The rapidity with which they can be erected and the economical use of materials in a semi-underground structure would make it possible to build sunken huts for temporary or relatively unimportant uses. The Breton peasants of Morbihan were still making a type of sunken hut around their houses in the nineteenth century in order to store their excess potatoes when the harvest was larger than usual.

In many cases sunken huts could have served many purposes – to house young animals, food stocks, supernumerary members of the family, or the whole of the serf workforce of the early Middle Ages. There is no doubt that Germanic Europe, as well as the Europe that inherited Roman law, maintained a considerable slave population up to the tenth century. This is well attested by documentary sources: out of 498 texts of laws promulgated by the Visigothic kings between 642 and 700, 299 were partly or wholly concerned with slaves, and the same proportions apply to the laws of the Salian Franks and the Burgundians.

Although the sunken hut, even in western Europe, can be seen as a dwelling, albeit temporary or marginal, it was nevertheless not the traditional form of dwelling for that period. Moreover, it must have been used as an ancillary building for sheltering various domestic activities, such as spinning and weaving, or even more specialized crafts.

The sunken hut is thus, by virtue of its rather systematic distribution, a fundamental component of early medieval rural settlement. Its almost complete disappearance around AD 1000 is even more interesting.

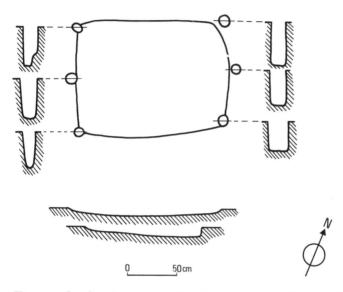

Fig. 43. *Sunken hut at the Brébières settlement (Pas-de-Calais), sixth to seventh centuries*
Thirty sunken huts were identified at this site: 13 were six-post and 13 two-post. Mechanical stripping before the excavation began had reduced the structures to the depths shown. Rescue conditions made it difficult to observe possible ground-level structures.

(P. Demolon, *Le village mérovingien de Brébières*, Arras (1972); fig. 27, p. 93)

3 Date of use

According to the definition of the sunken hut given above (a semi-underground structure that was not covered with a floor and which formed a building in itself), it appeared as early as the La Tène period. One of the earliest known examples would seem to be that at Ochterging (Kr. Main, Federal Republic of Germany), from the fourth century BC. In Gaul, sunken houses appear to have been in use from La Tène III, just before the Roman conquest. Structures of this type are known at Villeneuve-Saint-Germain (Aisne), from the first century BC. Sunken huts spread gradually over the rest of the Empire, often following the routes of Germanic peoples.

In the Netherlands, the earliest examples date from the first century AD, as at Diphoorn, but they only become common around the middle of the Roman period. They appeared in Britain with the first Germanic invaders in the late fourth or early fifth century AD. It is essentially the Germanic and Slav region that appears to have been the favoured region for the sunken hut from the early first century AD.

The period of the great migrations is undeniably the time when this structure became widely distributed over the British Isles, France and southern Sweden. By contrast, it was absent from areas of Norse colonization such as the Faroes, the Shetlands, or Greenland, and it was rare in the Frisian *Terpen-Wurten* sites. In the north-west of free Germany, beyond the Imperial frontiers and during the Roman period, sunken huts appear to have been very common, but with significant variations which seem to be related to soil characteristics: out of 30 settlements in this region without sunken huts, nine (30 per cent) were established on heavy clay soils, whilst of 46 settlements with sunken huts only six (13 per cent) were on soils of this nature. Heavy clay soils thus appear to discourage the construction of sunken huts, which are to be found in abundance in this region on light, sandy soils. This example serves to demonstrate that the functions performed by sunken huts could just as easily be discharged by ground-level buildings.

Further south in Europe, early medieval sunken huts are to be found in Switzerland and the French Alps, but the situation in southern France and Italy remains unclear, in the absence of excavations of rural sites of this period.

These different observations make it possible to define more clearly the uses of sunken huts, and show in particular that, according to the soils on which they settled, contemporary populations could do without them. The subsequent history of the sunken huts sheds further light on this aspect.

The British Isles, where many rural excavations have been carried out covering the whole medieval period, allows us to follow the history of the sunken hut. By 1965 sunken huts had been found at 22 different sites of the Pagan Saxon period (400–650), two of the Middle Saxon period (650–850), and four of the Late Saxon period (850–1066).

On the basis of data available in 1952, sunken huts had been found on the continent at 76 Roman-period sites, 28 from the fifth to seventh centuries, 30 from the eighth to tenth centuries (see Figure 44), and four from the eleventh to twelfth centuries.

In 1968, out of some 200 villages studied more or less intensively in England for the period 1066–1570, two twelfth-century villages were found to have sunken huts, three from the twelfth century, and a few later examples.

During the Middle Ages and later, in the British Isles (e.g. in Somerset and Ireland) as in France, sunken huts continue to occur. But the circumstances of their use are always the same, and rather different from those of the early Middle Ages. Sunken huts were uncommon, and never consistently present, as in the first millennium AD. They were usually temporary dwellings – for shepherds, for example – or specialized ancillary buildings – for cheesemaking or the occasional storage of various foodstuffs by a poor peasantry.

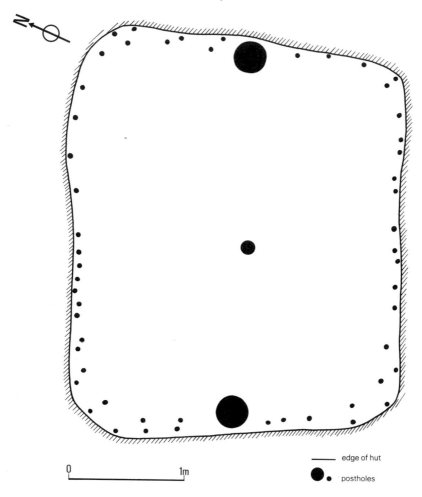

0 _____ 1m

—— edge of hut

● ● postholes

Fig. 44. *Sunken hut with wattle and daub walls at Dieue-sur-Meuse (Meuse)*
With its two axially disposed posts, this sunken hut belongs to one of the two classic types. Around the pit small-diameter stake-holes represent traces of vertical elements of the wattling. Several eleventh-century sunken huts, all with the same traces of wattle and daub, have been excavated on this site. They are reminiscent of similar structures used at Gladbach several centuries earlier.

(After J. Guillaume, *Le peuplement de Dieue-sur-Meuse (Meuse) au haut Moyen Age*, Mémoire de maîtrise, Nancy, 1972 (unpublished): with the author's permission)

There was thus a change in rural settlement, apparently between the Carolingian period and the tenth or eleventh century, which resulted for western Europe in the abandonment, apart from some rare exceptions, of the sunken hut. There were several reasons for this, closely connected with the overall development of rural settlement at this time, which will be discussed later. It is possible to say, in conclusion, that the sunken hut was, throughout the early Middle Ages (except for the Slav lands), a temporary or ancillary structure, the existence and use of which bear witness to the frequently unstable and always simple nature of rural settlement at this time. It is for this reason in particular that it is an important subject of study as a characteristic that defines an epoch in the history of rural settlement.

IV   CONCLUSIONS

For the period between the fifth century and the tenth or eleventh century, it is difficult to give a precise description of rural settlement over the whole region that we are considering. Throughout the entire southern part, and especially in the countries of the Mediterranean, the transition from Roman settlement to organized village, very often located high on a hill and dominated by a castle, as was the case from the twelfth century onwards, is at present difficult to reconstruct, owing to the lack of excavated data.

The situation is better understood in respect of the northern half of Europe, especially in countries such as Great Britain, the Netherlands and Germany, not to mention Scandinavia and Ireland. In all these areas, rural settlement is characterized by a measure of instability so far as location is concerned. All the countries under review provide evidence of more or less long and clearly defined periods of abandonment of settlement sites between the first century AD and the great classic desertion phases at the end of the Middle Ages. It would, however, be a mistake to believe that these two phenomena, at either end of the medieval period, can be explained in the same way. The early medieval desertions seem to have an altogether different context: they may be attributable (especially in Germany) to migrations of peoples who abandoned their original settlement areas, but they may also occur in a period of general demographic expansion.

Another classic aspect of rural settlement at this period, in addition to the instability of sites, is their small size and the almost general absence of those characteristics which defined the village of the later Middle Ages and subsequent periods: the church, the castle, and the construction of houses in an organized way around these two elements, which form, together with the village square and in certain cases the walls, specific nucleation points.

Small population units were general before the tenth century, although there are some examples of larger rural aggregations. However, this small size did not preclude a gradual, significant growth in population. A measure of demographic pressure, combined with concentrations in certain special sites, existed throughout the period. It was a precursor of the general demographic expansion that characterized the whole of western Europe from the tenth to eleventh centuries onwards.

A final important characteristic of this settlement must be stressed: even though the habitation sites were mobile, in many cases they moved within territories that were delimited by that period, and may even have been established in Roman times. Settlement instability, and the creation of a growing number of new population centres, brought with them – and this is especially clear in Great Britain and Germany – the fragmentation of older territories or estates. Thus, a period of instability and regular increase in the size of settlements, leading to the growth of new centres, led to the establishment of the settled landscape and the population distribution of the second half of the Middle Ages.

This settlement in the course of development, which begins to resemble that of the later medieval period, is characterized, at least in the part of Europe that is best known and understood, by a number of common factors so far as the house and its ancillaries are concerned.

The population and farming unit seems generally to have consisted of several buildings, ranging from two or three to more than ten in the most favourable cases.

These buildings, which in architectural terms belong to two distinct groups, built at ground level or below ground level, correspond with specific functions: housing of free peasants or slaves, protection of animals, harvests, equipment etc. This fragmentation of the settlement and of farming activities over several buildings varying in form and size appears to be typical of rural settlement over the whole of north-western Europe at this time, as is the presence of some form of enclosure around each of the units.

Houses proper seem to vary between two extremes – on one hand the large Frisian byre-houses, sheltering under the same roof men and several scores of domestic animals, and on the other the smaller houses, for human beings alone. The former seem to have been used principally in continental coastal regions around the North Sea (with some later examples in Britain), but the smaller rectangular house was the more general type, though it varied somewhat in size. It was the latter type which made up the classic rural settlements in the Saxon areas of Britain or central and southern Germany. Alongside these structures, sunken huts, used for housing the lower classes of rural society or as ancillaries for working or storage, formed a very common element.

What best typifies early medieval rural settlement in the best known part of Europe, the north-west, is the small size of the settlement nuclei, combined with the differences between these and later medieval villages and the pronounced instability of at least part of this type of settlement. This last-named phenomenon goes hand-in-hand with the use of constructional materials, extracted on the settlement site itself, of limited durability: raw earth or vegetable matter in the form of thin tree trunks, branches, and foliage rather than squared-up timbers. All these factors, including the materials and methods of construction, will be seen to undergo considerable changes in the following period. As a result of these transformations, the classic village form begins to appear.

Chapter Four: The dominant factors of the high Middle Ages

I THE BIRTH OF THE VILLAGE (ninth–eleventh centuries)

To relegate the origins of essential facts to those twilight zones where they cannot be seriously discussed is a temptation with which historians of less well-known periods are familiar. But it is in no way a wiser course to eschew them completely. We must, therefore, confront this particular dilemma: even as late as 850, cottages of manor tenants, priests' *villae*, and random scatters of huts did not constitute villages. Yet before the end of the eleventh century, in both Poitou and Latium, in Catalonia and Bavaria, grouped settlements had taken on the aspect of villages as we know them. In only two centuries a process of change was accelerated and finally completed – a change which was fundamental but which is in general not understood. The archaeologist may have his suspicions about this decisive process, but it is up to the historian cautiously to explore this hidden turning point of European history.

For so delicate a task we must renounce the consolation offered by the inductive methods that are usually highly prized by historians, who are concerned with causes: merely to list the evolutionary factors in total documentary darkness would be too artificial a procedure. Let us be content merely to observe.

A The regrouping of peoples

The first and most general observation that a historian can make is the multiplication of nucleation points for rural settlement. Those often quoted phrases about the West 'bristling' with castles or 'covered with a white robe of churches' once again will serve their purpose, but no longer to illuminate a power hierarchy or a flowering Christianity.

1 *The moated castle*
The phenomenon of the castle is indubitably the most important of all. It has for many years been associated by historians and their readers with the 'feudal period'. In fact, it takes little time to dismiss the simplistic political or military explanation. As a nucleating point for men, the castle appears nowadays to constitute a determining factor and, as a result, more questions are posed relating to the chronological stages of a castle or the local circumstance of its

construction, than about its juridical basis. The case where a castle buds off from an ancient stronghold – Celtic *oppidum*, Roman *castrum*, or Saxon fort – is naturally of secondary importance. They are certainly of significance in cases where a previously scattered settlement becomes concentrated in the interior of a defended enclosure, which until that time had harboured no permanent civilian settlement. So far as France is concerned, the work of Michel de Boüard or Gabriel Fournier has made it possible to set up a preliminary typology of those castles that are the successors of an earlier establishment, often of considerable antiquity, such as the re-use of an enclosure from late prehistory at Millançay (Loir-et-Cher), or a sacred place (first pagan, then Christian) such as the Grand Caux. More often it is the adaptation of a Gallo-Roman or Merovingian *curtis* which has been enclosed and heightened: there are many examples of this in the Caux (Gravenchon), the Auvergne (Escorailles, Ennezat), the Charente (Villejoubert), the Netherlands (Borssele), Germany and Picardy (Hamblain). The case of Doué-la-Fontaine (Maine-et-Loire) is one of the most instructive in this respect. It shows that after a *palatium* (royal residence), documentarily attested in 830, was removed elsewhere, an *aula* with service rooms was built; this was burnt down around 960, quickly rebuilt, and then buried in the early eleventh century within an artificial earthen mound or 'motte', which served as the base of a keep.

This phenomenon is of no less importance in connection with the present study than the creation of an entirely new motte.

It would be going outside the terms of reference of the present book to make a detailed study of the origins and typology of the motte (Figure 45), which is so tiresomely characterized as 'feudal'. We shall confine ourselves to what is relevant here, above all the period when this phenomenon first developed. This needs little discussion: the handful of documentary sources that refer to a *dunio*, a *munitio* or a *castellum* (and more infrequently to a motte) place its first appearance between 1000 and 1080. Estimates by archaeologists push this back a little earlier, and this is explicable in terms of the inevitable time-lag between the birth of a new phenomenon and its first documentary references. It might even be stated that, in theory, it dates from 864, when Charles the Bald protested against the unauthorized building of *firmitates* and *haiae*, presumably against the Normans. It can also be seen to be earlier in certain threatened regions such as Lorraine (Pierrepont in 940, Fins around 954, Chantereine-les-Mouzon in 974) or Puisaye (Toucy and Saint-Fargeau between 976 and 980), or in isolated areas such as the Auvergne (Brioude in 980), Quercy and Rouergue. Elsewhere, the rush to build local defences depended either on the level of princely power or the degree of development of seigneurial institutions: 1030 to 1075 in the Saintonge, Angoumois, and Anjou (Saint-Florent-le-Vieil 1030), 1020 to 1070 in Artois and Flanders, 1045 in Provence and Picardy, 1030 in Calabria under Norman influence, but not until 1080 in Guyenne. Outside France, there are more than 30 examples in Catalonia earlier than 1025, but they did not appear in England before 1060, and in Germany until 1080.

Fig. 45. *The motte at Montmiral (Drôme)*
In the foreground can be seen the half-moon-shaped escarpment of the promontory.
This was cut back from the natural slope and was levelled in the interior, so as to form
the bailey, defended by a palisade. In the background is the motte proper, with a later
square keep.

(Photo C.A.H.M.G.I., Grenoble)

The question of the numbers of mottes is more divisive of historians than
that of the time they first appear. Michel de Boüard considers that his
generalized statement is applicable to every region and that it relates to natural
defensive sites (steep spurs, such as the *puigs* of Catalonia or the *rocca* of
Provence and Italy) or structures that are more 'civilian' in character. In fact
surveys that have been carried out seem to justify this view: these surveys have
shown that many can be dated to before 1100 – more than 30 in the Chartres
area, 80 in Auxois, nearly 50 in Quercy, 30 in Puisaye, 80 in the northern part
of the Caux, 35 in Calvados, 30 in the Apt region etc. We should be quite clear
about terminology in this context: the stronghold (*ferté: firmitas*) and the tower
(*dunio* or keep – doubtless an older Celtic word) could be very modest
structures. There is a wide range between the 8 m (26 ft) diameter platform at
Louvetot (Seine-Maritime) and the 800 sq. m (957 sq. yd) of Goindreville in
the Eure. The role of the motte as a residence often seems to have been
important. The famous description (admittedly from the twelfth century) of
the tower built at Ardres shows the existence of a dwelling that is much more
like a *curtis* such as that at Annappes, at least so far as the layout of rooms is
concerned, than a fortress.

above all else, that Christianity effected its penetration by means of belief in the hereafter and reverence for natural forces rather than through the power of dogma. This, however, is a phenomenon that has no connection with those that concern us here. It can be accepted that the parochial network, which had long been loose, or even non-existent, in the Germanic and Slav lands that were the subject of missionary activities, was in operation in the tenth century (cf. Figures 62, 64). Carolingian legislation on tithes, followed by the gradual return, starting in the ninth century, of altars from lay or private hands (*Eigenkirche*) to those of the clergy, testifies to the completion of the process of Christianization. The church then became elevated to the status of a communal building: the development around the church of a zone of asylum and peace, the *atrium*, which comprised the village of the dead, the cemetery, and the meeting place of the living, dates from this time. The fact that in north-western Europe the church was, moreover, the only building in stone, the only one that could provide a safe haven for men and animals, could only serve to strengthen its role as the nucleus for rural settlement. There is no catalogue of the earliest references to parishes in Christian Europe, but an analytical scrutiny of Papal bulls confirming monastic privileges or listing donations to the Church would certainly produce one. From those few documentary sources which throw light on this aspect of history, it would appear that it was in the tenth century that fusion took place between ecclesiastical parish and village agglomeration.

Without wishing to over-generalize these comments – since there are certainly discontinuities and gradations – it is possible to identify from them one constant factor in the history of the countryside. It is undeniable that ancient sites – mere collections of huts or better organized *vici* – disappeared without our being able to know what replaced them; contrariwise, the persistence, at the level of straightforward distributions – of place names ending in -*court* or -*y* in northern France, for example – confirms that an ancient form of isolated settlement has survived which, although much weakened, proved capable of resisting – but why and how? – the general movement towards nucleation. To throw some light on this problem, it is necessary to examine, for ancient sites that were enlarged at this time, the structure of the village itself and to identify the various nuclei of which, over successive periods, it was comprised. This has been attempted – by Gabriel Fournier in the Auvergne, for example – and the picture derived from these observations is of a living village, built up very slowly over two or three centuries. Let us, therefore, try to create a general view. Whether it is a matter of continuity from an ancient site or an agglomeration below a castle, within a wall, or around a church, in every case a prescribed area is defined, as manor or royal creation or parish. This delimited area transcends the built-up section, extending over the surrounding countryside, hitherto only weakly controlled, with its scattered *casae*. The reordering of the countryside thus constitutes the second component of this fundamental transformation.

B Reorganization of the countryside

In the absence of property registers, detailed terriers, or cadastral surveys, the dating of early land allotments poses problems that are very difficult to resolve. Even the Domesday Book, the eleventh-century survey of English land holdings – itself a very exceptional document – gives no more than an indication of the situation applicable to large blocks of land and tells nothing of the layout of the countryside. This leaves only two possible approaches, both equally unsatisfactory.

1 *Redistribution of land holdings*

First, there is the study of changes in land tenure, in the event of there being any trace of them preserved in written records. The exchange of holdings or the reassignment of revenues may, in fact, be considered to be a very likely indication of the reorganization of the countryside; on the one hand as a result of the breaking up of the large farming units of the early Middle Ages, and on the other, attributable to growth in the number of 'economically viable' operations based on the land. These two aspects are amply illustrated by contracts lodged in registers of deeds or cartularies and by bulls confirming land holdings: the successive changes in these in relation to a single occupier, say between 1000 and 1150, make it possible to study the development of the system. Before 1100, of course, these apply only to churches. However, such donations admirably demonstrate the break-up of the early medieval *villae*. Dissolution of the earlier family unit, the *manse* or small manor, no doubt proceeded more rapidly in north-western Europe, where its structure appears to have been less firmly based. To this phenomenon can be attributed the dispersal of ancient estates of a complex type, which were only held by a single lord because of the more or less permanent coherence of the basic unit. In Domesday Book – in the county of Cambridgeshire, for example – more than a quarter of the estates inventoried had already been split up in 1066. Documents from Catalonia list the profusion of micro-holdings, encouraged in this region by the contract of *aprisio*, a form of planting lease, which provided for long-term cultivation and planting and which led in effect to a gradual transfer of rights in the land. It is often terminology that attests to the division of land allotments in the Netherlands: terms such as *bercaria, curtile, carrucata, diurnale* and *portiones* replace the words *mansum* or *villa*. In the Auvergne, *villa* came to have no more than a territorial significance. So far as the present study is concerned, the reorganization of the land into farming units better adapted to intensive agriculture – those *diurnales* that could be ploughed in a single day, the *carrucates* that a single team could cultivate in a season, and which will be discussed later – could only be implemented if there was a fundamental transfer of basic or relevant property rights. A redistribution of this kind, not apparent until 1000–1080, is a natural concomitant to the regrouping of peoples that we have just been discussing: one cannot take place without the other, and the magnitude of the change is astonishing.

2 *Reclamation of waste land*

A second study might be carried out on the fringes of the cultivated landscape, as additional evidence of the newly constituted village community seizing all the possibilities available to them: the reclamation of the *saltus*. This is important for our study in so far as it often led to the establishment of new settlements of a special type, or because it confirms that the older landscapes had become saturated with people and entirely under cultivation. It was not so much a matter of bringing under the plough land that had remained untouched until that time – high Pyrenean or Hercynian valleys, coastal areas reclaimed from the sea, encircling forests – but rather of taking over and adding to the existing cultivated areas, stretches of scrub and grazing land which had hitherto been left to animals and stock rearing. Expressed in another way, the reorganization of settlement and land allotment brought about a transition from a form of agriculture that was itinerant, wide-ranging and semi-pastoral, to a static form in which animals were banished to the woodlands or to land that was temporarily not being planted. Thus the bringing into cultivation of waste land was a corollary of the process of redistributing land allotments. In practice, this movement has left behind less evidence in the documentary sources than the clearing of thick forests or the creation of polders, on the one hand because it did not produce contractual arrangements, and consequently deeds that would be retained by the contracting parties, and on the other because logically and in practice it is a much older process. We only have indications to help us evaluate it, and these are insufficient to permit a quantitative appraisal. However, they do give at least a general idea of the phenomenon. There were inequalities in terms of status and responsibilities that can be detected in the documentary sources as between old and new holdings: the latter were more quickly and more heavily burdened with taxes, payable only in coin, or more rapidly excused from obligatory labour service.

It is admittedly no more than an impression, but it does seem that the scanty references to the rural landscape in documents of the eleventh or early twelfth centuries bear witness to a distinction, apparently manifest from that time, between the *bosc* (woodland) and the *plain* (the cleared area). However, this observation does not extend to Mediterranean Europe: one of the characteristics of this major phase is the divergence, which continued to grow, between the two main climatic zones of the Christian world. In fact, the reclamation and eventual disappearance of areas of waste land in northern and central France, in the British Isles, and the Germanic and Slav lands endowed this geographical region with a food-production basis that enabled it to support a permanent economic and demographic expansion. By contrast, in the barren, broken-up, arid soils of Spain, the Pays d'Oc, or the Italian peninsula, there was no alternative to leaving vast uncultivated regions to wasteland, scrub and flocks of sheep. After having dominated in a period of slavery and an extended economy, the Mediterranean lands gradually slipped, even in the rich mountain-girt river valleys, from a straitened economy into simple subsistence.

This poverty of rural life consequently encouraged urban and mercantile development. The gulf between north and south – predictable but long masked by the poor development of production methods over 'barbarian' Europe – should not be underestimated.

C   The causes – men or technology?

Within the terms of this study, several observations may be advanced. Between 900 and 1050 – from as early as 850 in regions under greater threat than others, but not until 1080 in those regions that were late in joining the Christian world – that is to say, over about two centuries, very profound changes can be discerned in the fabric of the rural world. A non-intensive economy, based on *latifundia* or enormous agricultural enterprises, generally dispersed over regions that were weakly governed and without any real organization, was replaced by an ordered economy, more orientated towards the systematic exploitation of natural resources, in some areas earlier and more determinedly than elsewhere and in others within the context of an ancient and persisting urbanization. This abrupt change, which brought with it an intensive mode of production, was especially characterized by the stabilization of settlement and structuring of the village and the countryside that supported it. The most salient feature of this change was the appearance of mechanisms within which this domestic or seigneurial economy could operate: parishes and manors.

It is relevant to seek the reasons for these changes. The study of the dominant features of rural life in the early Middle Ages, which must shortly be defined again for the high, final medieval period, shows that there were very strong links between the structure of land tenure or the type of settlement, on the one hand, and the main features of social life and material resources on the other.

1   *Human societies in flux*

The first fact that becomes evident is the increase in population. Whether this was a cause or a consequence of the economic phenomena we shall be discussing, a simple decline in mortality, or an increase in birthrate, is of no direct concern in this study. What is important is the resulting pressure which led to or maintained the rational exploitation of the land, the development of new settlements on new lands, and the expansion and redistribution of older settlements. Wherever the traditional reluctance of medieval historians to deal in numbers has been swept aside and attempts made to measure this growth, a clear correlation with the creation of new, organized villages becomes apparent. The earliest evidence comes from the ninth or tenth centuries in the Mediterranean lands: the final demonstration, in rural terms, of their superiority. It can be observed before 1000 in central and northern France, around 1100 over the whole of north-western Europe, and a little later in

Fig. 46. *Mediterranean and northern agriculture: threshing of corn*

a In his fresco in the communal palace of Siena, painted around 1338, Ambrogio Lorenzetti depicted a vast landscape at harvest time. This detail summarizes various characteristics of Mediterranean agriculture: the two-storied stone house, the small enclosure of fruit trees alongside it, asses used for threshing, and the landscape itself are all reminiscent of Italy or Provence. Close to the house, in front of a barn made out of branches and foliage, analogies for which are to be found much later in European rural architecture (cf. Figure 102), threshing is being performed in the classic way for those regions: two pairs of peasants are working rhythmically in an open area. The crop is threshed immediately after being harvested and the grain is stored.

Germany. These discrepancies, which may perhaps be the result of limitations imposed by the available documentation, do at least have the merit of defining the role played – a minor one – by the 'invasions' of the ninth and tenth centuries. Hungarians, Saracens and Normans neither impeded nor encouraged demographic expansion, and the time has come to see the biased lamentations of monks for what they are. The accumulation of great masses of people in villages, crowded together in houses designed for many fewer, would certainly have led to some diversification in buildings and a reorganization of the structure of the village itself, and the far-reaching changes in these two areas, which will be discussed in detail later, can be attributed to this cause. It should be remembered, however, that the essential characteristic of this growth is not so much its scale as its duration – two centuries at the least – which makes it the longest-lasting demographic expansion in the history of Europe.

b This miniature from a Flemish manuscript shows a completely different situation in the early sixteenth century. Near a dwelling house, which appears to be built in wood and has an upper storey (obviously representing the most recent phase), there is a timber-framed barn. The contrast between the materials used for these two buildings is strengthened by the roofs – flat tiles for the house, thatch for the barn. Within the barn two threshers are working rhythmically whilst a third man is winnowing the grain outside. This miniature, which illustrates November, as the hunting scene in the foreground clearly demonstrates, introduces another form of grain storage: the ears are kept for threshing well after the harvest, in autumn or winter. The storage capacity must therefore be considerably greater than in the first example (cf. Figure 50d).

(*a:* Fresco from the Palazzo Communale, Sienna (Italy) by Ambrogio Lorenzetti (*c.*1338). Photo: Alinari, No. 53086
b: Flemish calendar, early sixteenth-century. British Library, Add. MS. 24098, folio 28b)

Pressure exerted within the family group played a decisive role in the gradual abandonment of the clan structure. Here a second dynamic factor comes into play, clearly linked with the former, with the establishment of new obligations which accord a low priority to ties of blood. It might be said that the social apparatus of the human group went into a phase where horizontal obligations of this type began to play a role that was equal to that of earlier

Fig. 47. *A peasant feast: dance of the Shepherds and Shepherdesses (fifteenth century)*
In their leisure moments, medieval peasants knew how to practise the traditional rites
of rural sociability of the post-medieval centuries.

(*Missel à l'usage de Poitiers*, Bibliothèque Nationale, Paris, MS. Latin 873, folio 21
recto: photo Hachette)

vertical obligations: the coming together of fellow parishioners, legal peers or
landowners of equal status.

The relationship with the appearance of the new village communities –
parish, manor or cultivated land – becomes clearly apparent. The constriction
of men in this way can only be explained in terms of relaxation of the older
tribal links. In this respect, the movement towards the creation of *paix* – the
word eventually came to denote the village territory over which its protection
was extended – and communal manors (i.e. without any judiciary powers) are
complementary, and led to the same outcome: circumscribing men with
collective obligations, whether religious or judicial, economic or moral. It so
happens that both the phases of this phenomenon and the hostile reactions
that it engendered are well known. It is possible to date with some accuracy the
appearance of the earliest obligations for manorial service, a sure sign of the
constriction of men's freedom of action, and that of the oaths of peace which,
after various vicissitudes, combined to create a Christian society that was
subject to the Church and to the military and landed aristocracy: 975–990 for
Atlantic Europe, 1020–1080 for the whole French region, Italy and Spain and,

a little later, across the Rhine and the English Channel. This echoes the chronology for the appearance of mottes, enclosure walls and churches that has already been discussed.

2 Tools and implements

One further factor to be considered relates to tools and implements. Once again it would be possible to discuss the antecedents of technical developments that generate improved production or are capable of launching an exchange economy, either of which could promote demographic expansion rather than being its corollary. Let us, however, stick to hard facts: the availability of good-quality iron tools is, without any dispute, one of the basic factors in the introduction of intensive cultivation, the systematic clearance of virgin land, and the erection of better buildings. Unfortunately, it is difficult to catalogue technical aspects of this nature before the twelfth century, when iconography provides a more accurate picture, in the form of a number of practical manuals.

It is true that this aspect of the problem is of less importance in this context than the date when these innovations were introduced. In this respect archaeology, though often not able to provide firm dates for tools (see Figure 48), can identify evidence of the introduction of innovation in different buildings. Research has been attempted in this field, but the results – those obtained by A Sené, for example – whilst confirming the importance of the eleventh century, inevitably fall down over an inexorable inherent weakness: with certain exceptions, those churches, fortresses or ramparts which are available to be studied in this way form part of structures that are hardly typical. No technical innovation can have economic or social effect unless it is in general use, right across the social scale. Agriculture and tilling of the fields in general elude archaeological survey. The study of residual floras, buried plough-furrows, and the spreading of domestic refuse, as at Wharram Percy, can certainly provide certain data, but such data are still rather few in quantity. This type of work is, however, lightly touched upon in documentary sources: not, admittedly, in terms of descriptions (which were, in any case, usually out-of-date when they were written) but through those fugitive indications, the uses of words – references to methods of harvesting or, better still, the appearance in villages of smithies and mills. These are data affecting the economy as a whole, however, and it would be outside the scope of this study to consider them in detail.

II VILLAGE LIFE

Why should we try to hide the paucity of our documentary knowledge? The reader has already been warned about this problem at the start of this interpellation in the overall study. We are confronted, as will by now be better appreciated, with two types of agricultural exploitation and settlement. The

a

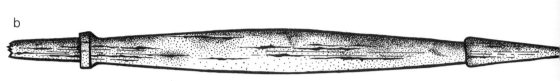

b

scale 1:1

scale 1:2

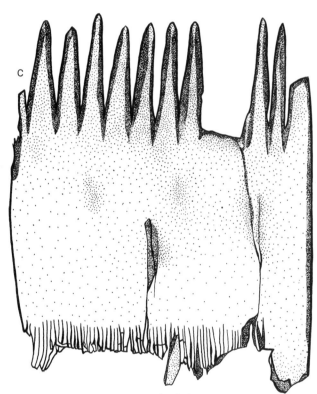

c

scale 1:1

d

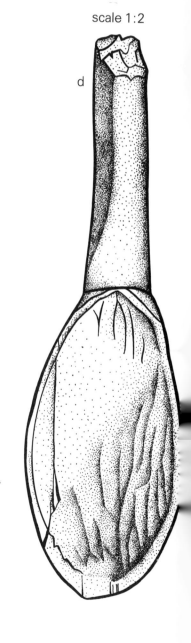

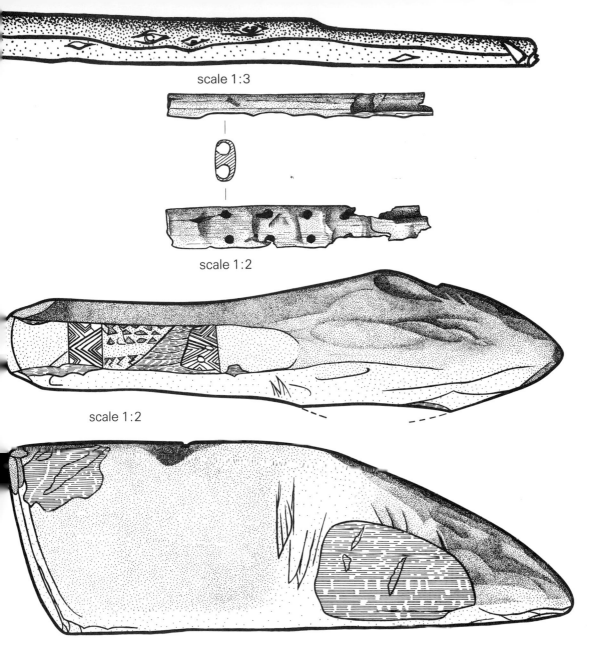

scale 1:3

scale 1:2

scale 1:2

Fig. 48. *Wooden tools and artefacts from Charavines (Isère) – eleventh century*

This settlement was covered by the waters of the Lac de Paladru and abandoned for this reason; it has produced some exceptionally well-preserved wooden objects. The example shown here illustrates traditional activities on rural sites: the transport of water, using a shoulder beam (a); spinning, with a lathe-turned wooden spindle (b); wool-combing (c); cooking or similar activities, using a wooden spoon (d). Other objects relate to activities that were doubtless also very common but which only rarely leave traces in the archaeological record: a double flute (e), and a shaped piece of wood, decorated on the back, which was used in making the sewn leather shoes common at that period (f).

(By kind permission of the excavator, Michel Colardèlle: from the archives of C.A.H.M.G.I., Grenoble)

one derives from antiquity – perhaps as early as the Neolithic period – and gradually disintegrates in the early Middle Ages. It is to the other tradition that medieval Europe owes its reputation as a land of villages, the broad outlines of which can be clearly distinguished in the twelfth century, or perhaps even in the eleventh century. Between the two traditions there is a clear cultural discontinuity, at least as significant as the urban explosion which has steadily been emptying our latter-day countryside over the last century. When we emerge from the documentary obscurity that accompanies it, where we have been able to grapple with a handful of facts, a new rural landscape becomes apparent between 950 and 1100, very similar to that of our own time, and it is to this that we must now turn.

The essence of what twentieth-century man knows of the Middle Ages is to be found in the central, 'classic' period, between 1050 and 1350. It is in no sense a paradox that our documentation for this period – and by this should be understood both excavation data and written sources, they are all one – is among the worst understood of all historical data. The historian, drawn to written sources that permit a quantitative view or to the meticulous analysis of very rare documents, tends to concentrate on the very early or the very late medieval period. For his part, the archaeologist works on sites that are rich in hut remains or Merovingian graves, or on buildings that still survive to a greater or lesser extent but they date back to no earlier than the fifteenth century. For the former, twelfth- and thirteenth-century documents seem to be abundant, but they offer little that is striking; for the latter, however, villages of the 'invasions' period or the Hundred Years' War are richer in information yield. The first effect of this neglect is to obscure in the most extraordinary way the two essential centuries of the Middle Ages; the second, and more serious, effect is the persistence of the illusion that nothing of importance occurred and that the rural world remained stable, unchanging, or even inert. In addition to studying the constant and general characteristics, it is therefore necessary to highlight the evolution of the living organism that is the village (Figure 49).

A   The seigneurial cell

1   *Overall aspects*

The seigneurial 'cell', which gradually became established between 950 and 1100, provided a framework for rural life, covering one or more districts, one or more villages. Naturally, as has already been noted, the creation of this network of dependencies was not uniform in either space or time: it survived right to the end of the Middle Ages in marginal Christianized regions that remained socially at the level of chieftainship or the clan, such as Frisia, Ireland, Sweden or the valleys of the Pyrenees. It may also be considered (though this lies outside the present study) that urban seigneuries apparently conformed with the village model: however, there were gradations in the

Fig. 49. *Montaigut-le-Blanc (Puy-de-Dôme) in the second half of the fifteenth century*

In a striking panoramic drawing, the medieval artist shows all the elements of medieval or post-medieval villages over a large part of Europe. Perched on a slope, below a castle and surrounded by a wall, the village of Montaigut-le-Blanc is made up of low houses, roofed with tiles. A large church, roofed with flat stones and surrounded by a group of tiled houses, forms its own quarter of the village. The countryside, with hedgerows in the background and the bridge with its calvary on the right, corresponds wonderfully well with what is still to be seen today in this region. In the foreground, the shepherd guarding his sheep and accompanied by his dog makes use of two classic elements available to his post-medieval colleagues: a portable enclosure and a wheeled kennel.

(*Armorial de Guillaume Revel*, Bibliothèque Nationale, Paris, Fr.22297, p.308)

---

towns. Finally, the fact should not be overlooked that the seigneurial (or 'feudal', if that is preferred) institution corresponds with the triumph of a new mode of social relationships or production, the evolution of which could only have been very gradual: however, this viewpoint has little relevance here. On the other hand, there are three specific points that relate to the problem of settlement itself, the subject of the present study.

If the presence of an overlord, whether lay or ecclesiastical, count or modest squire, justifies, by reason of the powers that he exercised, the concept of a framework – a seigneurial 'district' – it is at the lowest level of everyday life, that of the relationships which unite or protect men, that the basic 'cell' must be located. So far as this is concerned, the household, the *ostal*, the *domus*, the *casa*, whether of the king or the humble churl, is the medieval atom. The authority of the master, whether father or husband, the links with dead ancestors, whose portraits and relics were venerated, in due course the presence of a family cult location, and in any case the accumulation of material possessions, confer a sacred character on the houses of men and animals. As it happens, additionally, that in most cases the means of production were the responsibility of the family or servant workforce, without any obligation to exploit it fully or to produce a disposable surplus, which would constitute a source of rivalry within the group, it can immediately be seen that the household constitutes, in economic and moral terms, a micro-seigneury within the larger. There is no doubt that the house-as-organism has a role to play within the structure of the house-as-building.

Without contradicting this view, but changing the standpoint somewhat, it can, secondly, be affirmed that the lordship of pastures, of transhumance lands, or of small, isolated, impermanent clearings in the Scandinavian forests or in the scrublands of the southern islands, cannot be subject to the same rules that apply to the great peasant seigneuries of England, Picardy or Lombardy. In the former, the absence of a fixed or permanent geographical framework – huts for milking or shearing sheep or sawing timber – would seem to exclude a living style of this kind from our study. However, in addition to the role, always essential, of byres and store-sheds, the complex relationships between pastures and cultivated fields, the networks of roads for exploiting the land, or, better still, the links with the markets to which wool, timber and cheese are sent, all have a direct influence on the forms of landscapes and even the structures of villages built as components of these contrasting economies.

Finally, the antithesis that we have already encountered between the two great geographical and cultural zones of the medieval west must once again be taken into account – not so much in the structures or juridical characteristics of seigneury, which have no relevance to the present subject, as in the much greater fragmentation of southern landscapes, and, consequently, the much more important role played by the house, the *casal*, the isolated custodian of seigneurial rights.

2 *The importance of the church*

Typical both of the village and of the medieval period, the church and the castle are the twin anchors of settlement, and it would be paradoxical not to begin the study of the seigneurial cell with them.

The church, in practice, presents a more complex picture than appears at first sight. In the first place, its role in attracting settlement would appear to derive rather from the presence of baptismal fonts than from its liturgical function. As far as one can judge, in fact, a simple chapel without baptistery did not act as a nucleus for settlement, at least in the period when the parochial seed was taking root. A large number of fonts and altars were, however, set up in the very hearts of large farms in the early Middle Ages, which poses the problem of the progress of these to the rank of village. In such cases, the church seems to operate more as an element of seigneurial power than as a nucleus for bringing men together.

A second aspect of the role of the church which is often overlooked derives from its economic function. Historians have naturally subjected the church to intensive study, whether in its monastic, episcopal or canonical form, as the centre of a large rural estate, source of production and exchange, or as distributor and consumer of labour. The establishment of a peasant centre alongside an abbey or collegiate church is well known from Saint-Denis, Saint-Bertin, Saint-Riquier, Saint-Rémy, and elsewhere. The development – admittedly in the thirteenth century for the most part – of a *dos* or territorial endowment, consisting of land holdings or rights of use, in addition to the right to levy tithes, transformed the modest village church into a cell for the exploitation and disposal of agricultural surpluses. Little is known, before the end of the Middle Ages, about the role played by village fraternities in the exploitation of these communal properties, or by the vestry (*fabrique*), made up of local worthies and responsible for the administration of the revenues and the buildings. This is not a matter of denouncing the seizure, under the guise of communal parish interest, of these revenues by the richest members of the village community. However, it is not difficult to envisage the conservation of the 'parish' equipment and crops, bringing in its train the erection of buildings that were not connected with religous practices and which formed a complex surrounding the church, so as to constitute a special district within the village.

Since it clearly justifies the attractional role of the church, we should end by recalling the importance, in countries that habitually built in wood, of a stone building which could shelter countryfolk, and even provide them with protection in time of war where there was no nearby seigneurial bailey at the foot of a strong keep. An analogous role was played by hospices and gatehouses in the free distribution of food and in providing asylum, around which the huts of refugees would cluster. All these elements, many of which are to be observed in the changes of the tenth century, are prominent features in village landscapes.

3   The importance of the stronghold

It is not necessary here to discuss the typology or internal arrangements of the castle, that other nucleus which polarized human groupings, though its part in influencing the form and location of settlements cannot be disregarded. It can be seen that expansion around the motte proper of a spacious bailey, where men and animals could come together, would undoubtedly have encouraged the development of a settlement. The military function of fortresses assimilated and superseded the social role played by the development of mottes, which had been of greater importance in earlier periods. However, the castle, like the church, appears to have been essentially a mother economic cell, distributing work and receiving the production surpluses that were, from that time onwards, harshly exacted from the villages.

Read, for example, the famous description of the castle at Ardres by the early twelfth-century author Lambert d'Ardres: it is not a simple matter of garrison and defensive works, but rather of granaries, cowsheds, bedchambers and kitchens. The castle is the central nucleus of a family that remains very extensive, augmented by retainers, stewards, vassals who owed guard service (*estage*) and who were fed and housed for three months or more at the lord's expense, poor relatives, penniless younger sons, servants of all grades, and the common folk providing labour service; it gives the impression of being the main driving force of the seigneurial economy. To support this view, despite growing and sometimes very oppressive control over the peasant economy through levies, taxes for protection or the felling of timber, and later the obligation to pay for the use of installations erected by the lord, there is no evidence for a considerable time of any overlordship. Indeed, the less well organized the seigneury, the less rapid and productive the economic development. And here, once again, the solid rural lordships of north-western Europe – Picardy, the Ile-de-France, England – increased the social development of village communities in these countries by comparison with those of the Mediterranean lands.

It is, therefore, not the fortified structure and its changes over time that should detain us, but rather the symbols of the domination by the stronghold, the *ferté* of the castle. Ecclesiastical lordships were many and they reveal the same picture. Prime importance must be accorded to tithe barns, where tithes and rents in kinds were stored, to areas for the communal threshing of corn, to the seigneurial mill, and to the dovecote, where the lord alone could raise pigeons and collect their rich droppings. The absence of all or some of the ancillaries is a much surer index than the motte itself of the role of a seigneurial residence: in 1298 at Cagnoncles, near Cambrai, the appraisal of the village after it had been destroyed by fire valued the seigneurial barn at over 300 livres, whilst the value of the richest of the cottages did not exceed 40 livres, the average value of fifty burned dwellings being between 15 and 20 livres. Erected mainly around or within the seigneurial precincts, these auxiliary elements attest to the existence of exchange or craft activities based on labour service or paid employment. The absence of these relegated a village to the status of a hamlet, a subsidiary organism, as was the case with chapels that did not possess baptismal fonts.

4 *Within or beyond the pale*

A settlement cannot be deemed to be mature, in terms of the tenth-century main phase, if it is not provided with a seigneurial residence or a parish church. There is a third element, delineation of the built-up area, whether by a continuous enclosure work in solid materials, a lightly built structure, or simple boundary markers. In this respect, contact with the cultivated or grazing lands raises a legal question. It is readily acceptable that the stone walls of a Provençal or Sabine village, an incontrovertible separation between the village and its lands, has a legal function as well as a military one. However, this is not true of the Saxon enclosure, which was barely effective against wild boars and wolves, and even less so the crosses or boundary markers laid out round the *tours de ville* of Picardy. In such cases, which form the majority, it is the structures lying outside the boundaries (*hors du ban* or *hors de la paix*) which pose problems – those flimsy huts for guests, strangers, or aliens (*aubains*), the building used to house presumed lepers or madmen, which constitute a satellite settlement not subject to the community's rules and quickly transformed into the quarter of the serfs (an aspect that need not concern us here). These dwellings would not, therefore, be subject to the rhythm of development of the village proper: the parcels of land that they occupied would play no part in the collective organization of the land which will shortly be discussed. In their lack of cohesion, they are reminiscent of the structures of early hamlets and, as such, constitute anarchic nuclei or enclaves. The fact that they are always later than the village proper, since they usually developed in response to its economic evolution, is of no importance, since this does not represent a step backwards but rather the adaptation of the settlement to a primary function. Strung out, like town suburbs, along the roads leading from villages, these ribbons stayed almost inert in economic terms so long as the village communities remained strong, i.e. over virtually the entire medieval period. However, those that were established without any legal structure and located far from early villages – as for example in a woodland clearing or alongside a sheep run (*bercaria*) of polders and marshland – produced a special type of secondary settlement, the structure of which we shall return to.

5   A community of men

In various guises – as a parish complex, as a group of peasants required to give service in clearing out the seigneurial moat, waiting at the door of the mill, or living within the walled enclosure – a fundamental characteristic of medieval life can be seen to emerge: a manor or seigneury, the basic cell of all social and economic activity, is above all else a community. Of course, the tribe or the clan of earlier periods already displayed such characteristics, and the household reproduced the same fundamental connections at the primary level. However, the special attribute of the seigneurial society, and of the 'domestic' economy of the classical period, is the interlacing network of reciprocal obligations. This is no place to enumerate the different elements and the equally diverse grades within these communities: we will content ourselves with stressing the factors that condition such a mode of settlement. First, there are the economic constraints that emerge: voluntary constraints are linked with the internal organization of the land, which become stronger when subjected to the pressures resulting from crop rotation or communal use of woodland, waste lands, or upland pastures. In this respect, there are no differences between transhumant pastoral groups in the Briançonnais (*escarterons*), Picard arable farmers or Thuringian forest dwellers: everywhere the need to bring flocks together, to appoint shepherds and harvest overseers (*messiers*), to apporton out the tithes, or to agree with the seigneur the time for haymaking or the wine harvest, extends the collective responsibility of the human community over the whole of the land. No better proof of this is needed than the tenacity of peasants, in every region, in seeking to ensure the preservation or extension, preferably in writing, of their collective rights. It would not be going too far to assert that a major part of the road network in the village lands was determined by these communal obligations. It is not certain whether the ancient duty, military and fiscal originally but become purely economic, of the *adjectio sterilium* – i.e. the collective responsibility of the whole group in respect of land that was temporarily not being cultivated – had persisted or was reimposed at this time. A lack of manpower during periods of unrest or demographic recession (for example, the *mansi absi*, or houses without owners, which abound in the later polyptychs of the ninth century, or the 'ruined' and deserted lands of the fifteenth century) might preclude the implementation of this compulsory cultivation. However, where it can be identified in the twelfth and thirteenth centuries, it was certainly a potent factor in the 'full' exploitation of the countryside.

The interdependent responsibilities, whether voluntary or obligatory, economic or spiritual, that encompassed men are not easy to descry. Some are in evidence but difficult to make out clearly in legal documents: communal labour in forced-labour teams, guard duties on forest margins, the queue at the mill, work in the wash-house, or attendance at village general assemblies, the manorial courts or *plaids*. Others revealed by documents did not perhaps play a significant role, such as residence by churls (*manants*) within the confines of a village, theoretically the only method of acquiring rights of tenure and communal privileges in the woods and pastures. Through the medium of police examination in the early fourteenth century of the inhabitants of Montaillou, in the Ariège, Emmanuel Le Roy-Ladurie has recently demonstrated that, even at this period, ad hoc relationships constituted in the last analysis the most binding fabric of village life so far as their inhabitants were concerned: discussions round an elm tree or in a house, the inn, threshing on seigneurial land, sheep shearing, milking.

To summarize, and so as not to lose sight of the connection between the village and the seigneurial cell, let us reiterate that it was the interdependent relationships within a group, even an itinerant group, that shaped the basic constraints affecting human life: the household as the primary unit, the meeting places where villagers converged daily – graveyard, mill, smithy, wash-house, market place, the lord's workshops – which were fixed points in the community to which the church, the boundary, or the castle acted as precursors.

B Domestic economy

A group of men – relatives or those providing service, if need be servants or paid men – worked the land, either entirely on their own account or as 'settlers' on it. They did not use their entire labour force, except when seigneurial or fiscal pressure demanded a level of production greater than their own subsistence requirements. If they accepted this additional burden without too much complaint, it was because it secured for them protection or various services from the lord in return, by virtue of the links that bound them to him. Most of them were not motivated solely by the urge to survive: their only concern was to realize the agricultural capital that they held and, in case of need, they would increase it if the implements available to them allowed them to bring to market the surplus that remained after they had paid their taxes and fed their group. Voluntary over-production for profit was not the basis of their personal efforts, even if in terms of economic reality they combined to achieve this for the benefit of the seigneur. Naturally, bearing in mind the variable potential of different soils, all men were not protected against hunger, even famine: a quarter, perhaps a third, of them were constantly fighting against this. However, these included those who lived outside the walls or beyond the pale, excluded from the village community and, strictly speaking, fringe dwellers. This was the nature of the classic peasant economy throughout the long period when western Europe, though barely protected against general famines and epidemics, was building up its reserves of men and tools over a century and a half at the very least, from 1100 to 1250, one of the longest periods of continuous growth in the economic history of Europe.

1   Terracing and clearing

This harmonious development was founded upon a series of factors that demand consideration. First, there was the reclamation of virgin land, the conquest of the entire landscape. Marc Bloch once characterized the 'great clearances' of the Middle Ages as representing the most important stage in the expansion of the cultivated area in Europe since the Neolithic period, when massive clearances also took place. This statement needs modification, but not outright rejection: it can be accepted that the eleventh and twelfth centuries marked the time when western man became unquestioned master of the land. Without going too far down this road, some comments are needed by way of illustration. First, it is necessary to stress the pronounced geographical variations. Were the degraded vegetable soils and the climate of the Mediterranean lands, the scrubs and marshes, the remnants of a much denser shrub cover, modified – perhaps before the Christian era – either by climatic changes that cannot easily be understood nowadays, or by uncontrolled, disastrous grazing? Whatever the cause in these southern lands, with the exception of the slopes of the Alps and the Pyrenees, clearance – usually by burning – was carried out right up to the edges of the river valleys, the bottoms and the terraces being dominated by man, and the plateaux and the hills left for free grazing. Strong indications are naturally somewhat rare in these latitudes: reclamation of the *saltus* must have been the result of individual enterprise and very limited in scope, with no obvious effect on the village community. On the other hand, the broken nature of the upland areas, hardly affected by the bushes and scrub that grew there, would probably have prevented it from being brought into cultivation. This is why we must establish a link between the clearances in Mediterranean lands and the mammoth task of embankment, in the form of terraces held in place by low walls, so many of which are today still visible and in use. Here, in dealing with a landscape which is both agricultural and economic, we touch on a fundamental problem. In view of the fact that the Moslems made widespread use of them in the Iberian peninsula and the islands, they cannot be linked directly with a crop such as the vine. Nor does it appear that the enormous effort imposed upon the peasantry, in hoisting earth and stones in baskets on steep slopes, could only result from the use of slaves. This would seem to be medieval work, often in family groups, certainly adapted to local physical conditions but also a relatively lax seigneurial structure. The *huertas* of the Levante or Andalusia, the *revas* of the Cévennes or Corbières, the Provençal Alps, the Sabine Hills, or Campania appear in the twelfth century as high-density cultivated lands, a condition which could only be achieved, in the face of demographic pressure, by the laborious conquest of these steep slopes. Siting the village on the line of

a

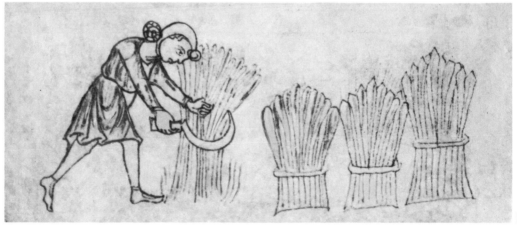

b

d

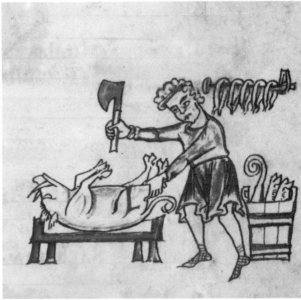

e

Fig. 50. *Jobs and days from a thirteenth-century manuscript*

Traditional tasks regularly mark the peasant year, and are frequently represented in manuscripts and in the porches of cathedrals. In February the soil is dug over and the seasonal cycle begins (a); the harvest is in August, using sickles (b); the grapes are harvested in September, with bill hooks and woven baskets (c); threshing of the corn takes place in October, for this is Burgundy (d: cf. Figure 46b); and finally, in November the year comes towards its end with the slaughter of the pigs and the preparation of preserved meat (e).

(Photos: Bibliothèque Nationale, Paris)

contact between cornfields and vineyards, as at Pélissane (Bouches-du-Rhône), is partly explained by the need to be close to both types of agricultural activity. In theory, all the land available for cultivation should have been cleared and incorporated into the village lands: when, as in Latium and Sabina, the distinction was maintained until the thirteenth century between the infield (*tenementa de intus*) and outfield (*tenementa de foris*), the difficulty and long-term nature of this effort is well demonstrated. The general course of the Mediterranean economy followed the same arduous road.

In those lands where the hawthorn and the oak hold sway, the picture changes to a 'classic' one, and the only problems are ones of degree and emphasis: attacks on bushes and shrubs before those on the beeches and oaks in those regions of vast cultivated landscapes supporting village life, such as the corn-growing prairies of northern France, southern Germany and the London basin. It was a matter of extending cultivation into those marginal lands that had hitherto been used as wild pasture or for ad hoc cultivation: a voluntary and massive penetration into the forest mantle of the mountains of Germany and Bohemia, or across the dense thickets on the alluvial plains of the Slav territories in Silesia or Moravia, or, again, clearance of the groups of woodland on the Alpine slopes.

All this effort led to the extension or new creation of the traditional farming landscape: arable agriculture or natural pasturage. It was only in the colder regions facing the Atlantic – Armorica, Wales, Scotland – that clearance led to the creation of a special type of discontinuous occupation, the *bocage*, to which we shall return later.

Although opposite in their effects on farming structures, those different aspects of the conquest of the land nevertheless display certain common characteristics. In chronological terms, they were earlier in southern than in northern Europe and later in the east than the west, with certain exceptions, such as Catalonia, where they did not exist before 1000. They clearly slackened off in the thirteenth century, except in Scandinavia and Poland. The pace varied from region to region, but this is attributable rather to differing chronological phases than to inequalities in the implements available. It is difficult to measure the general extent of land made available to the plough in this way: methods of approach such as the study of assarting contracts, micro-toponymy (field-name studies, for example), variations in pollen counts, and remanent flora are not well adapted to quantitative treatment. In the heavily populated grain-producing areas such as Picardy, Brabant and Swabia, the maximum increase seems to have been 15–20 per cent, but in Silesia, the Perche, or the Ardennes it is possible to postulate a doubling of the cultivated area.

However, it is at the level of its effects that the pushing back of the outfield seems to have been consistent and homogeneous. It manifestly brought to an end the isolation of the ancient forest clearings, which were the seat of a restricted, wretched economy and way of life. It acted as the mainspring for an exchange economy. By permitting men and beasts to make use of woods and copses, it reinforced the village community and encouraged the exploitation of natural resources. On a more modest scale, the peasant working alone at this task, whether legitimate copyholder or entrepreneur biting into the surrounding wasteland, was able to provide a securer basis for his future. How is it possible to prove that the population expansion of Christian Europe was not directly attributable to this phenomenon?

2 Mastery of tools

In touching on this causal hypothesis – if it was not due to a surplus of hands, it was because of the possession of better tools – and in evoking above man's assault on the giants of the forest or the heavier soils and the construction of *huertas* (terraced fields), we encounter a second factor underlying the domestic economy: the mastery of high-quality tools and implements (Figure 51). It is not part of this study to evaluate the role of invention or empiricism in the use of a fertilizer, the choice of a better cereal, a method of harnessing draught animals, or the use of a mould board. Nevertheless, it can readily be seen that mastery of iron, wood and water remains the precondition for more effective tools and implements. The smithy, the sawmill and the cornmill thus appear to have been the nuclei for village expansion, and the men who ran them acquired high social standing, the source of a positive influence on the orientation and volume of sales in local markets. The lord who owned the ironworks, the timber supplies and the water-course, used these to exercise control over production. It is, therefore, surprising that prospection for, and appropriation of, the sources of wealth and power, with complementary control of roads or waterways, along which tree trunks and 'sheaves' of iron were transported, are not more prominent features of the documentary sources – surprising also that so little scholarly work has been done on them. Certainly we shall touch on, here and elsewhere, materials of all kinds used in building, an essential element in this study. However, research is only just beginning on rural craftsmanship in iron and wood. The effects of the movement of raw materials are known well enough for more recent periods for us to suspect that, when a medieval settlement was stabilizing its location, the proximity of running water, of a pocket of iron ore, or of an easily accessible wood was as important as the need for a defensible site or a light soil.

3 Mastery of production

Production freed from isolation and the simple necessities of subsistence, supported by an increase in the labour force, expansion of cultivated land, improved quality of tools, and communal constraints, means a development of the land on which pastoral demands and the requirements for cereals are in balance. Let us recall the principal factors. Traditional medieval nutritional practice gave pride of place to cereals, the basis of porridges and bread. In second place were dairy products, with meat third. A balance therefore needed to be struck between corn and livestock, those two mainstays of subsistence: if ploughing tended to occupy the entire arable area, and even pushed back the

Fig. 51. *Ploughing equipment in early sixteenth-century Flanders*

Successive autumn tasks are shown in this scene, which represents September: in the background, ploughing with a typical wheeled mould-board plough drawn by two horses; in the middle distance, right, broadcast sowing; in the foreground, harrowing with an implement drawn by two horses, working at right angles to the furrows so as to cover the grain. This is a region of developed agriculture, as shown by the quality and strength of the implements and by the use of horses. The individual in the background should be noted, knocking down acorns to feed the pigs that are grazing freely, a traditional medieval practice which gradually disappeared on the recommendation of agronomists from the thirteenth century onwards.

(Flemish calendar, early sixteenth-century, British Library, Add. MS. 24098, folio 26 verso)

---

woodland where many types of domestic animals were sent to graze freely, there was a risk of reducing stock raising in both volume and quality. However, driving out nursing sows or working horses in order to reserve the woods for hunting or timber felling meant that the stalling of animals had to be developed, along with artificial meadows or leys: the vicious circle of the medieval economy which was only rendered possible by reducing arable land.

The balance of the countryside was therefore a delicate one. When the scrublands and copses had disappeared under the combined influence of human pressure and the opportunities offered by improved tools, the balance could only be safeguarded by crop rotation and by codification of the use of the woodlands. The removal each year of half or a third of the fields from ploughing, leaving them for grazing, was the concomitant of the removal of the woodland. However, if the loss of grain was not to be too severe, sowing and ploughing practices had to be improved. This leads to the view that more sophisticated techniques of agriculture – deeper ploughing, cross-ploughing, ploughing in lands – which had hitherto been reserved to certain manorial estates, became the norm wherever an open, deep soil permitted them.

The progress of these practices can only be judged from a handful of examples, such as the fossil fields in England dating from the enclosures or the evidence of some fifteenth-century miniatures. They are enough to show that research into the efficiency of working practices was linked with the improvement hoped for from land that had to feed more mouths from a smaller area. It can be seen more easily that the gradual increase of grain production could only be feasible where a pressing demand and easily-worked soils came together: on the cold slopes of the Harz mountains, or above the Alpine valleys, even more so as the Mediterranean grew nearer, need and potential grew less distinct. Grazing land was less restricted, the dry, sandy soils produced only poor crops, and the need for the economy to develop disappeared. Barns, cowsheds and dovecotes are not symbols of power in a village, and even the press and the wine cellar do not seem to have played the role that is too easily attributed to them.

4 Grazing rights and stock rearing

So far as the codification of grazing rights, the natural corollary of intensive exploitation which reduced the wooded area, is concerned, it can be seen that it assumes different guises according to the relative preponderance of arable land. Where arable cultivation made a triumphant progress, it was first a matter of reserving a place for the *breuil*, the woodland reserved for hunting, where warriors hunted large game animals, then for felling *en defens*, protected against misuse, which could not be outside the law, and finally for the woodland that was essential for the poorest folk, who had no resources but those offered by nature, because they could not hitch on to the progress of the rest of society. After 1250 the *gens du bosc* were no longer only outlaws, hermits, woodcutters or brigands, but also humble folk, living by picking fruits and nuts and poaching, like those at Neubourg (Normandy), described contemptuously in the aristocratic literature of the thirteenth century as 'charcoal burners', outside the law. Not much is known about the cabins, the rock shelters, or the *bories* (stone huts) of these misfits and rejects of the system of crop rotation, grazing on 'waste' lands, and the customaries which set out men's established rights.

If, on the other hand, the cultivation of rare fertile tracts of soil was to be a defence against poverty, it required strenuous efforts against the excesses of stock raisers. On the Iberian plateau or the limestone marls of Languedoc, along the slopes of the Apennines and the Pyrenees, from the top of the mountains of Provence to the bottom, transhumance along drove roads, *bacades*, or *mesta* of thousands of animals, different species mixed together, threatened the small cultivated plots painfully hacked out of the short grasslands, which had to be protected by low walls. The landscape bristled with enclosures of this kind and the peasant archives bulge with reports of legal actions. In this struggle between two forms of agriculture, it was almost always the immobile one that suffered. Land trampled over by sheep or buffalo was irrecoverable. The only way to restrict the damage was to abandon large areas that might have been fertile to livestock, so that they could be kept at night far away from the cultivated fields (cf. Figure 49). Elsewhere, especially in the fourteenth and fifteenth centuries, speculation in wool – from Shetlands or the Spanish Merinos – gave the prospect of such enormous profits that the lay and ecclesiastical aristocracies decided to reserve it to themselves: English Cistercians and the military orders of Santiago and Alcantara, London woolmen and kings of Castille, all did not hesitate to block the extension of arable holdings, and sometimes to reclaim or abolish them, for the benefit of their profits. Whilst the general economic consequences were of enormous moment – think of the English enclosures and the sterilization of the Iberian plateau – it is the inhibition of fixed settlement that concerns us here, and we shall return to this.

5   *Village craftsmen*

One final element must not be overlooked, the village craftsmen. Wherever raw materials – iron, wool, clay or wood – could be collected together, the domestic workshop was raised to the level of village craft centre to meet the need. There is evidence that a major farming establishment of the eight and ninth centuries would have its own smithy, weaving sheds, leather or wood workers, brewers and millers: these are known from Corbie, Saint-Rignier, Prüm, Saint-Gall, Annappes and Tilleda. There is no doubt, also, that throughout the whole of the early Middle Ages, as recounted in so many saints' lives, itinerant smiths or brewers of beer journeyed from village to village. The prestige of the craftsman who alone was capable of working iron and forging swords can be judged from the Germanic legends, which made him into a being on the fringes of the supernatural: the man buried with all his tools in the richest grave at Hérouvillette (Calvados) was probably both chieftain and smith.

However, we are referring now to the development in the heart of the village itself of individual workshops whose clientele did not solely comprise the lord and his *familia* (using that term in its fullest sense) but also included all the surrounding country dwellers. Two chronological phases can once again be recognized. From their first certain appearance in the tenth century, up to the end of the thirteenth century, those villagers, whether recent immigrants or not, who opened shops or workshops had dual interests. They cultivated plots of land and remained peasants, but their unquestioned specialization made of them men apart, to be envied or feared, because one could not do without their skill and they had to be paid dearly. These were smiths, these *fèvres* and *maréchaux*, who alone would dare to work iron, and knew how to shoe animals or retyre a wheel – 'village artificers', as Georges Duby has called them; they were also butchers, more rarely bakers, potters, tanners, clog makers. All the rest – shearing or spinning the wool, smoothing down a plank, or sawing up a tree trunk – was the province of every man. To judge by the little that documents reveal to us, their first appearance – above all in lists of witnesses, where they little by little elevated themselves to the level of worthies (*notables*) – seems to date to around the end of the eleventh century, when weekly local markets gave them the opportunity to acquire tools or sell their products to the peasants, who had hitherto not possessed any money. From that time on the smithy became a meeting place, where, surrounded by sparks, one could question, consult, listen to the man who had the lord of the manor as a customer as well as the common man. The material importance of those buildings possessing remains of forges in deserted villages, demonstrates the place assumed by this technician in the rural world.

After 1300 the situation changed, though with no diminution in the role of the place where animals were slaughtered or iron was forged. However, competition from the town and its products became much more substantial. Sometimes, in order to add rural profits to those they already commanded, townsmen would sell hardware in the flat surrounding countryside like Barral, a notary from Riez (Alpes de Haute-Provence). Since the villagers in their turn were attempting to put their technical skills at the service of the townsmen, they too developed a wide range of specialist tilers, carpenters, curriers, potters, weavers, and, naturally, iron workers and food producers, who would chance their luck in the town during periods of bad weather, sleeping in ditches or even staying in the village and working secretly on commissions from urban entrepreneurs, who were most often those who had taken their trade from them. The rivalries created in this way between town and country dwellers eventually reached the stage of open violence, but this is not within our subject.

C The village as a living organism

Nothing would be more mistaken than to consider the factors that have been brought together so far as immutable or original. Although it cannot be denied that a structure that is in the main homogeneous made its appearance over the entire medieval, Christian cultural zone, the characteristics of the life which animated it underwent significant changes over the centuries.

1 *The pressure of circumstances*

It is not difficult, for a start, to identify the factors which exert unequal pressures on the structure of the village or the appearance of the countryside, so as to be able to evaluate them. It is necessary only to recall the ravages of war which have traditionally been held responsible for peasant miseries: the raiding of the Vikings and the Hungarians, incursions – whether Christian or otherwise – on the Spanish table-land, wars between nobles and cities, invasions and pillage by armed horsemen in the closing years of the Middle Ages – these succeeded one another almost without interruption, yet life went on just the same, even in those places where violence struck most often, such as river crossings, regions of rich soils, and densely populated areas. Of course the immediate impact cannot be gainsaid, particularly when it resulted in the destruction of tools and implements, mills and ploughs, and the killing or carrying off of animals. But men returned, the corn grew again, and the house received a new thatch.

Changes in technology also seem to have had little influence after the mid-twelfth century. It was before 1150 that this factor had its greatest effect, in enlarging the cultivated area and improving crop yields. In this respect, it is not difficult to prove that the fall in the number of ears of corn and heads of livestock after 1350 has nothing to do with a fall in the technological competence; on the contrary, the fourteenth century witnessed the general application of crop rotation, closer sowing, the planting of fallow land with trees, and the growing of vegetables and fruit trees. It should rather be asserted that the displacement of the cereal base of the economy, or its reduction in favour of other material resources, and the imbalance that this caused in the traditional revenues from the land, led to a crisis that was in fact social rather than economic, but the consequences for settlement were only minor.

2   Numbers of men and social relationships

Fluctuations in population must be given pride of place. However, this is not a simple factor: it is obvious that population decline began well before the famines and plagues to which tradition always attributes it. In England, for example, where the Black Death of the mid fourteenth century is held to have carried off a third of the population, it can be demonstrated that population decline began as early as 1250–1260. In the counties of Berkshire, Norfolk and Oxfordshire, five to eight per cent of the villages abandoned before 1500 were deserted during the thirteenth century, if not the twelfth century. The same applies in other regions: excavations at Rougiers in Provence well illustrate phases of desertion, but one of the reoccupations took place right in the middle of the population decline of the Black Death.

Care should, therefore, be taken to evaluate the fall in population numbers – which is an unquestionable fact – in absolute terms; it is appropriate to introduce relative weightings for town and country. This correction is necessary in order to understand the phenomenon of abandonment followed by reoccupation of sites, evidence for which is especially noteworthy in the fourteenth and fifteenth centuries. In the first place, rural populations could, under the stress of events, whether fortuitous and transitory (devastations, wars, or epidemics) or more lasting (deficiencies in the system of production), find refuge in the suburbs of neighbouring towns, which they would leave as soon as the normal situation was restored. The suburbs of Rheims or Chalons-sur-Saône, when studied in this way, seem to act like lungs, taking in and expelling people from the *cité* and from the neighbouring villages. Secondly, emigration affected not the towns but the flat countryside, in favour of places reputed to be safer: in southern Champagne, over more than a century, there was a 60 per cent migration to villages deep in the forest or on distant high ground, far from the valleys, where bands of mercenaries roamed. In Alsace, 250 sites between the Ill and the Rhine were drained in this way in favour of the large towns of the Vosges foothills. In this respect the migration movements, which are better known in the fifteenth century, seem to represent more a redistribution over the countryside than an absolute numerical fluctuation. Robert Boutruche, studying the population of the Entre-deux-Mers region, Jacques Heers for the Ligurian Apennines, and Edouard Baratier for the Provençal plateaux have demonstrated this perfectly. Naturally the effect on the settlements' lands are of major importance: in regions that remained in the rudimentary stages of urban development, such as Poland, the flowering of towns was dependent on the socio-economic development of the rural world.

However, as during the population growth of the eleventh and twelfth centuries, demographic events as a whole or on the ground cannot be separated from the structure of production. Having reached its optimum level of development and organization by the mid thirteenth century, the rural seigneurial system presented in theory the image of a delicate balance between various types of farming activity (agrarian or husbandry), the different aspects of production (self-consumption or seigneurial production), and different forms of economic production (paid workers or indirect exploitation). The rural world seemed too full, at the limits of its capacities for production and exchange. For this reason the fall in profitability of landed capital, or, alternatively, the 'failure' of the seigneurial system, was inevitable. The small-farmers (*laboureurs*), already partly controlling the market and dominating the under-equipped part of the village community, could not adjust to a check to the growth of their revenues, less still to a seigneurial or 'feudal' reaction which would tend towards the seizing of new sources of income by means of a system of justice, and a demanding fiscal programme which they no longer had the fortitude to bear. It may be considered that the violent changes that this led to, more or less rapidly between 1270 and 1360, not only brought about transformations in relationships but also – and this is the main point in the context of this study – in some areas introduced new, more profitable economic models and transformed the countryside, whilst in others it resulted in the creation of fortunes and of economic disasters, in both cases excessive, traces of which are visible in the houses that survive to the present day.

3 'Deserted villages'

The phenomenon of village desertion, known for many years in Britain (see Figure 52), but only recently recognized on the Continent, intrigues historians.

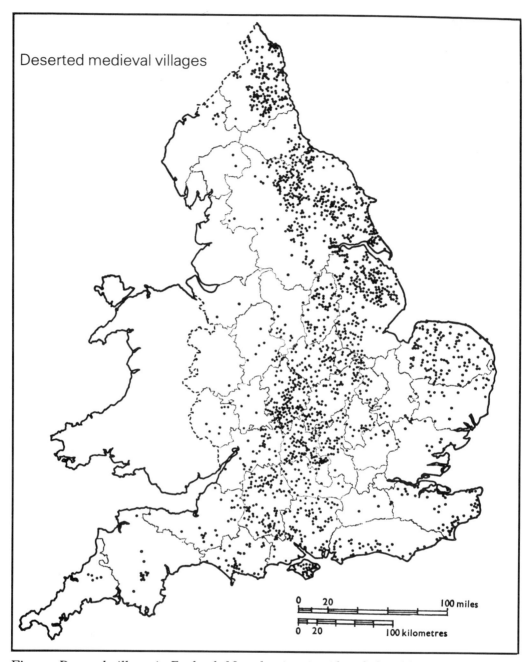

Deserted medieval villages

Fig. 52. *Deserted villages in England. Map showing sites identified and located by the end of 1968 by the Medieval Village Research Group*

Survey work is still in progress in the western counties, which explains the relatively small numbers of sites. In those counties most affected by the phenomenon and well surveyed in 1968, there was more than one deserted site in every 40 sq. km (15 sq. miles), the figure being double this in the most affected area.

(M. W. Beresford & J. G. Hurst, *Deserted Medieval Villages* (1971); fig. 13, p. 66)

At first sight it is of great importance. Wilhelm Abel has put forward huge figures for Germany: 40 per cent of the villages between the Elbe and the Weser and in Silesia; more than 20 per cent in Alsace, Swabia, Franconia, Prussia and Brandenburg. In England the phenomenon, which was accompanied by the enclosure movement, to be discussed later, affected all the central and south-eastern counties and well over a thousand villages.

Desertion is less striking on the southern flank of Europe, but it is not negligible for the fourteenth and fifteenth centuries: nearly 250 sites in Tuscany, more than 200 in Sabina and Latium, 225 on the Castilian plateau, and almost the same number on the rich coastal plain of the Levante and Catalonia. In France, 130 examples have been recorded in Artois and the same number in Champagne. Ten years ago a balance sheet was drawn up for the whole of Europe and produced a hatful of figures. However, even at that time among French historians, and subsequently more widely, since R. Hilton took the offensive against this 'catastrophism', there has been a reaction in favour of a less simplistic approach.

In the first place – and this has already been referred to in its demographic aspects – the movement lasted four centuries and only speeded up at the very end of the Middle Ages. Thus in Norfolk the proportion of 'desertions' was only 5 per cent in the fourteenth century and 8 per cent in the fifteenth, as against 45 per cent between 1485 and 1548. Moreover, excavations carried out on several available sites (which, in addition, have supplied virtually all the information we possess about houses and villages after 1300) have shown that these abandonments were often temporary during the final stage of the medieval period. Hilton estimates that sites that were never reoccupied represent no more than 20 per cent of the total, and even less perhaps on the continent. Figures of six to seven per cent have been put forward for Hurepoix, the poorest part of the Ile-de-France, 10 per cent in the seneschalships of Beaucaire and Carcassonne, and 1 per cent more in Quercy. Abandonment was decided upon communally and at a stroke, if the relative poverty of what was left behind is an accurate indicator, and it often affected poor sites that were too exposed, isolated, and far from any market. Many *sauvetés* (new villages), such as La Tour d'Avance (Lot-et-Garonne), or *bastides* (new towns with a military function) in Gascony lost their inhabitants when these were unwisely established on cold soils around 1190. In Chartrain, the area that was affected lay between the silts and the clay-with-flints, whilst in Italy the poor Tuscan region provided 55 per cent of the desertions known.

It is, however, impossible to generalize: in the English Midlands the good clay and forest soils, producing wheat and cattle, resisted better than the areas given over to sheep, it is true, but in Norfolk the poorer soils contributed less than a quarter of the losses, whilst they contributed barely 7 per cent in Oxfordshire. Moreover, a simple act of transplantation can explain away the difficulties: in Provence there was a move down into the valleys, from Saint-Geniès to Jonquières, for instance. In Liguria it was merely the deliberate choice of a new site: Belvedere became Albiano, Pieve di San Venerio became

Castro Boverone. The changes in farming practice referred to above are also significant: not only in England but also in Calabria, Sicily and Castille, the advance of animal husbandry at the same time changed the countryside and gradually ruined the peasantry. The reductions in taxes recorded in written sources testify to this progressive bleeding process. In the second half of the fifteenth century this was the case in 75–80 per cent of the villages in Norfolk and Leicestershire, and the coasts of the Boulonnais and northern Brittany furnish other examples.

Men who had been ruined or gradually chased out of their fields and vineyards and had resigned themselves to yielding their land to scrub or grassland, returned to the older villages, thereby enlarging them in size and changing their structures. It is possible, of course, only to excavate the dead village, not the receiving village, which is often still extant and inhabited. Even in these circumstances, however, the subdivision of houses, which can be observed at Rougiers as well as in England, must surely result from a demographic overloading, fortuitous and perhaps temporary, complementary to the abandonment of a neighbouring village: however, we have not yet reached the point when we can be categorical about this.

Coming after a period when the history of village desertions was essentially written on the basis of documentary sources, the growth of archaeology over the last two decades and its growing contributions have greatly helped to change the approach of historians to the phenomenon and to draw attention to its complexities.

Against the picture of the village grown larger as a result of an influx of people fleeing from threatened sites has to be put that of hamlets and dependencies which, at the same period or a little later, multiplied in the migration zones: this phenomenon has been studied in the Aquitaine basin. However, it is discernible over the whole of Atlantic France and a considerable part of the Mediterranean plains. Here the break-up of the older forms of settlement led to the creation of a new type, which more often than not remained at the hamlet stage, unlike so many pioneer sites of earlier periods, which generally attained village rank. Place names will sometimes make it possible to understand the origins of this secondary settlement, the work of incoming strangers or of a local who separates himself from the community. This is a very eloquent example of the ties that unite the settlement to social and economic structures. Whether resulting from the break-up of a family group, leading to fragmentation of the settlement's holdings, the suppression of the seigneurial system, allowing a new estate to be created, or redistribution of holdings as a result of a reallocation of resources, all these possibilities obviously mean that the traditional schema for rural desertion has to be modified.

It is, in fact, often difficult to establish correlations between, on the one hand, written sources which directly or indirectly prove that settlements were abandoned, and on the other, archaeological data which describe the life of these settlements, often in detail, but always provide very few certain indications of the causes for their disappearance or the precise date. This disappearance, contrary to the impression sometimes given by the written sources, could be gradual, slow, and the result of cumulative processes that are difficult to demonstrate. The example of Dracy is illuminating from this point of view.

This small village on the Côte d'Or is first referred to in documents in 1285. Then it had 15 hearths, which implies a population of 50–70 people. From 1423 the various written sources show that it had been abandoned and that its inhabitants, following a classic procedure, had re-established themselves at a better location that was older and larger, some distance away: the present village of Evelle.

After 15 years of excavations, beginning in 1965, the archaeological results enable us to be precise about the chronology, though not about the mode of or the reason for abandonment.

Twenty-three different houses were studied. They were laid out in three parallel rows, on a slope below and to the east of a high limestone cliff. It is possible that there may have been other houses on the site lying outside the area excavated.

It appears that in 1348 the village entered a period of recession connected with the general conditions, and the Black Death in particular. However, a little later, more than half a dozen houses were burnt or destroyed, no doubt as a result of the passage through the area of the Grandes Compagnies in 1360. Several were certainly rebuilt later, but not all. In 1396 documents refer to only four hearths, and this had fallen to two in 1400: the desertion had nearly run its course. It would appear that here, as no doubt elsewhere, can be seen the results of a process that spread over more than half a century, the consequence of a general state of crisis, especially in terms of population, allied, to an extent difficult to determine precisely from the archaeological data, to historical accidents – in this case the Hundred Years' War.

Did abandonment of a village also mean abandonment of its lands? Abel and his disciples have been somewhat hasty in creating *Wüstungen*, those lost lands in Germany, one of the prime components of village history in that country. Here, again, moderation must intervene: in abandoning to scrub and heath the light soils that are no longer needed to feed such a large number of mouths, the movement of withdrawal has essentially rectified the effects, at times excessive, of cultivation at whatever cost. Unfortunately it is much more difficult in this case than it is for built sites to identify this process, and even more so to measure it. There is no lack of terriers for the last two centuries of the Middle Ages, but there is no way in which we can compare these with the twelfth and thirteenth centuries, when documents of this type are very rare indeed, except perhaps in England. In the light of what can be deduced, it would appear that the phenomenon of change consisted overall more of a change in the type of agriculture practised than a pulling back from the forest (cf. Figure 10). It was the expansion of pastures or the development of speculative crops – vines, dye-plants, hay-fields etc. – which led to changes in the landscape. The effects of this transformation on the organization of the land should not be understated, and this will be dealt with later. But so far as settlement land allotment was concerned, this phenomenon of the closing years of the Middle Ages seems to have been more a process of reordering than a failure.

III CONCLUSIONS

Although the lifespan of the pre-medieval or early medieval village, which, being loosely structured, if at all, cannot be measured, there were only five centuries from 1000 to the disappearance of 'feudal' society. This is undeniably a long period – as long as that which separates the present day from its end. Village life was no more immutable then, however, than it was between 1500 and the present day. For the convenience of this survey, it has been necessary to distinguish the constant features of cellular peasant life, because these are closely related to a particular social structure or to the technological capabilities that were established and came to be dominant after the eleventh century, after which they remained more or less constant. However, it is self-evident that regional variations, inequalitites in the rate of development, and the variety of types of landscape and settlement according to natural constraints, impart to the history of the village a dynamic character that a more detailed study will substantiate.

Chapter Five: The opening up of the land and the village

In a new nation, aware of the potentials of grain production, every modern landscape invokes the impression of an organized quest for efficiency. By contrast, most European landscapes, even though they may have been reorganized and reallocated in recent years, present the appearance of chance and irrationality, and the villages one of disorder and arbitrariness. This is because the accumulation in the same area over a thousand years of techniques and preoccupations special to each chronological stratum overlie and blur its features. It is necessary to make the effort to identify each of these ancient impressions, since it is, above all, organization that is the dominant feature in the history of the European agrarian landscape.

I EUROPEAN LANDSCAPES IN THE HIGH MIDDLE AGES

A Organization of the land

Two factors played a leading role in the shaping of the land. Both are closely connected with the dominant features of the period, and both were certainly desired by the workers on the land: gradual adaptation to the quest for productivity, and redistribution of land allotment as intensive agriculture developed.

1 *Productivity*
The comprehensive exploitation of the land and the reclamation of uncultivated areas by the plough in no way represent random effects, under pressure of circumstances; they were voluntary activities, generally collective in nature, the object of which was the adaptation of agricultural life to productivity. This can be confirmed by studying the considerable mass of documentation, which bears witness to the role played by entire communities working together and in harmony, usually with the seigneur. The regular flow to market of products obtained either through the use of seigneurial levies or by deliberate production of a surplus can only be conceived as being the result of rational organization of the land and prior agreement.

In these circumstances, crop rotation appears to be deliberately linked with the seigneurial system. It is for this reason that we believe that it is artificial, even absurd, to seek the origins of rotation in a period anterior to the establishment of the seigneurial system. However, its expansion takes place in the main period of medieval growth. It is amply demonstrated in the mid thirteenth century over the great corn-growing plains of northern France or England, a little later in Germany, earlier but in its rudimentary, two-yearly cycle form in Provence, Latium and Catalonia. The introduction of a fourth change of crop, or even the abolition of the fallow year, were barely medieval, although they can be observed in Flanders, the Ile-de-France and around London about 1420. The fact that this major improvement was essentially possible only as the result of technological developments in harnessing and draught or metal working, and by refinement of manuring and sowing practices, does not diminish its social dimension. It is not easy to understand how it came about. However, some examples that have been studied show that it was a matter of empirical adjustment, in the first instance the work of certain innovatory seigneurs: the admittedly partisan written sources suggest that these were ecclesiastics, probably Cistercians. In order to achieve maximum efficacy, that is to say, crops that were consistent in volume with fallow and pasture years, it was obviously necessary to bring together, into two or three holdings that were equal in surface area and as large as possible, former parcels that were hitherto variable in size and location. The problems encountered by powerful modern administrations in trying to impose a rational redistribution of land holdings give some idea of the difficulties inherent in carrying out a reorganization of this kind in medieval times. Add to these both technological inadequacies and geographical obstacles, and the difficulties could well have seemed insurmountable in many regions, justifying the slow rate of implementation and the check to the introduction of rotation. It was impossible to bring it in over the entire landscape: there is no lack of compulsory injunctions to individualists or recalcitrants recorded in four-teenth-century documents. In the task of adapting each plot to optimum production, attempts were made in places to establish concentric zones around the built area: rotation was only practised on those closer to the village, the others being reserved for purposes that did not require fallowing – hemp, vines or meadows.

2 Specialization, speculation

To a certain extent, the example just quoted might be considered a tentative step towards specialization in crops, something which seems quite natural to us but which was not generally acceptable in the Middle Ages, owing to the permanently poor state of commercial relations and the risk of famine that monoculture implies. The vigorous movement towards specialization at the end of the medieval period, which opened a new phase of agrarian history, must therefore be accorded a high degree of importance. A concern for profit, and even for speculation, linked this development with that of the market economy. Four sectors profited most from it. First, vine growing, which was both concentrated and intensified in the most advantageous regions: the *offensive des vins forts*, as Roger Dion has termed it, was perhaps a matter of taste, but it quickly became one of money. The citizens of Genoa, Paris or Lyons were not the only ones to invest their capital in this form of agriculture with high returns and low costs. The dukes of Burgundy saw the advantages of developing the Arbois, as did the dukes of Savoy in the Alpine piedmont. *Boire son vin* is a mark of the successful man. Did the extension of vineyards around towns and along rivers have an effect on the economic development of a region comparable with the similar explosion of the nineteenth century? Robert Boutruche strongly believes this to have been the case for Bordeaux, as does G. Fourquin for Paris. However, this view has been contested in respect of the Rome region and Barcelona. Whatever the case, the reorganization of the landscape is undeniable.

The same holds good for dyestuff-producing plants – woad and saffron, for example – the assured markets for which in weaving towns led to a sudden invasion at the expense of food crops in the Toulouse region, the Levante, around Cambrai and in the Abruzzi. This was a significant factor in making the fortunes of merchants in Toulouse, in Ravensburg, in Welser (Thuringia), and even that of the Medici in Florence.

The rapid growth rate, multiplicity of uses, and hardiness of conifers explains, if not their recrudescence at the expense of cultivated fields, at least their triumph over deciduous trees in the many mountainous regions in the Hercynian region, where we nowadays get the impression that they have been growing since time immemorial. In grubbing out oaks and beeches to plant firs and larches, the burghers of Nuremberg and elsewhere were able to come to profitable arrangements with shipyards, but they also profoundly changed the tree cover of central Europe. If one thinks of the role of oak and beech woods and of the rich undergrowths replaced by the sterile carapace of bark and needles from resinous trees, it will readily become apparent that this change in the appearance of the forests is accompanied by the loss of its value as a producer of food, and thereby a major disruption of the traditional but delicate balance between woodland and cultivated fields. Driven out of the forests, domestic animals were forced to seek pasturage elsewhere, and it is logical to link this development with the rise of two further factors – permanent pasture and hay meadows (cf. Figure 10). In this case, however, the resulting changes were so far-reaching and so lasting, especially in the Atlantic lands of Europe, that they will need more detailed consideration later.

It would be wrong to underestimate the simple desire to adapt crops and practices not to financial profit, but to the needs of the local topography and of the soil itself, especially if they are very restrictive. Growing corn at the foot of the mountains, vines on the slopes, and hemp along the forest margins represents a tradition transmitted from generation to generation over a very long period of time. However, the migration of vines to the more clement latitudes and the sunnier slopes, or the withdrawal of agriculture in Germany from the best soils (*Entsiedlung*) resulted from a preoccupation with yield and profit. We may, therefore, assert that the main characteristic of European agrarian history between 1000 and 1500 was a slow progression towards productivity on the land. If technological development is also taken into account, it can be seen that the agrarian societies achieved at that period a mature stage of development that was not to be improved upon, after the long period of 'modern' stagnation, until the mid eighteenth century, if not, indeed, later.

B Transformation of the land allotment system

All these changes did not take place everywhere or immediately. In some areas there were difficulties due to isolation, in others an older system would persist for a long time, leaving archaic structures and methods of working mixed up with more up-to-date ones. The two systems could even exist side by side: this has been observed in Silesia and upper Poland in fossil field systems in the low, marshy plains. For the most part, however, the landscape evolved in a regular manner, and three aspects of the reorganization are worthy of note.

1 · Concentration

The concentration (*commassation*) of holdings seems to have been basically favoured by the low price of land during periods of population decline or the introduction of new social structures, as, for example, over the whole of western Europe in the eleventh and fifteenth centuries. However, this grouping phenomenon was only a legal façade: it was more often a matter of reallocation of holdings. This can be seen in the continual growth of profitable operations, which has already been touched upon, or in the disposal of remote holdings. As has already been stated, the development of the small manor or *manse* constituted an excellent basis: wherever it formed a coherent grouping, in the Languedoc or in Italy, it assumed independent status, and often a name of its own. Round it collected its dependent plots and escheated freeholds. Thus it formed a large block of contiguous holdings, both fields and meadows, known as a *cap mas* in the Massif Central. It was the possession of several of these around a church or a castle that, from the twelfth century onwards, allowed so many 'seigneurs' without ancestors to assert economic and political control over the less fortunate members of their entourages. From this time the old Carolingian terminology lost its meaning: the *villa* became no more than a village, the *casa* only a defended dwelling – the *mansio* or *maio* of Comminges, Rouergue, or the Auvergne. Where, by contrast, as in north-western Europe, the *manse* broke up into disjointed plots, their incorporation into the neighbouring lands of other manors that were similarly foundering brought about the destruction of any kind of 'domanial' memory and favoured regroupings on a purely economic basis.

At the beginning of the twelfth century it has to be accepted that, in any region that may be selected, all significant links with the Carolingian land tenure system had been broken. There were still large seigneurial 'reserves' –

great stretches of woodland, vineyards, meadows, rich gardens beneath the fortified residence (*ferté*). But the remainder of the demesnes had been effectively broken up, and no longer had any link with the overlord other than the feudal obligations. The gradual abolition of labour service, which by the fourteenth century had been reduced solely to haymaking, lends credence to the view that the assigned holding, the *censive* or copyhold, brought its owner more than the rights of use. By the end of the Middle Ages the development of different types of tenant farming in central France and in England, *métayage* and *mezzadria* around the Mediterranean, seems to have been an attempt to recover ownership rights over the land, but in the development of the land tenure system the expansion of these rights did not have an impact on the course of that development. The Church, for its part, played a decisive role in this process, especially by its refusal to integrate its goods into the common welfare. From the eleventh century, the Cluniacs had provided an example by evicting villagers from holdings that they wished to regroup. In the twelfth century, the military Orders seized vast areas of pasturage in the Causses, the high lands of the Toulouse region. Buying up of land by the Church in the thirteenth century was accompanied by expulsions and even the distribution of entire villages: in Champagne, in Lorraine, in Germany, and especially in England, the Cistercians brought together lands purchased at low cost into vast *bouverots* or estates. Later, when the monastic estates (*granges*) could no longer be exploited directly, they were not returned to the communal land holding system: leased out *en bloc* at Vaulerent or in parcels as at Gergovie or in Burgundy, they continued to disrupt the tenurial system.

2 *Dispersal*

The phenomenon of fragmentation of the land allotment system might be considered to be the converse of what has just been discussed. In practice, however, it often operated in parallel with it, but its effect was on the smaller holdings whose low profitability thereby deteriorated still further. Nothing can be said about the first two centuries of the high Middle Ages, since the situation is too obscure. However, from the mid thirteenth century, and again, after a check due to population decline, after 1450, the fragmentation of holdings reached a critical level, less than two or three hectares per hearth in Normandy, Picardy and Provence. This is explained by, first, an excess of people resulting from population growth and later, after 1350 and for a long time thereafter in certain places, by a return to the better-quality land by peasants who gave up working the poorer soils or who could find no new land in the forests that had been substantially encroached upon or too effectively protected against them. The practice of dividing holdings up among heirs, which operated against the best interests of the group involved, also played a part, as did circumstances which, temporarily or otherwise, led to crowding on to the land that remained viable – the marine transgressions in Flanders and Zealand of the fourteenth or fifteenth century, for example, or Aquitaine when it was ravaged by war. This shows how concentration and fragmentation, working alongside one another on the same landscape, could militate against the establishment of a system of intensive exploitation of the soil.

3 The framework

Rural roads were an essential component of the structure of the landscape, since the network of roads sustained rural production and the movement of produce towards the market or the town. The absence of precise topographical data earlier than the fourteenth century, apart from rare references to boundaries, introduces a good deal of uncertainty over early routes. Nevertheless, what can be extracted bears witness to an unmistakable intention of maintaining an almost exclusively rural role for roads. This characteristic not only runs counter to the Roman road system, the basis of centuriation and more heedful of towns than the countryside, but also to the pre-Roman tracks which, in so far as they can be reconstructed, were intended for the use of various warriors and merchants rather than peasants. Above all, roads served as boundaries: the limits of woodland, seigneurial boundaries, and parish pales were based on them. They took up the course of the *tour de ville*, where the rights of the community ceased, and they enclosed fields and tofts. Finally, they provided a service: works of the imagination and legal reports depict roads as thronged with carts laden with wood and hay, oxen bearing the corn tithe, flocks of sheep being brought back from forest grazing, and peasants with hoes on their shoulders.

When the road network was so diversified as to serve each individual holding, as in Latium, this is evidence for a fanatical degree of individualism, and it is not very common. However, the use of headlands in the fifteenth century, to enable the heavy plough to turn round, was very widespread, and it cannot be considered to have been feasible without the presence of a strip for free passage between the holdings or blocks of land. The laying down of roads as a result of a seigneurial decision or on new lands or, as in twelfth-century Rieti, when a vineyard was being planted, proves that chance played no part in this process. It would be wrong to be too categorical: the manorial courts would not have been choked with cases about boundaries, had there always been permanent fixed roads which everywhere discouraged those *rogneurs de royes* and *fauteurs de bornes* who secretly ploughed beyond their own holdings, or went at night to move the stones which delineated their boundaries. Discussions and enquiries are always concerned with the landscape of the countryside, and so it would seem appropriate at this point to examine what we know about medieval farming landscapes.

4 Field shapes

Ever since the appearance of Marc Bloch's famous work, nearly half a century ago, medievalists have been discussing the shapes and disposition of plots in the Middle Ages. Observations made on the fossil field systems in England and Germany, the ridges of Brittany and Limbourg, and the few reliable indications in iconography or written sources which have supplied details of field sizes, have produced some reasonable findings which reinforce what we know of this problem in the seventeenth and eighteenth centuries.

Let us begin by putting on one side the period before 1100, when the as yet incomplete exploitation of the land would certainly have produced a mixed landscape, with a few cultivated patches distributed over the outfield, some enclosed and others not. It has just been suggested that this primitive stage of exploitation could survive either in regions that were especially remote or sparsely populated, as in the colder areas of Atlantic Europe, or in areas of deforestation. To a certain extent this incomplete state is very well adapted to the practice of non-intensive animal husbandry, especially transhumance. In mountainous regions or the Mediterranean plains, arable farming took refuge behind low walls or fences – *drailles* and *cañadas* – for protection, it is said, against the ravages of flocks of domesticated animals. In an economy of this kind, therefore, the structure of the arable landscape may be seen to be a secondary effect of pastoralism.

Where the whole landscape was being exploited, two problems become apparent. The first is the shape of the fields. Basing their stance on the very clearly defined situation in the seventeenth century, some historians have been eager to set up the strip field, which is more widely distributed over north-western and northern Europe, in opposition to the larger open field of the south. The determining factors, put forward first by Marc Bloch, are dependent upon the methods of draught and the technique of ploughing, as well as the system of inheritance. However, leaving aside the objections that might be raised to each of these explanations, we cannot be sure that they applied systematically in the twelfth and thirteenth centuries. In fact, one has the feeling that before the beginning of the fragmentation discussed above, fields would have had the appearance of large compact blocks, roughly square in shape: the 'Celtic' fields in England, those found near Spicymierz in Silesia, the boundaries of the Sabine fields, and the plots cleared around the new towns on the Somme, the Gers, or the Aude provide clear evidence of this. Moreover, the triumph of the mouldboard plough, which is difficult to handle if it has to be turned too frequently and so favours a smaller number of longer furrows, was neither universal nor sudden in its effect. Finally, the practice of cross-ploughing, required by shallow cultivation, obviously cannot be reconciled with strip holdings, and this technique is known to have lasted a long time.

It would seem reasonable to accept that the earliest form of ploughed field in a fully cultivated landscape would have been compact, and that division into strips, which becomes apparent in the late eleventh and twelfth centuries, was due to the abandonment of cross-ploughing, an intermediate stage in the development of cultivation practices. Naturally, geographical requirements – the terraced fields of the south, and lynchets on the chalk and limestone slopes of the north – made a contribution to the process of division into strips. Elsewhere, in regions that had to be drained and where culverts and ditches superimposed a matrix on the landscape such as eastern Flanders or the Adige flood plain, strip cultivation quickly came to dominate. The same applied in deforested areas, where the access tracks into the woods had run parallel behind the woodmen's huts, producing the 'fishbone' layout well known to geographers. Rather than falling back on a conflict between horses and cattle or between different types of plough, where it is not difficult to find aspects which rule out such an approach, it is more appropriate to examine methods of ploughing. Those landscapes that remained faithful to older techniques retained a land-holding system based on a widely spaced lattice, with low outputs, for a much longer period; this resulted in their becoming economically non-viable, even where adverse soil or climatic conditions had not already condemned them from the start. For these regions, the mechanized ploughing which would have helped them came too late, in the twentieth century, when vines, olives or woad had already replaced most of the arable crops.

5 *Field boundaries?*

The second problem is no less important. Were these fields enclosed by some permanent boundary? This seems, in fact, to have been the case: in Beauce, for example, in the manner of enclosed woods ('*en defens*'), the fields were probably protected, after sowing, against the incursions of animals by rapidly erected structures (see Figure 53). From the earliest days of their order, the Cistercians had frequently prohibited access to their lands. However, since the open field was apparently the usual form in use in grain-producing countries, it is essential to know under what general circumstances it would give way to the *bocage* landscape of small hedged or walled fields, whether arable or pasture, which is typical of the present-day landscape in many parts of Atlantic, Alpine and even Hercynian Europe (cf. Figure 49). Unfortunately, once again we find ourselves in a twilight area. To be sure, there are certain clear facts. The establishment of this type of landscape pattern on cold soils, with abundant rainfall but relatively scattered populations, gives the impression of an incomplete form of agrarian enterprise. The human communities lived on the defensive, near water, in small isolated groups, and with an economy that was restricted because it lacked outlets and production surpluses. It is also necessary to distinguish between different cases. The extended family structure, living in proximity to the ancient clan and resistant to the fragmentation that threatened it after 1100, may have preserved a form of settlement in hamlets, with its *courtils* and enclosed pastures. Around the *herbergements* (new farming establishments of the later Middle Ages) of the Perche and Corbonnais, A. Chedeville has found traces of this up to the mid thirteenth century, and the word *haya* there assumed its present-day meaning of hedge. In Brittany the Celtic *ran*, the holding consisting of a house surrounded by a rampart, constituted an early family unit within a wider administrative group, the *plou*, reproducing 1000 miles away the *plebs cum oraculis* of the Italian countryside. This dispersed structure of cultivation seems to have taken hold of the whole peninsula in the early twelfth century. The low population may have played a similar role, preserving a pre-Carolingian

Fig. 53. *August harvest scene in early sixteenth-century Flanders*
The pair of harvesters partly hide the light fence which, as so often at this period, would have been set up as soon as the corn began to ripen. The use of the sickle and the presence of a four-wheeled cart should be noted; this is from the region where up to the present day this type of vehicle was common, in preference to the two wheeled vehicle used elsewhere.

(Bibliothèque Nationale, Paris, MSS Facsimile 4, 298: photo Hachette)

---

structure into the high Middle Ages. This has been demonstrated for southern Scandinavia, where the grouped farm known as *bol* underwent a process of redistribution which isolated houses from their holdings. Finally, excessive forest clearance may have resulted in the enclosure of ploughed fields against grazing by wild animals expelled from the woodlands.

6 Enclosures?

Although all these forms of delineation and defence may appear to have been either archaic or ad hoc in character, in well-defined periods (and especially in the fourteenth and fifteenth centuries), there was a deliberate process of creating a *bocage* landscape in countries that were in no way backward and which had hitherto been covered with open fields. This was, as we have said, especially the case in midland England: the enclosure movement played a decisive role in that region (Figure 54). This is not the place to dwell upon the social and economic consequences of this phenomenon – for example, the

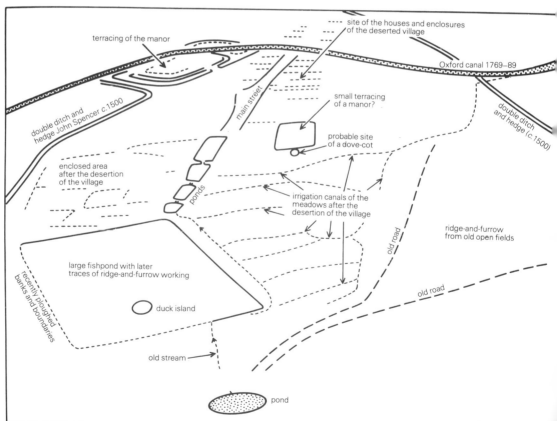

site of the houses and enclosures
of the deserted village

terracing of the manor

Oxford canal 1769–89

double ditch and
hedge John Spencer c.1500

main street

small terracing
of a manor?

double ditch
and hedge (c.1500)

probable site
of a dove-cot

enclosed area
after the desertion
of the village

ponds

irrigation canals of the
meadows after the
desertion of the village

old road

ridge-and-furrow
from old open fields

large fishpond with later
traces of ridge-and-furrow
working

recently ploughed
banks and boundaries

duck island

old road

old stream

pond

Fig. 54. *The deserted village of Wormleighton (Warwickshire)*

The aerial photograph (a), taken in 1953, shows a whole series of structures: they tell the history of this area, which is very typical of the development of the English landscape.

The first reference to the Wormleighton site dates from 956. In 1086 the parish was inhabited by 50 families, owning 23 teams, and contained three manor houses. It may be assumed that there were very probably two settlements in the tenth to eleventh centuries, one near the church (below and left in a), the other above the manorial castle, between that and the stream (above and centre, b), the line of which is emphasized by a line of trees.

In the fourteenth century, here as in many other parts of England, there was a very heavy demand for wool; this is near Coventry, which was the centre of a large textile industry. Moreover, the village of Wormleighton appears to have been badly affected by the Black Death in the fourteenth century. Depopulation seems to have commenced at this period.

It was speeded up in the late fifteenth/early sixteenth century by a fortuitous event: in 1495 the principal of the three manors passed to the Crown. In 1498 it was granted to one William Cope, who bought the secondary manors, and then sold the whole holding in 1506 to a local cattle farmer, John Spencer. He and his family made a remarkable rise up the social scale: ennobled shortly before his death in 1522, John Spencer left behind him a family which, in less that 100 years, was to become one of the most influential in England.

From 1499 onwards, William Cope had expelled the peasants who were practising mixed farming, and that was the end of the settlement. John Spencer completed the reorganization of the site by planting hedges around his lands, reconstructing houses for his own workers, repairing the church, and planting trees in an area that was otherwise totally bereft of them for several kilometres around.

The air photograph and its interpretive sketch clearly show this history as preserved in the soil.

First, there are the remains of the village before it was abandoned in 1499: obliquely, in the centre, on either side of the main street, can be seen the long rectangular enclosures (crofts) within which the peasant houses were built. Below and to the left this street abuts upon a series of adjacent ponds, which are difficult to date. These then open out into a large square fishpond, which may date to before or after the depopulation.

Above and in the centre of the photograph, the terracing of the main fortified house, abandoned at the latest by the early sixteenth century, can be made out. Between 1516 and 1522, John Spencer in fact built a large red-brick manor house in the Tudor style, substantial remains of which survive in the village to the right of the church (bottom left of the photograph).

Almost in the centre of the photograph a second small square terrace is all that is left of one of the two secondary manor houses that existed at Wormleighton from at least 1086.

After the abandonment, the landscape was considerably remodelled. In place of a landscape of open fields, worked in the ridge-and-furrow system still visible in the photograph, John Spencer substituted a landscape of pastures enclosed with ditches and banks surmounted by hedges, in order to practise animal husbandry. To the left he put in a system of double hedges and ditches which enclosed a large field. A series of irrigation ditches was laid down in the valley to supply water to the meadows.

Around the church (bottom left in the photograph), part of the tower and nave of which is twelfth-century, John Spencer built a dozen houses for his own workers.

In addition to these two great phenomena in English agrarian history, desertion and enclosure, the photograph shows some more recent changes to the landscape. The canal between Coventry and Banbury was completed in March 1778, and its route can clearly be seen running across the photograph. It clips one of the corners of the manor house, then follows the line of the ditch – a good example of reuse of an earlier feature. Finally, between the time the photograph was taken and the present day, renewed ploughing has destroyed one of the sides of the fishpond, a good illustration of the vulnerability of the archaeological remains which, nevertheless, when taken together, as here, with written sources and field survey, can throw so much light on ancient landscapes.

(Harry Thorpe, Air, ground, document, in D. R. Wilson (ed), *Aerial reconnaissance for archaeology*, CBA Research Report 12 (1975); fig. 6, p. 147 [photograph from Cambridge University Collection, no. 145/443542, 3 May 1953] and fig. 9, p. 151)

---

abandonment of ruined villages, the crowding of fleeing villagers into the towns, and the industrial and commercial expansion that it produced. However, a study of the probable causes should throw some light on the development of the *bocage* landscape elsewhere – in Normandy, Aquitaine, and parts of Bavaria. By chance we know these causes well. A great deal of importance has long been attached to the social evolution factors: the small size of the English peasant population certainly facilitated the fragmentation policies of the lords of the manor and the urban merchants. From 1235 onwards there is evidence of attempts, often successful, to appropriate waste land, well before the enclosures of the seigneurial holdings with hedges and walls, a phenomenon which assumed catastrophic proportions for the pea-santry in the fifteenth and sixteenth centuries (Figure 55). The defensive measures demanded by the lesser clergy and part of the gentry after 1480 and 1510 were ratified in theory by Parliament and the Tudor monarchs. However, the profits from sheep raising and the great increase in the consumption of fresh meat rendered any return to the earlier situation out of the question. It would, however, be going outside the limits of the present study to examine the evolution of the phenomenon which transformed an English countryside, once very similar to the plains of the Ile-de-France, into a grassland landscape.

However appropriate this explanation may be in English terms, though, it is not equally valid on the Continent. It would be better to stress the element just referred to – the demand for meat, for leather, and for wool – which raised the profitability of hay-fields and made the price of hay and animals soar. In other words, a reversion to animal husbandry gripped part of Europe in the fifteenth century. Whilst this was more marked in Britain than elsewhere, for reasons connected as much with the history of its economy as with its natural

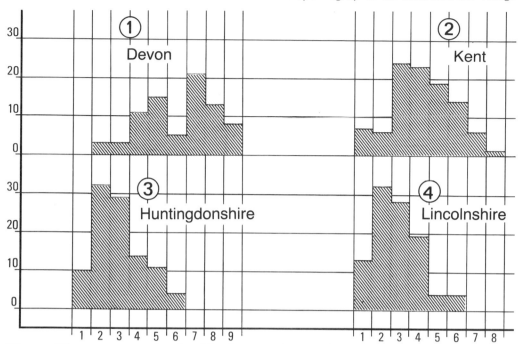

Fig. 55. *The appearance of enclosed landscape in four English counties, based on the number of tree species in modern hedges*

The study of the flora of modern hedges, a technique proposed by the botanist Max Hooper, makes it possible to study the evolution of an enclosed landscape. He postulates that, in general terms and with regional variations, a hedge should contain one tree species for every century of its age. Using a unit of 27m (30yd) a tree species count was carried out for a number of hedges in each county. It would appear that in Devon more than half the hedges surveyed contained five species or more, which means that they are earlier than 1400, as compared with only 40 per cent in Kent, *c.*16 per cent in Huntingdonshire, and less than 5 per cent in Lincolnshire. These botanical data correlate perfectly with data from written sources, which show that the enclosed landscape is relatively recent in the two latter counties and earlier in the other two, especially Devon.

(M. D. Hooper, *Hedges and Local History* (1971), fig. 8)

---

geographical predispositions, on the Continent it encouraged the demarcation of pasture lands. It was logical, therefore, from that time onwards that a juxtaposition would develop between an older *bocage* of fields enclosed by walls and hedges, but archaic and still in the hands of the peasant farmers, and a modern system of enclosed hay fields and pastures.

Whether open field or *bocage*, the face of the landscape does not merely reveal the application of one or another method of production. As we have already pointed out more than once, man moulds his habitat to the best of his ability to suit his economic interests. From the moment that he began to dominate his landscape in this way and set about organizing it, the medieval peasant endowed the village with the structure that it had hitherto been lacking.

II MEDIEVAL VILLAGES

A The layout of the village

After various digressions and different modes of approach, the reader has now reached the core of the subject, perhaps better equipped to appreciate it. The study of the village itself remains none the less a difficult one, for there are many areas of uncertainty and many questions remain to be answered.

1 *Temporary settlement*

Right at the outset we come up against one of these questions, which is an essential preliminary to any study of the subject: did man abandon the practice of building temporary settlements, the consequences of an incompletely controlled economy or a source of refuge against external threats? Unfortunately, owing to their transitory and fugitive nature, temporary settlements are difficult to grasp. These are not sites that were occupied or abandoned by herdsmen or hunters according to need; such temporary shelters – shacks, huts, or *aumuches*, destroyed or abandoned in forests or marshes – testify only to an annual mode of settlement. The long periods spent by shepherds in upland pastures re-created on the higher ground the material structure, and sometimes even the social hierarchy, of the villages in the valleys below. However, in the times of terror, of war, of plague or of famine which occurred almost everywhere in the eleventh and fourteenth centuries, and in southern France in the thirteenth century, temporary settlements became common once again, as in the last days of the classical world. The study of souterrains is clouded by re-occupation in later centuries – by the victims of religious persecution in the sixteenth century, by starving peasants in the eighteenth century, by fugitives from military service in the nineteenth century, and by *maquisards* in the present century – whilst the occupation layers in them have been disturbed by weekend treasure hunters and mushroom growers as well. However, they have been studied so far as possible within the context of the present subject, and the slopes of many valleys in western France – the Vienne, the Charente and the Gartempe – have provided evidence of long periods of organized occupation which duplicate the village hierarchy of the above-ground. This 'underground civilization' has evoked many interpretations, based, for example, on religion. It would seem wiser to see it simply as a reproduction of peaceable settlement in reverse.

2 *The anchoring points*

It can safely be assumed that settlement ceased being itinerant after 1100. This permanent quality has endured up to the present day, apart from the phase of abandonment followed by reoccupation that characterized the end of the medieval period, which has just been mentioned. It is the external boundaries of the village which are first noticed, whether a solid undressed stone wall in more hazardous regions, as in the *bastides* of Aquitaine, the *byl* of the Scandinavian forests, the Silesian *Dörfer* or the Sabine *borghi*, or the simpler boundary delineated by marker stones or a palisade, the role of which has already been discussed.

However, once this boundary has been crossed, it becomes more difficult to distinguish the constituent elements of the village unit than it is for those of an urban district. Certain factors do, nevertheless, stand out, such as the *atrium*, at first an enclosed area that was usually alongside the church and sometimes covered with the huts of people outside the law – fugitive serfs or strangers to the community. The importance of what was, in the eyes of the villagers, a 'neutral' place of refuge can be judged from the fact that they demanded that one should be established as soon as they assumed a legal identity. Thus the absence of an *atrium* may indicate that the village has no such legal status. This has unfortunately been the case in the sites so far excavated in France. Likewise, the development of a secondary settlement outside the boundaries, along the roads, may be seen as a symbol of economic vitality, pushing the village outwards, or it may be evidence of a solid social cohesion which drives those who do not partake in the privileges of the community outside its walls.

One would like to be able to locate in each village the site of the mill and the smithy, the nuclei of craft activity, and to find out whether their establishment modified the structure of the built part of the settlement. However, this is rather ambitious, given the present state of excavations. At Saint-Victor-des-Oules (Gard), the pottery kilns form a group, but this does not occur on other sites. At Saint-Jean-le-Froid, the smithy that was identified is difficult to distinguish from the neighbouring buildings by virtue of its size or the material found in it, but this is the smithy of a priory. A good example of clustering of settlement round rural workshops is the village of La Chapelle-des-Pots in the Saintonge. A document from 1320 shows that potters settled in a wooded part of this region, some kilometres to the north-east of the important Roman and medieval town of Saintes, and gradually cleared it. This settlement by craftsmen must have taken place in the second half of the thirteenth century, or perhaps a little earlier. Very careful field survey of the land around La Chapelle-des-Pots has shown that there is apparently no Gallo-Roman occupation, but there were some eight or nine workshops producing decorated floor and roof tiles and, especially, pottery, widely separated from one another. Only two or three workshops appear to have been found around the church, which was founded in 1320. In the fifteenth to seventeenth centuries, however, it is striking to see these scattered workshops disappearing and a smaller number than there were in the twelfth to fourteenth centuries becoming grouped within the village, around the church. This is a classic example of settlement clustering around a newly founded rural church. Pottery manufacture, which leaves abundant, closely datable surface evidence, by the craftsmen of La Chapelle-des Pots makes it easy to follow this process. It also shows that during the eighteenth century, although a number remained in the village, there was a second dispersal of craftsmen over the surrounding countryside, which corresponds with the introduction of the dispersed form of settlement that is characteristic of this region.

It is likely that in many cases, which cannot unfortunately be quantified, this reorganization of village settlement represents the abandonment of older sites, as, for example, when peasants settled around a new feudal residence or motte or near a parish church. However, it is even more likely that where the general occupation took the form of scattered settlement, composed of small centres of population, one of these would predominate over the others and grow into a village. The example of England makes it possible to follow this phenomenon. At the time of Domesday Book, in the late eleventh century, many relatively old and large areas of Saxon occupation were characterized by a dispersed form of settlement based on the presence on the land of two, three, or sometimes more population units. Subsequent population growth, which should not be overlooked, later obscured this picture, which can nevertheless still be seen quite well in Cambridgeshire, for example, in the late eleventh century. The effects of William the Conqueror's invasion of these regions may well be adduced, but it is also certain that the introduction of the feudal system made an additional contribution, if not the main one, to this process, together with the generalized introduction of the parish church.

It is striking to observe that many late Saxon villages were abandoned in England, even though this was a period of demographic expansion, at a time when many new villages were being created and that, out of 209 English village sites dating to the late eleventh century and afterwards that had been explored and excavated by 1968, only four produced any evidence of Anglo-Saxon structures. This would appear to offer conclusive proof of a very pronounced change in settlement within the areas already under cultivation.

B   Village topography

It may be premature to attempt to sketch the geography of the village: an economic geography is possible, perhaps, but not a social geography. There are, however, certain examples which indicate that there are certain preferred locations within the built-up area, which for this reason would have been occupied early by the rich and influential: near the seigneurial residence, the church, or the open space where the markets were held. At Cagnoncles near Cambrai, a village that was burnt down in 1298, the inventory of houses shows admirably that the *manoirs* valued at 40 livres and the *maisons* valued at 10–15 livres clustered near the barn of the overlord, the Abbot of Saint-Aubert. In a number of villages in Gascony or Picardy, the detailed charters of which survive, it can be seen that the central plots were allocated and built on first (and were, indeed, sometimes the only ones to be built on). These were the plots at the intersection of main roads or facing the church. The houses on these plots were aligned with and abutted upon one another, like town houses.

Only very careful study of representative examples will enable the true situation to be revealed and the overall topography of villages to be analysed.

The phenomenon of the creation or relocation of villages influenced the whole medieval world; however, it followed different chronologies and assumed various forms in different cases. Two major specific zones can be distinguished: the Mediterranean region, where this phenomenon was usually associated with the location of settlements on high ground and with *incastellamento* – the establishment of a castle and an enclosing wall round the village – and the more northerly region, where the relief did not allow high-ground settlement and where *incastellamento* is rare or appears only later. Although these two phenomena may have a number of factors in common – chronology, organized mode of settlement, and seigneurial presence in particular – they nevertheless result in the evolution of very different rural landscapes with contrasting subsequent histories – the elevated Italian or Provençal sites were gradually abandoned from the later Middle Ages onwards in favour of flat-land sites – and with different forms of rural architecture. To illustrate this difference, let us consider the almost complete excavation of Rougiers, a Provençal high-ground village, and several excavations on English villages (Figure 56).

1 A Provençal hilltop village, Rougiers (twelfth–fifteenth centuries)

The village excavated at Rougiers (Rougiers commune, Var *département*) is of exceptional interest from several points of view. In the first place this work, initiated by Gabrielle Démians d'Archimbaud and the Laboratoire d'Archéologie médiévale of the University of Aix-en-Provence, was the first modern excavation project of a medieval village in France. Secondly, this is still the most considerable French archaeological project designed to explore a medieval rural site (which happens in this case to be very large and rather complex) as comprehensively as possible. Finally, this settlement, by virtue of the length of time it was occupied, the high quality of the archaeological work, and its regional context (the Mediterranean region, which has been poorly studied in this respect), is of considerable scientific importance. Moreover, Rougiers is very representative, from the Roman period to the early Middle Ages, of the phenomenon of high-level settlement followed by a descent to lower-lying land, the classic evolutionary pattern in the southern regions of Europe.

The site

Excavations were carried out principally on the ruins visible at the top of the limestone massif of the Sainte Baume, which looks down from its height of 600m (656yd) on to the present-day village and the plain at an altitude of 350–360m (383–394yd) (see Figure 57).

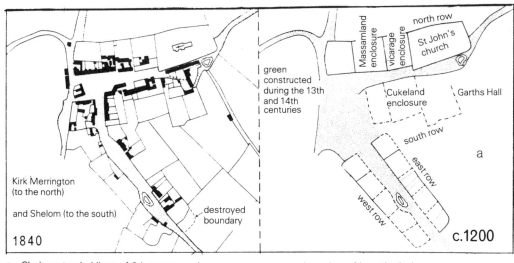

green constructed during the 13th and 14th centuries

Massamland enclosure

vicarage enclosure

north row

St John's church

Cukeland enclosure

Garths Hall

south row

east row

west row

a

c.1200

Kirk Merrington (to the north)

and Shelom (to the south)

destroyed boundary

1840

a   Shelom: ten holdings of 2 bovates, each of 8 × 20 ft facing on the street

———— boundary of medieval property still visible

— — — boundary of reconstructed medieval property

—·—·— boundary of hypothetical medieval property

····· boundary of present property formed by the subdivision of a former estate

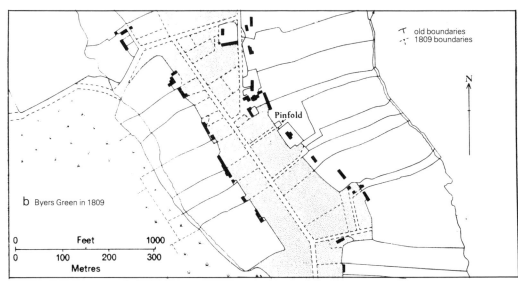

old boundaries

1809 boundaries

N

Pinfold

b Byers Green in 1809

0   Feet   1000

0   100   200   300
Metres

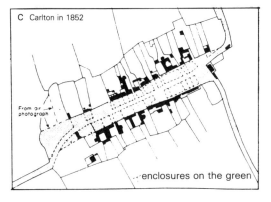

C Carlton in 1852

From air photograph

enclosures on the green

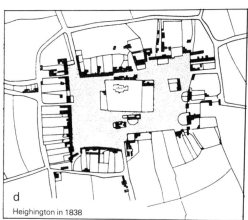

d

Heighington in 1838

184

Fig. 56. *Some village plans from County Durham (England)*

It is normally very difficult to establish a typology for village plans in Europe, whether medieval or post-medieval. However, research in Great Britain, Scandinavia and Germany has succeeded in defining some basic types, the distinctions between which are, however, sometimes rather flexible. They can be defined as follows: *street villages*, where there are one or two rows of buildings or tofts on one or both sides of a street, with a maximum length of 250–500m (273–547yd) (Kirk Merrington-Shelom); *villages with greens*, which cover a vast area of Europe, where the holdings are disposed round a wide open space of common land – this may be a square or green or an especially wide road (Byers Green, Carlton); and *agglomerated villages*, with more or less complex intersecting street plans (Heighington). To this classification should be added the Mediterranean high-ground village.

The basic question is when these regular, even planned, layouts first appeared. They often relate to settlements that are known from documentary sources to have existed since the early Middle Ages. In these circumstances it is usually difficult to know whether these layouts go back to the origins of the settlements or whether they relate to a more recent creation, the view of many historians and archaeologists.

The study of Durham villages on the basis of early nineteenth-century documents (tithe awards), reveals certain elements that hold good for other regions of Europe: a certain regularity in plan, as in the categories listed above, and agreement between the information from the plans and that from twelfth-century and later written sources.

Thus, various fiscal documents of the early or late twelfth century show that, for certain villages such as Byers Green or Kirk Merrington-Shelom, there were, at that time, holdings with houses on each side of a street. It is thus possible to affirm that a street-village or green-village plan existed at this time; these are not unique examples in this area.

If the toft street-frontages are studied, it can be seen that they still conformed in the nineteenth century with multiples of medieval units of measure. For Byers Green, the relationship between street-frontage widths on the east-west axis is, from north to south, 2:1:2:2:1:1:3. These relationships, and the total length of the row of plots, are in agreement with the historical data in providing a basic unit of multiples of a known unit of measurement from that period of 16 perches 5 feet (5.03 m).

Similar calculations can be made on other plans, such as that for Kirk Merrington-Shelom: the ten east and west tofts mentioned towards the end of the twelfth century, or perhaps even earlier, and all apparently identical in area, can be reconstructed on the basis of a unit of measurement of 8 perches (8 × 20 ft [2.4 × 6 m]), a unit in use locally.

This shows that fiscal information of the twelfth to thirteenth century or later, combined with the more recent layouts, permit medieval village plans to be analysed and their origins to be studied. This does not resolve the question of the original dating of these planned, regular layouts. In the case of Durham they were already in existence in the twelfth century, and it is likely that they were created with the reconstruction of earlier settlements after the devastation that followed the Norman Conquest. It may be that, over a large part of Europe also, planned village layouts were adopted at the same time, between the eleventh and twelfth centuries.

(Brian K. Roberts, Village plans in County Durham: a preliminary statement, *Medieval Archaeology*, 16 (1972); figs. 20, 21, pp. 38, 40)

Settlement before the late twelfth century

Medieval settlement did not take place at Rougiers in the later twelfth century in a landscape devoid of earlier occupation. To the west of the village, on the edge of the same limestone massif at Le Piégu, there was a much older promontory fort, with important occupation in the La Tène II period.

A classic *villa*-type Gallo-Roman settlement was developed in the plain below. Finds of the first and second centuries are relatively abundant, but there are fewer from the third century. Two distinct settlement areas developed, both near the present-day village on the plain. One is close to the road leading to the *oppidum* and near the Camp-Long hill, which was the site of the first fortified medieval *castrum* at Rougiers, destroyed around 1550.

However, before that date, towards the end of the Roman period, an initial phase of settlement on higher ground, for reasons of greater security, can be observed, as in other southern early medieval sites already discussed. The La Tène II fortified promontory was reoccupied and refurbished, though probably for only a short period. It was quickly abandoned by its inhabitants in favour of another site, not yet located, somewhere on the Camp-Long hill.

References to cultivated land at Rougiers first appear in documentary sources around 1020, at the same time as the first castle. This land was at that time partly owned by the monks of the abbey of Saint-Victor at Marseilles, but ownership soon passed to a local seigneur, who seems to have been related to the founders of the abbey at Marseilles. This transfer, which was only partial up to the middle of the twelfth century, was soon accompanied by quarrels and demolitions; it was completed a little after the disappearance of the first castle and the subsequent growth, around a new stronghold, of the village that was subsequently excavated.

Rougiers well illustrates the slow course of development – first settlement on the high ground and then the protection of the rural settlement with a fortified enclosure, the process of *incastellamento*. It can be observed here, as in most of Provence, as occurring in the second half of the twelfth century; in Italy it dates from the same period, or in certain cases somewhat earlier. Moreover, the history of the medieval settlement of Rougiers, according to current research, notably that of Michel Fixot, is in good agreement with the two phases of the phenomenon recently defined for other parts of Provence: a cautious beginning in the eleventh to twelfth centuries, followed by a more decisive and systematic process from the late twelfth and thirteenth centuries. This was the time, in particular, of the erection of the Provençal stone *castella* and the appearance of the village excavated at Rougiers, which will be described in some detail.

Fig. 57. *The village of Rougiers (Var) – twelfth- to fifteenth-century*
Plan of structures revealed by excavation.

(By kind permission of the excavator, Gabrielle Démians d'Archimbaud)

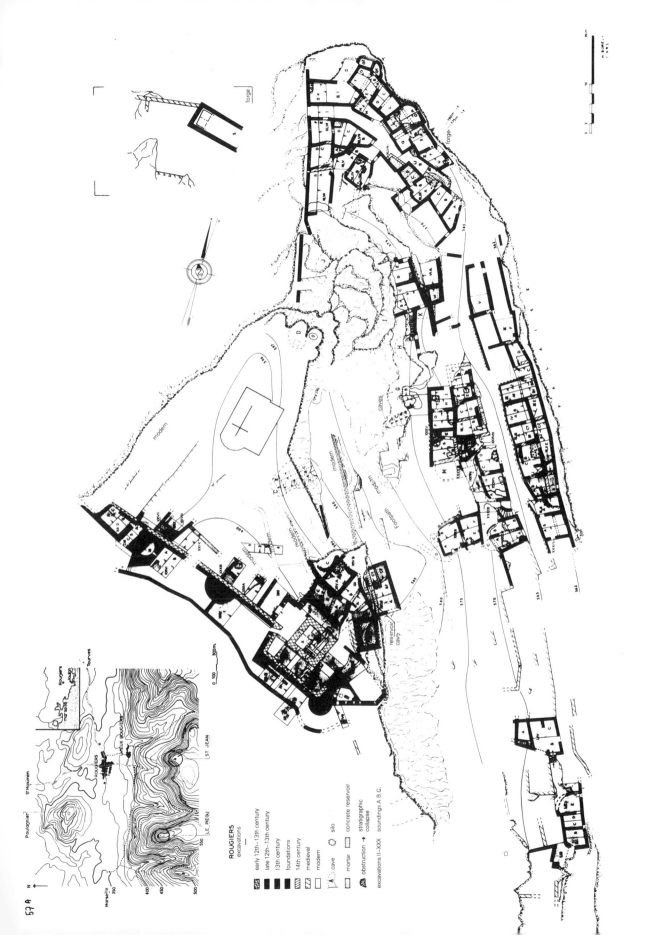

57 A

N

Poulognier St Maximin

Rougiers
Tourves

Marseille 350

LE REGU ST JEAN

VIEUX ROUGIERS

ROUGIERS
excavations

early 12th–13th century
late 12th–13th century
13th century
foundations
14th century
medieval
modern

cave silo
mortar concrete reservoir
obstruction stratigraphic collapse
excavations II–XXX soundings A B C.

forge

forge 170m

caves

reservoir cave

modern

modern

modern

Forgath

Forgath

0 100 500m

The twelfth- to fifteenth-century village
– Settlement chronology

A new castle was built towards the end of the twelfth century. At the same time an enclosure wall, shown by examination to be very homogeneous in construction, was put up to protect the future village. The land was divided up and a rural population appeared very quickly after this preliminary phase: the earliest datable coins are of 1177. It is, therefore, reasonable to see this as an act of creative will, and at the same time as a reflection of the classic phenomenon of high-level settlement. In addition, here as elsewhere, this seems to correspond with a classic twelfth-century trend, the proliferation of new castles or the creation of secondary or peripheral fortresses.

This high-level village was apparently occupied from the end of the twelfth century until the early decades of the fifteenth century; dated coins and tokens range from 1177 to 1420, the latter date apparently marking the almost total abandonment of this upper site. In accordance with the classic sequence for this type of settlement, it was gradually abandoned in favour of a settlement on the plain below, though possibly in discrete stages and according to certain modes. There are documentary references from 1308 to a settlement halfway down the slope. At that time the total population of upper and mid-slope settlements was 34 hearths. The mid-slope settlement was probably considerably earlier than that in date, probably going back to the late thirteenth century.

One rather curious fact, in which the history of Rougiers may differ from that of other high-level villages, is that this movement towards settlement on lower ground was reversed during the fourteenth century, and it is possible to observe, in the decades before 1350, the intensive reoccupation of the upper site, not in terms of new building, since the area was already entirely occupied by 15 blocks of houses dating back to the late twelfth century, but by the parcelling up of older buildings (see Figure 58): the 17 unitary dwellings of around 1200 had grown to 28 by about 1400.

This phenomenon is curious, since it appears to run counter to the general trend of this period, characterized by heavy depopulation. It is tempting to see this as evidence of a growth in population, the consequence of a need for protection following the unrest of the second half of the century. There are a number of examples of inhabitants of lower-lying sites reoccupying the dwellings in the higher settlements, ownership of which they had retained; where they did not own houses already, they would seek to build on new holdings or to divide up earlier buildings. This explanation would suit the situation at Rougiers, as elsewhere, and justify the dividing up of built-up areas, which led to a reduction in the average number of rooms per dwelling from three to two between 1200 and 1300–1350, and a marked reduction in the average area of rooms; in some cases a single house was split into three different dwellings (see Figure 58). Written sources show that at Rougiers in the years between 1360 and 1370, even though the main settlement was lower down, its inhabitants seem to have maintained ownership of houses in the upper village. Here the influence of another phenomenon must be recalled:

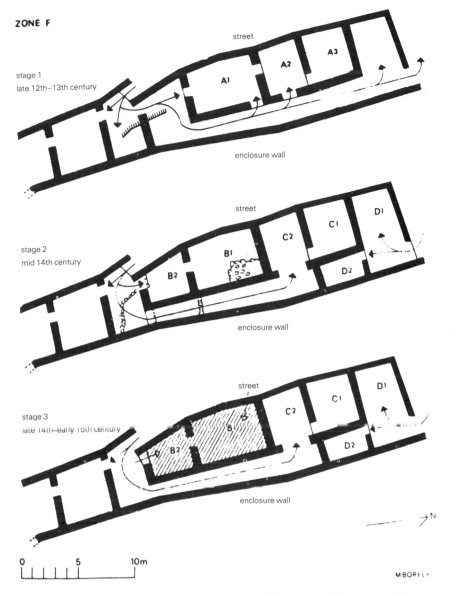

ZONE F

stage 1
late 12th–13th century

street

A1

A2

A3

enclosure wall

stage 2
mid 14th century

street

B2

B1

C2

C1

D1

D2

enclosure wall

stage 3
late 14th–early 15th century

street

B2

B1

C2

C1

D1

D2

enclosure wall

N

0   5   10m

M BORELY

Fig. 58. *Evolution of a block of buildings at Rougiers (Var) from the late twelfth to the early fifteenth century*

In this sector (block A), located up against the village enclosure wall, one building was in existence in the late twelfth to thirteenth century, with three communicating rooms, a lane in front, and a courtyard at each end. Around the middle of the fourteenth century, this complex was reconstructed so as to accommodate three different households. The dense occupation of the ground area is obvious: there was a reduction in the surface area available for living in and in the exterior open spaces – the courtyard and circulation area, the latter being blocked. The buildings in this sector still survive to a considerable height (cf. Figure 78).

(G. Démians d'Archimbaud, L'habitation rural en Provence, *La construction au Moyen Age*, Paris (1973); pp. 59–122, fig. on p. 107)

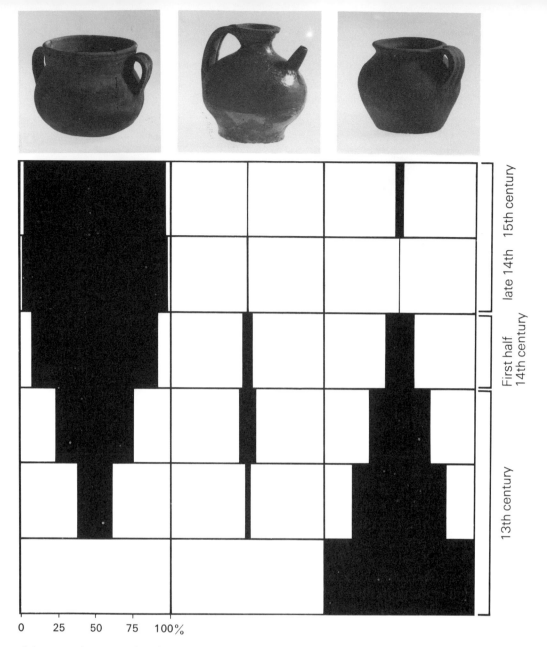

this trend towards the reoccupation and division of the upper settlement precedes the period of unrest, and is probably to be explained by the development, from around 1320 for about two decades, of a glassworks near the upper site, producing good-quality glassware. This is in good agreement, too, with the quantity and quality of the archaeological material, which testifies (the pottery in particular: see Figure 59) to a development of commercial contacts and exchange activities in general, which is very noteworthy in this otherwise troubled century.

However, this did not prevent the settlement in the plain from continuing to be occupied, since its inhabitants clearly had two residences – something which is rather tiresome so far as the interpretation of the results of excavations at the upper site is concerned. Round the beginning of the

Fig. 59. *Development of the usage of the three main pottery types in common culinary and table use at Rougiers (Var), twelfth- to fifteenth-century*

Alongside some less common groups of high-quality pottery, largely imported and which mainly come on to the site around the end of the thirteenth century, three pottery types were in general culinary and table use among the inhabitants of Rougiers:

1 Unglazed grey-wares
2 Glazed white-ware cooking pots
3 Glazed red-ware cooking pots

The first type is the only material on the site when occupation begins. Its use gradually declines in favour of the second type (which remains, however, relatively uncommon), and above all in favour of the third type, which is almost the only ware present by the fifteenth century.

(G. Démians d'Archimbaud, Monnaies, céramiques et chronologie: essai d'analyse des fouilles de Rougiers (Var), *Provence historique*, 25 (1975 [1976]), p. 235; photos L.A.M.M.-Foliot)

---

fifteenth century, the phenomenon of high-level settlement was reversed for the final time. The lower settlement, established in mid-slope around the middle of the thirteenth century, began to develop round the priory founded in the late thirteenth or early fourteenth century, which from that time became the parish church of the two settlements, upper and lower. Another characteristic element was the creation of a third centre of population down on the plain and near the main highway at the beginning of the fifteenth century. It had dwindled to a few houses by around 1424, but it reached the same size as the mid-slope settlement in due course, and became the main settlement centre and the core of the present-day village in the seventeenth century.

The history of Rougiers is a very characteristic example of what must have been the development pattern for a large number of settlements in the Mediterranean region, and one that was very different from what is to be observed in northern Europe – in the British Isles, in Germany, or in northern France. Although this contrast should not be over-systematized, it does illustrate two different modes of rural settlement history between the twelfth and the fifteenth centuries.

In other aspects relating to the construction and layout of its buildings, Rougiers is also very representative of rural settlement in the Mediterranean lands.

– *Village layout*

By the time excavation ceased in 1968, it was estimated that three-quarters of the *castrum* (the area enclosed by the castle and village walls) had been excavated and that every block of the buildings observed in the ruins had been investigated (cf. Figure 57).

The village seemed to have been established with a minimum of free choice in its organization, which suggests this was a 'new village', the result no doubt of seigneurial pressure of some kind.

Whilst the settled area was voluntarily confined to one part of the hilltop, with the object of ensuring protection against the wind, all the available space was utilized, open spaces being kept to a minimum – a single street (probably originating as a cart track), some narrow lanes between the houses and along the walls, but no gardens (cf. Figure 58).

This high occupation density, which contrasts strongly with what is to be observed in contemporary medieval villages over a large area of Europe (northern France, Britain and Germany), with tofts around the houses, is accentuated by the use of high blocks of houses, surrounded by ancillary buildings that abut on them, the classic layout of rural settlement in Provence, defined by the origins of the village of Rougiers.

These buildings were erected on the hill slope, after some levelling of the limestone rock to form platforms at four different levels, plus an underground level of grottoes and caves that were adapted in varying degrees to different uses. These rocky terraces, where a fourth wall was often not needed in the buildings, resulted in the erection of several different types of building. It was only the use of small interior staircases that enabled the buildings to function properly as dwellings, making it possible to gain access to the upper levels. In some cases the upper storey was reached through a door opening to the back of the building on the higher level, whilst in others wooden staircases were probably used.

Occupation density was not uniform over the whole site. The western sector, exposed to swirling winds, which can be very strong around this particular hilltop, was only lightly settled, by contrast with the dense occupation of the central area. At least in the earlier period of occupation, this central area contained the largest houses in the village, near the walls. To the south there are larger houses, less divided up internally but fewer in number, and this part of the site does not seem ever to have been so intensively occupied as the centre.

– *Building materials and techniques*

From its foundation in the late twelfth century, the village was entirely constructed in stone, using limestone blocks quarried by picks and hammers. Walls with internal rubble fillings were built using lime mortar throughout the life of the village. This is a characteristic which strongly distinguishes this village from contemporary examples known from England, Germany or northern France. In all these countries, although the drystone technique was not properly speaking in use, in that clay was used as a form of mortar, lime mortars are never to be found in the somewhat rare cases of the use of stone in building at that period.

The quality of the mortar and, indeed, of construction in general, declined considerably in the new buildings, repairs and reconstructions at Rougiers from the late thirteenth to early fourteenth centuries onwards. This contrasts with the earlier period, when the hard mortar, with little ash or charcoal in its composition, testifies to the use of high-quality lime kilns.

It would appear, in this context, that specialist workers, living in the village itself, were involved in building and fitting out the houses. The successive phases of building or fitting out in the castle and the dwelling houses must have played a role in the diffusion of technology and in the techniques and utilization of different types of material or interior fittings.

– The houses

The houses at Rougiers should, however, not be thought of as high-quality buildings: although they were tall, averaging 6–8m (20–26ft) (because of the general use of an upper storey), their walls were not thick, averaging 0.6–0.7m (2ft–2ft 4in.). Whilst efforts were usually made, especially in the older structures, to build directly on the solid rock, this concern to build on solid foundations disappeared in the late thirteenth century and especially in the fourteenth century; moreover, these foundations were never bonded in any way, which significantly reduced their solidity.

The treatment of the interior remained simple: bare rock in ancillary buildings and kitchens, beaten clay floors in the internal rooms. Cooking and heating arrangements displayed, alongside a rustic simplicity, a very clear indication of human activity orientated towards the exterior of the house or its outbuildings. Out of 57 fireplaces or hearths studied on the site, 47 were located outside the houses, on the rock or the soil. Very often there are abundant material remains around these hearths, including evidence of meals, and they were frequently reconstructed, which well illustrates their importance in everyday life. It is only in the higher buildings that there is evidence from the late thirteenth and fourteenth centuries of a movement towards the improvement of installations connected with fire: the appearance in the centres of certain rooms, or up against their walls, of hearths with dressed stone or flagged bases. However, following the general rule for rural dwellings over the whole of Europe at this time, there are no stone-built chimneys, except in the castle, where an installation of this type was put in with the construction of an external kitchen in the early fourteenth century. There is one very probable example in the village of a passage for evacuating smoke over a hearth. The general absence of ovens is also noteworthy at Rougiers.

– Ancillary structures and services

Until the late thirteenth century a large cistern with a capacity of about 45 cu. m (59 cu. yd) supplied the castle, whilst another, of 80 cu. m (105 cu. yd) capacity, was the communal source of water for the villagers. The latter was abandoned around this time and was not replaced by a single installation. The problem of water supply was as pressing on this site as in those down on the plains.

Although the animal bones from domestic refuse that have been partially analysed seem to indicate that sheep played the major role in food supply (they represent 40–45 per cent of the meat consumed, as compared with 13 per cent goat's meat), and the existence of flocks of sheep in Provence at this period is widely attested by contemporary documents, there is nothing in the village that suggests a sheep fold, with the possible exception of an isolated structure below the village site.

There are a number of pits of different kinds in the village which pose similar problems. Some of these are simple holes dug into the rock, often with some care; those which are designated as storage pits (*silos*) are to be found both in the castle and its bailey and in the village itself. Pits of this kind are characteristic of sites in southern Europe, and in particular in the south of France, as demonstrated by finds from Montaigut (Tarn-et-Garonne), Sannes and Cucuron (Vaucluse), and Condorcet (Drôme); these correspond with the post-built granaries known from Germany and the Netherlands, and to a lesser extent in Great Britain, in a different climatic context. It should be noted that there are relatively few of these (14 in all – nine in the village and the remainder in the castle) and they are small (1–7 cu. m [1¼–9 cu. yd] capacity). An observation that should be linked with this is the clear absence of a threshing floor or floors, which are traditional in medieval Provençal villages in the plains according to written sources.

Taken together, these observations show that the inhabitants of Rougiers depended for their everyday life and their survival on a group of varied buildings or installations, of which the village on the high ground constituted only one element. Finally, in considering this overall structure, it should be noted that the only church in the village was the small chapel of the castle, until the priory founded in the lower settlement in the early fourteenth century took over that role; this is perhaps a significant factor in locating the true centre of the settlement as a whole at that time. Moreover, there is another even more characteristic element, the fact that no burials (with the exception of a child behind the altar and two foetuses or neonates found in the mid fourteenth-century rubbish dump) were found in the vicinity of the castle chapel, which indicates an early concentration of peasant settlement in the lower site.

– Craft and agricultural activities
Nevertheless, it would be wrong to underestimate the importance of the upper site in the settlement history of the territory of Rougiers. In the fourteenth century, when the lower site was already in existence, there are indications of considerable craft activities – not only a glassworks but also probably a smithy on the hillside below the upper site, along with the working of leather, wood and even stone, since various tools relating to these crafts have been discovered. Agricultural implements (reaping hooks and sickles) show that the inhabitants practised agriculture, and also most probably viticulture, since the presence of a vineyard has been noted, and the upper site played some part in these activities. Another important factor, which ensures that the role of the upper site in the life of the Rougiers settlement is not underestimated, is its relative prosperity, especially in the fourteenth century. Although it is not easy to make full use of this observation, in the absence of excavations on comparable contemporary sites, one cannot but be impressed by the presence of many shoes for horses, asses and oxen, which demonstrate the use of

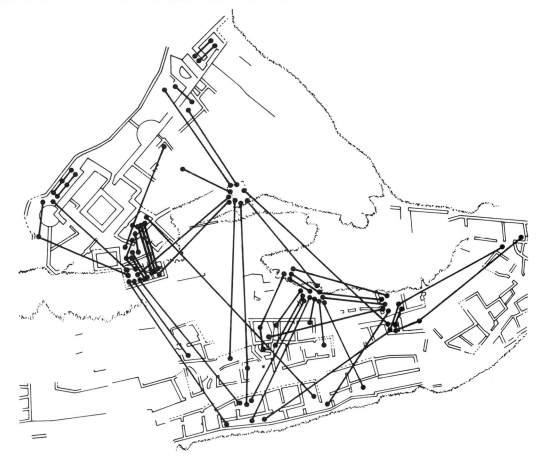

Fig. 60. *Location of pottery dumps in the village of Rougiers (Var) – twelfth- to fifteenth-century*

Among the tens of thousands of potsherds collected on the site, it has proved possible to establish links between sherds belonging to the same vessels. If the sherds from a single vessel found at different locations are plotted on the village plan, this simplified distribution (which covers material from all periods on the site) of dumping places is obtained. On an upland site, with somewhat uneven relief, rubbish was not transported far: certain places – four caves and one abandoned building block – played the role of dumps.

(G. Démians d'Archimbaud, Monnaies, céramiques et chronologie: essai d'analyse des fouilles de Rougiers (Var), *Provence historique*, 25 (1975 [1976]), p. 231)

---

draught animals, and by the quality of some articles of dress and pottery, often imported from as far away as Spain or Italy, in the fourteenth and early fifteenth centuries. It was more than a marginal settlement and/or a place of refuge: this must be seen as settlement duplication, the upper site being more orientated towards craft activities and the lower based more on agriculture.

Conclusion
In this probable dissociation between place of residence and place of work, between the upland site and the site (or even sites) in the plain below, between

Fig. 61 *Relative importance of iron and bronze at Rougiers (Var) – twelfth- to fifteenth-century*

The majority (66.3 per cent) of the 1640 metal artefacts discovered on the site, covering the whole period of occupation from the late twelfth/early thirteenth century to the fifteenth century, were iron, the remainder being copper or bronze. It will be seen that more than half of the surviving objects date from the final phase of occupation (late fourteenth to fifteenth century), even though this was a period of depopulation and ultimate abandonment of the site; few metallic objects derive from earlier periods, evidence of the care with which they were looked after and of their being melted down for reuse when they were beyond repair. The higher figures for metal objects in the final occupation phase may be explained by the greater diffusion of metals at the period, a phenomenon known from other sites but not yet fully understood.

	Late 12th–1st half 13th	2nd half 13th	1st half 14th	Middle & 3rd quarter 14th	Late 14th–15th	Total
Iron (1061 objects)	42	53	57	71	74	66
Bronze and copper (538 objects)	58	47	43	29	26	34
	100%	100%	100%	100%	100%	100%

This table shows another interesting factor, that is to be seen elsewhere: the fairly common use in the Middle Ages of copper and bronze for many objects and tools in everyday use. In the thirteenth century, copper and bronze objects outnumbered those of iron, but the latter grew in importance and predominated in the latter occupation phases.

(G. Démians d'Archimbaud, Artisanat et échanges en Provence médiévale d'après les fouilles d'habitat rural, *Atti del Colloquio internazionale di archeologia medievale 1974* [1976])

the houses and the sheep folds or enclosures set up outside the inhabited places, Rougiers is very typical of villages in Provence and, no doubt, over a much wider geographical area. It illustrates the complexity and the interest of rural settlement history in these regions. With its houses huddled together without gardens or tofts, the marshalling of structures above one another on a slope, beneath a castle, and enclosed with a wall, the use of stone and lime mortar for building, and the common use of two-storied construction, it provides a very characteristic picture of one type of medieval village.

These characteristics link Rougiers directly with the typical rural medieval settlement in the Mediterranean regions and make it a structural model without equivalent, save in northern Europe. Other examples can be quoted from elsewhere in Provence, from all over Italy, and from Spain. There is, however, a lack of excavated examples on a scale that makes it possible to reconstruct, as at Rougiers, the general history of this type in this region. Nevertheless, the recent development of archaeological research in Spain and, more particularly, in Italy augurs well for the future. In the Levante region of Spain and in Sicily, several sites are beginning to provide complementary data on the history of Mediterranean rural settlement.

The Sicilian *castrum* of Brucato of the thirteenth to fourteenth centuries, abandoned around 1340, occupied a classic location, within a walled enclosure below a castle. Excavation has revealed buildings in clay-bonded stone, very probably single-storey, covered as at Rougiers by rounded and hollow tiles on double-pitched roofs. The same simplicity is apparent internally as at Rougiers, with floors usually of beaten earth. Certain other characteristics of Mediterranean upland sites, such as dense occupation without open spaces, and roads that are narrow and winding (with the exception of the main street), are also present, together with some flexibility in internal furnishings and a growth in density over the course of the history of the village.

These Mediterranean upland sites represent a specific form of rural settlement, the history of which is broadly homogeneous over a very wide geographical region. As yet there are no gradations within the general type, but they will certainly emerge in the years ahead.

To characterize the modes of rural settlement of northern France, Great Britain or Germany is relatively simple: it is possible to use the results of several large-scale English examples. In practice several examples are needed, because what typifies medieval villages in this region, by virtue of the much greater flexibility offered by landscapes that are not bounded by fortifications and which are usually flat, is on the one hand, the relative mobility of houses within individual holdings, and on the other, changes in the character of rural houses, especially in the closing centuries of the Middle Ages: much larger, more complex and better built houses often appear around this time.

In order to characterize the northern type of village it is proposed to use several examples, nearly all of them from England.

2   An English village, Wharram Percy (tenth–seventeenth centuries)

The significance of the site

The site of Wharram Percy (Yorkshire), where the first trial work took place in 1950, has been excavated each year regularly since 1952. This is one of the major British excavations, at the present time the largest and most important study of a medieval village in Europe and one of the richest in information yield. The site is of special importance for various reasons, which relate primarily to the history and origins of medieval archaeology in Great Britain and, indirectly, on the Continent. Wharram Percy is the result of scientific collaboration between two of the leading personalities in English medieval archaeology: the historian Maurice Beresford, who undertook the original exploratory work in 1950, and the archaeologist John Hurst who, in 1952 and 1953, introduced on this site, for the first time in Great Britain, the method of large-area excavation used by German archaeologists before 1939 and introduced on English medieval sites during World War II by Gerhard Bersu, director of the Deutsches Archäologisches Institut, who was dismissed by the Nazis for racial reasons and took refuge in Britain. This method, which was tested on sites of this type, has subsequently been applied widely in medieval village excavations.

In addition to this aspect, Wharram Percy has played a very important role in the history of European medieval archaeology, since it has made an indirect contribution to the foundation of this discipline in Great Britain. John Hurst was trained in prehistoric archaeology at Cambridge, and began his excavations and research relating to the medieval period at Wharram Percy in 1952. It was there, too, in the August of that year, that the Deserted Medieval Village Research Group (it has subsequently dropped the word 'Deserted') was founded; this Group was one of the main founders, five years later, of the Society for Medieval Archaeology, of the first specialist journal (*Medieval Archaeology*), and of the subsequent evolution of medieval archaeology in Great Britain.

Another interest of Wharram Percy is the objective of excavating as much as possible of a medieval site for the first time. Before, and indeed since, that date, only parts of sites, of varying sizes and for a variety of reasons, were excavated. Attention has already been drawn to the number of such sites that are often of questionable value when it comes to drawing general conclusions. It is, of course, not always feasible to excavate the whole, or almost the whole, of a site, because of lack of material resources, but the possibility of doing so must always exist for certain typical sites.

Fourthly, Wharram Percy is an exceptional site in itself. There are two main factors, as we shall see: a settlement which began very early, in the Anglo-Saxon period, overlying substantial traces of Romano-British occupation; and the existence of two classic medieval village structures – the seigneurial manor and the parish church – both equally accessible to excavation. Excavation of both of these has been one of the major contributions of the village of Wharram Percy.

The final important characteristic of this excavation is the initiative taken in 1970 to relate the information from the houses being excavated to the wider context of the environment. Since then attempts have been made in various ways to determine the limits of the site, the extent of the cultivated fields, the dates when their boundaries were fixed, and the introduction of manuring, and to study various other ancillary activities, such as the creation of a fishpond.

Although this excavation is of the first rank it is, unfortunately, as yet difficult to show its full importance because the results are still for the most part unpublished. It will thus be possible here to present only some of its aspects.

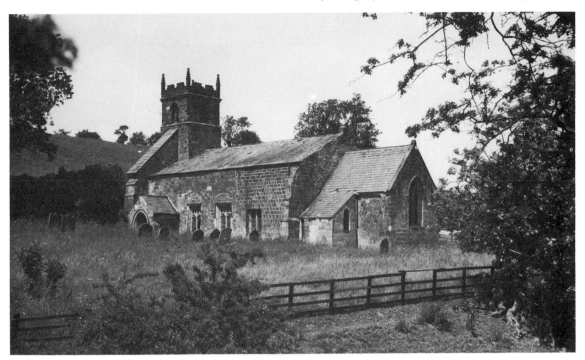

Fig. 62. *The church at Wharram Percy (Yorkshire) as it stood before 1960*

This building represents more than 1000 years of architectural development (cf. Figure 64). Since this photograph was taken the tower has collapsed.

(*Photo:* Deserted Medieval Village Research Group)

Chronology of medieval settlement

Wharram Percy forms part of a group of five settlement centres, served by the same parish church, which is still standing on the site of Wharram Percy itself (see Figure 62).

This is a classic process, that of the village that has been totally deserted and fallen into ruins but whose parish church still stands, surrounded by fields, and in use until very recently.

Four of the five centres were abandoned in the course of the sixteenth century, and Wharram Percy itself around 1510, leaving the area to sheep grazing, a very common development in Great Britain around that time.

The site

Before excavation, the site appeared as a group of abandoned fields covering a plateau overlooking the church on the west, orientated east-west and abutting on a series of four-sided enclosures aligned on a north-north-westerly axis, on the edge of a slope that overlooks a small river, formerly controlled by a weir that has been destroyed (see Figure 63). These four-sided enclosures, bounded by clearly visible low banks, were obviously the boundaries of

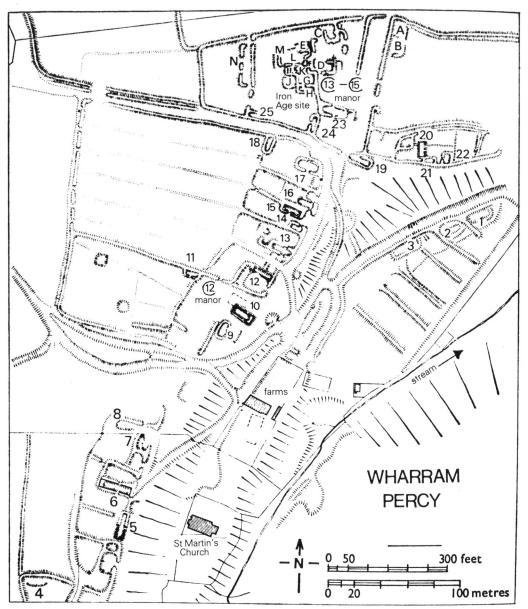

Fig. 63. *The village of Wharram Percy (Yorkshire) – twelfth- to sixteenth-century*

In the centre is the twelfth-century manor house, which was then abandoned and replaced by a second, situated to the north of the village, which was built in the thirteenth century and was in use until the fifteenth century. Between the two are the tofts occupied by houses with strip fields lying behind them, to the west. The village extends to the south with further tofts. These overlook the river, lying to the east, and St Martin's church (cf. Figure 62).

Even before excavation, the field and toft boundaries, in the final fifteenth- to sixteenth-century form, and the house ruins, were visible on the ground. This plan shows those surface remains with the results of subsequent excavations superimposed. Excavation was first concentrated on tofts 6 (to the west of the church) and 10 (near the site of the first manor house).

(M. W. Beresford and J. G. Hurst, *Deserted Medieval Villages* (1971); fig. 25, p. 120)

individual holdings or tofts, each containing a house whose ruins could easily be distinguished under the grass. Above the church to the south and up to the site of the ruined manor house to the north, the site appeared as a relatively well-ordered group of enclosures, each containing a house, ranged along a street running along the edge of the plateau.

Romano-British occupation (first–fourth centuries AD)

Careful survey and several excavations have shown that there was some Iron Age occupation. Four Romano-British sites of the first and second centuries are at present known. The first, and largest, dating from the first century, is a farmstead in a trapezoidal enclosure, lying to the north-west of the medieval village. The second lies beneath the second ruined manor house, to the north of the village. The bank enclosing this manor house may, in fact, represent the course of the Romano-British enclosure.

There is a third Romano-British site beneath the medieval church and a fourth located under houses 8 and 9, on the plateau to the west of and above the church.

These four settlements, which were doubtless small, seem to have been merged into a single, larger estate around the end of the Roman period, a classic process in this region and elsewhere.

Saxon occupation (seventh–eleventh centuries)

There seems to have been a break in settlement of several centuries at Wharram Percy after the end of the Roman period. It was not until the Middle Saxon period, around the seventh to eighth centuries, that new settlers arrived there. They installed themselves in a deserted landscape, but one in which the earlier boundaries were clearly visible enough for these to determine the layout of the fields and the general orientation of the new settlement.

Up to the present, as for the Romano-British period (excluding the church, dating from this period, which was found beneath the present stone church), only one structure, a sunken hut, has been excavated, but many potsherds and coins are evidence of settlement.

The most recent discoveries indicate that there were two centres of population in the seventh to eighth centuries: one round the church and the other beneath the second manor, to the north of the medieval village.

In the case of the latter, the discovery in 1975 of a sherd of Tating ware, a continental type of pottery that is very rare and exceptional in England, usually only coming to light in the great eighth- to ninth-century ports, may perhaps explain the presence of these two Saxon settlement centres. Documentary sources show that there were two seigneurial manor houses at Wharram Percy at the end of the eleventh century. It is possible that there had been two distinct settlement centres from the Saxon period, one to the north and the other to the south, round the church. The same phenomenon is attested from other sites, such as Mucking, referred to above. In such circumstances, the later history of the village and the building of new houses on the site in the thirteenth to fifteenth centuries may be interpreted as a continuous evolution of these two centres, with buildings going up along access roads to merge into a single village with a relatively ordered plan, its houses arranged along a main street running north-south. The archaeology and history of the medieval landscape, especially in Britain, yield a number of examples of this type of polynuclear development around the end of the Saxon period and the beginning of the Norman. In 1976 a Saxon-period sunken hut was discovered beneath the bank delineating the northern boundary of the second manor house now excavated. All the finds from this area point to the possibility that occupation at this point was continuous from the Roman period to the Middle Ages.

The twelfth- to fifteenth-century village

Apart from the Saxon period, the earliest peasant houses excavated on the site do not date from earlier than the twelfth century. They appear around a manor house, doubtless built after the arrival of the Percy family in 1186–88.

– The church

Although excavation has not as yet produced any evidence of peasant houses earlier than the twelfth century, study of the church has shown how old the settlement was (see Figure 64).

The earliest church, in wood, seems to date between the eighth and very early tenth centuries. As with most early wooden churches, this was replaced, at a date that is difficult to establish but certainly before the tenth century, by a very simple rectangular building in mortared, well-dressed stone. By the early eleventh century, this church had been enlarged by the addition of a square chancel.

This first stone church was demolished and completely replaced by a new building, again in stone and much larger, which probably dates to the late tenth or early eleventh century. Thus, before the Norman Conquest there had already been three phases of building in stone, plus an earlier wooden construction, at Wharram Percy.

Before the end of the medieval period there had been five substantial additional phases of enlargement or rebuilding: the addition of a bell tower at the west end of the existing church in the late eleventh century; the building of a new semi-circular chancel and of a south aisle towards the end of the twelfth century, at the same time, significantly, that the first manor house was erected, probably by the same builders; the addition of a north aisle, probably shortly after the previous extensions; rebuilding of the chancel in the late twelfth/early thirteenth centuries; and modification of the chancel arch in the early fourteenth century. This brought the medieval works to an end, no doubt coinciding with the highest population level achieved in the village. The church attained its maximum size at that time and, in the centuries that followed after the village was abandoned in the sixteenth century, it was reduced in size by successive demolitions. The aisles were removed in the sixteenth century and the chancel was rebuilt on a smaller scale in the seventeenth century; finally, during restoration work in the nineteenth century, a small vestry was added. This brought the evolution of the church to an

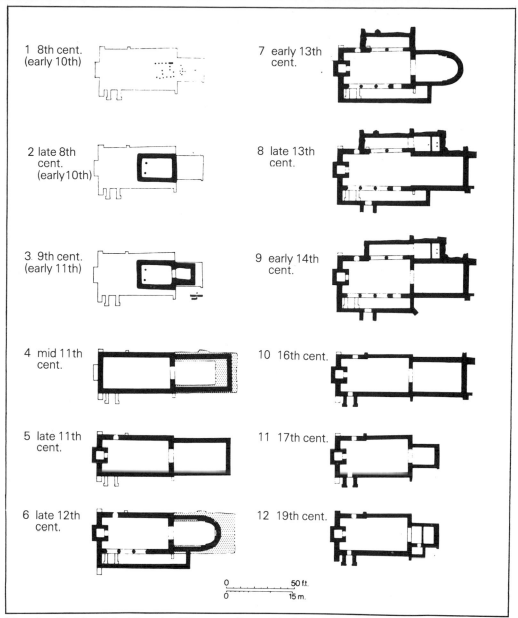

1 8th cent. (early 10th)	7 early 13th cent.
2 late 8th cent. (early 10th)	8 late 13th cent.
3 9th cent. (early 11th)	9 early 14th cent.
4 mid 11th cent.	10 16th cent.
5 late 11th cent.	11 17th cent.
6 late 12th cent.	12 19th cent.

0 ____ 50 ft.
0 ____ 15 m.

Fig. 64. *St Martin's Church, Wharram Percy (Yorkshire) from the eighth to tenth centuries to the present day, based on excavation results*

The first church was built in the Anglo-Saxon period, in wood like most of these early buildings (1). Before the end of the Anglo-Saxon period, in the eighth to tenth centuries, this was replaced by the first stone church (2), which was rebuilt once (3) and then replaced in the tenth to eleventh centuries by a much larger new stone church (4). There followed many phases of rebuilding and extension throughout the Middle Ages, as in most churches of this period. It is interesting to note that it was in the early fourteenth century (9) that the church attained its largest size; after that date, like the village itself, it regressed to its present ruinous state (Figure 62), though it did not disappear altogether, as the village did.

(J. G. Hurst, Wharram Percy: St Martin's Church, in P. V. Addyman and R. K. Morris (eds.), *The Archaeological Study of Churches*, CBA Research Report 13 (1976), fig. 13, p. 38)

end, and it became a typical example of those religious monuments that stand alone in the countryside which, like the church on the site of the ancient village of Saint-Jean-le-Froid (Aveyron), so often indicate the location of deserted villages.

This example of a church is, as other excavations have shown, not exceptional. It highlights a number of phenomena which must have had an influence on the medieval village. The number of building phases – three before the Norman Conquest, five subsequently and before the end of the medieval period, is very significant. It is evidence of the involvement of specialist workers, since each phase reveals the use of techniques in stone dressing and mortaring that are not to be found in the houses of the village itself. It is inevitable that these programmes of works at the church and the arrival of specialists would have affected the building methods known and used by the inhabitants of Wharram Percy, and in particular the use of stone.

– The first manor house (late twelfth century)
Although it was known before excavations began, from the visible remains, that there had been a manor house in the northern part of the village, the discovery of another, older one, built on the plateau in the late twelfth century, some 150m (164yd) to the north of the church, was completely unexpected. Its existence was unknown until excavation revealed a large underground store-room measuring 8.2 × 5.4m (27 × 18ft) internally, which underlay a ground floor with moulded sandstone doors and windows. Around this manor house, which was abandoned when a new seigneurial family, the Chamberlains, bought the village in the first half of the thirteenth century, there was established, at the same time, an initial group of peasant houses in rectangular tofts.

– The house enclosures
One of the most interesting results of the excavations at Wharram Percy has been the variations in enclosure sizes. It had been thought that the boundaries visible before excavation began must have been laid down when the site was first settled, and that they were maintained thereafter. This view was based on the urban example, where tenement boundaries effectively remained stable once they had been laid down, as early as the Saxon period in the case of Lydford (Devon), as revealed by excavation.

Careful excavation of two of the enclosures at Wharram Percy, enclosures 10 (excavated 1953–60) and 6 (excavated 1961–70), has shown this not to be the case: the indications visible before excavation began relate to the situation in the fifteenth century. Before that date, boundaries and sizes were variable. Two reasons may be adduced for this phenomenon: on the one hand, a variation in the total number of houses in the village as a function of population pressure, and on the other, changes in the orientation of the houses. For example, three houses were found in area 6, each within an enclosure, which were abandoned and replaced in the fifteenth century by only two houses, with the consequent erection of new enclosures with different boundaries.

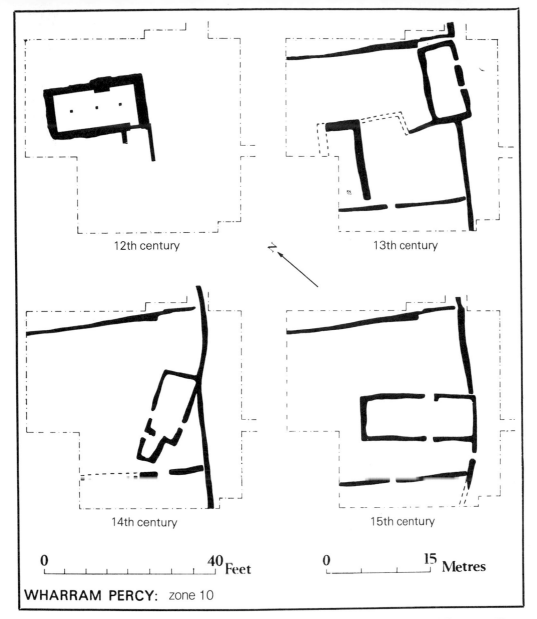

WHARRAM PERCY: zone 10

Fig. 65. *Simplified development of buildings within enclosure 10 at Wharram Percy (Yorkshire) – twelfth- to sixteenth-century*

A twelfth-century manor house was succeeded by two thirteenth-century peasant enclosures, one with a house lying parallel to the street. These were joined to form a single enclosure in the fourteenth century, the house being built with a similar alignment. Finally, later in the fourteenth century, the house was rebuilt at right angles to the street and the axis of the two earlier buildings.

(Wharram Percy, *Current Archaeology*, 49 (1975), p.42)

– *House orientations*

The change in orientation of houses observed at Wharram Percy is another very important aspect of the excavations, as shown by area 10 (see Figure 65). In this area, very near the manor house built around 1186–88, no less than nine successive phases of superimposed houses were found on a thin occupation layer. These nine houses correspond to a period of about 325 years, between the late twelfth century, when the first was put up, and the abandonment of the site around 1510 – in other words, one reconstruction roughly each generation.

Whilst this phenomenon of regular and rapid replacement is interesting in itself, it becomes even more significant when the plans and orientations of the houses are considered. In area 10, all the houses were built to the same plan, as long rectangles, with one half of the building lower than the other: the lower part was for animals, the higher for humans. These houses were 15–23m (49–75ft) in length (see Figure 65). Still in area 10, the three latest houses to be built, in the second half of the fourteenth century and the early fifteenth century, were at right angles to the street, which ran north-south. All the earlier houses, on the other hand, were built parallel to and alongside the street.

These changes in the layout and size of enclosures and houses pose certain problems. It is not certain, however, that they run counter to the notion of a planned settlement of the village that was probably seigneurial in origin. The first houses in area 10 were put up at the same time as the manor house. When the latter was abandoned in favour of a larger establishment further to the north, the reason was probably the undesirable proximity of the earlier manor house to the peasant dwellings. A group of new plots was laid out between the old site and the new manor, which was built during the thirteenth century, to accommodate additional inhabitants. This means that the initial development of Wharram Percy was from the south, around the church, northwards to the area around the new manor house, from the tenth century to, at the latest, the thirteenth century. Then, as a result of the fall in population in the fifteenth century, new homes were built in larger enclosures between these two centres. This development would seem to represent a kind of overall settlement plan, related to the seigneurial establishments. At the same time, such reorganization could only have been possible for two reasons, which generally hold good for rural settlement at this time: first, the availability of land on sites that were not enclosed by walls or restricted physically by broken terrain, as at the upland villages, and secondly, the use of insubstantial buildings and low-quality materials, resulting in periodical reconstruction, which facilitated change. Until stone was used for building, from the thirteenth century onwards and then only in certain areas, both these factors explain the greater flexibility of rural settlement outside the Mediterranean lands. In this respect, therefore, Wharram Percy is less representative than other examples.

– *The houses: materials and building methods*
The houses at Wharram Percy were, like so many others of the same period, apparently built in a simple fashion, using poor-quality materials.

In the earliest period, as with many English or German examples from before the late twelfth century, they were built of wood. Many postholes, often overlaid by later buildings, have been found, and it is therefore difficult to make out the exact plans or dimensions of these early buildings. Buildings of this kind were being erected until the beginning of the thirteenth century.

During the first half of the thirteenth century, chalk begins to come into use in the construction of houses with walls 0.6–1m (2ft–3ft 3in.) thick (Figure 66b). The stone comes from the sub-soil of the village itself. Many quarries – simple, roughly circular pits a few metres deep – have been found around the houses; there were about ten in area 10, for example. For the most part, these quarries date from the first half of the thirteenth century, when there must have been a significant change in house-building methods in the village. Some of the quarries must, on the other hand, have served for lime-burning as well, most likely for the construction at this time of the manor house, since clay and not lime mortar was used for bonding the chalk of the peasant houses. Some part of this chalk may also have been used for liming the fields.

Another change in house-building technique came at the end of the fourteenth century. A relatively shallow stone wall-footing of a few courses was built and a timber frame was erected on this – the timber-framed house (Figure 66a). This discontinuation of building in stone is worthy of note, since examples are known from elsewhere.

– *House typology*
All the houses at Wharram Percy were rectangular, 15–23m (49–75ft) long by 4.5–6m (13–20ft) wide and divided into two sections, one for animals and the other for humans (see Figure 66). In some cases this division is emphasized by the provision of two facing doorways in the centres of the longer sides, thus producing a kind of passage at right angles to the long axis of the house.

There were other types of building at Wharram Percy. One late thirteenth- or early fourteenth-century house, considerably smaller than those just referred to, was found in area 6. It was divided into two rooms, one containing a hearth, and would not have housed animals.

– *Sunken huts*
It is interesting to note that a medieval sunken hut was excavated at Wharram Percy, close to house 5, to which it must have been related. It was dug down into the earth to a depth of about 45cm (18in.) and was very similar to the Saxon examples. It was probably a simple working place, so as to leave more room inside the house. In form, date and function it is reminiscent of the (admittedly rare) discoveries in other English late medieval villages, such as Gomeldon, where the sunken hut was dated to the fourteenth century.

– *Around the village: weirs and fishpond*
Studies are in progress in an attempt to identify residual floras, especially in the valley to the east of the site. The stone weir that is still extant in this area has been investigated. There was an initial construction of wooden piles, followed by a primitive wooden weir, and finally a stone structure in the

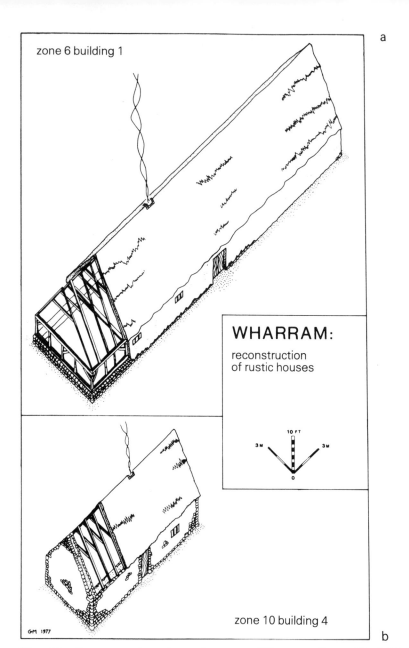

zone 6 building 1

WHARRAM:

reconstruction
of rustic houses

zone 10 building 4

GM 1977

Fig. 66. *Reconstruction of two houses at Wharram Percy (Yorkshire) – fourteenth-/early fifteenth-century*

These were mixed houses, with doorways in the centres of the longer sides and half of the building reserved for animals (cf. Figures 71 and 73). The timber-framed house shown in *a* is the largest so far excavated – 4.6m (15ft) wide by 27m (88ft) long overall. The other mixed houses on the site were 12–24m (39–78ft) long. The second example (*b*) was built entirely of chalk blocks. The chalk came from the sub-soil in the village, with some sandstone elements from a quarry 3–4 km (2–2½ miles) away. Between the building of *b* in the fourteenth century, and that of *a* in the late fifteenth or early sixteenth century, Wharram Percy passed from entirely chalk-built houses to timber-framed houses with stone footings.

(J. G. Hurst, *Wharram* (1979), London, p. 70, fig. 25)

208

thirteenth century, all intended to create a fishpond or a reservoir.

– *Refuse, manuring, and distant contacts*
The absence of rubbish pits, characteristic of a number of British villages at this period, led to consideration of the practice of manuring fields with refuse. The collection of sherds on fields around the site that are currently under cultivation seems to confirm this hypothesis, which is very illuminating in relation to medieval farming practice. Systematic research is being carried out on this at Wharram Percy.

Several finds indicate that the inhabitants had external connections over quite large distances. Coal has been found: the nearest mines are about 100km (62 miles) from the site. Cod bones have also come from the excavations, but the sea is about 30km (19 miles) distant from Wharram Percy.

Conclusion: characteristic features at Wharram Percy

Various aspects of Wharram Percy seem to be characteristic: the erection of houses within enclosures, very typical of rural settlement at this period; the mobility of boundaries and of the location and orientation of houses within them; and changes in building materials. These are all important points and are duplicated, more or less clearly, on other English sites. One final point relating to Wharram Percy must also be stressed: the almost exclusive occurrence of a single house type, a long rectangular building housing humans and animals beneath the same roof, from the thirteenth century to the early sixteenth century (Figure 66). It will be seen that other types of building are to be found in various English villages of this period.

Let us consider these points further. The enclosure around the medieval rural building is a constant feature, predating the establishment of the aggregated rural settlement. Whatever the village plan (along a single street or two parallel streets, around a green, etc), the existence of an enclosure, for use as a kitchen garden, is almost invariable. This conforms with the planned nature of villages at this period and represents a clear break with early medieval rural settlement, where such provisions appear not to have been made as a matter of course around dwelling houses. It would be tempting to see this as an indication of the importance of leguminous plants, or more widely of vegetables, in the food supply of this period. However, the finding at Wijster of a large kitchen garden sounds a note of caution in this respect.

Other examples of villages demonstrate, as at Wharram Percy, the simultaneous modifications of boundaries, alterations in house orientations, and changes in building materials.

3 Changes in village plans and house orientations

The site at Wawne (Yorkshire), recently destroyed in the course of construction works, was the subject of a rescue excavation which made it possible to trace the development of settlement and house-construction materials from the twelfth to the fifteenth century (Figure 67). The land was covered in the

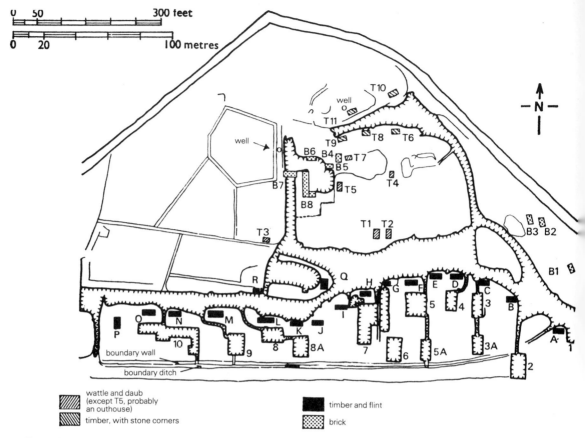

Fig. 67. *The village of Wawne (Yorkshire) – twelfth- to fifteenth-century*

This plan, made after the site had been destroyed by mechanical excavators, shows the successive phases of the village. In the twelfth to fourteenth centuries, 12 wooden houses were dispersed rather at random over the northern part of the site. They were abandoned in the second half of the fourteenth century and replaced by houses that were all built in the same style, with stone foundations, on the same side of a street and almost all parallel to it.

(M. W. Beresford and J. G. Hurst, *Deserted Medieval Villages* (1971), fig. 29, p. 126)

Middle Ages by four metalled streets.

In the earliest period, there were some 12 houses, disposed rather irregularly, either parallel or at right angles to the streets. Their structures were of wattle and daub or timber-framing. The latter measured *c*.15 × 4.5m (49 × 13ft).

All the houses, including some which were probably only barns, were occupied from the twelfth century to the first half of the fourteenth century. The irregular layout of the site suggested that the settlement had grown somewhat haphazardly.

Those buildings were, in due course, abandoned and demolished, the sites where they had stood being brought under the plough, as the remains of furrows and ditches show. Sixteen new houses were built to the south of the earlier ones, parallel to the main street on an east-west axis. All except two lay to the south of this street. They were of timber-framed construction on footings of boulders; they had tiled roofs and hearths with brick bases. The regularity in size of these houses reinforces the impression given by the village plan of an ordered settlement: all were 5.2m (17ft) in width and all except one consisted of two rooms separated by the fireplace. Although they varied somewhat in length, from 10 to 13m (33 to 43ft), the westerly room was always of the same size – 5.2 × 5.7m (17 × 19ft). The pottery discovered dated from the later fourteenth and fifteenth centuries. It is tempting to see this as a seigneurial initiative, perhaps resulting from a new settlement after the Black Death in the mid fourteenth century or the succeeding decades.

C The medieval house

The preceding examples have illustrated some of the main characteristic features of the later medieval village. However, when considering changes in layout, it is necessary to consider another factor, in addition to seigneurial initiative, displacement of manor house or church, demographic pressure, or insubstantial construction resulting in rebuilding, namely the appearance of new types of rural building layout in the twelfth or thirteenth century.

Only one type of structure was used at Wharram Percy – the large, long, rectangular, dual-function building, housing both humans and animals (Figure 66). This was not the case everywhere.

1 New technological and socio-economic conditions

Starting in the eleventh to twelfth centuries, but pre-eminently in the thirteenth century, a series of phenomena directly influenced rural architecture, or at least those houses belonging to the more affluent peasants. These phenomena were the diffusion of the mouldboard plough, which needed more powerful teams; general use of the horse by the rural population; the growing trade in milk and its products, which led to greater production; the increased demand, especially in Britain, for wool and, more widely, for meat; and the greater care given, for all these reasons, at least at certain levels of the peasantry, to livestock, whether draught animals or those raised for wool, meat, or milk. At the same time, the creation of large agricultural estates as a result of growing wealth among some of the peasantry, led to much larger stocks being built up for supplying urban markets in particular.

All these phenomena resulted in new and more highly developed buildings being erected around the dwelling house itself, with the object of housing domestic animals (which were more numerous or better cared for), farming implements and gear (and eventually carts and other vehicles), and finally corn crops. This was the process whereby agricultural buildings evolved, ultimately attaining the level of the great monastic farms of the thirteenth to fifteenth centuries, with their enormous barns.

2 The rectangular-plan farm

Growth in the wealth of a section of the peasantry led to the appearance, within some villages, of farming units similar to those visible today over large parts of Europe – true farms in which the ancillary buildings occupied an area that was much larger (sometimes by a factor of three or four) than the dwelling house. In addition to this contrast in size between dwelling and outbuildings, a tendency can also be observed towards laying the buildings out in a regular fashion by grouping them round a square or rectangular open space. These are the rectangular-plan farms, with open or closed yards, still to be seen in the countryside in France and other European countries.

The main element which distinguishes these late medieval farms from early medieval farming units such as Warendorf, where the various activities are scattered over 12 or more buildings, is not so much the existence of diversified buildings (dwelling house, barn, cowshed, stable etc) as the contrast in surface area between dwelling house and ancillary buildings. This is typical of late medieval farms and distinguishes them from early medieval farming units, which covered a large area because they were composed of many elements, each small in size, apart from the house proper.

The village of Hangleton

The appearance of structures of this kind profoundly changed the plans of certain villages in the later Middle Ages. At Hangleton (Sussex) four houses each occupied their own enclosures in the thirteenth century, but two centuries later the same area was filled by a single farm, composed of several buildings, which completely transformed the remains of enclosures, and thus the plan of this part of the village.

The village of Gomeldon

Excavation revealed an even more interesting evolution, with the same ultimate result, at Gomeldon (Wiltshire) between the twelfth and fifteenth centuries (see Figure 68).

Four successive phases of building on the western slope of a small hill were revealed by the excavations: these structures were built of drystone flints without foundations; the walls, which probably stood about 90cm (3ft) high originally, were 60cm (2ft) thick.

Only one twelfth-century rectangular building was found on the site, measuring about 7.8 × 4.2m (25 × 14ft), with a doorway in the centre of each long side, as at Wharram Percy. There was a hearth in this house, which had a cruck roof, a special type of which it is the first dated medieval example in Britain (cf. Figure 103).

During the second phase, in the thirteenth century, this building was demolished and replaced by two parallel buildings, larger than their prede-

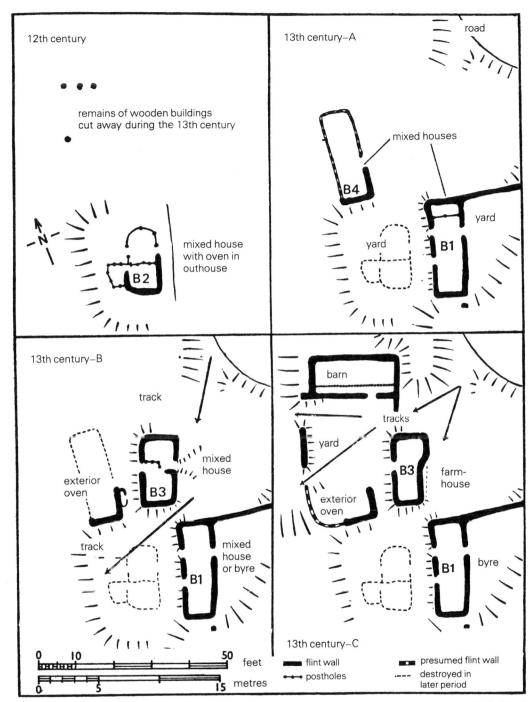

Fig. 68. *Evolution of the closed rectangular-plan form in the village of Gomeldon (Wiltshire) in the twelfth to thirteenth centuries*

There is a transition here, between the twelfth and thirteenth centuries, from the mixed house, partly built in wood, to the farm with several buildings laid out in a regular way around a closed rectangular yard.

(M. W. Beresford and J. G. Hurst, *Deserted Medieval Villages* (1971), fig. 22, p. 111)

cessor: the bigger of the two measured 12.6 × 4m (41 × 13ft). The existence of a drain in the northern half of building 1 of this period suggests that this part of the building, as at Wharram Percy, was used to house animals, the humans living in the other part; building 2 was similar in form. These are comparable with those from Wharram Percy and a number of English sites of this period (cf. Figures 66, 71, 72, 73).

In the following phase (thirteenth to fourteenth centuries), there was a profound change in the character of the settlement. One of the buildings from the preceding phase was demolished, but part of its wall was left standing in order to support an exterior oven. A new dual-purpose building was put up, with entrances at the centre of each of its long sides: this was smaller than the two earlier buildings, one of which was retained but possibly given a new use as a barn. This phase is important because it shows the creation of a kind of farm with multi-purpose buildings, certainly arranged irregularly, but very typical in the ratio of dwelling area to working/barn area.

The most profound change came in the fourth phase, in the fourteenth century: the dual-function building of the previous phase was converted into one exclusively for human habitation, one of its entrances being blocked up: the barn to the south retained its function, but a very large cowshed, 12m (39ft) long by 5.1m (17ft) wide, was built on the north of the site. A stone enclosure wall sheltering an oven imposed an ordered layout on these structures, which formed a very typical rectangular-yard farm.

An increase in livestock was probably the decisive factor in this final phase. From a few beasts housed at first in the dual-function house, they grew in number to the extent that a special building had to be put up for them. In an earlier phase it was the barn that needed to be created, and that on a large scale. Thus, in the final stage of the history of these buildings in the fourteenth century, we find together, around a rectangular farm yard, the two fundamental elements in the large farms of the later medieval and subsequent periods: the barn and the cowshed. There is another interesting aspect of this example: the rapidity with which buildings were converted or rebuilt.

Spread of the rectangular-plan farm

Gomeldon well illustrates the evolution of the mixed or dual-function house into the farm with an organized layout and closed yard, that is to say, the creation of a very characteristic type of European rural architecture, and, moreover, provides a chronology for this process. But it should be realized that this development was neither unique nor accidental: it is a classic phenomenon and indicates the increase in wealth of a fraction of the peasantry in certain villages and regions that were specially favoured. Alongside these peasant establishments, of great interest but restricted in size, much larger farm complexes developed in the later medieval rural world, which left a profound impression on the landscape and on society in succeeding centuries, in the form of monastic farms and fortified manor houses.

These establishments had twin functions – as residences for the steward or feudal lord and as working buildings – and they evolved in the twelfth and, more especially, the thirteenth centuries. They were dominant elements in economic and social terms, so far as the rural society around them was concerned, and they probably reflected the spirit of the age and defined its architectural framework. The overall resemblance with the development recorded at Gomeldon, especially in its final stage, is a remarkable one.

Whether it is the strongholds of the Perche or the great farms of the Soissonnais, often monastic or ecclesiastical, that are being considered, the most outstanding feature is the enclosure or *pourpris* round the group of building. In the Perche, this enclosure on average measures 50 × 50m (55 × 55yd), a total surface area of 2500 sq. m (3000 sq. yd). It is usually four-sided in plan and may be fortified and defended by corner towers. In the case of the defended sites, the buildings are on a low platform 1–2m (3ft 3in.–6ft 6in.) high, constituting a sort of low four-sided motte. When the buildings have been demolished this is often all that remains visible – examples are known from Yorkshire, inland Flanders, Burgundy, and elsewhere.

Within the enclosure, or on the square motte, there are buildings ranged round a central courtyard, with the barn, associated with corn production, being given pride of place. This is especially typical of the large religious farms of the later Middle Ages, less so of the fortified manor houses. The type and size of other buildings varies according to circumstances and region.

What is remarkable about these relatively large and exceptional establishments (though most villages had one, either ecclesiastical or manorial) is that regular layouts appeared only gradually, and often very late. In the Soisson nais, the buildings were laid out in the sixteenth century rather haphazardly within the enclosure, without any particular plan and rarely joined together. It was only by chance, from rebuilding, enlargement or conversion, that regular four-sided layouts of contiguous buildings round a courtyard slowly emerged. In such regions, this process was not effectively complete until the nineteenth century. The same applies to the large peasant farms that evolved first in the later Middle Ages. In the Somme region, the characteristic square layout of linked buildings was apparently not created until the nineteenth century.

The appearance of these large farming units with developed buildings, relatively regular layouts, and, in particular, enclosed yards, obviously corresponds with the needs and potentials of a small section of the later medieval peasantry. The crisis of the late Middle Ages, with cultivated lands being abandoned, followed by the need to bring them back into cultivation in the later fifteenth and sixteenth centuries, favoured the concentration of land in the hands of a small fraction of the peasantry, and therefore made the construction of very large buildings more feasible. The creation of large farming enterprises and the concentration of land holdings in the last two centuries of the medieval period had an important effect on the development and definition of post-medieval architectural forms that will become apparent later. It is enough here to emphasize that the enclosed farm with specialized ancillary buildings evolved under the influence of ecclesiastical or manorial

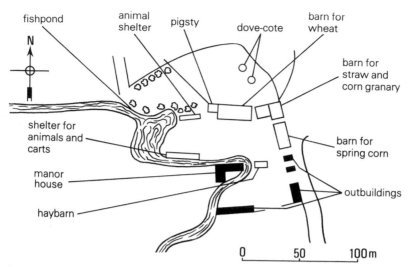

Fig. 69. *Layout of a large Oxfordshire farm in the early fourteenth century*
From written sources it is possible to reconstruct the various buildings that made up this large farming unit, typical of the bigger establishments of the end of the medieval period. Worthy of note are the number and diversity of the ancillary buildings, which occupy a built-up area considerably larger than that of the dwelling house.

(N. Harvey, *A History of Farm Building in England and Wales* (1970), fig. 5, p. 40)

---

models from the late thirteenth century at least (Figure 69). Gradually, over several centuries, the same conjunction of conditions being maintained, regular evolution towards the rationalization of layouts continued. This phenomenon appeared early in grain-producing areas (Beauce, Soissonnais, Somme, to quote some French examples), but it seems not to have occurred elsewhere – in Brittany, for example. Even though the phenomenon was later or absent in some parts of Europe, it nevertheless did have its effect: outside France and England, the farm at Sindelfingen (Kr. Boblingen, Federal Republic of Germany) is an outstanding example.

The Sindelfingen farm
The initial farming unit was composed of several buildings dispersed randomly over quite a large area, and dated from the mid eleventh century to the first half of the fifteenth century. In the second half of the fifteenth century, a palisade appears round the buildings, and there is a very marked tendency to put up buildings that are parallel with one another, i.e. towards a regular layout. This marks the appearance of the classic type of farm with buildings disposed round a yard (*Mehrseithof*) of central Germany in the post-medieval period. Other examples from the eleventh to fourteenth centuries are known from Königshagen in the Harz.

This type of farm represents a response in building terms, always easy to identify and interpret, to those influences which seem very largely to have conditioned changes in rural settlement in the last four centuries of the Middle Ages, either by changing the use and occupation of earlier types of building or by introducing new types of building more widely. In the former case, this means the unitary house of one or two rooms, exclusively for human habitation, and in the latter the mixed house, sheltering both humans and animals under the same roof, which became one of the classic forms of rural house in north-western Europe from the twelfth century onwards.

3 *The unitary house*

The unitary house, the most simple form of dwelling, is the classic type in Europe, outside the Frisian region and the Mediterranean zone, and, indeed, almost the only rural settlement type in the first half of the medieval period. This is what has been observed wherever there have been sufficient excavations – in the fifth to twelfth centuries in central and southern Germany (Gladbach) or England (Chalton, West Stow), as shown in Figures 32, 34, 99, and 105; they usually have one, or sometimes two, rooms.

Even after the twelfth century and through to the present day, the one- or two-room unitary house is, if not the basic type of rural dwelling, one of the most common forms (see Figure 70). With local variations, frequently dating back to the last one or two centuries of the medieval period, it often constitutes the main regional house type from an early period.

One of the lines of development of the unitary house is, at least from the twelfth century, the appearance of types in which two rooms can be distinguished. One, the larger, has a fireplace (a hearth that is usually central, or more rarely up against one of the walls, and ultimately a chimney proper on a wall), and the other, the smaller of the two, used normally as a bedchamber and without a hearth.

This type of house is to be found from the second half of the medieval period onwards over a very large part of Europe. Contemporary texts often contain examples. Thus we know that in the Forez in the fourteenth century, the most common type of rural house consisted of one room with a hearth (*chauffage*) and an adjoining one (*cellier*) At Montaillou and its surrounding villages in the late thirteenth-century Ariège, we again find this large room with hearth (the *foganha*), which is the living room *par excellence*, and a smaller adjoining room, used both as sleeping chamber and storeroom (the *cave*). The houses from Dracy (Côte-d'Or) with two rooms, one containing a hearth or fireplace, are related to these examples.

The importance of this type of house, the bipartite nature of which is based on the presence of an installation for fire in one of the rooms, makes it necessary to examine the role of the hearth or fireplace in medieval rural dwellings.

Open hearths and fireplaces in medieval rural houses
Two main problems result when fire is introduced into a house. The first is the

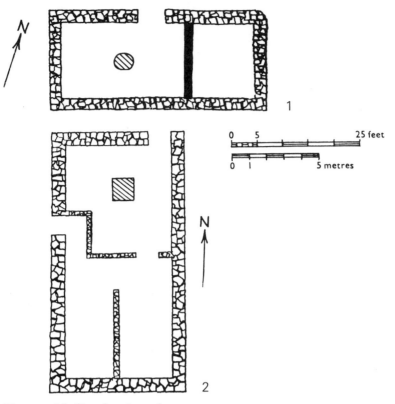

Fig. 70. *Medieval unitary houses*

1 Two-roomed house: Riseholme (Lincolnshire)
2 Two-roomed house with entrance passage: Muscott (Northamptonshire) – late
twelfth- to late thirteenth- or early fourteenth-century

(M. W. Beresford and J. G. Hurst, *Deserted Medieval Villages* (1971), fig. 21, p. 110)

---

hazard aspect, which leads to the fire being sited in the centre of the room,
until such time as walls came to be built in fire-resistant materials (i.e. stone,
either for the entire wall or at least the part around the hearth itself). The
second is that of smoke removal. To avoid filling the house with fumes, there
are three possible solutions: either the fire is situated in an outbuilding or
ancillary room, or, more simply, outside the building (as, for example, at
Gomeldon – cf. Figure 68), or a hood is installed over the hearth (i.e. the use
of chimneys, either on the wall or centrally located).

The first alternative, as we have seen, often explains the existence of sunken
huts around the house proper, especially in the Slav lands. Another solution,
as at Hohenrode, is to put the hearth in a separate external room at ground
level, which serves as a kitchen, possibly following the model of earlier or
contemporary manorial residences.

The use of a fireplace with chimney, of course, solved both these problems.
The introduction and general application of this type of installation in rural

settlements occurred very gradually, and always at a late stage, especially in certain countries. The earliest examples of wall fireplaces that can be quoted occur in palatial stone buildings – at Broich near the Ruhr (Federal Republic of Germany) and Doué-la-Fontaine (Maine-et-Loire) in the late eighth and early tenth centuries respectively.

The earliest wall fireplaces are of two types: either a chimney built up against the wall itself, usually as a later addition, and sometimes simply made of planks coated with clay, or a flue incorporated into the stonework at the time it was constructed – the classic late type of stone-built wall fireplace.

However, a number of excavations have revealed the existence of a transitional type between the centrally placed hearth and the wall fireplace proper. This is a hood mounted on four uprights placed over a central hearth. Examples of this type of construction are to be found in stone buildings that do not belong to the rural tradition, such as the Cistercian abbey at Longpont (Aisne), as well as various medieval rural settlements. Chimneys of this type continued in use in certain rural areas, such as the Bresse, right up to the nineteenth century.

Independently of the typology of the wall fireplace, it is very important to study the chronology of its introduction into rural dwellings, which is in general very late and varies from one country to another. Hohenrode in Germany, with its hooded chimneys dating from the later twelfth century, is the earliest example so far known.

At the Burgundian village of Dracy, the fortuitous preservation of organic materials has revealed the existence in a fourteenth-century house of a vertical wooden chimney of small cross-sectional area, built up against a wall over a hearth. This first appearance of a wall fireplace, made of planks lined with clay, is important. Contemporary documents describe installations of this type which must often have preceded the stone wall fireplace proper, designed and built at the same time as the house and incorporated into the wall.

There was certainly a time-lag between France on the one hand and Italy and Great Britain on the other, where the wall chimney appeared much later. In the fourteenth century, large manorial reception halls were still being erected in these countries with central hearths, as, for example, at Penshurst Place (Kent), built in 1341 by John de Pulteney, great merchant and Lord Mayor of London.

In conclusion, it is important to stress that the wall fireplace, a fundamental element in traditional rural architecture and an installation which occupied an essential place in the everyday life of peasant peoples up to the nineteenth century, was introduced very gradually, most probably after the Middle Ages and certainly at times that varied considerably between one European country and another.

Whilst the unitary house was, over a long period and in many regions, one of the most common forms of rural dwelling, it none the less conforms with the socio-economic evolution which we have seen in the later Middle Ages and the influence of which has been shown in the development of farm types. The example of Hohenrode in the Harz Mountains serves to demonstrate the vital role played by the unitary house in this region of central Germany in the twelfth to fourteenth centuries, and also how it may have evolved.

The village of Hohenrode: unitary and mixed houses
– Periods of occupation

There were two periods of occupation at Hohenrode (Kr. Sangerhausen), separated by a short period of abandonment, the first in the tenth to twelfth centuries and the second from the twelfth century to the end of the fourteenth century. In the first phase of occupation, the inhabitants of Hohenrode were still using sunken huts, but these were not in use in the second phase, an interesting illustration of the point at which these buildings went out of use in the Middle Ages. These sunken huts contained two groups of pottery – Germanic and Slav – which is surprising, since Hohenrode lies beyond the eastern limit of Slav expansion in the Middle Ages, the river Saale. They contain hearths in their corners, as at other sites such as Tilleda.

However, the most interesting aspect of this village is the second phase of occupation, dating from the second half of the twelfth century until the end of the fourteenth century. The houses were built on stone foundations, which supported wooden sill beams and cob walls. Within stone enclosures roughly 50m (55yd) square, which defined the farming units, three types of building are to be found side by side: dwelling houses, buildings reserved for cooking, and storehouses. The dwelling houses, 12.4–15.6m (40–51ft) long by 7–8m (23–26ft) wide, invariably consisted of two rooms, the larger housing the hearth and serving as the living room and the smaller being the bedroom, with occasionally a stove for heating purposes (see Figure 71a).

Stoves for cooking or heating are unknown inside houses, especially in Britain and Germany, until very late in the medieval period. The earliest German example yet known is in fact Hohenrode, from the later twelfth century. However, ovens for these purposes are frequently to be found in eastern Europe, from the Iron Age onwards. This is particularly true of the sunken huts, which were the only form of rural dwelling among the Slav peoples east of the Vistula, until late in the Middle Ages: from the sixth century onwards these sunken huts almost always had ovens (cf. Figure 38).

– Fossil land allotments

Abandoned fields have been observed a little way to the south-east of the village of Hohenrode: these belong to the twelfth to fourteenth-century village, which must have comprised eight to ten farms. Since there are 19 strip fields, between 7.1 and 9.2m (23 and 30ft) wide and about 180m (560ft) long, it may be concluded that each farm cultivated two fields. Fields that are similar in shape and size have been observed in other regions of Germany, especially the central part. However, the most interesting aspect of the excavations at Hohenrode concerns the functions of the buildings.

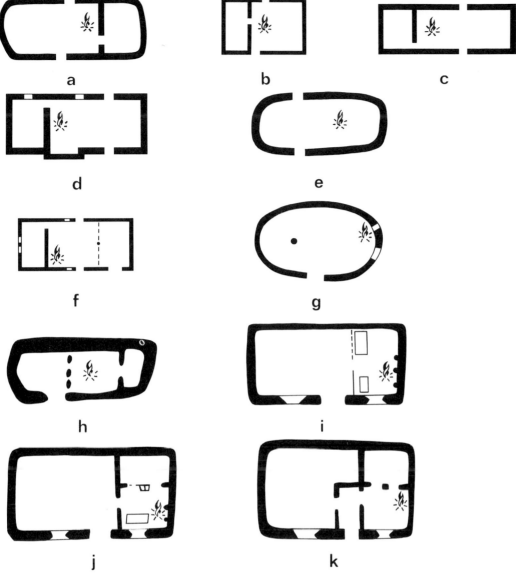

Fig. 71. *Some medieval and modern European mixed houses*

Medieval examples:

a   Hohenrode (East Germany)
b   Königshagen I
c   Wharram Percy

Post-medieval examples:

d, e Surviving Irish houses
f   Contemporary house at Kohlgrube (West Germany)
g   Contemporary house in northern Spain
h   Contemporary house in the Hebrides
i–k Three houses at Villars d'Arène (Oisans) at the end of World War II. They illustrate three possibilities, increasing in complexity, for access to the building and separation between its two parts (cf. Figure 72).

(*a, b, c, f*: Karl Baumgarten, Ethnographische Bemerkungen zum Grabungsbefund Hohenrode, *Ausgrabungen und Funde*, 16 (1971), pp. 49–53 (p. 51)
d, e, h–k: Techniques et architecture, 7: 1–2 (1947), p. 14)

– The buildings and their functions
The buildings used as kitchens were generally 7m (23ft) square whilst the stockrooms, built in a form that was to become traditional in these parts of Germany and which persists to the present day, were *c.*6m (19ft) long by 4.5–5.5m (15–18ft) wide. What is of greatest interest is the appearance of two-room dwellings, the larger of which always contained a hearth. This is the type of house that was to become characteristic of the later Middle Ages and of rural dwellings in central Germany. From the medieval period alone examples of comparable buildings can be quoted from Janssen's excavations at Königshagen, very near Hohenrode and close to it in date (see Figure 71b), where they were associated with rectangular farm plans, or the twelfth- to fourteenth-century stone house excavated at Schönfeld (Kr. Tauberbischofsheim).

The use of internal space in the Hohenrode houses has posed a number of problems since they were excavated before World War II. According to the excavator, Paul Grimm, these houses were reserved exclusively for human habitation. However, following a recent reassessment of the excavation and phosphate analysis of the occupation layers, it is now considered that the use of parts of some of the houses for sheltering animals cannot be excluded. This is the case in house 1, which is strongly reminiscent, with its two doorways each in the centre of one of the long sides, its general layout, and in particular its rounded corners, of comparable English and Irish buildings.

This is in excellent agreement with various ethnographic observations made in Germany. In several regions of that country there are houses, some going back to the sixteenth century, that have been identified as belonging incontrovertibly to the mixed house type, sheltering both men and animals – for example, in the hilly areas in north-west Germany, around Düsseldorf.

It is, therefore, probable that certain of the Hohenrode houses may be of the mixed house type, whilst the remainder belong to the unitary house type, used exclusively for human occupation.

– Conclusion
This interpretation of the Hohenrode dwelling houses is confirmed by the results of the excavations at Königshagen in the same area of the Harz, not far from Hohenrode. At this settlement, which will be discussed in greater detail later, the simultaneous presence of unitary and mixed houses has been attested, with, in at least one case, that of the farmhouse, a mixed-house type being used as a dwelling house (which recalls one of the phases at Gomeldon). Thus Königshagen reveals, in a simple village, the effect of the major socio-economic trends that have just been described, in diversifying settlement form into the three classic types found in central Germany at the end of the medieval period and through into the present day – the square-layout farm, the mixed house, and the unitary house.

The unitary house at the end of the Middle Ages: the case of Germany
At the end of the medieval period, or in the early modern period, central

Germany provides two types of possible development for the unitary house.

In the former case, the main living room or hall decreases in size, becoming in effect a kitchen, whilst the bedroom is enlarged. Later a room is added on the first floor and a corridor and staircase are inserted in the centre of the house in front of the kitchen, which occupies no more than one corner of the building. This represents the late appearance, after the medieval period, of the two-storied rural house, with its resultant internal rearrangements.

The other possible mode of development of the medieval two-roomed rural house in central Germany is interesting, especially in the light of what will be discussed later relating to the origins of the mixed house. In this region after the end of the medieval period, this once again consists of adding a byre at the opposite end of the building to the bedroom; the entrance to the building is still in the centre of one of the long sides and provides access by means of a corridor, either to a staircase giving access to the upper storey or, more simply, to the kitchen, located at the rear of the building. Thus in this region in the post-medieval period, animals and humans were lodged under the same roof in a new type of building, which is distinguished from the mixed house by the fact that the two parts of the building are physically separated and each is entered by a separate door. The present-day village of Grillenberg (Kr. Sangerhausen, near the Hohenrode site) in the Harz is one of several German examples that include buildings of this type. They are interesting because, in parallel with the general evolutionary process which brought about the appearance of the mixed house, a phenomenon that will be discussed later with special reference to Britain, it demonstrates the birth of a type of house that often came into use in the rural architecture of many regions, notably France in the post-medieval period. It would be interesting to attempt to study the dates at which this type of house made its appearance in those regions where it constitutes one of the traditional forms of post-medieval rural architecture. In any case, it is essential to distinguish it from the mixed house.

4 *The mixed house*

Definitions

The term 'mixed house' should be reserved for those buildings that provide shelter under the same roof and at opposite ends of the building for human beings and livestock respectively. They may have one or two common entrances. Where there are two such entrances, they are often located opposite one another towards, or in the centre of, the long sides of the building.

The large Frisian houses, which might seem to belong to a special category of mixed house, belong, by virtue of their large size and the presence of a large number of animals, to another architectural tradition. They illustrate the house-barn-byre type, still so characteristic of those wetter regions that are favourable to grassland and *bocage*, such as the Vendée, the Jura and the Vosges, as well as Friesland.

In Britain and certain other regions, such as medieval Brittany, there are

Fig. 72. *Internal arrangements of a mixed house in the Val-d'Isère at the end of World War II*

Humans and animals lived beneath the same roof, without any enclosure or wall between them, as in many medieval or post-medieval examples (cf. Figure 71 i–k, Figure 76).

The hay stored in the loft acted as an excellent insulating material. Since hay was scarce and expensive, the cattle were bedded down on the floor without litter. Their tails were tied to a steel wire so that their urine did not spray over the whole room! A manure gully at right angles to the long axis of the building, which was emptied each morning, separated the part reserved for humans from that of the animals. Sheep were housed beneath the enclosed bed.

(*Techniques et Architecture*, 7: 1–2 (1947), p. 10)

---

mixed houses where the separation between the two parts is either non-existent or denoted by no more than a light partition. Since post-medieval houses had no ceilings, the partition stopped short at roof-timber level and the rooms were open to the roof space, even where a loft was installed. In those areas where the recent history of these buildings can be studied, such as Savoy, a gradual transformation can be discerned, with the partition tending to become more solid and more permanent.

Another development is the addition of a ceiling that closes off both rooms. However, architectural analysis of existing buildings in Devon, which have ceilings in their present-day form, shows that the roof timbers still bear traces of sooting, which militates against the notion that the ceilings were an original feature. This must therefore represent a measure of internal reconstruction as a post-medieval development. Nevertheless, these are all different types of mixed house.

However, the term 'mixed house' cannot be used for the type of building known from after the medieval period, especially in central Germany, as described above in the case of Grillenberg. Here men and beasts are lodged under the same roof but in rooms that do not communicate with one another, being separated by a wall and provided with individual entrances. It would appear that the byre was added to the dwelling house, perhaps to reduce and simplify building work, and this is confirmed by the evolution that can be seen in certain German villages. Post-medieval rural France provides many such examples.

The case of the mixed house is altogether different. It is acceptable in these circumstances to envisage a common origin for the appearance of both types of house: a concern to provide shelter for a few domestic animals whilst restricting the size of the whole structure. However, in one case it is appropriate to speak of the mixed house; the other is the unitary byre-house.

Mixed house and unitary house

The term 'mixed house' must be reserved for buildings conforming with the precise definition set out above, and in particular for those which house both humans and animals beneath a single roof and using the same entrance. Buildings of this type do exist, as in nineteenth- and twentieth-century Brittany, where neither part is reserved for animals. In certain fishermen's houses, fishing gear is stored in one half of the building. Ethnography shows, moreover, that the use of certain mixed houses can vary. Thus it is necessary in both terminology and excavation to distinguish clearly between *plan* (i.e. architectural description) and *function* – proof of the presence side-by-side of human beings and livestock. It is reasonable to doubt whether in certain cases the use of the term *longa domus* (long house) in medieval documents was systematically used to designate dual-purpose houses of this type. In such circumstances it is better to talk of a *mixed house* when this dual function can be proved, and of *mixed-house plan* in other cases, not overlooking the fact that, in this case, the plan is the same as or close to that of a two-room unitary house. This clearly shows the potential for transition between one and the other by a simple increase in size. In this connection it is important to recall the discussion above of the Hohenrode houses.

Mixed house and long house

In its classic sense, to denote an aisleless rectangular house, in which men and animals were lodged at either extremity under the same roof, with a common entrance on one of the long sides and without a permanent and integral division between the two parts, the term *long house* (for what is called the *mixed house* here) was first used in the 1930s by the British ethnologist I. C. Peate to describe the typical Welsh house. This was, in fact, a translation into English of the term used by Welsh countrymen for their houses, the equivalent of which can be found in linguistic terms in medieval Welsh documents in the form *tŷ hir*. From these observations it appeared that this form of dwelling was typical for a long period in Great Britain of the Highland Zone, occupied at the present day by Celtic peoples – Wales, Cornwall, and the Scottish Highlands. It required only one step further – and one that was taken by some scholars – to establish a relationship between the present-day distribution of buildings of this type and an ethnic origin, which defined the 'long' house as a characteristically Celtic house type.

The mixed house in Britain: its origins and spread

Excavations in the inter-war years revealed the antiquity of this house type in the Celtic lands, notably those by Lady Fox at Gelligaer Common (Glamorgan) in 1930. These were insubstantial buildings with turf walls; there was a central row of postholes in the part reserved for animals and two rows in the human dwelling area.

Another medieval excavation, under the direction of E. M. Jope at Great Beere (Devon) in 1938, produced more mixed houses of classic type, with two facing entrances in the centres of the longer walls (see Figure 73d).

Since that time, a number of similar finds have been made in the Celtic parts of Britain, which show that this type of house was current in these regions of the British Isles, at least in the thirteenth century. In Scotland, however, the poor development of medieval archaeology means that it is not possible to give examples earlier than 1750.

The considerable growth of medieval village excavations in the British Isles revealed, very soon after World War II, the fallacy of attributing this type of building exclusively to the Celts. More and more excavations are demonstrating the characteristic presence of the mixed house from the thirteenth to sixteenth centuries over the whole non-Celtic area – Sussex, the west and central Midlands, Northamptonshire, East Anglia, Kent, Dorset, Wiltshire, and the stony areas of northern England, Yorkshire, Lincolnshire and the Cotswolds. It can now be affirmed that this type of house existed throughout the whole of the British Isles in the later Middle Ages.

The post-medieval history of this type of dwelling explains the fallacy of the argument put forward by ethnologists, who did not have at their disposal those data needed for a historical overview of the problem.

As has just been shown, the mixed house appeared in the British Isles around the end of the twelfth century, so far as the earliest known examples in the south-west are concerned. It was in common use in the thirteenth century, but by the end of that century it was beginning to be replaced by another type of building, the farmhouse. This phenomenon became widely diffused and it may be assumed that, towards the middle of the sixteenth century, with the great rebuilding phase in England between 1570 and 1640, the mixed house lost a great deal of ground. A striking illustration comes from Yorkshire: at Wharram Percy, abandoned around 1510, there were only mixed houses, whilst at Towthorpe, one of the four inhabited sites that constituted, with Wharram Percy, a single parish served by the church at the latter village, there are several rectangular-plan farms. This is doubtless to be explained by the fact that Towthorpe was not abandoned until around 1600, and that in the intervening period, in the course of the sixteenth century, the process of transition from mixed house to farm had reached Yorkshire.

In the Highland Zone proper, by contrast, the mixed house remained in use

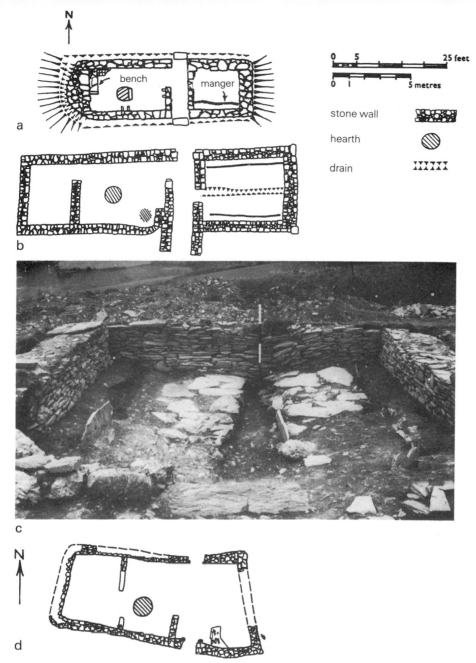

Fig. 73. *Medieval mixed houses in south-western Britain*

a   Garrow (Cornwall) – thirteenth-/fourteenth-century

b, c Trewold (Cornwall) – plan and photograph showing stone feeding troughs *in situ*

At Garrow and Trewold, the presence of stone feeding troughs indicates that animals occupied the right-hand part of the houses. At Great Beere, the dwelling part of the house comprises, as is often the case, one large living room with its hearth and a form of bedroom at the end of the building.

(M. W. Beresford and J. G. Hurst, *Deserted Medieval Villages* (1971), figs. 19 and 20, pp. 108, 109; photograph Medieval Village Research Group, London)

after that date, up to the present day. This relates once again to one of the reasons for the appearance and subsequent disappearance of this type of dwelling in favour of the farmhouse: the relationship between dwelling and type of agriculture, and more particularly, the role of animal husbandry. The mixed house survived in the Highland Zone of the British Isles because a relatively poor form of peasant agriculture predominated there, based on grain production and a backward form of stock raising. The mixed house is the type of dwelling best adapted to this type of farming.

The mixed house in France

The French example also illustrates this evolution quite well, from its origins to the survival of the mixed house in the mountainous or poorer regions of France, such as Brittany or Savoy.

— Brittany in the twelfth–twentieth centuries
Pen er Malo (Morbihan)

Excavations took place from 1969 to 1972 on the site of a deserted medieval village at Pen er Malo (Guidel commune, Morbihan). Like so many Breton coastal sites from the Neolithic onwards, this settlement, some 250m (273yd) from the sea, was covered by the wind-blown sand dunes that occur along the coasts in this region. Excavation has shown that the dunes were formed in the mid twelfth century. This was doubtless the reason for the abandonment of the village and of a nearby field, which was in effect fossilized. This field, measuring roughly 200 × 100m (219 × 109yd), seems to have had some stone buildings in its centre, and excavation revealed surviving traces of cultivation in the form of strips 1.10–2.45m (3ft 6in–8ft) wide (the average width of eleven strips was 1.76m [5ft 6in]).

The village of Pen er Malo seems to have covered about 3ha and was only partially excavated. Seven buildings were found, of which only three were studied in detail. They were all occupied in the first half of the twelfth century.

Building A, elliptical in plan and with its major axis lying east-west, measured 11.75m (38ft) long by 6.70m (22ft) wide (see Figure 74) The area enclosed by the walls was of the order of 50 sq. m (60 sq. yd). Apart from a few quartz pebbles and slabs of schist, the wall was built of granite blocks; these constituted the inner and outer facings, which were filled with granite chips and clay. A bonding of mixed clay and soil was used instead of mortar. This wall, still standing to a height of 0.6–1.2m (2–4ft) when excavated, varied in thickness between 48–80cm (1ft 6in.–2ft 6in.) (average 60–70cm [2ft–2ft 3in.]). It was built directly on the underlying rock, with stone filling in places where there were depressions in the rock. This form of construction was found in all the buildings excavated.

Building A was divided into two unequal parts internally by a very dilapidated partition wall. The western part, measuring about 30 sq. m (36 sq. yd), contained two centrally placed and well-constructed circular hearths with a third, less elaborate, lying to the west of them. The eastern part had no hearth and very little pottery was found in its floors; it was only 20 sq. m

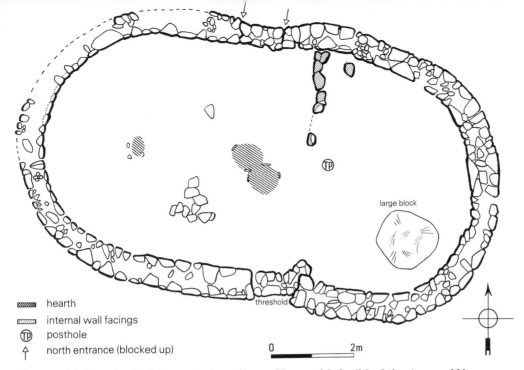

Fig. 74. *Medieval mixed house in the village of Pen er Malo (Morbihan) – twelfth-century.* This oval plan should be compared with that of other mixed houses (cf. Figure 71e, g)

(R. Bertrand and M. Lucas, Un village côtier du XXIe siècle en Bretagne, *Archéologie médiévale*, V (1975), fig. 3, p. 80)

(24 sq. yd) in area and lay slightly lower than the western part, since the house was built on a slope.

There was a doorway between these two rooms, 1.25m (4ft) wide and opening to the south. Almost exactly opposite this doorway there had been another which was subsequently blocked up.

Reconstruction of the roof and roof timbers of this building, as for the others on the site, can only be hypothetical. A single posthole was found lying on the long axis of building A, but there was nothing comparable in the other buildings excavated. By analogy with more recent examples of this type of building that survive in Brittany, it is possible to reconstruct the likely roof structure as having been composed of two or three pairs of collar rafters.

The other buildings on the site, whilst comparable in construction, were a little smaller than building A. Although certain of them, such as building C, contained well-constructed hearths, some had a second doorway. Those buildings of this type excavated were arranged in pairs (A and E, B and C), joined by a wall several metres long which may have constituted part of a form of enclosure for poultry, for example.

The archaeological data give an indication of the resources and way of life of the inhabitants. Some 30 quern fragments (both saddle and rotary querns) were discovered. It is unusual to find so many domestic querns on a medieval rural site: when the feudal system became established, seigneurial communal wind or water mills were quickly set up, for the use of the peasants on payment of a small fee. The use of domestic hand querns was in consequence forbidden, and this is no doubt the explanation of the rare occurrence of such objects in rural settlements after the twelfth century.

Finds of animal bones reveal that cattle, sheep, pigs, rabbits and chickens were all sources of food, although it is impossible to establish in what relative proportions they were eaten. This is evidence of animal husbandry and the presence of poultry. Seafood, obtainable very close at hand, was also eaten, as shown by finds of limpet, mussel, and other shells, fishbones, and remains of crustacea.

The pottery provides some very interesting information about the village's economy (see Figure 75). Out of some 1500 sherds found on the site, only 60 were not in the ware known as 'greasy'. This was a special fabric containing talc, and easy to distinguish by touch for this reason. Present knowledge indicates that it was made in the Middle Ages in Finistère, especially in Cornouailles, perhaps at Bodérès-en-Plonéour-Lanvern (Finistère); it is known from the eleventh to twelfth centuries as far south as Lannion (Côtes du Nord) at the mouth of the Loire, and in the thirteenth century as far north as Dover. This distribution implies sea transport, mostly coastwise. It is therefore very interesting to find so large a quantity of this type of pottery at a village such as Pen er Malo, at some distance from the only place of manufacture at present known: this is an indication of at least indirect contact between the inhabitants of this village and the coastal trade.

In the light of very recent excavation and fieldwork on deserted Breton settlement sites, the buildings at Pen er Malo would seem to be characteristic for southern Brittany – so much so that it is permissible to ask whether these stone elliptical-plan buildings were not typical of this region from the twelfth century onwards.

Plumelec

Trial excavation took place in 1973 and 1974 on the site of a deserted village, now covered by woodland, at Kerlano-en-Plumelec (Morbihan). Two buildings forming a group, as at Pen er Malo, were revealed. The larger had an elliptical plan and dimensions (11.6 × 5m [36 × 16ft]) similar to that at Pen er Malo; it had two doors opening to the north and south respectively and almost opposite one another. The building was thus divided into two sections of unequal size, the larger (eastern) section being lower down the slope than the smaller. Although the Kerlano buildings were very similar to those at Pen er Malo, they were different in two respects: Kerlano seems to have been occupied and abandoned later than Pen er Malo – probably in the later thirteenth century – and the 'greasy' ware which predominated at the latter site represented no more than a tenth of the 400 sherds found at Kerlano, no doubt owing to its later period of occupation.

Nineteenth- to twentieth-century Breton mixed houses

Field survey has revealed other houses of this type. At Malguenac (Morbihan)

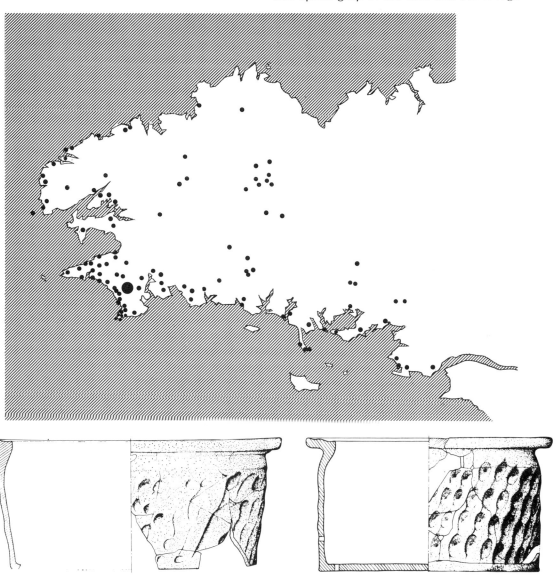

Fig. 75. *Pottery from the medieval village of Pen er Malo (Morbihan) – twelfth-century*

These two cooking pots, from the midden of house A (Figure 74), are typical of a special ware whose distribution is essentially confined to the south and west coasts of Brittany, and which was probably traded largely by coastal shipping. A possible production site appears to have been located at Bodérès (Finistère), shown by the large dot on the map.

(R. Bertrand and M. Lucas, Un village côtier du XIIe siècle en Bretagne, *Archéologie médiévale*, V (1975), fig. 10, p. 89; map based on P.-R. Giot, La céramique onctueuse de Cornouailles: contribution à l'étude de l'économie médiévale *Bull. Soc. archéol. Finistère* (1971), fig. 2, p. 123, brought up to date with material from 1978 investigations, with the kind help of the author) there were two elliptical buildings, joined as at Pen er Malo by a straight wall, and accompanied by a smaller building. In the forest of Pont-Callek (Morbihan), a group of ten such buildings was found, which may have survived until the nineteenth century. As at Pen er Malo and Plumelec, all these buildings measured about 12 × 6m (39 × 20ft).

The interpretation of these buildings from the socio-economic point of view becomes more interesting when account is taken of the fact that buildings of this type have survived in use very late in Brittany, as shown by the examples from Pont-Callek or others that are still standing, and were still in use in World War II.

Analysing the economic structure of nineteenth-century Brittany shows it to have been a region of smallholdings, largely dominated by farming on behalf of a landowner under the system of *métayage* (whereby the farmer pays rent in kind, the owner supplying seed and stock) or by tenant farming. Breton houses in this period were for this reason usually small, or at best modest in size. Two-storey houses, which were reserved to the rural middle class or to the richer peasant farmers, were rare: they possessed a measure of prestige and status, which to some extent persists.

This nineteenth-century peasantry, whose livelihood was based on corn production from their own smallholdings and a few animals, lived in rudimentary houses. The outbuildings were often even more primitive. Generally in lower Brittany, even in the first half of the present century, stocks of fodder and bedding for the animals were kept in stacks in the open air, without any protection. Grain was threshed in an area open to the skies. Whilst the introduction of lofts within the house itself is quite common in many Breton regions, for storing grain and fodder reserves, this was still not the general rule in the first half of the twentieth century: thus in Léon there were normally no lofts in nineteenth- and early twentieth-century buildings, no doubt owing to the shortage of timber. A more general reason was probably the difficulty in installing a loft with certain types of roof construction. One of the most widely used forms of roof construction in rural houses of this type in Brittany, even in the nineteenth century, consisted of collar rafters or crucks, which will be discussed in more detail later. These very primitive forms of roof construction, especially the latter, are ill-suited to the construction of lofts.

This is all the more remarkable when it is remembered that these rectangular buildings were usually inhabited by both men and animals. This holds good equally for the *longères* – the largest rectangular houses, often 12–16m (39–52ft) or more in length – and for the smaller examples, not exceeding 8–10m (26–33ft) in length, and also for those houses – the *loges*, for example – built with wooden poles and branches.

The area reserved for animals is as well-defined in the layout of these houses – at a lower level than that for the human occupants – as in the terminology. The *pen dreh* (high end) was reserved for humans and the *pen traon* (low end) for animals. Guests were invited to *sourd'ous diqu'an fouyer* (step up to the hearth) to occupy a place of honour. The smallest rectangular houses, between 8m (26ft) and 10m (33ft) long, were called *ti bihan* (ends of houses), which well illustrates the fact that the standard, common house would be a certain length.

The mixed houses were still the most common type in Brittany in the nineteenth and early twentieth centuries. They were even used by fishermen, who utilized the section usually reserved for animals to accommodate their equipment. They are now disappearing at a great rate. Certain examples recorded towards the end of World War II, as at Plumelin (Morbihan), shown in Figure 76, give a very accurate picture of these structures.

The relationship in the nineteenth and early twentieth centuries between these houses and the socio-economic situation of their inhabitants is very important for a study of medieval houses. They were occupied by the poorest section of rural society, and in particular by day labourers, peasants who were compelled for lack of lands of their own to offer themselves for hire. These houses, lying alongside roads, were very often located close to a large farm. For the present study, the interest does not lie in projecting this socio-economic structure and way of life backwards into the Middle Ages, but rather in understanding that it is because of this structure, which followed the breaking up of land ownership patterns in Brittany in the post-medieval period, and the survival of a subsistence agriculture based on the cultivation of certain cereals and the raising of a few animals, that this form of mixed dwelling continued in use after the end of the medieval period in Brittany, as in the Celtic areas of the British Isles. The medieval Breton houses, with their similar building techniques, probably the same primitive roof structures, access through two doorways (or sometimes only one) centrally placed in the longer sides, and a difference in level between the two sections of the building, are very close to these nineteenth- to twentieth-century examples. It is, consequently, legitimate to assume that, on the basis of various archaeological observations such as the absence of hearths and the small amount of pottery in their lower sections, the medieval examples housed both men and beasts. This is a very important case of the survival of a form of dwelling house, linked with a specific mode of farming economy, from the Middle Ages through to the nineteenth century, which is evidenced in the Celtic zones of the British Isles as well as in Brittany. The relationship between farming systems and house types, which is infinitely complex in other respects, is here very strong in that the persistence of such systems in these regions has resulted in a failure on the part of house types to change.

– Other French examples
The existence of comparable rural houses in other regions of France which present the same characteristics in relation to farming systems is proof of the absence of demonstrable relationships between race and building type, and at the same time provides a clue, based on nineteenth- to twentieth-century examples, to those areas where the mixed house must have made its appearance in the Middle Ages.

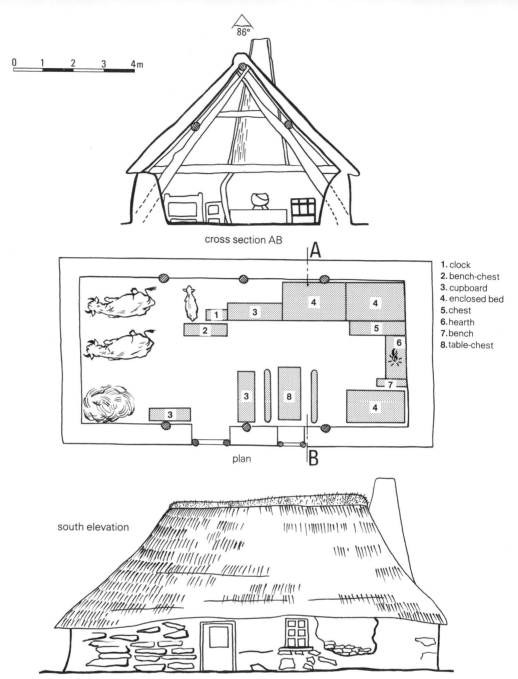

cross section AB

1. clock
2. bench-chest
3. cupboard
4. enclosed bed
5. chest
6. hearth
7. bench
8. table-chest

plan

south elevation

Fig. 76. *Contemporary mixed house at Plumelin (Morbihan)*

This small farming unit, studied in 1944, reveals several characteristics of comparable medieval buildings: an outbuilding near the dwelling house or *cave* (cellar), which is in fact a sunken hut; the plan, method of construction, and dimensions of the building itself.

There is no separation between humans and animals beyond that constituted by the furniture, and access for both is through a single common doorway. The roof is of cruck construction, without loft or staircase, and the roof is hipped.

(*Enquête sur l'architecture rurale*, doc. 44.215.7; Archives du Musée National des Arts et Traditions Populaires, Paris)

234

Savoy

In mountainous areas such as Savoy – in the Val d'Isère, for example, or in the Oisans, especially at Villars d'Arène – the same types of building, with the same characteristics (size, communal doorways for humans and animals, each occupying their end of a simple building), existed in the nineteenth century, surviving in places until the mid twentieth century. Records of buildings surviving at Villars d'Arène around 1940 even make it possible to trace the development of the mixed house, according to a model observed in certain cases in thirteenth-century Britain. At that time there were still existing, side by side in this Savoy village, mixed houses with a light but permanent partition between the two sections and a single doorway opening into the animal section (cf. Figure 71); buildings with a full wall between the two sections, but still with a single entrance giving on to the animal pens, and – the ultimate phase of development – a form of corridor behind the communal doorway, with access on one side into the dwelling part and on the other to the animals.

Ethnographic studies have established the existence of rural buildings of the same type in various other regions of France in the mid nineteenth century – Normandy, the Pas-de-Calais, the Ardennes, north-eastern France, the Massif Central, especially the Cantal, and the Lozère and Dordogne in the south-west.

Medieval mixed houses: the Forez

Analysis of medieval documents for a given region can furnish very important information, especially if this study is linked with excavations. An example is the Forez, a region on the north-eastern edge of the Massif Central.

A very large number of fourteenth-century wills provide an indication of rural houses, or at least of the terminology used to describe them. The most commonly used term is *domus*, mentioned in 1329 out of a total of 3228 units. This was the classic type of house, which could be urban or rural, consisting of one or more rooms, one of which contained a hearth or fireplace. These were thus houses very similar in this respect to, for example, the later medieval house of central Germany, i.e. the unitary house.

However, another type of house, styled *hospitium*, occurs in these documents. In 93 cases this refers to the rural residence of members of the urban middle classes, and in 33 cases to those of knights (*chevaliers*). This word is also used to designate the houses of peasants, but with a different meaning: the farm buildings, larger in size than the general run, of a well-to-do peasant. This is thus a case of a clear terminological distinction based on the strong social differentiation between two types of rural building. Thus a document of 1314, which by chance describes one of these *hospitii* more precisely, makes it possible to establish a typical plan which consisted, under a single roof, of centrally located main rooms, with fireplace and oven built into the wall which separated this room from a bedroom or *cellier*. The animals were housed at the other end of the building. Over all three sections there was a loft communicating with the outside by means of a window through which hay could be

235

brought, to be distributed to the animals through a hole in the ceiling. It is not at all certain that this was in fact a mixed house, although for various reasons it very likely was one: men and beasts were certainly living beneath the same roof, at different ends of a single building that was in all probability rectangular, but we know nothing of where the doors were and in particular of what provision was made for access and communication between the house and the exterior, or between the sections reserved for humans and animals respectively. It is not possible to assert that the Forez houses fit in well with the long house typology discussed above, though this would appear to have been the case, in all probability.

Other French medieval examples

The same kind of problem arises in other parts of France, where medieval documents describe various types of rural building, unfortunately always in an all too summary way, so that the houses cannot be assigned to precise categories with certainty. Take, for example, the houses of the village of Montaillou in the Ariège during the later thirteenth century. There are many references to animals – sheep, lambs, mules, swine, draught oxen – being stalled in the houses overnight, or sometimes permanently. There are also quite precise indications that dung from the stalled animals was taken out of the building through the doorway used by humans, some of whom, especially when they were ill, slept with the animals in the part reserved for the latter. As in the Forez, but perhaps with more certainty, these were mixed houses. However, the same documents seem to show that there were also, in the village or its immediate surroundings, houses that did not shelter animals, which provide interesting parallels with the *domus* of the Forez. These had, similarly, a main room with a fireplace (in this case a central hearth), the kitchen or *foganha*, which opened through a doorway into the *cave*, equivalent to the *cellier* of the Forez, which contained the bed or beds as well as wine casks and sundry other items. It would seem that there was a form of unitary house in use alongside mixed houses.

The close study of medieval documents from other regions of France might provide interesting material that would help to throw more light on the problems of the origin and distribution, at least over the last two or three centuries of the Middle Ages, of the mixed house and unitary house. In the Oisans region of Savoy, fourteenth- and fifteenth-century archives appear to prove that there were at that time mixed houses of the type we have seen to have existed in the early twentieth century.

Whatever the degree of accuracy in these written documents, data of the kind they supply are very important in so far as they attest – for example, in the fourteenth century Forez – the probable existence of the mixed house type that is recorded ethnographically several centuries later in the same regions. Moreover, these documents are invaluable, especially for the Forez, since they give an idea of the relative rarity of buildings of this type and of the social status of their occupants. They appear to have housed the richer fraction of the peasantry, who designated their dwellings with the term used also to denote the residences of the urban middle classes or the gentry. The presence under the same roof of men and animals in the Forez in the fourteenth century thus appears to be a sign of higher status in the peasant hierarchy and a mark of social success, at least in this region. This demonstrates the importance of a combined use of documentary and archaeological sources, and in particular of the potential value of documentary studies for the interpretation of archaeological data, especially in fields, such as rural buildings, where socio-economic implications are significant.

The example of the mixed house also demonstrates the close links that should exist between archaeological and ethnological observations – the complex but vital relationships between farming systems, socio-economic data, and house types. The history of medieval rural architecture should be based on and interpreted in the light of such data: the careful study of documents, ethnographic investigations of surviving monuments, and excavation in the case of earlier ones. In this way it should be possible to identify the major house types, the social stratification of the peasantry in the later Middle Ages, and the specific nature of regional types of traditional rural architecture, which gradually evolved, only to disappear in the post-medieval period, particularly in the eighteenth and nineteenth centuries.

Decline and abandonment of the mixed house

In the thirteenth and fourteenth centuries, as at Gomeldon for example, and later elsewhere, the mixed house yielded its place to the farm (cf. Figure 68). However, even in those regions where this new form of house appeared, the mixed house could remain in use (see Figure 77). It sometimes survived to the mid twentieth century, in north-western Ireland or Brittany for example (cf. Figure 71), inhabited by an impoverished peasantry.

It can thus be said, in conclusion, that the mixed house and the farm had a common origin: the developments in agricultural production after the eleventh to twelfth centuries, along with the growth in affluence of a section of the peasantry. This phenomenon affected a variable proportion of the peasants, in different regions, at different times and to different degrees. However, it was an analogous form of development, stemming from the same causes and bringing with it the same consequences. An observation by John Hurst even allows us to state that the two successive phases in the development of rural buildings correspond well with two hierarchically distinct grades of peasant. He has pointed out that, whereas in certain regions, such as Hangleton, the fourteenth-century abandonments caused by the general economic crisis affected villages that included farms, the enclosure movement, characterized by the expulsion of the peasantry and the demolition of villages by their overlords to make way in the sixteenth century for sheep pastures, affected villages such as Wharram Percy, consisting only of mixed houses. Whilst the former group of desertions were simply the result of a general situation which led to the reorganization of the rural economy, the process was possible in the

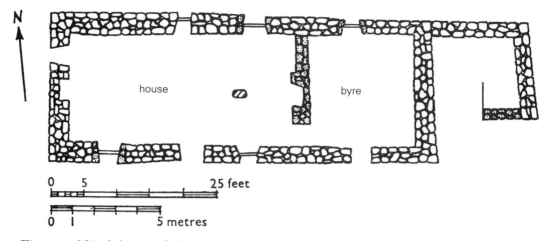

N

house · byre

0 5 25 feet

0 1 5 metres

Fig. 77. *Mixed house of the eighteenth to nineteenth centuries at Auchindrain, Argyll (Scotland)*

There were several buildings on this site, all thatched and of cruck construction. This one shows two phases. In the first there was a single room with a hearth on the floor, the smoke being evacuated through a hole still visible in the thatched roof. In the second phase, a stone partition was built in which a wall chimney was set, and three additional windows were pierced. Thus the building developed from a mixed house towards a two-roomed house, a progression to be seen elsewhere in Scotland, and in this village during the twentieth century.

(M. W. Beresford and J. G. Hurst, *Deserted Medieval Villages* (1971), fig. 35, p. 241)

---

latter case only in so far as the lord had the capability and the right to chase off the peasants, by virtue of their occupying a lower place in the medieval peasant hierarchy. These were, for example, smallholders who were compelled to cultivate the seigneurial lands in order to survive, whereas the occupants of the farms at Hangleton owned their lands and produced crops that were large enough to justify the erection of ancillary buildings. This idea, which John Hurst points out needs to be confirmed by further excavation, is very interesting because it shows to what extent the problems of the mixed house and the farm are two aspects of a single phenomenon which affected the rural world to differing extents and at various times in the Middle Ages and afterwards.

Conclusion

Between the twelfth and fifteenth centuries, types of rural architecture developed or spread which were to become classical elements of traditional rural architecture or the basis for social differentiation in a given region. To interpret these types of rural architecture correctly in these circumstances, it is essential to study not only the main building, that which serves entirely or partially as a dwelling, but also the ancillary buildings. Only in this way can the roles of the farming units or the activities of their inhabitants be established.

This poses the question of the agricultural basis of the existence of these villages, and in particular the presence or absence of livestock. It is, unfortunately, often difficult to be positive, because in many cases – as, for example, at Rougiers – the existence of structures with specialized functions, such as cowsheds or sheepfolds, outside the village proper cannot be ruled out. This is, in particular, a problem in the case of villages in the Mediterranean region. Ethnography shows that in this region animal husbandry had played, and continues to play, only a minor role in farming. There are only a few small animals such as goats, sheep and donkeys which take up little space in houses when they are kept within them. In fact they are usually left to roam outside, and so they deposit little dung and require little fodder, which means that there is no need for ancillary buildings such as barns.

Ethnographic data on farming in this zone allow us to go much further. The examples of Sardinia and Syria, amongst other countries, clearly show, in addition to the minor role of animals, the relative poverty in farming requirements, composed of a few tools and some reserves of food, often reduced to a few baskets of grain. At the same time, another classic characteristic of agricultural life in this region becomes apparent – the importance of activities that take place outside the house in the open air. As a result the house itself is often not specifically rural in character and is similar to the urban house. In this respect Rougiers, with its closely packed houses and the other features already described, is close to this type of rural settlement, which poses complex problems for the archaeologist who wishes to go beyond the mere architectural analysis of buildings found by excavation.

This highlights one of the difficulties of the archaeology of rural sites, especially when the study is concentrated on buildings and the inhabited centre of a cultivated landscape. It is difficult, on the basis of excavation alone, to reconstruct an economy and thereby to explain, so far as rural architecture, is concerned, the socio-economic bases of regional distinctions or those within a single village. Only a combination of the study of archaeological data detailed analysis of the cultivated or fossil landscape, and a knowledge of documentary sources permits any progress in this essential field, and in most regions research has not yet unfortunately progressed to this point. This explains the importance of excavations such as those at Rougiers or at Königshagen (Kr. Osterode).

Königshagen is a village established on newly cleared land around 1130–50; it was abandoned in the early fifteenth century following destruction by fire resulting from war. This village, which possessed a stone-built church, was built with a circular layout, and was composed partly of two-roomed houses, with fireplaces in the larger rooms built up against the wall that separated living room and bedroom, as at Hohenrode, and partly of farms made up of several buildings disposed round a yard. This represents the appearance alongside the unitary house of the courtyard farm (*Mehrseithof*) of central Germany, which became the classic type after the early medieval period. As at

Hohenrode, all these buildings were timber-framed, built on stone foundation walls.

The existence at the same time of both farms and two-roomed houses is of primary interest in this village, because a considerable part of its economy was based on craft activities and not solely on animal husbandry and agriculture. There was a pottery near the eastern entry into the village, and also a smithy producing tools for the inhabitants. A glassworks was situated in the surrounding woodland during the fourteenth century. Finally, salt extraction certainly played an important role in the economy of the village. This echoes, perhaps more strongly, the place of craft industries noted in villages such as Rougiers. Activities of this kind would certainly have fitted in better with the unitary houses than with the farms, where the main dwelling houses are strongly reminiscent of those buildings at Hohenrode that may be interpreted as mixed houses.

Furthermore, pollen diagrams show that there was a very significant change in the farming system at Königshagen towards the end of its history. The curve for cereals drops sharply in the closing decades of the fourteenth century, whilst that for plants associated with the development of pasture increases. There was thus a transformation in farming practice, with stock raising taking over from grain production, a phenomenon familiar from other parts of Europe in these troubled centuries. It was doubtless from this time, and more especially after the settlement had been abandoned, that the many narrow terraced fields, which can still be found in large numbers when carrying out field surveys around the site, were abandoned. These constitute the fossil cultivated lands of this deserted village.

Such transformations most probably explain, at the same time, the evolution of rural settlements in the later medieval centuries, the appearance of new types of building or the conversion of earlier types, and architectural differentiation in single villages or the creation of regional building types. The socio-economic foundations of these architectural phenomena are certainly decisive factors, and it is more important to understand them than all the ethnic factors which have often (in particular in the years before World War II) been put forward directly or covertly to explain certain regional types of architecture. It has been the ethnologists, using as their starting point the existing realities of surviving buildings, usually of the nineteenth century and rarely more than one or two centuries earlier, at least so far as the more common rural architecture is concerned, who have attempted to put forward interpretations based on considerations of this nature. Paradoxically, explanations of this kind are still being hawked around France. This leads to a delay in accepting the knowledge of medieval rural buildings derived from archaeological research, and to a consequent ignorance of the complexity of their types and development.

This leads us on to attempt, on the basis of the numerous examples that have been discussed and the resulting main lines of development, to define the common types of rural house in the period from the eleventh to the fifteenth century.

Fig. 78. *Ruins of a house at the village of Rougiers (Var)*

General view of buildings A1, A2 and A3 in block A (cf. village plan, Figure 57, and details of the development of this block, Figure 58), built on the edge of the cliff.

(Photograph kindly supplied by the excavator, Gabrielle Démians d'Archimbaud)

---

5 *The principal types of late medieval rural house*

The two-storied house

The two-storied house was, in the medieval rural world, pre-eminently a southern type of building, closely associated in particular with the enclosed hilltop villages in Provence and Italy, such as early thirteenth-century Rougiers (see Figure 78).

It was only very late, in fact as a result of developments in carpentry, that the two-storied house made its appearance in the more northerly regions of Europe – principally in the fourteenth century, but even later, in the fifteenth to sixteenth centuries, in Great Britain and Germany. In addition to the carpentry factor, the installation of an upper storey seems often to have been linked with the emergence in villages of some socio-economic differentiation, and the appearance of peasants who were capable and desirous of demonstrating their privileged status by means of their houses. Thus at Montaillou (Ariège), at the end of the thirteenth century, there were only a few houses with a bed chamber in the upper storey. It is significant that, around this time, a village shoemaker is recorded who wished to mark the

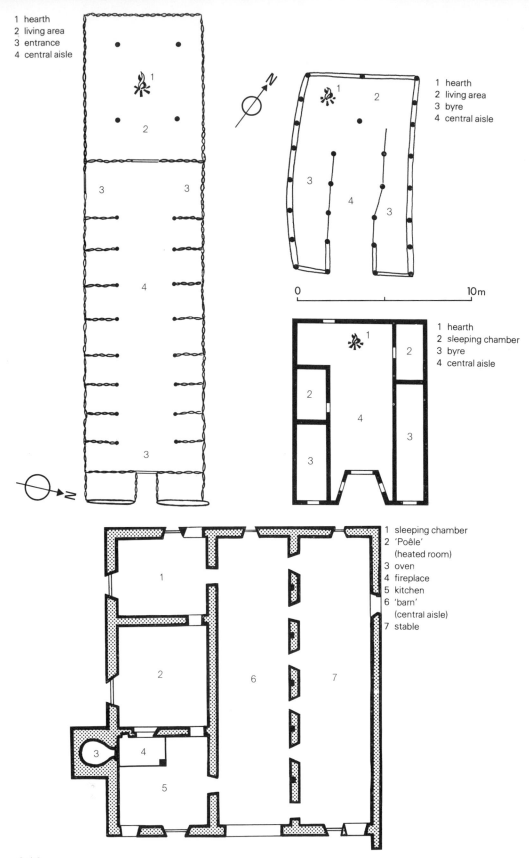

1 hearth
2 living area
3 entrance
4 central aisle

1 hearth
2 living area
3 byre
4 central aisle

0   10m

1 hearth
2 sleeping chamber
3 byre
4 central aisle

1 sleeping chamber
2 'Poêle'
  (heated room)
3 oven
4 fireplace
5 kitchen
6 'barn'
  (central aisle)
7 stable

Fig. 79. *Evolution of the Frisian byre-house from the first century AD to the present day*

a Feddersen Wierde (West Germany): first-century AD
b Ramm bei Lübtheen (East Germany): thirteenth-century 'Early Saxon' house from deserted village
c Traditional Dutch house with central aisle traversing the length of the building
d Moulin des Prés (Doubs, France): traditional farm (post-medieval)

In the region where a form of rural settlement developed in the Iron Age, composed of large rectangular buildings housing both humans and animals in relatively large numbers under the same roof, this house type, the *Wohnstallhall* (cf. Figure 29), persisted through the Middle Ages to the present day: these are 'old Frisian houses' (*altfriesische Wohnstallhallen*).

The Feddersen Wierde houses (a) are representative of this building type for the first to fifth centuries AD. Some of them could have housed several dozen head of cattle (cf. Figure 30). Access was either through the centre of one of the short sides or through one of the two openings that faced one another on the long sides; this defined a cross-passage that divided the roofed area into two parts, the larger for livestock, the smaller for humans. The latter was demarcated by a light partition and a hearth always occupied the centre of the open space.

This type of house persisted in this region during the Middle Ages, whilst in northern Germany a very similar house type (cf. Figure 29) appeared in the thirteenth century, the 'Lower German house' (*niederdeutsches Haus*). Medieval and post-medieval examples show the main characteristics of this type: the central passage was enlarged to accommodate vehicles, and the doorway in one of the short walls, giving access to the byre section, becomes the main entrance, and even the only means of access (b, c).

The section reserved for human occupation is usually central within the building, or sometimes on one side, especially in post-medieval examples. The hearth is, as a general rule, placed centrally. In various regions of France there are eighteenth- to nineteenth-century houses belonging to the same rural building type (d), although this betokens no more than the fact that a certain form of rural economy led to the adoption of the same building types in various places.

(*a:* B. Trier, *Das Haus im Nordwesten der Germania Libera*, IV, Veröffentlichungen der Altertumskommission im Provinzialinstitut für westfälische Landes- und Volkskunde, Aschendorffsche Verlagsbuchhandlung, Münster/Westfalen (1969), Tafel 8
b, c: W. Radig, *Frühformen der Hausentwicklung in Deutschland*, Berlin (1958), figs. 136, 137
d: Jean Raffi, Structures, *Techniques et architecture*, 1–2 (1947), p. 22)

---

improvement of his socio-economic status by erecting an upper chamber on his house.

The unitary house

This was the simplest and most widespread house type, and became the classical form from the early Middle Ages onwards, except in certain specific regions such as Frisia, where the large three-aisled house was preferred. The unitary house is to be found in all the early medieval villages of central and southern Germany and the whole of Anglo-Saxon England. It evolved gradually in the course of the Middle Ages – although an exact chronology is not possible nor can the phenomenon be regarded as a general one – generally in the direction of partition into two rooms, one with a hearth and the other without, usually interpreted as a bedroom. This can be observed in a number of Anglo-Saxon sites, and it becomes very pronounced from the eleventh to twelfth centuries onwards, both in German settlements such as Königshagen and on French sites like Dracy. In examples from the last three or four centuries of the Middle Ages, the replacement of the centrally placed open hearth by the wall fireplace, with a wooden or, much less commonly, stone chimney, is a characteristic feature, especially at the two sites just mentioned. Then come the buildings described in documents – at Montaillou in the late thirteenth century or the Forez in the fourteenth century. This distinction between the room containing the hearth (the hall) and the smaller bedroom (the chamber) alongside it, is to be observed in the various German sites of the thirteenth to fifteenth centuries.

There is no doubt that the unitary house remained a basic element in rural European buildings until the nineteenth century, with, naturally enough, many regional variations.

The mixed house

In its general layout, the mixed house often closely resembles a large unitary house. As soon as the developed plan of the latter, as set out above, becomes established, it is only possible to affirm that a building belongs to the mixed house type if the presence within it of both humans and animals can be demonstrated. From the archaeological point of view this is not always easy. However, given the implications of the appearance of this type of building in medieval Europe, as John Hurst has shown for the British Isles, it is essential to seek this double function rather than pursuing studies of house plans, which are largely meaningless in this connection.

The byre-house

As with the mixed house, the large Frisian byre-house is characterized by a double function and a specific building style (see Figure 79).

This is an early house type which antedates the mixed house; furthermore, it developed in the homeland of the Germanic peoples who invaded the British Isles in the early Middle Ages. In consequence, the notion of a relationship between byre-houses and mixed houses has been put forward. However, a connection of this kind is not required to explain the origins of the mixed house in the British Isles: indeed, this would seem to be altogether improbable.

One of the main arguments in this regard is the actual structure of the byre-house. In all the Frisian examples these are three-aisled structures (Figure 79b), whereas in Britain and elsewhere they are always single-aisled. Furthermore, the large byre-house is always to be found in regions where stock raising is of considerable importance: it was designed for flocks and herds numbering several dozen animals, just the opposite of the situation in respect of the mixed house. The appearance of the latter in the late twelfth or thirteenth century was, moreover, not a specifically English phenomenon but was apparently, as we have tried to show, a European phenomenon of which abundant evidence has survived. Thus there were two distinct traditions of buildings that housed men and beasts under the same roof which have persisted down to the present day: the large three-aisled byre-houses and the single-aisled mixed houses. Even though the former diffused over a larger area in the later Middle Ages and after that, they did not overlap with the latter. Again, the period when large three-aisled byre-houses began to appear outside Frisia in northern Germany is just that in which mixed houses came into general use in other regions of Germany and elsewhere, the thirteenth century. A form of three-aisled house made its appearance in Lower Saxony around this time, as H. Hinz has shown. Like the mixed house in the Celtic regions of the British Isles and in Brittany and other parts of France, it was to remain the basic form of traditional rural building until the nineteenth century.

The fact that these two phenomena – the coming into general use of the mixed house and the enlargement of the surface area of the byre-house – came about simultaneously, suggests that they resulted from a single cause, the growth in importance of stock raising. There is an additional factor affecting the simultaneous development of both types of building: in the case of the Lower Saxony house, the influence of the Frisian byre-house cannot be demonstrated, contrary to what might be expected. It would appear that the Lower Saxony three-aisled byre houses, which first appeared in the thirteenth century, formed the buildings of large-scale farming enterprises, especially those connected with monastic foundations. This is a fundamental point, because once again it becomes necessary to consider building types developed earlier, in response to the requirements of a specific type of farming economy, in order to understand the origins of an enlarged rural building that assigns a major importance to the housing of livestock. In Lower Saxony, as in the case of the mixed house, the crucial factor is not the introduction of a copy of a house type from some other region, but rather those general socio-economic factors that have already been emphasized, all exerting pressure in the same direction.

The farm

In the same way it can be said that the appearance of the farm, where the dwelling house, whether at Gomeldon or Königshagen, was often originally a mixed house, is merely another manifestation of the same evolutionary process, in this case through to its conclusion. In most of the regions under consideration in this study, in fact, the type of rural settlement that constitutes the farm proper was always established at around the same time, either in conjunction with or in competition with the mixed house.

In the course of this survey of late medieval house types, we have seen the traditional rural building types evolving rapidly and those categories of building appearing that were later to provide the bases for traditional rural architecture. However, they should not be defined solely in terms of building plans and functions: the materials and techniques used constitute another element which plays a very important part in the definition of regional forms of architecture. Did the later Middle Ages, in this field also, represent a period of transition, even a direct break, from the materials and techniques of earlier times? Will the same phenomena of regional differentiation and establishment of local forms of rural architecture become apparent?

Chapter Six: Medieval building materials and techniques

So far as materials are concerned, the medieval house of all periods remained closely dependent upon local resources that were immediately accessible, obtained either directly or by exercising user rights. In the latter case, this meant in many regions of France that timber for house building could be taken without charge from the thirteenth century onwards. However, in most cases the possibilities open to the peasants were limited, in that they were restricted to timber for repairs, and only very rarely extended to material for building new houses; moreover, material taken in this way had to be second-quality timber. Thus there were often problems in getting hold of some materials such as timber, to say nothing of stone, which was even more difficult to procure. This certainly explains the high values put on some later peasant houses, as shown by documents of the later Middle Ages, from Worcestershire, for example.

In these circumstances the dependence of some peasants on the natural environment becomes evident; it also explains the role of manorial buildings or communal edifices such as the country church. They were often sources of material for rebuilding – timber offcuts, for example. Indirectly they were of considerable importance, because they attracted skilled craftsmen to a village who would communicate new technological practices, since the peasant population always played a large part in various ways in the construction of exceptional buildings of this kind. These, moreover, also resulted in significant investments being made that were of value to the rural community – the opening up of quarries, for example, or the laying down in a more or less summary way of service roads.

The medieval peasant was dependent on wood above all else. He made use of it in various ways, but principally for timber framing, and later for foundations, and of course regularly for roof timbering.

A Foundations

1 *Individual upright posts*
Medieval houses can display various types of foundation according to the types of material used, especially for walls. In many cases – throughout the whole of the early Middle Ages, at least up to the ninth to tenth centuries in Anglo-

Saxon England (see Figure 80a) or the German Rhineland, for example – no foundations at all were used: the only building elements bedded in the ground were the upright posts of walls, the bases of which were set in holes dug for them, then filled in different ways and compacted.

2 Posts in foundation trenches

Some improvement was brought about by bedding the uprights, not directly in individual postholes, but in holes dug into the bottoms of foundation trenches which marked out the layout of the building in the ground. This gave better insulation because the walling materials were inserted into the ground instead of lying on top of it. Some of the latest Anglo-Saxon houses at Chalton had foundations of this type, whereas the earlier buildings fell into the first category, like those in almost all the known German and Dutch villages earlier than the eighth century (see Figure 80).

Both these building methods would certainly have made it difficult to conserve the walls properly. Being essentially constituted of degradable materials, particularly wattle and daub, or of planks arranged horizontally or vertically in various ways, walls were vulnerable to direct contact with the soil and humidity. Nevertheless, such techniques remained in use until a relatively late date, even for buildings that used more elaborate materials elsewhere in their construction – Yorkshire manor houses (see Figure 81), for example, or the tenth- to eleventh-century Scandinavian churches known from excavations, such as that of St Maria Minor at Lund (Sweden).

3 Interrupted or continuous sill beams

It was this major disadvantage, which all house builders would doubtless have experienced, that led to the introduction of the technique of construction on sill or sleeper beams, especially when tongued and grooved boards were being used for the walls. In this case the walls rested on beams lying directly on the ground, and later on a stone wall base. Two different systems were in use. In the first of these, the structure of the walls included large-diameter vertical bracing elements, designed to support the roof timbering either directly or indirectly through a wall plate. This produces a system of short lengths of sill beam linking vertical elements that are sunk into the ground. The tenth-century site at Husterknupp is a good example of this type of construction, as are some wooden Scandinavian churches of later centuries (cf. Figure 88).

In the other system, the wall is made up entirely of homogeneous materials, particularly tongued and grooved boards, without separate bearer elements, the roof timbering being carried on posts inside the building. In this case, there is no need to break up the sill beam, which is therefore continuous, the walls resting on a rigid frame set into the ground – e.g. the eleventh- to twelfth-century buildings at Büderich, constructed like those at Husterknupp out of vertical tongued and grooved boards (cf. Figure 90).

In normal conditions of preservation, a structure of this kind will leave no

Fig. 80. *House at the Anglo-Saxon settlement of Chalton (Hampshire) – sixth to seventh centuries*

Several house-building techniques were used at Chalton, and these left different below-ground traces. The simplest method used posts sunk individually into the ground, each with its own posthole (A). In some cases another technique was used: first a foundation trench was dug corresponding with the outline of the building, and posts were set in this to support the walls. The features in B are both foundation trenches and individual postholes. These two types of foundation represent different types of wall (cf. Figure 105).

(P. V. Addyman and D. Leigh, The Anglo-Saxon Village at Chalton, Hampshire, *Medieval Archaeology*, 17 (1973), pl. v)

249

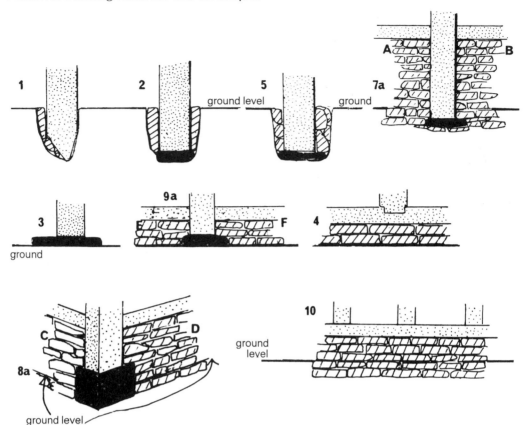

Fig. 81. *Types of foundations used in moated houses in Yorkshire, thirteenth to fifteenth centuries*

The simplest system was that of individual posts, as in the first building phase at Newstead (1). The same system was used again on this site later, but with the posts resting on flat stones at the bottom of the postholes (2). The same can be seen at East Haddlesey in the building that antedates the moat and which must be dated to the thirteenth century (5).

In the course of the thirteenth to fifteenth centuries, the use of stylobates became general in buildings of this type in Yorkshire, including later buildings on the two sites referred to above: the posts rested on flat stones lying directly on the ground surface (3). This technique has the disadvantage of leaving little trace if the stones are subsequently removed.

In the fourteenth to fifteenth centuries, interrupted sill beams began to be used, resting on a stone wall base that varied in height; the wall was partly buried in a foundation trench and interrupted at intervals by vertical posts. This system is to be found, in various forms, at East Haddlesey (7, 8).

Finally, in this part of Yorkshire at least, the fifteenth century saw the introduction of the continuous sill beam on a stone wall base at Rest Park, where the wall was partly below ground (10). This can be seen in the sixteenth century at Newstead, which is the model for the traditional building method of this region, with its wall base built above ground and a continuous sill beam.

(H. E. Jean Le Patourel, *The Moated Sites of Yorkshire* (1973), fig. 30, p. 69)

trace in the ground. It is, therefore, difficult to recognize the existence of such structures, or to get any idea of how this technique was diffused. It would appear, however, that the sill beam method (*Ständerbau*) was common in Germany as early as the Carolingian period, especially in the middle and upper Rhine regions – at Zimmern, Burgheim, Weimar, and a monastery at Bonn. This was possibly an early measure of differentiation between these regions and northern Germany, which remained faithful to the post form of building and which preferred the interrupted sill beam method in the later Middle Ages to the *Ständerbau* technique.

These two systems were obviously used in association with various walling materials, including the use of wattle and daub made from raw clay or cob.

4 Stone wall bases

It is probable, though not certain, that the use of a low stone wall base to support the sill beam, which in turn supported the frame and walls of the building, was introduced after the ground-level sill beam (Figure 81). To judge from the known examples from England or southern Germany, where this technique was relatively common, it began to be used in the eleventh to twelfth centuries on rural sites. There are good examples from Wharram Percy (cf. Figure 66a) in England, and from Wülfingen, Tilleda, Hohenrode, Königshagen, Sindelfingen, and elsewhere in Germany.

Finally, there are types of structure which are specific, for various reasons, to certain geographical regions or to later periods and which pose different problems in connection with their foundations: these are the 'log cabin' structures and those built in stone.

5 Walls of horizontally laid logs

This technique, analogous to the contemporary log cabins of foresters in Canada, for example, is well known from Slav sites and, in a more sporadic way, from Scandinavia – at Sigtuna, for example. There are those who would have this to be an essentially Slav technique, used by Scandinavian peoples under Slav influence. However, examples of this technique are known from southern Germany, and even in the Alps and the Vosges, from before the medieval period. The eleventh-century building at Colletière, Charavines (Isère) makes partial use of this technique. In fact, the distribution of this form of construction is more closely related to problems of raw materials than to ethnic problems. The trees that are best suited to this technique are the conifers, which have long straight trunks, with relatively small and constant diameters and low densities. Thus the technique is logically restricted in its application to these well wooded regions. The larch, for example, was widely used in this way in the post-medieval period, especially in regions of France such as the Queyras or the Briançonnais.

Post-medieval examples such as this, like others from outside the Alps or the Massif Central – in the Agenais, for instance, where such houses exist – raise the question of the extent of the utilization of this technique in France in the Middle Ages. Unfortunately there is very little information on this point. In the Lot-et-Garonne or the Dordogne, some houses built in this way may date back to the sixteenth or perhaps even the fifteenth century.

Finally, there is an important point relating to the consumption of timber. A house and its ancillary structures built in this way require hundreds of tree trunks, and so the use of this technique necessitates a very dense forest cover. It is for this reason that it is often associated with pioneer settlers in a heavily forested region, such as North America in the nineteenth century. The transition from the horizontal tree trunk house or log cabin to the plank-built house not only lightens the problems of transporting raw materials but also reduces the consumption of timber fivefold.

6 *Stone walls*

The medieval stone house poses some relatively complex problems. All that need be said here is that in those villages that are built in stone – i.e. essentially later than the twelfth or even the thirteenth centuries, except in the Mediterranean region – there is a general absence of foundations. The walls are often set directly on the existing ground level, as shown by many English, French, and German villages of the thirteenth to fifteenth centuries.

B Wall construction

The medieval rural building often consists primarily of a wooden framework showing varying degrees of development in construction and assembly. The walling material is inserted into this framework. Thus, except in the case of stone buildings, this is essentially a frame architecture. The methods of jointing and preparation were in general somewhat crude. The work of Bendix Trier on the houses of north-western Germany shows how it is, none the less, possible to erect large and even grandiose buildings using this technique.

1 *Primitive structure*

The construction of the simplest wooden frame, without mortices and tenons, usually making use of undressed posts rather than squared beams, is known as a primitive structure. It dominated rural building until very recently, the actual date being somewhat variable – indeed, it can still be seen in use, admittedly for ancillary buildings, in France, Germany, and the Netherlands.

2 *Primitive timber framing*

The appearance from the tenth to eleventh centuries onwards in rural building of new possibilities, such as the use of mortices and tenons and a more developed method of joining the structural elements, was probably a gradual process. Jointing took place when the frame was being erected, and the elements of the frame, even when they were squared up in cross-section, were very often not straight. The general practice of squaring up timbers and the use

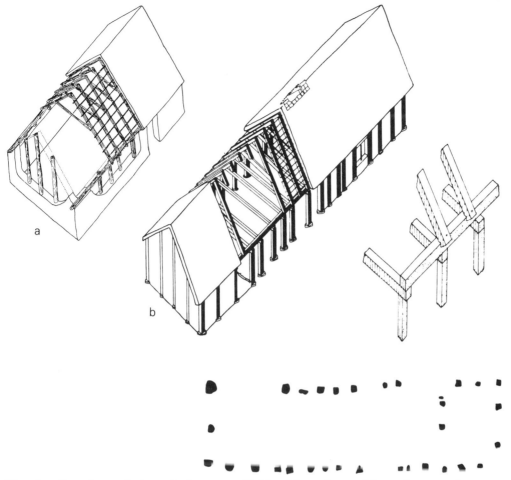

Fig. 82. *Framing techniques in houses at Goltho (eleventh- to thirteenth-century)*

The houses of phase 1 (a), which correspond to the end of the Anglo-Saxon period and the early Norman period (eleventh to twelfth centuries), were built of unsquared timbers set directly in individual postholes. The posts were aligned longitudinally, since they supported wall plates on which the roof timbering was carried. In phase 3 (thirteenth-century) (b), the upright posts, now of squared-up timbers, were aligned transversely in pairs, but not along the long sides. This means that the wall plates were no longer carried by the uprights but by the tie beams, the ends of which were now supported by the wall posts and which carried the wall plates. This house is typical of primitive framing. A fully developed timber-framed building has a logical jointing assembly between wall plates, collar rafters, and wall posts.

(G. Beresford, *Clay Land Village: excavations at Goltho and Barton Blount* (1975), fig. 18, p. 38; fig. 19, p. 42)

of wall plates can be associated with this development. These different elements would have been introduced gradually, but they are not to be found all in use at the same time in rural buildings earlier than the twelfth to thirteenth centuries (see Figure 82). It is in this way that it is possible to reconstruct the chronology of framing techniques in villages where the opportunity exists to study houses dating from the early Middle Ages until at least the thirteenth century, such as Barton Blount or Goltho.

3 Timber framing

Around the time that primitive timber framing became established in rural building, i.e. the twelfth to fourteenth centuries, a more developed form of building structure was evolved. This was a more complex structure which developed further after the end of the medieval period, but which retained its distinctive characteristics: rectangular frames of squared timbers, using mortices and tenons for elaborate joints; often very complicated prefabrication of the frame in the craftsman's workshop for subsequent re-erection on site; and a degree of standardization of types of structure, jointing techniques, and modular components. There is evidence of a system of assembly of complete elements in the structure, or bays (*chas*): houses were described in documents by a number of internal volumes, expressed in material terms by four load-bearing posts in the walls (or corner posts) which supported two trusses. A house would normally consist of two or three bays, sometimes more.

It is likely that this developed form of timber framing began in the towns and spread into the countryside. Various discoveries and documentary references suggest that this type of construction reached the rural world in the fourteenth century; it was certainly there in the fifteenth century, though only marginal in its application. It was, doubtless, its arrival in the countryside that explains the decline in or abandonment of building in stone (at Wharram Percy, for example), a phenomenon which can be observed in several regions in the fourteenth and fifteenth centuries. This proves that the transition from primitive framing to building in stone in the twelfth and thirteenth centuries was one form of progress, but not the only one: for a variety of reasons the subsequent abandonment of stone in favour of timber framing also represented a new step forward.

In this form of construction, the walls could be filled with wattling more or less evenly coated with clay daub, and also with squares of fired clay or bricks, as seems to have been the case in some towns, such as Cambrai as early as the fourteenth century. This confers greater strength and a longer life on walls. Whilst this transition did take place in rural architecture in the last two centuries of the medieval period, its application was nevertheless very restricted and partial, for reasons which will become apparent later.

C Walling materials

Considerations of climate and soil play an important role in this field and strongly influenced rural building, resulting in distinctive regional styles developing as far back as the early Middle Ages.

1 Wattle and daub

One of the most common walling materials must have been wattle and daub –

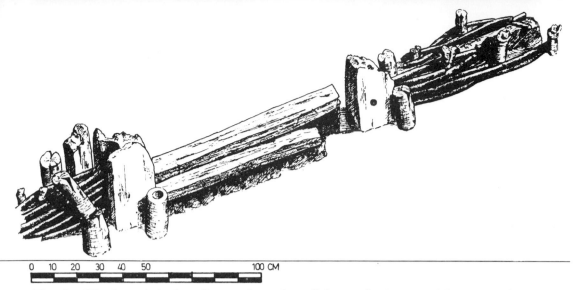

```
0    10   20   30   40   50              100 CM
```

Fig. 83. *Wattle and daub walling and wooden sill beam of a house in Winetavern Street, Dublin (Ireland) – eleventh to twelfth centuries*

The walls were constructed by setting straight branches upright in the ground, to support an interlace of thinner, supple branches of hazel, ash or elm. A coating of clay probably ensured that the walls were wind- and watertight. On either side of the door sill, two upright beams of oak formed the jambs of the doorway. These were grooved on the sides opposite the doorway to accommodate and hold the wattling. Two pairs of small uprights, one inside and the other outside the building up against the wall and touching the jambs, served to strengthen this point.

(B. O'Riordain, Excavations at High Street and Winetavern Street, Dublin, *Medieval Archaeology*, 15 (1971), fig. 25, p. 82)

---

interlaced tree branches coated with raw clay – both for sunken huts and for structures built at ground level. It is sometimes possible in excavations to observe indications of the small upright stakes around which the branches were entwined, situated between the large wall posts: there are examples from Hound Tor (Britain), the Carolingian settlements at Oberbillig and Gladbach (Germany), and Dieue-sur-Meuse (France). In some exceptional cases the circumstances of the destruction of a building and the nature of the soil were such that all the wattling is preserved: excavations in the medieval port of Dublin (Ireland) have produced such evidence (see Figure 83) – in town houses, of course, but nevertheless thoroughly representative of the materials used in contemporary rural buildings. It is, notwithstanding, difficult to be sure to what extent the developed techniques of wattle and daub, such as those used in rural buildings of the eighteenth and nineteenth centuries, were in use in the Middle Ages.

2 Cob

There is another way in which unfired clay can be used, in addition to wattle and daub, but unfortunately this leaves very little trace: that is cob. To construct cob walls a mixture of liquid clay, chopped straw, and gravel is

Fig. 84. *Cob house at Wallingford, Oxfordshire – late twelfth-/early thirteenth-century*

The construction in the thirteenth century of an earthen rampart preserved this remarkable earlier building, which was buried under the material brought in for this new feature. No windows can be seen in the walls as they now stand. The roof, the nature of which is not known, was probably tiled. The precise function of this building is difficult to determine; it is, however, the best preserved specimen known to date of a medieval cob building.

(Photograph by kind permission of the excavator, Robert Carr)

---

poured into plank shuttering in successive layers. This gives a wall of a certain thickness which does not need supporting with upright posts. Walls formed in this way are surmounted by wall plates. Such walls, which are relatively thick – often more than 50cm (20in.) – are normally given a protective coating externally, on surviving specimens at any rate. This method of building walls is well known in certain regions of Europe through more recent structures, notably in Great Britain and France. It is difficult to identify this technique in excavations except in exceptional circumstances, and so to establish its antiquity. This was the case in the excavation of a motte built around 1250 at Wallingford Castle, Oxfordshire (England), illustrated in Figure 84. A cob building was found measuring 8.5m (28ft) by 12.5m (40ft) externally, divided into three rooms, each with its own hearth and constructed at ground level; it was buried by the rampart, which in effect fossilized it. The walls were remarkably well preserved, up to a height of some 1.8m (6ft), which made it possible to observe that there was no provision for windows up to this level. In other regions of England where cob is still a traditional material, such as Cornwall, Devon, Norfolk, Buckinghamshire, Huntingdonshire, Northamptonshire and Lincolnshire, excavations have shown that it was already in use in the Middle Ages.

The situation in France is the same, although there are fewer data because so few villages have been excavated. Nevertheless, examples of the use of cob are known from the twelfth century in Limagne, notably in the sunken huts at

Lezoux (Puy-de-Dôme). The urban excavations at Tours by Henri Galinié have revealed a Carolingian building constructed in this material.

Some technical aspects of the use of cob, known from recent structures built in this material, are worth stressing, since they make it possible to characterize this building technique in relation to a given socio-economic context. First, the use of cob normally assumes a certain level of humidity in the material when it is used, coupled with a fairly rapid drying rate. Rainy seasons must, therefore, be avoided for building operations. For these reasons the normal period for building in cob in the last century was from May to August or September.

Another important factor is that building walls in cob needs a sustained working rate and, consequently, a fairly large labour force – at least a dozen people. Up to the beginning of the present century, this labour force was obtained by a collaborative effort on the part of villagers. Cob was probably used in many regions of Europe in the medieval period, particularly in the south. In the alluvial plains around the Mediterranean – Italy, Spain or Egypt – a very ancient tradition of building in cob or mud was still maintained in the early years of the present century.

In the Levante of eastern Spain, the technique of *tapial* or building in *cajones* (caissons), especially for fortifications, is of some antiquity, since it was known to the Moslems there in the tenth century. This was a high-grade form of cob, consisting of a large quantity of lime added to the clay and gravel, which produces a very hard fabric. This was a classic technique throughout the Moslem period from the tenth century onwards – in the Castellón region, for example.

In some cases unfired bricks were used instead of cob. The regions in which this technique could be used were obviously circumscribed by climatic considerations. Ethnographic studies have shown that it was used in certain southern regions of France, such as Bresse and the Agenais. Once again it still has to be proved that this technique was in use in these regions or elsewhere in the Middle Ages. However, these are clay regions where the soil itself must have constituted the most favoured building material in the Middle Ages, in one form or another. In exceptional cases it has proved possible to demonstrate the use of unfired bricks in the Gallo-Roman period – in the recent excavations in the rue des Farges at Lyons, for example.

3   Turf blocks

This material was still being used widely in the eighteenth and nineteenth centuries in the colder, windier regions of Europe and those with clay soils, where grass grows very densely – Denmark, Norway, the northern coastal regions of Germany, Iceland, the provinces of Drenthe and Veluwe in the Netherlands, Ireland, the Campine in Belgium, and several parts of France and Britain. In Scotland, for example, most peasant houses were still being built in this material in the eighteenth and nineteenth centuries, as contemporary descriptions and reports by travellers testify.

The turf was cut, using a special tool, into rectangular blocks a little larger than a brick. The English village of Hound Tor provides a good example of construction using turfs up against a wattle framework (cf. Figure 94). In German settlements on the North Sea littoral, turf was often used in the form of a wide low wall. The best preserved example so far known is the Danish site of Solvig (see Figure 85), since the outlines of the turfs could still clearly be made out when the walls were sectioned or cleaned down. In certain cases turf was also used as a roofing material, with the grass uppermost.

The use of this material for building is linked with a type of farming that was dependent upon an abundance of grassland. The rich terminology associated with turf in German, and more particularly in English, is direct proof of the importance of this type of farming, at the same time testifying to the wide use of turf for building in these regions.

In the British Isles, there are eight different terms used for the same material, according to whether it is undisturbed, removed to permit ploughing, or cut and lifted for building purposes. Words such as turf, sod, sward, flag and flaw (the last-named in northern England) are used in this way to designate precisely blocks of turf that have been cut and lifted for various purposes. An even more specific vocabulary is used in Scotland: the thick blocks for walls are feals and the thinner ones used for roofing are divots. The terms flag and flaw are used more widely in England to apply to flat stones as well as turfs (*lave* and *lauze* in French, and occasionally *gazon*, the general word for turf). Similarly, in German there is a distinction made between *Torf* (undisturbed turf or peat) and *Sode*, a cut block of this material, used for building walls, for example. The abundance and specific nature of this turf vocabulary leaves no doubt as to the importance of this material, particularly for building, in at least two cultural regions (the British Isles and northern Germany), even though the usual level of preservation makes archaeological observations rare and fortuitous.

4   Wood

Whilst timber plays a very important role in rural architecture as a constructional element of walls and roofs, as we have seen, it is often also used to form the walls themselves – as a bracing material for wattle and daub, for example. In some cases wood alone is used to constitute walls.

Vertical trunks and plank palisade walls

The use of tree trunks stacked horizontally has already been described. However, there are some examples known of vertical thin-section trunks, sunk into the ground and ranged closely together, so as to form an enclosure wall rendered weathertight with cob. An example of this form of construction was found at Stammheim (Kr. Calw, West Germany). This building (cf. Figure 97) has been dated very accurately to 1288 by dendrochronology.

In a sense, this building is heir to the wall building technique using thin tree trunks, either whole or split, to form a wall, known from well before the

Fig. 85. *Turf block wall at Solvig (South Jutland) – fourteenth-century*

A wall some 2.8m (9ft) thick was built from turf blocks averaging 60cm (24in) long by 10cm (4in.) thick, bonded to one another by long wooden stakes, which had also survived.

a Vertical view of building; b oblique view of wall; c vertical section of wall.

(Photographs by kind permission of the excavator, J. Hertz)

259

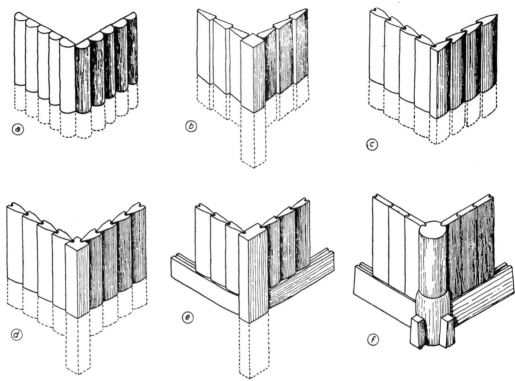

Fig. 86. *The palisade wall and the vertical plank wall in the Middle Ages*

Primitive forms of vertical plank wall (*Stabbau*):

a Palisade wall (*Palisadenbau*)

b Palisade wall with posts (*Pfostenbau mit Palisadenwand*)

Development of vertical plank wall:

c Tongued-and-grooved plank wall (*Stabwand-Bau*)

d Tongued-and-grooved plank wall with posts (*Pfosten-Stabbau*)

e Interrupted sill beam with posts and tongued-and-grooved planks (*Pfosten-Stabbau mit Schwellriegel-Konstruktion*)

f Tongued-and-grooved planks on continuous sill beam (*Ständer-Stabbau*)

(A. Herrnbrodt, *Der Husterknupp, eine niederrheinische Burganlage des frühen Mittelalters* (1958), fig. 78, p. 189)

Roman period in southern Germany and the Alpine region (see Figure 86). Good examples were discovered at Aichbühl (2500–200 BC) and Goldberg (c.600 BC). This form of construction can be termed the *palisade wall*; it was in use for a very long period, extending into the Middle Ages. Medieval examples from Germany in addition to Stammheim that may be quoted are from Husterknupp (building 4, tenth century), Haithabu (ninth to nineteenth centuries), and Emden; there are others known from Wolin (Poland) and Sigtuna (Sweden). A Merovingian example on a low foundation wall, excavated at Saint-Victor-de-Massiac, may well be assigned to this method of building in

Fig. 87. *Greensted Church, Essex*

The southern wall of the church is made up of vertical timbers; this dates to the eleventh century, but the rest of the church is largely later in date.

(National Monuments Record, London)

---

wood (cf. Figure 95). The technique appears to be Continental in origin, more specifically from central Europe, and it seems to have spread gradually northwards. Two different forms of palisade wall can be distinguished, depending on whether or not there are large posts at intervals along the sides and at the corners.

Jointed vertical planks (Stabbau)

There was a development of the palisade wall, which may have begun in the same area – southern Germany and the Alpine region. The chronology is not well understood, but several excavations (especially on German sites) have shown that the technique was widely used in the ninth to twelfth centuries. It is usually designated the *Stabbau* technique (building with vertical elements), using the German term. This is a development of the palisade wall consisting of the introduction of joints between the vertical planks that make up the wall, in this case tonguing and grooving (see Figure 86). The use of this technique made walls especially weathertight.

Before studying the chronology of the use of this method of wall construction and the regions in which it was used – two questions which pose complex problems that are as yet difficult to resolve – let us first examine the various types of *Stabbau* known from the Middle Ages.

– *Types of Stabbau*

The palisade wall techniques developed from the two forms described above into two types of *Stabbau*, based on the presence or absence of wall posts at corners or spaced at regular intervals (see Figure 86). Into the first group, without wall posts, fall a number of Scandinavian churches, notably those of St Maria Minor and St Clement at Lund, Sweden (tenth to eleventh centuries), Jelling, Denmark (tenth century), and Greensted, England (eleventh century: Figure 87), along with secular buildings, such as those in the town of Lund (eleventh century), at the great fortress at Trelleborg, Denmark (early eleventh century), and at the rural settlement of Lindholm Høje, Denmark (eleventh century). In all the cases it was necessary to use interval posts to support the roof structure.

The second group, which is less common and which makes use of wall posts, is represented by house 1 at the twelfth- to thirteenth-century German settlement of Emden (Ostfriesland). Here the upright panels between the posts were set in a wall trench, as was the case with all the examples of the first group.

The evolution of *Stabbau* construction followed the classical mode of all forms of wall frame building: from post-built structures with filling, to the use of interrupted sill beams and then a progression to an integral frame based on a continuous sill beam, or *Standerbau* (cf. Figure 86).

The use of interrupted sill beams between earth-fast posts is known from

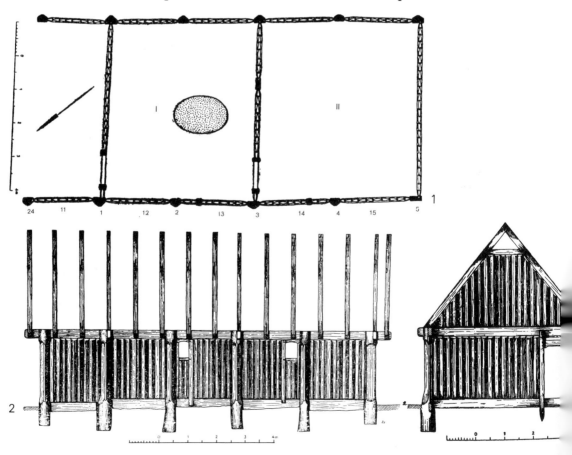

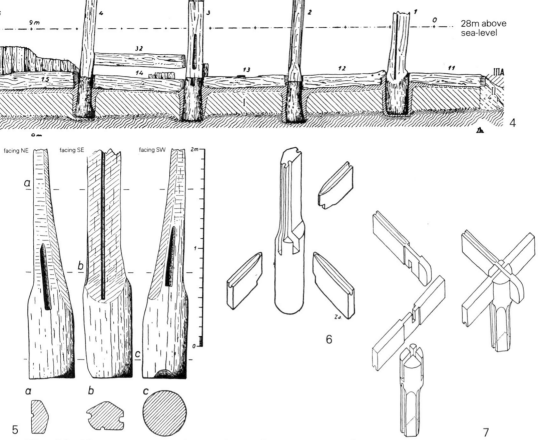

Fig. 88. *House 3 at Husterknupp (West Germany) – tenth-century*

This is one of the best preserved examples of construction using vertical tongued-and-grooved boards.

1 Plan (partly reconstructed) of the building *c*.1 m (3ft 3in.) above occupation level

2, 3 Elevations (reconstructed) of the north-west wall (2) and north-east gable (3). The slope of the rafters was calculated to be 51°. The rather small windows were at the top of the plank walls, immediately beneath the wall plate, so as to avoid excessive complexity in building.

4 Elevation of the remains of the north-west wall, after excavation (drawn from the interior). The foundation trenches for the interrupted sill beams and deeper circular postholes can be distinguished. Posts 1, 3 and 5, to which both the external wall and the internal partitions were tied, show clearly the grooves for the latter (cf. 5)

5 Elevation and section at three levels of one of the posts of the north-west wall. It was circular in section at its base and rebated above, with two grooves to accommodate the boards of the external wall on either side, and an additional groove for the internal partition.

6 Detail of jointing between post 3 and the three sill beams that converge on it. The latter are grooved to receive the vertical planks making up the external and internal walls.

7 Reconstruction of the jointing between post 1, which formed the north-west corner of house 3, the wall plate, and the tie beam which defined the western end wall of the building.

(A. Herrnbrodt, *Der Husterknupp, eine niederrheinische Burganlage des frühen Mittelalters* (1958), figs. 13, 17, 63–5, 67, 73)

263

innumerable buildings of the ninth to fourteenth centuries, both sacred and secular. There are examples from German fortified sites of the ninth century (Stellerburg, Dithmarschen) and the tenth century (Husterknupp, Rhineland: Figure 88), from the tenth-century urban settlement at Haithabu (Schleswig), from the Danish churches of Nörre Hörning (eleventh century) and Bröru (eleventh to twelfth centuries), from twelfth-century urban contexts at Antwerp, Emden and Lund, from the thirteenth-century Weoley Castle in England, and from many other sites, not least in the fourteenth century.

This type of *Stabbau* with interrupted sill beams may be considered to have evolved more or less directly from the type just described from, say, twelfth- to thirteenth-century Emden, where there are posts at the corners and at regular intervals along the walls but no sill beams. A structure of this kind can take the load of the roof timbers and so eliminate the need for internal posts.

There is another type of *Stabbau*, constructed entirely on continuous sill beams. In this case, however, it is impossible to postulate a direct transition from the type described above. Unless the sill beams are very massive or highly evolved jointing techniques are used, it is often very difficult to mount heavy-section vertical elements on the sill beam, whether at the corners or along the walls. This explains why some examples of *Stabbau* on continuous sill beams have walls that are no more than screens, incapable of bearing loads, this function being taken over by posts within the interior of the building, as at Büderich (eleventh to twelfth centuries), for example (see Figures 89 and 90). When this type of *Stabbau* was used, there were usually posts only at the corners and not along the walls.

Stabbau construction on continuous sill beams represents the most developed form of this technique. It became the classic method for Scandinavian church building, especially in Norway, between the later eleventh century and the middle third of the twelfth century, when this type of architecture had its heyday. Among secular buildings in this style were the ninth-century 'great hall' at Haithabu, buildings I and V in the Petersberg artisan quarter of Basle in the tenth to eleventh centuries, and several urban buildings of the twelfth century in Lund.

A change in the types of planking used for walling materials was associated with the evolution of *Stabbau* construction towards the use of continuous sill beams. Two distinct groups can be identified, one characterized by the use of two types of element and the other making exclusive use of a single element. No chronological or regional differences can be distinguished between these two techniques. There is, however, a very clear transition between the ninth to tenth centuries and the eleventh to twelfth centuries from the use, in both cases, of thick planks – effectively split tree trunks – to the use of much thinner planks. The former were very difficult to mount on sill beams, whether interrupted or continuous, and so they had to be bedded in trenches.

With thinner planks, however, both types of sill beam could be used. Whether the reduction in plank thickness was a cause or an effect of the use of sill beams is difficult to determine, but it is incontrovertible that this

Fig. 89. *Photograph of building 1 at Büderich (West Germany) from the south-west (eleventh to twelfth centuries)*

(M. Müller-Wille, Eine Niederungsburg bei Haus Meer, *Rheinische Ausgrabungen* (1968), Tafel 2)

development was essential if they were to be used. The introduction of the continuous sill beam must, naturally, have resulted in a more weatherproof and better finished building, as at Büderich, but it also became impossible, without using a very robust sill beam, to incorporate the corner and wall posts in the framework to support the roof timbers. This difficulty doubtless explains the abandonment of *Stabbau* construction in urban, manorial, and even rural architecture from a certain date: it corresponds with a wish to clear the interiors of buildings, a general trend that will become more apparent later in this study and which was very marked in the medieval period. By contrast, this constraint was easier to accommodate in church buildings, the supporting elements serving to define the side-aisles.

Another factor which may have played a part in the abandonment of *Stabbau* construction everywhere (apart from the Scandinavian churches or some outbuildings of rural houses in certain Alpine and sub-Alpine areas) is the problem of obtaining timber for planking. A large *Stabbau* construction requires a considerable amount of timber and a major effort in sawing it up. When the example of Canada is considered, it can be seen that timber sawn

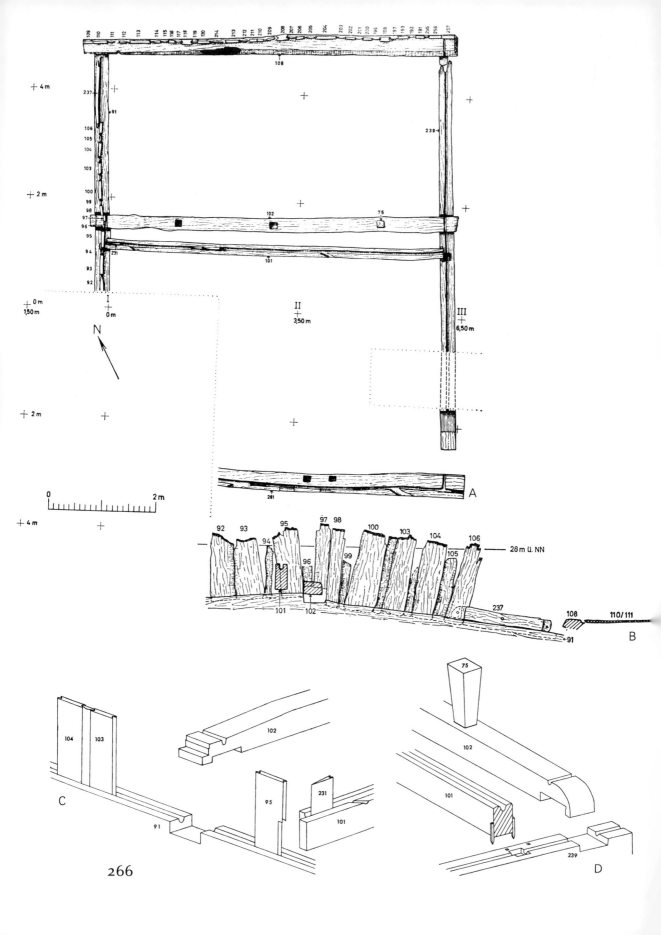

266

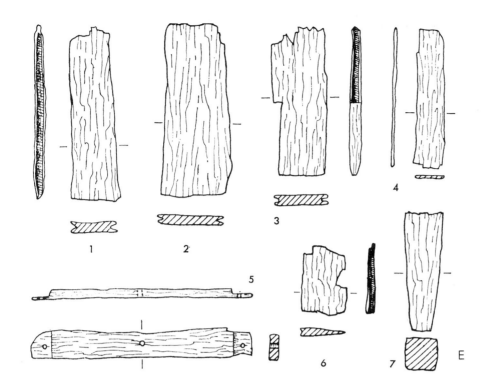

Fig. 90. *Building 1 at Büderich (eleventh to twelfth centuries)*

A. Plan. In the centre the grooved beam 101 supported a partition wall, whilst the heavier beam 102 received three vertical roof supports.

B. Elevation (from interior) of the west wall at the junction between the western external wall sill beam (91), the internal partition sill (101), and the roof support beam (102).

C. Interpretive sketch of the jointing between the western external wall sill beam (91), the internal partition sill (101), and the roof support beam (102). The joint between 91 and 102 is a very solid one, so as to prevent any movement, but that between 91 and 101 is less firm, since 101 was not load-bearing.

D. Ditto for the eastern wall. Although the jointing techniques are somewhat different, the same comments can be made in respect of the joints between 239 on the one hand and 101 and 102 respectively as under C.

E. Planks from the north wall. These were naturally longer in their original state.

(M. Müller-Wille, Eine Niederungsburg bei Haus Meer, *Rheinische Ausgrabungen* (1968), Tafel 7–11)

---

into planks, a material that is infinitely superior to stone in winter conditions, did not in fact become widely used until sawing techniques improved in the eighteenth century, first with pit sawing and then the introduction of the hydraulic sawmill. Despite its advantages, especially in cold climates, the diffusion of *Stabbau* construction was no doubt restricted, especially in rural application, by virtue of this technical problem, which was difficult for ill-equipped peasant societies before the twelfth to thirteenth centuries to overcome. Examples of the use of this type of building are therefore usually to

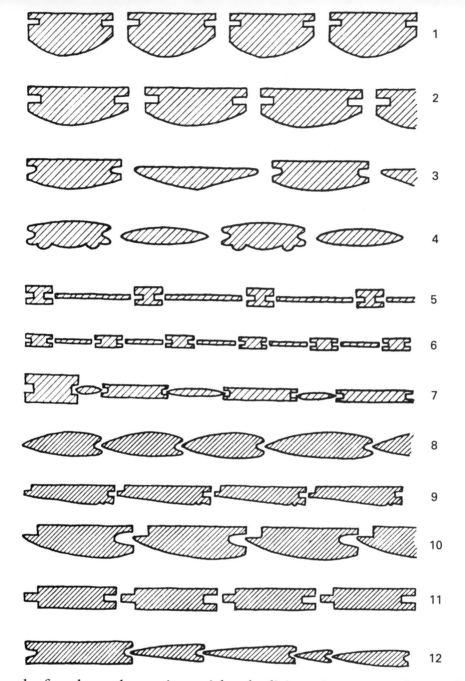

be found on urban, seigneurial and religious sites – not a chance phenomenon – until other techniques of building in wood (timber framing, for example) or the wider availability of stone for building in Scandinavia, especially in Sweden and Denmark, from the twelfth century onwards led to its gradual abandonment; a process that was almost completed by the end of the medieval period.

– The regions of origin of Stabbau construction
This leads on to consideration of the origins of this building technique and of the regions in which it was used. Until just before World War II, almost all the examples earlier than the twelfth century (from which Scandinavian churches

Fig. 91. *Techniques of tongued-and-grooved construction*
There were two alternative methods available in the Middle Ages:
a. Alternate double-grooved planks and thin planks
  1 Greensted (England): eleventh-century church (cf. Figure 87)
  2 Santa Maria Minor, Lund (Sweden): eleventh-century church
  3 Vänga (Sweden): twelfth-century church
  4 Hånger (Sweden): twelfth-century church
  5 Petersberg, Basle (Switzerland): eleventh-century urban buildings
  6 Torfkirche (Iceland): modern church
  7 Büderich (Germany): north wall of building I, eleventh to twelfth centuries (cf. Figure 90, E)
The difference in thickness between 1 and 2 and the remainder is apparent. The walls at Greensted (Figure 87) and Santa Maria Minor do not have sill beams (cf. Figure 86, c or d), whilst the others, notably Büderich, do possess them (cf. Figure 86, e or f), and this limits the use of thick planks if they are to be set into the sill beam.
b. Quoining
  8   Hedared (Sweden): thirteenth-century church
  9   Urnes (Norway): eleventh-century church
  10,11 Norwegian medieval stave churches
  12   Büderich (Germany): north wall of building III, eleventh to twelfth centuries

(M. Müller-Wille, Eine Niederungsburg bei Haus Meer, *Rheinische Ausgrabungen* (1968), Tafel 23, 24)

---

have survived) known from excavation were in northern Germany, always apparently from sites where Scandinavian influence was probable, if not certain, such as Haithabu. For this reason, and also for ideological reasons that are not difficult to understand in the context of that period, bearing in mind as well the decisive political role that early medieval archaeology has always played in Germany, a Scandinavian origin was put forward for this method of building.

However, it is ironical that around the same time Scandinavian specialists engaged on studies of the many Norwegian medieval churches built in this way – the stave churches – were putting forward the hypothesis that it derived originally either from the Continent or from the British Isles.

Although the problem has not been settled, more light has now been thrown upon it. First, it is necessary to take account of the role of the conditions for preservation. Most of the north German finds came from very wet contexts, which facilitate the preservation of wood and therefore identification of the walling techniques used. However, these ideal conditions are not so easily realized outside this area, particularly in regions such as Britain, France, Switzerland etc., or even over large parts of Germany. This fact very considerably influences the possibilities for study: a *Stabbau* building on continuous sill beams leaves virtually no trace in the ground, whilst the use of interrupted sill beams will only be shown by postholes: an example of this is Warendorf, where the use of the *Stabbau* technique would seem to have been very probable in the larger houses.

We also have a better understanding of the ethnographic data now, as a result of which it can be seen that there are in northern Europe, and particularly in Scandinavia, a large number of modern buildings constructed in this way, especially churches. Alpine Europe – Germany and above all Switzerland – also possesses many examples of the same type. However, for the practical reasons set out above, these are confined to ancillary buildings such as granaries or barns. It is well known that rural outbuildings represent repositories of older building technologies or materials, formerly used in dwelling houses but abandoned for this purpose in the course of time.

Data arising from sources other than archaeological excavations indicate, moreover, that before the ninth century, *Stabbau* construction may well have had a more westerly distribution than that disclosed by the excavation of the ninth- to twelfth-century sites or by Scandinavian churches. It appears that the earliest parish churches, especially those built before the eleventh to twelfth centuries, were usually wooden. Documents of the fifth to tenth centuries often use two forms of wording when describing them – *ecclesia lignea* (wooden church) or *ecclesia ligneis tabulis fabricata* (church made of wooden planks). It is reasonable to ask whether the former were not religious buildings of post and wattle and daub construction, of the type found on several sites, and whether the latter, which are more specifically characterized, were not entirely plank-built. Attempts have sometimes been made to identify these 'plank' churches with edifices built using the *Stabbau* technique at Husterknupp and Büderich. The possibility must also be borne in mind that horizontal planking was used, at least in Britain, even though the surviving wooden church at Greensted (Essex) testifies to the early use of the classic *Stabbau* method of construction in the British Isles. If all the documentary references to early medieval 'plank' churches are plotted on a map, a distribution appears which seems to correspond to the archaeological data, but with a much wider extension westwards (see Figure 92).

Thus two regions seem to be possible candidates for the origin of the *Stabbau* technique: the Alpine regions of Germany or perhaps France or Switzerland, and the British Isles. There are additional documentary indications so far as the latter are concerned. Some Scandinavian authors believe that they have been able to recognize *Stabbau* buildings in references to churches built by Irish or Anglo-Saxon missionaries in Scandinavia, designated in contemporary texts as *opus scotium* (Scottish work), i.e. the work of inhabitants of the British Isles. Although this is a somewhat tenuous hypothesis, it may receive indirect confirmation from various recent English excavation results, which prove that, from the Anglo-Saxon period and especially in the sixth and seventh centuries, either the *Stabbau* technique or a method of building walls using tongued and grooved horizontal planks between wall posts at 30–40 cm (12–16 in.) intervals was being practised.

Chalton is an example of the use of horizontal plank walling in the sixth to seventh centuries, whilst Thirlings (Northumberland) is one of the sites that

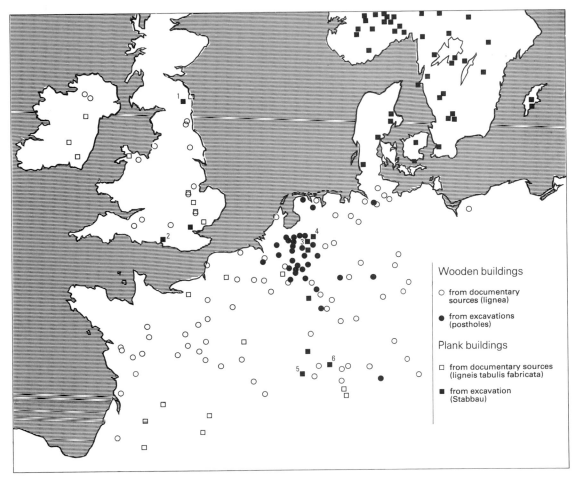

Fig. 92. *Building with vertical planks between 500 and 1000 (data from surviving structures, archaeological excavation, and documentary sources)*

In addition to the many surviving wooden churches of tongued-and-grooved vertical plank construction, mainly in Norway, excavations have produced a large number of examples of buildings constructed in this way. The analysis of documents that describe early medieval wooden churches demonstrates that two different expressions were used: either simply *ecclesia lignea* (wooden church) or, more infrequently, *ecclesia ligneis tabulis fabricata* (church made of wooden planks). All these data reveal an interesting distribution of plank-built constructions: Scandinavia, as is well known from the many surviving monuments, but also the British Isles, the Rhine region from the North Sea to the Alps, Normandy, Picardy, and south-western France.

A map of this kind poses various problems of interpretation: the small number of excavations, and therefore the lack of archaeological data, in certain regions, and the wide chronological span that the map covers, which rules out certain interpretational possibilities. Nevertheless, it does show what the proper study of documentary sources can yield, even for the earliest medieval periods.

(W. Zimmerman, 'Ecclesia lignea' und 'ligneis tabulis fabricata', *Bonner Jahrbücher*, 158 (1958), with the addition of data from recent English and German excavations)

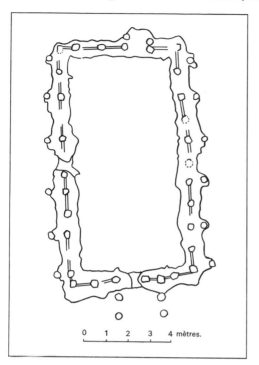

Fig. 93. *Plan of a house from the Anglo-Saxon settlement of Thirlings (Northumberland) sixth to seventh centuries AD*

Like some of the houses at the contemporary settlement at Chalton (cf. Figure 105), several of the buildings found on this site seem to have had plank walls. Here, however, the excavated below-ground features seem to suggest that the planks were vertical, whereas horizontal planks were used at Chalton.

(*Medieval Village Research Group, Report 22* (1974), fig. on p. 26A; excavation directed by R. Miket)

---

has produced several examples of the use of vertical planks from the sixth to seventh centuries (see Figure 93). These two sites are especially relevant to this problem, since they are very early and because they fit in with various documentary sources from this period which describe churches in Britain as being *ligneis tabulis fabricata* (made of wooden planks) (cf. Figure 105).

So far as an origin in the Alpine region is concerned, in addition to ethnographic data, which are incontrovertible but difficult to use for elucidating this point, there are similar documentary references to churches, plus at least one recent discovery dating to the early medieval period. This came from the village of Unter Wassere in the commune of Erplingen, south of Württemberg, where the remains of a *Stabbau* building were found, well preserved by a waterlogged soil and dated by dendrochronology to AD 668 ± 6. Although this is an isolated find, it is of interest by virtue of its early date.

Stabbau chronology

The problems of the date and place of origin of the *Stabbau* technique are in no way resolved by the foregoing. From modern excavations it is known that it was widely used between the ninth and twelfth centuries for churches, and also for secular buildings, in the Rhine valley from Basle to Cologne (including Strasbourg, where examples were found many years ago), in northern Germany, and in the Scandinavian countries. However, these discoveries have resulted primarily from the development of medieval archaeology in these regions, and in particular from favourable conditions for the preservation of organic materials in the ground, rather than from reliable data on the true place and date of origin of this building technique. It is reasonable to assert that it was known at least as early as the Merovingian period and no doubt also in the western parts of Europe, the Alpine region, and the British Isles in forms that remain to be defined precisely. After that date it may well have spread into Scandinavia and northern Germany. Since it was a somewhat laborious building technique, in that it required the sawing up of a large number of planks, it was probably restricted at first to religious edifices, along with some manorial and urban buildings, as at Husterknupp, Büderich, Haithabu and Stellerburg, but it was also used for some rural structures. It is perhaps worthwhile emphasizing that among the earliest instances of the use of this technique there are to be found rural examples, such as Unter Wassere in seventh-century Germany and Chalton and Thirlings in sixth- to seventh-century England (cf Figures 93, 105). From the twelfth to thirteenth centuries onwards, however, the use of this technique gradually became restricted for the reasons outlined above, either to certain Norwegian churches (other churches in Norway and all of these in Denmark and Sweden were henceforth built in stone) or to rural ancillary buildings in the Alpine region. Although the use of this method of construction poses problems in use so far as rural architecture is concerned, such as the high cost of materials, the thermal insulation qualities of wood, generally recognized to be high even when only thin planks are being used, would certainly serve to explain its persistence to the present day in these two applications. However, it was for the most part superseded by more developed techniques that were more economic or more readily accessible, such as timber framing or building in stone.

5 *Stone*

The problem of the use of stone in medieval rural architecture is generally studied under two main aspects, independently of one another: its substitution for wood and the geographical distinction between northern Europe, the region of wood, and southern Europe, and more particularly Mediterranean Europe, the region of stone. Before surveying these two factors, it is worthwhile making the comment that in this case, as with many other aspects of rural building, several analytical approaches are possible – study of the precise availability of constructional materials, notably stone; climatic constraints; the influence of technology, and in particular the problems of tools;

finally, the effects on building methods of the colonization of new lands or temporary occupation of certain areas. It is tempting to substitute for an overall analysis, which at the same time covers the whole of Europe and contrasts north and south, a more detailed study which deals with a specific geographical, technological, economic and social context within a defined chronological framework.

It would seem, at first sight, erroneous to consider that the main question that the use of stone in medieval rural building poses the historian is its replacement of wood, a phenomenon that can be observed definitively during the twelfth and thirteenth centuries in certain regions that have been well explored by excavation, such as Great Britain. There is no doubt whatever that well before that period, and often continuously throughout the Middle Ages and beyond, there were certain areas of northern Europe where stone was being used for rural building.

Use of stone in the early Middle Ages: Scandinavia

Scandinavia provides an example in the village of Vallhagar, on the Swedish island of Gotland in the Baltic, which has already been shown (cf. Figures 24 and 25) to be made up of houses with stone walls. Another Swedish Baltic island, Öland, provides another example in the village of Eketorp, from an early period. From the first century AD, and perhaps a little earlier, stone buildings of this type predominated in these regions, even though there was no lack of timber. It is a very remarkable fact that on yet another Swedish island in the Baltic, Bornholm, which had a similar climate and vegetation, together with comparable stone outcrops, wattle and daub was always used for house walls during the equivalent period.

Gotland and Öland are not the only regions of northern Europe where stone was utilized for house building from an early date. Although it seems to have been used only very rarely in mainland Sweden and Denmark during the Viking period and earlier, the situation was altogether different in Norway. There was a tradition of building in stone in Norway which probably dates back to the first century AD, as illustrated by examples that are contemporary with Vallhagar, such as the sixth- to seventh-century farm at Sostelid (Aseral). This tradition has continued right through to the present day, at least for farm outbuildings. There can be no question of this being attributable to a lack of forest cover.

– The islands colonized by Scandinavians

Comparable timber resources are lacking in the settlements colonized by Scandinavians to the west, such as the islands around Scotland (Hebrides, Shetland, Faroes), Iceland, and Greenland (cf. Figure 31). It is therefore not surprising to find examples of building in stone dating from the earliest phases of Viking colonization (ninth century and later) in these regions. Courses of stone generally alternate with courses of turf: the farm at Stong (Iceland) is one of many examples. This represents contact with the Celtic civilizations, which were already building widely using dry-stone walling well before the Scandinavian settlers arrived. The two traditions doubtless met and merged in the Hebrides. In other Celtic regions such as Cornwall, Wales and Ireland, building in stone was just as ancient a tradition as it was on the Baltic islands. It is unnecessary to continue quoting examples: one need only bear in mind the innumerable ruins of buildings of all kinds in these regions – houses, fortified sites, churches – which have survived from the period from the first century AD to the Middle Ages. One particularly fine example is the small farm at Gwithian, near the north coast of Cornwall, with its two circular drystone buildings, probably sixth-century in date.

– Dry stone in southern Europe

Dry-stone construction was a well-established element of rural architecture from well before the medieval period in certain regions of Europe. This applies not only to those regions already mentioned but also to other southern areas, where limestone slabs are to be found that are well suited to this type of construction. Provence and Périgord in France, and Apulia in Italy are just a few examples of such regions.

When tackling the problem of stone and wood in the Middle Ages, it seems reasonable to distinguish a special case, that of those regions where building in stone is feasible and often of some antiquity. In Ireland, as in those French regions just mentioned, there is another factor, closely linked with the characteristics of dry stone (a poor building material when dried out because it becomes difficult to shape), namely the appearance at a very early date, well before the Middle Ages, of vaulted construction. The simple juxtaposition of the Europe of wood and the Europe of stone is profoundly modified by specific cases of this kind, not to mention the very early use in various Scandinavian regions of stone bonded with clay mortar, sometimes associated with turf blocks.

Moreover, this dual tradition – the Scandinavian regions and the dry-stone regions, where vaulting was often practised – does not preclude the use, where this was feasible, of wood or turf blocks – in the Scottish islands, for example, where this was the predominating technique – in the same geographical regions in the same periods. This stone-using tradition did not disappear after these periods; this holds good not only in the case of Norway, considered above, but also for the Celtic regions of the British Isles and the areas of Scandinavian colonization in the Scottish islands. The Jarlshof settlement on Shetland, for example, was reconstructed regularly between its foundation in the ninth century and the twelfth century, always in stone; the same is true of Scandinavian buildings in Greenland, right up to the abandonment of the colony in the fourteenth century. It thus becomes difficult to maintain the notion of two distinct homogeneous European regions, one of wood and the other of stone, whatever chronological framework is selected.

Although the simplistic north-south division has little relevance in this respect as part of a serious historical analysis, there was undeniably a transition

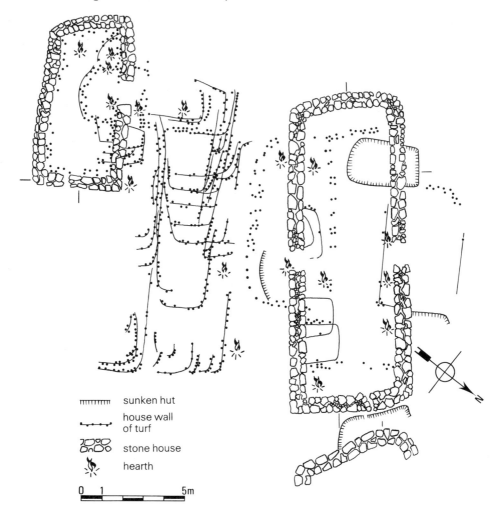

sunken hut

house wall
of turf

stone house

hearth

0 1   5m

from wood to stone in the twelfth to thirteenth centuries. However, it is important to define just what can be analysed in this way. The contrast between the two Baltic islands of Bornholm and Gotland serves to reinforce the point that study of the transition from one material to the other is pertinent only in respect of a defined geographical region, as part of an extended historical analysis, based on a sample that is large enough to be representative and which provides, if possible, evidence of long continuity of occupation. Transition from wood to stone – or, indeed, from stone to wood, since this phenomenon certainly took place – seems to be too complex a process to be exempted from caveats of this kind, and to be transformed into a general tendency that holds good for the whole of the rural architecture of geographical and historical groupings that are essentially distinct from one another. Moreover, if its full significance is to be realized, this phenomenon should not be separated from its motivations or its implications, especially in relation to

Fig. 94. *The transition from perishable materials to stone: the tenth- to thirteenth-century houses at Hound Tor (Devon)*

Three successive building phases can be observed on the plan:

1 Late Saxon: a series of sunken huts, only a few of which are shown on the plan, orientated NW–SE.

2 Early twelfth-century: rectangular houses 3–4m (10–13ft) long and orientated NE–SW (i.e. at right angles to the sunken huts). These houses were built of wattling mounted on closely spaced earthfast wooden uprights. Up against this framework, on the exterior, the wall proper was built of turf blocks. The traces left in the ground by these wooden uprights prove that 1) the houses were rebuilt frequently (they stood for about a century before being rebuilt in stone), and 2) at each reconstruction, planks of the previous house and the orientation were preserved.

3 Late twelfth- or early thirteenth-century: houses rebuilt in stone. The plan of the house in the top left of the plan shows that, in this case at least, the stone wall was an exact replacement of its turf predecessor, the uprights of which can be seen up against the inner face of the stone wall over its entire length. It is difficult to be specific about the reasons for this transition from wood to stone. It may be due, at least in part, to increasing difficulty being experienced in obtaining good-quality turf in the neighbourhood of the settlement.

(M. W. Beresford and J. G. Hurst, *Deserted Medieval Villages*, London (1971), fig. 14 and information from G. Beresford)

---

the underlying socio-economic factors. Before studying the latter, let us first examine the problem of the transition from wood to stone in a specific and well-understood context, that of certain regions of Britain, where the quality and abundance of the documentary material permits us to confirm the validity of observation on the ground.

In order to study this transition, the primary requirement is for excavations of villages where the continuity of occupation is sufficient to span the most significant period, essentially the twelfth and thirteenth centuries. Given such data, the phenomenon can be studied with some confidence.

Modes of transition from wood to stone in the twelfth–thirteenth centuries.

– Great Britain

Excavations at Hound Tor I, a site in Devon, in a region where turf was the general building material at the start of the Middle Ages, revealed remarkably continuous occupation from the end of the Saxon period up to the thirteenth century. Thus it admirably illustrates the transition from houses constructed of turf blocks on a light wattle foundation that were crudely built and frequently reconstructed – perhaps more than once every generation – to stone-built structures. This change is shown by several houses to have taken place in the late twelfth or early thirteenth century (see Figure 94).

At the site of Hangleton (Sussex), in the most southern area of Britain, wooden constructions were found dating from the second half of the twelfth century and the early thirteenth century. Around the middle of the thirteenth century these were replaced by flint-walled houses; it is not possible, however, to be certain whether these were full walls or merely wall bases to support a timber frame.

Gomeldon (Wiltshire) illustrates the situation in the English midlands. Timber structures were replaced in the thirteenth century by some of the stone buildings referred to earlier (cf. Figure 68). However, elsewhere on the site, stone houses had been built as early as the late twelfth century. In the same region, at Wythemail (Northamptonshire), timber buildings remained in use until the mid thirteenth century. Base walls of chalk appeared around this time and, in the final period of occupation in the fourteenth century, there were buildings constructed wholly in this material. This is a progression somewhat similar to that at Wharram Percy (Yorkshire), further to the north. There the twelfth- and early thirteenth-century timber buildings were replaced by houses entirely constructed of chalk, and finally with timber-framed houses on chalk footings (cf. Figure 66).

These and many other examples show that, in these English villages, the transition from wooden walls to walls composed entirely of stone or with stone footings, took place at the end of the twelfth century or during the course of the thirteenth century, though with some regional variations in chronology. This phenomenon seems to have begun in the south or south-west (e.g. Hound Tor I) and moved gradually northwards during the thirteenth century. It is usually found that in chalk regions such as Yorkshire (e.g. Wharram Percy), where the use of stone entails the opening up of quarries, wood continued to be used for as long as possible. However, it is somewhat perplexing to observe that in a region such as Dartmoor, in the south-west, where stone is very abundant on the surface and where it had been handled since very early times to clear fields for cultivation, it did not come into use for rural houses until comparatively late: the question of the use of stone must depend upon very complex factors.

– Germany

At the present time it is more difficult to study this phenomenon in other countries, especially in continental Europe, largely because of the lack of excavated sites with an adequate continuity of occupation over the twelfth and thirteenth centuries. It should, however, be noted that in the Merovingian and Carolingian periods, although stone seems to have been used rarely, and perhaps exclusively in certain areas of Germany, there are nevertheless a number of sites such as Zimmern, Weimar, Merdingen and Tilleda where it was in fact used for the walls of sunken huts and the footings of house walls (cf. Figure 35). Comparable observations have as yet not been made on Anglo-Saxon sites, which suggests that the use of stone for wall footings occurred relatively earlier in southern Germany than in Britain. However, this observation relates to sites occupied in periods that are too early for the present study or where the occupation was too brief to permit an adequate continuity to be studied. This was not the case at Hohenrode, where in the first period of occupation (mid twelfth – late fourteenth centuries) the houses had stone wall footings and timber frames. This covers a period analogous to that of several English sites. The German examples lead to the thought that it might be more appropriate to make a clear distinction between houses with stone footings, the use of which required only a small amount of stone and which may be associated with the parallel widespread diffusion of the use of wooden sill beams, and those built entirely of stone, which pose additional problems relating to supply of materials and building techniques.

– *France and Italy*

It is difficult to analyse the situation in France, for want of sufficient data. All the villages excavated in France to date – Dracy (Côte d'Or), Montaigut (Tarn-et-Garonne), Condorcet (Drôme), Rougiers (Var), Courtisigny (Calvados), Saint-Victor-de-Massiac (Puy-de-Dôme) etc. – are almost entirely settlements that were founded after the end of the twelfth century. Stone was used at all of them, but this observation does little to help solve the problem: it is essential to know the construction techniques used for earlier buildings on these sites or in nearby settlements. Nevertheless, using some of these examples, particularly Saint-Victor-de-Massiac (see Figure 95) or Ronzières (Puy-de-Dôme), it is possible to postulate the existence of structures earlier than the twelfth century which made use of stone, for wall footings at least. It is also interesting to note, moreover, that among these post-twelfth-century sites, only those in the Mediterranean region such as Rougiers and Condorcet have produced examples of houses in which lime mortar was used. Elsewhere only soil was used for bonding.

In the absence of a larger number of excavations, it becomes difficult to know how old this rural tradition of building in stone is, especially in the Mediterranean region. In Italy at least, to judge from the analysis of documents earlier than the late twelfth century recently carried out for Latium by Pierre Toubert, rural houses were more often built in stone than in wood. This picture doubtless needs some modification, but we have to accept as a hypothesis that, even though Mediterranean Europe possessed a rural architecture in stone from the twelfth to thirteenth centuries, it is not yet possible to assemble the chronological, regional and quantitative data that would permit such a modification to take place. In conclusion it can be said that the Mediterranean region of Europe is also one where limestone is abundant, even in the cretaceous form which provides northern Europe with its friable, shattered chalk, and is often of high quality and easy to procure. This must surely explain not only the early and widespread use of stone building techniques in this rural region, but also the early use of mortar, for which lime is essential. It is this factor which had led to the close identification of building in stone with the limestone areas, and in particular with southern Europe.

Fig. 95. *Saint-Victor-de-Massiac (Puy-de-Dôme)*
North wall of the earliest church (probably Merovingian) of this deserted village. The stone wall footings survive, between the two faces of which a wooden wall would have been anchored.

(Photograph by kind permission of the excavator, Luc Tixier)

Technological and socio-economic aspects of the transition from wood to stone.
This phenomenon will be better understood by taking into account its economic, social and technological components, both in the regions where it is manifestly present and in those where timber framing, wattle and daub, or cob have held sway up to the present day.

It has already been pointed out that the problem of the use of stone cannot be considered in isolation, without taking account of at least four factors: availability of building materials; climatic constraints; technological level and progress in this field; and specific aspects of settlement in colonized areas or regions under temporary or cyclical occupation. These factors are important, of course, not merely for building in stone but also for all other types of material.

Access to and availability of building materials are important factors. The presence of stone in the fields, as is frequently the case in certain areas of southern France or various regions of northern Europe, may have played a role in this respect. However, the examples of Bornholm and Gotland or of Dartmoor, referred to earlier, must once again be borne in mind: local resources are merely possibilities, which may or may not be exploited. Technological or socio-economic considerations and cultural practices clearly exercise a decisive influence, along with other factors that we shall go on to consider.

Climatic constraints are also obviously very important, especially for rural buildings in northern Europe: the best building material for protection against cold is wood, which is immeasurably superior to stone. This leads directly to a preliminary observation: the rural architecture of northern Europe does not exclude stone construction, even though wood seems to be the predominant material, as in Sweden and Denmark.

This apparent contradiction between the constraints of climate and the materials used in practice is easily resolved in regions such as Iceland, Greenland and the Scottish isles: stone was used because the inhabitants had no alternative, there being practically no wood apart from that washed up on beaches, the value of which to the inhabitants is well illustrated by the Icelandic sagas. However, it must be pointed out that in many cases, where the soil allows, houses were built of turf blocks on stone footings rather than entirely in stone. Referring once again to the Icelandic farm at Stong, we can see that the main building, which was used as a dwelling house, was built in this way; only an outbuilding, constructed up against the dwelling house, was entirely stone-built.

In practice the use of stone was restricted to the wall footings, which varied in height, often with turfs on the outside and always lined with wood on the inside, as recounted in the Icelandic sagas and confirmed by excavations in Iceland and Greenland. Turfs and wood panelling are materials with insulating properties far superior to those of stone. This is clearly a case of a local constraint, the shortage of wood, being overcome by the judicious use of thermal insulating materials.

The remainder of northern Europe appears to be a region that is favourable to the use of timber construction, with wattle and daub, horizontally laid logs, and horizontal or vertical planking. Does this represent a geographical antithesis, as some have described it, overlying a cultural division into Germanized north and Romanized south? This is assuredly not the case. Once again it is climatic considerations that are decisive. In the northern regions it is more logical, so long as local soil conditions allow it, to use wood, if possible in the form of planks, rather than stone. It would appear, moreover, that this is just the solution most widely adopted, even though there was a return to stone in certain parts of northern Europe, particularly in the early medieval period.

The use of stone, especially from surface collection, poses many fewer problems in terms of working and dressing than certain types of timber construction, especially the more developed plank techniques. In these circumstances it is reasonable to ask whether, as excavation appears to suggest, the more elaborately worked materials, particularly vertical planks, were not reserved for royal, seigneurial, urban and, above all, ecclesiastical buildings, as was the case with stone in Britain and France before the twelfth century. Compared with the contemporary rural buildings, the Scandinavian churches of *Stabbau* construction exhibit the same contrast as that between the romanesque churches of Burgundy and the Saintonge and the peasant houses in those regions.

– The problem of rural churches
It may well be that the problem of the materials used in rural churches provides a pointer to one of the principal causes of the transition from wood to stone.

Scandinavia
Let us look at the example of Scandinavia. Churches began to be built in the ninth century, when the Christian missionaries started to arrive. Excavations in Denmark of some 30 of these, both romanesque and gothic and all built in stone, have shown that they were all of wooden construction prior to the tenth to eleventh centuries. Their subsequent history proves that in both Sweden and Denmark they were replaced as quickly as possible by stone structures, especially from the twelfth century. In 1080 the king began the construction of a stone cathedral at Lund, capital of Sweden. This movement of change continued progressively and very little evidence of the earlier phase survives. Beginning in the eleventh century, but more particularly in the twelfth, this movement meant that in neither country did a school of religious architecture based on high-quality wooden buildings develop, as was the case in contemporary Norway.

In Norway, by contrast, not only did church building in wood continue throughout the twelfth century and perhaps subsequently, but – what is more important – very significant developments took place which resulted in the creation of a regional school of architecture in wood of high technological accomplishment.

The detailed study of the problem demonstrates very clearly why and how Norway preserved this type of ecclesiastical architecture. Medieval Norway was sparsely inhabited by a few hundred thousand people, who lived mainly on isolated farms in a dispersed form of settlement. There were few towns and the artisan and urban middle classes had not evolved to any great extent. In such conditions, in a thinly populated country that was too poor to permit the development of the infrastructure needed for building in stone, the evolution of the church and the parochial system in the twelfth century was therefore based on wooden churches. In due course, stone architecture developed, but later than elsewhere in Scandinavia. Wooden churches in the towns date to the eleventh or early twelfth centuries, being subsequently replaced by stone edifices or relegated to subsidiary functions. In the countryside the results of the development of building in stone are very evident and of considerable importance: the 322 wooden churches known in the early nineteenth century from various sources were all located in the most sparsely populated and least affluent areas of Norway, that is to say, in the regions of forests and mountains, the side branches of the great fjords, and the small fishing hamlets scattered along the coast. The 31 surviving wooden churches are all situated in mountain valleys or areas of primary forest on the lower-lying lands.

The rest of Europe
The history of the Scandinavian wooden churches is of prime importance in identifying the problem of the use of stone. In those regions with harsh climates, where demographic and economic development lagged behind that in the more westerly regions of Europe, the stone church appeared gradually and usually relatively late, after the twelfth century; the process was not yet completed by the nineteenth century. The uniqueness of these regions lies in the lateness of the replacement of wooden churches by stone structures. Elsewhere – in Britain and Germany, for example – those areas that were Christianized earlier and where socio-economic development made an earlier start, there are many examples of churches being built first in wood and then replaced by stone edifices. This phenomenon occurred in these regions at an earlier date – in the tenth to eleventh centuries at Zimmern or Saint-Martin-de-Pier (Rhineland), and at Wharram Percy around the same period. In these circumstances there was no possibility that a very developed form of architecture in wood might blossom, as was the case in Norway, which is important in itself. Furthermore, the opportunities for the use of stone in rural settlement arrived at a very early date. The links that must have existed between the use of stone for churches and its potential use in rural architecture generally have already been discussed. This act of replacement, as illustrated by the case of Scandinavia, serves as an index of a socio-economic change, for both churches and rural buildings, which made it possible to contemplate stone construction. It is also proof of the establishment of an infrastructure, the development of a skilled workforce, and the possible diffusion of technological knowhow. The medieval peasantry was to take advantage of the examples and opportunities that were available to effect a similar transformation, with an apparent time-lag of one or two centuries and only in certain

regions. The problem of the use of stone in the Middle Ages can probably be explained to a substantial extent in this way.

Thus it appears to be difficult to make a simple division of Europe into the north, as the region of wood, and the south, as the region of stone. It may be that it is necessary to make certain modifications, especially to the chronology, and, by proceeding to a more elaborate form of analysis, to assert that this apparent antithesis represents the difference between the Romanized part of Europe, which had been stabilized in antiquity and was well populated, and that more northerly part of Europe where a new form of socio-economic structure and the distribution and stabilization of land took longer to become established. It is only in this sense that it is possible to talk of two Europes, and then only after introducing further modifications to the picture. Although stone and lime mortar were being used in the Mediterranean region for rural buildings at a very early date – in the twelfth century at Rougiers, for example – traditional architecture in wood is still to be found in certain parts of this region, in places persisting until the nineteenth century. There are examples in southern Italy, in Périgord and the Agenais in the fifteenth and sixteenth centuries, in the province of Salamanca and various parts of north-western Spain. Another important factor which serves to modify the simplistic picture, especially in the later medieval period, is the probable coexistence of houses in both stone and wood in certain areas at that time. In the granite regions, for example, such as Brittany or the Limousin, the rural houses of the *Ancien Régime* were built in stone, but urban houses were timber-framed, since this technique was better adapted for high buildings on the small ground surfaces of urban tenements. The use of one or other building technique is thus not solely dependent upon basic factors related to the subsoil or the forest cover: there are more complex socio-economic problems that, once again, have an important influence.

In summary, therefore, when considering the problem of building in stone – as, indeed, other aspects of medieval rural architecture – it is important not to overlook a number of different factors, especially in the socio-economic field, which play their part in determining both the constructional material used and the types of building. The study of a long period of time and a vast geographical area – western Europe in its entirety – creates an awareness of the complex nature of the problems involved and of the dangers of seeking to reduce them to a few simplistic formulae.

D   Roof structures

Whilst we often know a good deal about the materials used for building a house, thanks to the remains that are discovered by excavation, it is an altogether different problem when it comes to reconstructing its elevation, and in particular its roof structure. Apart from a few rare manuscript illuminations or documentary descriptions, we are compelled to use the information that can be derived from a careful study of the roof supports, either within the building or incorporated into the walls, and the data provided by ethnology and technology in general. Such information may make it possible, in certain cases, to achieve reconstructions that are credible and specific enough to allow attempts to be made to set down not only the history, but also the geographical distribution of various methods of supporting house roofs. Among those who have made such attempts are W. Haarnagel, H. Hinz, A. Zippelius, B. Trier, J. T. Smith, and W. A. van Es.

There is no space here to go into these studies in detail, especially since the geographical area that they cover is somewhat circumscribed – essentially the Netherlands, the north German plain, and the North Sea coastal region. Elsewhere, notably in Britain and the southern parts of Germany, very accurate data have made it possible to reconstruct part of the history and the chronological and regional variations of this aspect of the subject.

It was the prehistorians who first showed, in the last century, that it was possible to reconstruct the plans, if not the elevations, of buildings from postholes. Holes dug into the ground to receive vertical or sloping supports produce anomalies in the soil, which can often be rendered even more apparent as a result of the decay of the post itself *in situ* or by the use of stone packing, which increase the contrast in colour or appearance between the posthole and the soil around it. Archaeological observation is thus not dependent solely on the mere identification of postholes – not always a simple matter when, for example, the structure was a relatively slight one or complicated by multiple phases of reconstruction – but it also involves the study of their dimensions, of their layouts, and sometimes, as we shall see later, of their sections, since posts were often bedded obliquely in the soil and it is of prime importance to recognize that fact.

It must be admitted, in conclusion, that it is not always possible to interpret the complex network of postholes found in excavations with absolute certainty. Furthermore, in some cases posts may not have been sunk in the ground but simply mounted on large stones. There are many examples of this type of arrangement, which may mean that there is no trace of load-bearing elements, especially if the padstones have been removed or displaced (cf. Figure 81).

The problem of roof structures in medieval architecture is a very important one for several reasons. It is important first because building in wood largely predominated, at least before the eleventh to twelfth centuries. Secondly, many questions appear that are related to the methods and forms of roofing used – social stratification, forms linked with functions, technological developments, regional variations etc. To justify the attention paid to these questions it should be noted that buildings were often reconstructed, particularly in the early Middle Ages, and this was in large measure due to the poor quality of the roof structures. This weakness persisted, even into the later medieval period and in aristocratic and religious buildings, as much because of the poor quality of the materials used as the level of technological development that had been attained.

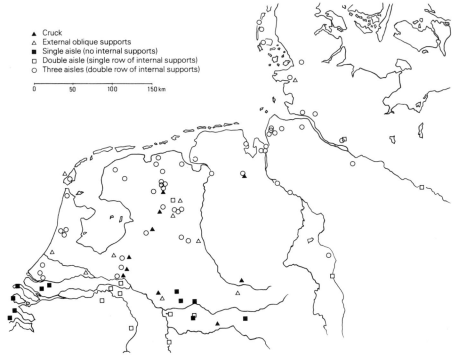

- ▲ Cruck
- △ External oblique supports
- ■ Single aisle (no internal supports)
- ▢ Double aisle (single row of internal supports)
- ○ Three aisles (double row of internal supports)

0   50   100   150 km

Fig. 96. *Types of timber construction in the Netherlands and northern Germany during the first millennium AD*

Certain phenomena are very striking: first, the coastal distribution of three-aisled buildings (cf. Figures 29, 79, 100).

In the Rhine valley, from its mouth to the central stretch, there is a notable absence of three-aisled buildings and a predominance of those with a single aisle. The two-aisled building with a central row of posts is to be found exclusively (in the area covered by this map) on the middle Rhine. Cruck-frame buildings and buildings with oblique external supports are to be found, albeit in small numbers, in contact zones between single- and two-aisled houses on the one hand and three-aisled houses on the other, in the Roman period and in the Middle Ages.

(Synthesis of data from B. Trier, *Das Haus im Nordwesten der Germania Libera*, IV, Veröffentlichungen der Altertumskommission im Provinzialinstitut für westfälische Landes- und Volkskunde, Münster/Westfalen (1969), Tafel 2, and W. van Es, Etablissements ruraux de l'époque romaine et du début du Moyen Age aux Pays-Bas, *IXe Congrès de l'Union Internationale des Sciences Pre- et Protohistoriques*, Nice (1976), colloque XXX, p. 144)

A final, and equally decisive, reason for the importance of studying roof structures is this: whilst it is not difficult to build a wall, adding a roof is a much more complex matter. For this reason, when attempts were made to extend the lives of buildings, the main research effort was more often than not devoted to technological improvements in the roof structure.

The main problem concerns the type of support used to hold up the roof. Three basic types can be distinguished (see Figure 96): buildings with a

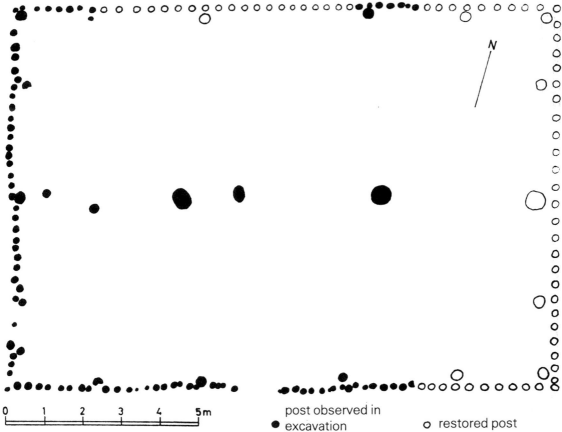

N

post observed in
● excavation   o restored post

0   1   2   3   4   5 m

Fig. 97. *Building with single row of posts on the long axis and palisade wall at Stammheim (West Germany) – thirteenth-century*

The uprights were probably coated with clay. Part of the building plan is hypothetical. The large diameter of two of the internal postholes indicates that this was a hipped roof, as would be expected in so long a building: it would be difficult, if not impossible, to obtain a single timber of this length.

(G. Fehring, Zur archäologischen Erforschung mittelalterlicher Dorfsiedlungen in Südwestdeutschland, *Z. für Agrargeschichte und Agrarsoziologie*, 1 (1973), fig. 9, p. 28)

---

central row of supports on the longitudinal axis; buildings with two rows of supports, which divide them up into three aisles, the centre one being on either side of the ridge; and buildings without interior supporting members, the roof being carried on load-bearing walls, using various forms of structure that will be discussed in the following pages.

1   Roof supported on internal posts

One central row of posts

In chronological terms, the use of a single central row of posts is the earliest technique known. This system is found in houses of the Danubian culture of 5000–2000 BC – at Köln-Lindenthal (Germany), Bylany (Czechoslovakia), or Cairy-les-Chandardes (Aisne, France). Although they were no more than 6–

7m (20–23ft) wide, these structures had not only a central row of posts but also auxiliary rows on either side, which thus constituted four-aisled houses (albeit houses that were cluttered with posts internally).

Developments in carpentry and joinery meant that, by the Hallstatt period, only the central row of the posts – which was in any case the most important one – was retained. This was the case with several buildings at Goldberg (Württemberg, Germany), dating from around 600–500 BC.

This is not only the oldest but also the simplest form of roof structure. It

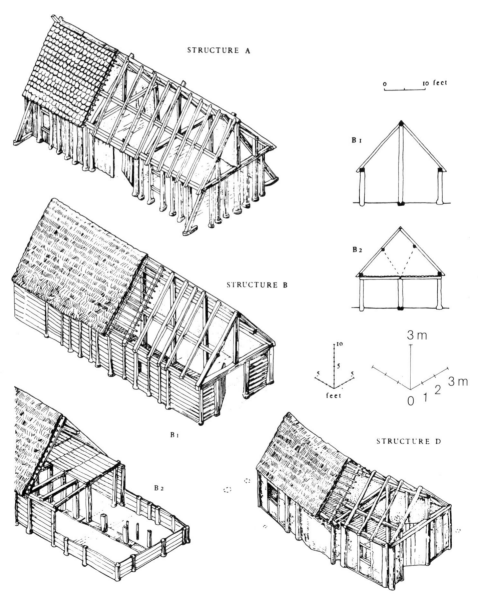

STRUCTURE A

STRUCTURE B

STRUCTURE D

B 1

B 2

B 1

B 2

0   10 feet

3 m

3 m

0 1 2

feet

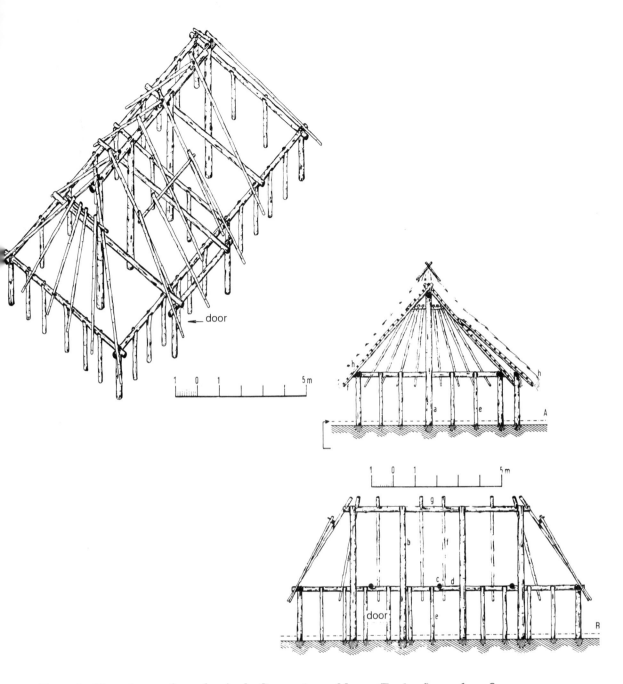

Fig. 98. *Three houses from the Anglo-Saxon site at Maxey (England) – c.650–850*

Building A is a single-aisled structure, but building B has a single central line of uprights. These reconstructions are partly conjectural. Although the presence or absence of rows of posts can easily be demonstrated by excavation, the use of tie beams, which are the basis of the reconstructions of building 1 and of building 2 in its second phase, is not certain in rural architecture at that period.

(P. V. Addyman, A Dark Age Settlement at Maxey, *Medieval Archaeology*, 8 (1964), fig. 11, p. 46)

289

consists essentially of a ridge beam carried on vertical supports and itself supporting transverse members or rafters (see Figure 99). Roofs of this type are to be found in medieval buildings, and in certain cases right up to the eighteenth century, a period when they became a traditional architectural type. This can be followed best in Germany, where the central and southern regions seem to have been attached to this form of roof from Merovingian times onwards: it is to be found in the Merovingian or Carolingian villages of Wülfingen and Zimmern in the south, and at Gladbach in central Germany, and later at Wittislingen and Stammheim (see Figure 97), dated to *c.*1288. A building with a single line of posts on the long axis at Sindelfingen, which is very characteristic of the local architectural tradition, has been dated by dendrochronology to 1447; it is built on the plan and in the style of an older building of the later fourteenth century. This is proof of the transition from a medieval architectural style to a specific regional tradition.

Central and southern Germany were doubtless not the only regions of Europe with this form of construction in the Middle Ages: it is known from the Roman period in the Netherlands and there are several eighteenth-century Danish examples. The situation in Britain is less clear, although some Anglo-Saxon examples are known, such as St Neots, Chalton, and Maxey (see Figure 98). It is to be found at Gelligaer Common (Glamorgan) from the later medieval period up to the fourteenth century. Two manorial halls, Huttons Ambo and East Haddlesey (Yorkshire), both of thirteenth-century date, also had roof structures of this type. However, these few examples are not sufficient to be described as regional traditions, unlike the situation in Germany.

The roof supported on a single row of posts no doubt developed for the same reasons as the evolution of roof design in medieval rural architecture – a wish to clear the interiors of buildings by eliminating as many posts as possible. There were two alternatives, so long as the principle of using a ridge beam borne on vertical elements and supporting the entire roof covering was retained. The first was to locate the vertical supports only in the two shorter walls, which would free the interior entirely but would limit the length of the building to that of the largest available ridge beams, a substantial constraint. Sunken huts represent examples of this type of ridge-beam construction (cf. Figure 33).

The other possibility was to support the ridge beam at each end on an upright post, as in the previous case, but to use a hipped form of roof, and in this way to increase the internal space. House 14 at the Carolingian site of Gladbach is a typical example of this alternative (see Figure 99).

Finally, in this consideration of ridge beam roofs attention should be drawn to the existence, from at least the Iron Age, of a series of houses where the ridge beam was supported, not by a row of vertical posts immediately below it, but by two lines of obliquely mounted posts that meet at the ridge to support the ridge beam – scissor posts (German *Pfostenscheren Konstruktion*). Examples of this type of construction are known from the Roman buildings at Kethel, near Schiedam (Netherlands) and the Carolingian structures at Haithabu.

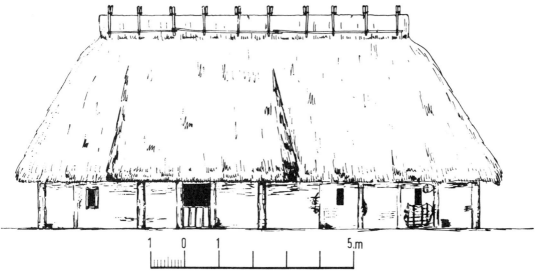

Fig. 99. *A house from the settlement at Gladbach (West Germany), seventh to eighth centuries*

There is a striking similarity between this building and that from Stammheim (Figure 97): they have the same dimensions, the doorways are similarly positioned, and the same double hipped roof supported on a single row of posts. This is the most likely reconstruction of the roof, since there is no vertical support in one of the shorter sides (there is an element of the internal partition wall in the centre of the other and again no ridge beam support). The excavated remains show that this building was walled with wattle and daub between relatively slender uprights at intervals of *c.*1 m (3ft 3in.). It was divided into five rooms.

(W. Sage, *Die frankische Siedlung bei Gladbach, Kr. Neuwied* (1969))

During excavation, buildings of this type may be thought to be of three-aisled construction, with two rows of posts, a very common form that will be discussed next. However, sectioning of the postholes makes it possible to distinguish these two forms one from another.

Double row of posts

The roof structure supported on a double row of posts (see Figure 100) is one of the most common medieval types. Although it is not as old as the single-row form, it nevertheless appears at a very early date. The oldest example known is from Elp in the province of Drenthe (Netherlands), dated to 1250–850 BC. It later became very widespread in certain regions, especially in the first millennium AD.

Basically it can be distinguished from the previous type in so far as it is normally not possible to use a ridge beam since there are no supports on the long axis of the building. The roof is therefore usually carried on collar rafters. A longitudinal timber (ridge purlin) joins the rafters to make roofing easier, but this is not a ridge beam in the strict sense since it does not support the rafters.

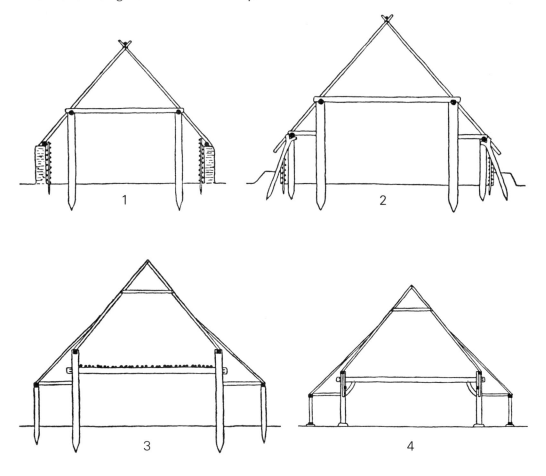

In a coastal zone which stretches from south-western Sweden through western Denmark and the whole of Frisia between the Danish peninsula and the mouth of the Rhine or the Zuider Zee, this form of roof construction is to be found in long houses – often more than 20m (66ft) in length – dating from the second or first centuries BC to the eleventh century AD and perhaps even later, since from the thirteenth century onwards this type of medieval house, in various guises, became the most typical German medieval building, the Lower Saxon or Frisian house (cf. Figures 29, 79). In addition to their three-aisled layout and size, these houses are characterized by the internal partitioning into two areas, one for humans and the other for animals. We shall return to this point later.

More or less in parallel with these houses, three-aisled structures made their appearance on the frontiers of the Roman Empire, from Hungary through Picardy to Britain: these were the basilica-plan buildings. Although in some cases, particularly in Britain, they may be deemed to have housed both men and beasts, this was not the general rule. This was effectively a different type of building, the later history of which is not at present easy to discern in these regions.

In addition to the large Frisian farms, three-aisled buildings were in use in

Fig. 100. *Three-aisled buildings from Frisia (first- to fifteenth-century)*

The earliest three-aisled buildings have two characteristics: the side aisles are wide relative to the central aisle and the roof consists of two flat sections. Rural architecture in these regions shows that these characteristics develop in the medieval period: the central aisle becomes wider, particularly in relation to the side aisles, and the two parts of the roof have a break of pitch. It is easy to demonstrate the former from excavations but the latter is more tricky. Judging from surviving buildings (4), this feature existed as early as the thirteenth century (Figure 106c), and seems to be associated with the use of false tie beams. Some German authors have reconstructed tenth–thirteenth-century buildings found in excavations with these two features – that from Wilhelmshaven-Krummerweg (3), for example. The first three examples shown on the figure (1–3) belong to the classic byre-house type of these regions (cf. Figures 29, 79).

1 Ezinge (Netherlands), first to second centuries AD. Turf walls on wattling.
2 Leens (West Germany), eighth to ninth centuries: turf walls without wattle support (which explains their thickness).
3 Wilhelmshaven-Krummerweg (West Germany), eleventh to twelfth centuries: reconstruction of excavated structures; false tie beams supporting an attic floor and broken-pitch roof.
4 Barn at Hardesbüttel (West Germany), thirteenth to fifteenth centuries: extant building, same features as 3.

(A. Zippelius, Das vormittelalterliche dreischiffige Hallenhaus in Mitteleuropa, *Bonner Jahrbücher*, 153 (1953), pp. 32–3)

Germany, France, Belgium, the Netherlands, the British Isles and Scandinavia during the Middle Ages for two main functions: seigneurial halls and monastic barns.

Although the three-aisled seigneurial hall disappeared early in Germany, it persisted in Britain until at least the thirteenth century, as shown by the bishop's palace at Hereford and the castles of Leicester, Oakham and Winchester, all of which date to the eleventh to twelfth centuries. Over the English lowlands there was a tradition of three-aisled halls in the countryside until the thirteenth century and the same is true of Scandinavia, where it persisted well after 1000, by which time it had disappeared in Germany.

Monastic barns are examples of buildings that were widely diffused by the religious orders and which were perfectly adapted to a specific function: the access of wheeled vehicles and the storage of large quantities of grain. It was doubtless this functional aspect of the three-aisled layout which accounts for its constituting, from the thirteenth century onwards, a classic type of German rural architecture, the Lower Saxon farm (*Niedersachsenhaus*) or by a comparable process, though at a date that is unfortunately not known with any precision, the typical large farm in several regions of France, such as the Doubs (cf. Figure 79).

In certain cases buildings with one or two lines of posts survived long after the medieval period, to become traditional types of rural architecture. This is doubtless explained by their functional nature, especially the three-aisled buildings. However, the increasing rarity of these types of roof structure after the eleventh century is a manifestation of a general phenomenon: a desire to clear the interiors of buildings of all vertical supports and at the same time to increase the roofed area, especially its breadth.

2   Roof without internal supports

This concern led directly to the house without internal supports, for which three types of roof structure are possible: the cruck roof, the roof supported on oblique external supports, and the roof borne on the walls.

The early cruck

The cruck is a form of roof structure composed of as many pairs of timbers as are needed to cover the building, the base of each either resting on or embedded in the ground and the apex being formed by the junction of these two elements, which are disposed on either side of the main axis of the building – in effect rafters springing directly from ground level. With a roof of this kind the pair of supports, which constitute not only the roof structure but also the walls themselves, are spaced at intervals, so as to create a construction divided into bays, whilst there is not normally a ridge in the strict sense of the word.

This type of construction is known from the first century AD in Germany (cf. Figure 96) and (from a single example) Great Britain. It seems to have spread in the Netherlands from the third century onwards. It is strange that the known examples all seem to have had no successors after the fifth century: this applies to the German examples at Haldern (early Roman period) and Milte, Kr. Warendorf (first to late fourth to fifth centuries), those at Wijster and Odoorn (Figure 101) in the Netherlands, and the Roman villa at Latimer (Buckinghamshire) in late fourth- to early fifth-century Britain. This technique appears not to have been used again until much later, in the thirteenth century.

In such circumstances it is very difficult to determine where and when this technique originated. All that can be said is that, with the cruck buildings of this first, Roman, period, it was technologically possible to build roofs that were wider than those possible at that time using any other form of construction without supports. They were all, in fact, 6m (20ft) and more in width – 6.5m (21.5ft) at Milte and nearly 7m (23ft) at Haldern, the traditional width of contemporary three-aisled buildings. This is well illustrated at Wijster, where there were long rectangular buildings for both men and animals that were 6m (20ft) wide. The part reserved for animals was a three-aisled structure, whilst in the other part the same width was achieved without difficulty by the use of a cruck frame. This example is also of importance in that it confirms the trend towards the freeing of the interiors of houses, which was apparent as early as 1250–850 BC at Elp, Drenthe Province (Netherlands), a three-aisled building which, as we have seen, housed both humans and animals. However, in the section reserved for humans, the uprights were more widely spaced than in the animals' section – concern for technological improvement tending in the same direction as in those referred to above from Wijster, where there were three-

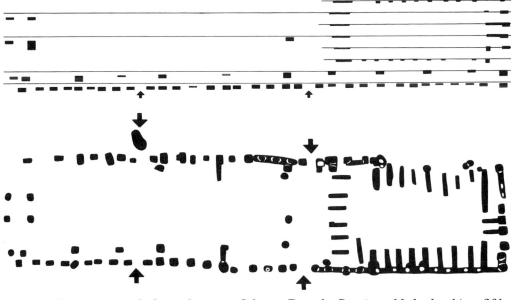

Fig. 101. *Primitive cruck-frame house at Odoorn (Drenthe Province, Netherlands) – fifth-century AD*

This is one of the larger houses on the site, which measured 19–25.5m long by 5–5.5m wide.

This is one of the longest, and is in two sections, separated by two doors (marked by arrows) facing one another. The dwelling section for humans is on the left, entered by another pair of doors, and that for livestock is on the right, where remains of the animal stalls are clearly visible. The interpretive sketch (above) helps to understand the roof structure better. For each posthole it shows: 1) the alignment (a thin line), 2) the location (the location of the rectangle), and 3) the width and depth of the posthole (the dimensions of the rectangle).

It is thus possible to distinguish the posts making up the wall framing (external lines) and those representing the ends of the stalls (small posts on the innermost parallel lines in the livestock section). To the left of the two doorways that separated the two sections of the building, and on its long axis, there is a large post intended, it would appear, to carry an internal partition wall. The main point of interest, however, is the group of posts on the alignment closest to the walls in both sections. Four pairs of posts can be made out in each section, in addition to those of the internal partition. These are located very precisely opposite one another and are comparable in depth and breadth: these are the bases of the cruck frame.

(H. T. Waterbolk, Odoorn im frühen Mittelalter – Bericht der Grabung 1966, *Neue Augrabungen und Forschungen in Niedersachsen* (1973), fig. 8, pp. 48–9)

---

aisled structures that showed the same features as those from Elp.

The most striking example from this point of view is unquestionably that of the village of Odoorn, Drenthe Province (Netherlands). In this settlement, occupied from the fifth to the ninth or tenth centuries, nine successive phases of occupation can be distinguished, exhibiting three main building types. During the earliest phase of occupation, the buildings were of the cruck-frame type discussed here, amongst the latest examples of the primitive form (see

Figure 101). In the next phase the buildings seem to be variants of the Warendorf structures already discussed, with oblique external roof supports and none in the interior. The buildings of the first group had an average width of 5–5.5m (16–18ft) whilst those of the second group varied between 4–6m (13–20ft) – usually more than 5m (16ft). However, in the three latest phases of occupation, these buildings with external supports were replaced by houses with a single central row of posts, a remarkable development, since it resulted in a reduction in the widths of buildings; the structures of this period, which represented the majority of the 72 houses found on the site, were 2.5–4m (8–13ft) wide.

The example of Odoorn and its succession of house types demonstrates the likely abandonment of primitive cruck-frame buildings at an early date. In the circumstances, therefore, it is not possible to talk of continuity in the use of this form of construction from the Roman period to the Middle Ages, but rather of a desire to disencumber and enlarge the interiors of buildings. Before studying post-thirteenth-century crucks, it is therefore worthwhile looking quickly at a form of construction that preceded it, between the primitive Roman crucks and the cruck-framed buildings proper of the Middle Ages – those structures with oblique external supports just mentioned from Odoorn.

Oblique external supports
This type is represented by Wittenhorst, Haldern (seventh to eighth centuries), and Warendorf (late seventh to eighth centuries: cf. Figure 17) in Germany, Kootwijk (seventh to eighth centuries) and Odoorn in the Netherlands, and the Danish fortified camps of the early eleventh century at Fyrkat, Trelleborg, Aggesborg, and Nonnebakken. Structures of this type have been discovered more recently at the sixth- to seventh-century Anglo-Saxon villages of Chalton (Hampshire) and Thirlings (Northumberland). There are also some examples from the Carolingian port of Haithabu (ninth to tenth centuries). Like the primitive cruck, this form of construction makes it possible to use large roofs on buildings without internal supports that are wider than the three-aisled structures – 5.6m (18ft) and 6.1m (20ft) in the case of the two buildings at Thirlings and 6–8m (20–26ft) at Warendorf and Kootwijk as well as the Danish examples and those from Odoorn.

Although this form of construction, which was a relatively simple one that gave excellent results, like the primitive cruck, appears not to have been used for dwelling houses after the eleventh century, it continued in use, according to the classic formula, for ancillary buildings, especially barns. A good example is the seventeenth-century barn at Hohenhorst, near Kiel (Germany), and there are others in France, such as the nineteenth- and early twentieth-century barns in the Touraine (see Figure 102).

The medieval cruck
Houses of cruck-frame construction are found from the thirteenth century onwards, especially in Britain (see Figure 103). The earliest example from the archaeological record is that from the village of Gomeldon, near Salisbury

Fig. 102. *Barn with externàl oblique supports at Courcelles-de-Touraine (Indre-et-Loire, France)*

This structure is of interest in so far as it shows the survival of this form of construction after the medieval period, and gives an idea of how excavated medieval buildings of this type may have looked.

(Photograph taken by Dominique Orssaud 1974)

297

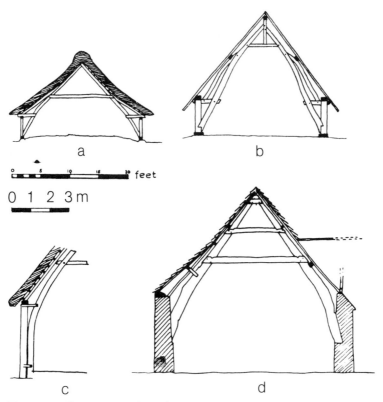

Fig. 103. *Some examples of medieval or post-medieval cruck-frame buildings in different European countries*

a Hummling region (Westphalia)
b Duclair (Normandy)
c Ramskapelle (Belgium)
d Enstone church (England)

Enstone is an example of a raised cruck, the members springing from the walls rather than from on or below the ground (base crucks). Many French post-medieval rural buildings use this technique – in the Corrèze, for example.

It will be seen that in almost every case these cross-sections show that there are no tie beams or wall plates.

(J. T. Smith, Cruck construction: a survey of the problem, *Medieval Archaeology*, 8 (1964), figs. 29, 33)

(Wiltshire), dated to the thirteenth century (see Figure 104). On the basis of observations during the excavation, the timbers used were 17.5 × 25cm (7 × 10in.) in cross-section and were sunk 50cm (20in.) into the ground at an angle of 60°. Although there are many examples of this type of building still surviving in Britain, they rarely date to earlier than 1450. However, in a region like Worcestershire, documentary studies have shown that the most common form of construction used timber framing for the walls and a cruck roof. The

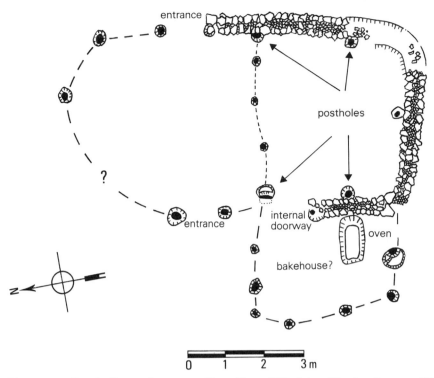

Fig. 104. *Cruck-frame house at Gomeldon, Wiltshire (England) – twelfth to thirteenth centuries*

Posts can be seen inside the stone walls, set obliquely in the ground and linked in pairs across the building: these are the bases of crucks. There are two facing entrances, one in the centre of each long side. This building, which was partly demolished after being abandoned in the thirteenth century, is a mixed house: the northern part was the human habitation and the southern separated from it by a partition indicated by postholes, housed the animals. The buildings that replaced this one developed into a rectangular-plan farm (cf. Figure 68).

This house, with its stone footings and rounded corners, must, as is often the case with oval cruck-frame buildings, have had a hipped roof, which is suggested by the absence of a pair of load-bearing posts up against the southern wall. This is thus a mixed house of recognized type, like those medieval and post-medieval examples from Brittany with and without crucks.

(*Medieval Archaeology*, 8 (1964), p. 290)

---

earliest reference to the cruck in this region dates to 1312.

Ethnographic data and the information from archaeological excavation demonstrate both the importance of cruck construction in Britain and its survival to the present day, especially in the mountainous Celtic peripheral regions – Wales, Scotland and Cornwall. This should not lead us, however, like some English scholars, to see cruck construction as being Celtic in origin, since the present-day geographical distribution is the result of recent

A

B

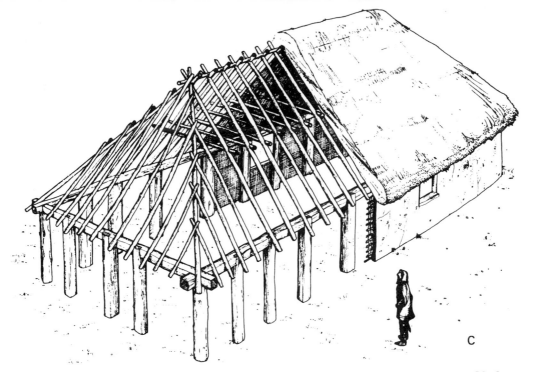

Fig. 105. *Reconstruction of two buildings from the Anglo-Saxon settlement at Chalton, Hampshire (England) – sixth- to eighth-century*

The walls of building B1 (C) are made up of identical posts. The evidence on excavation was similar to that shown in Figure 80A. A collar rafter roof structure can be postulated. The absence of a more substantial support in the centre of each of the two shorter sides, and above all the considerable length of the building, indicate that the roof was of hipped construction (cf. Figure 99)

In the case of building A1 (A and B), where the walls were made up of different-sized uprights in foundation trenches (cf. Figure 80B), two reconstructions are possible. They are differentiated essentially in terms of the shape and pitch of the roof in the two gables. The principal rafters are the same in either case, as were the tie beams, whilst the existence of a hipped roof is again demonstrated by the absence of central endposts on the long axis.

(P. V. Addyman, D. Leigh and M. J. Hughes, Anglo-Saxon houses at Chalton, *Medieval Archaeology*, 16 (1972), pp. 25–27)

---

developments, essentially post-medieval, the available documentation being based on surviving buildings. It is more a case of technological persistence than of evidence of place of origin.

In addition to certain problems of regional development in cruck construction in Britain, the most interesting aspect is its persistence since the Middle Ages in only certain regions of Britain and France, such as Brittany and the Limousin. There are several possible explanations, the most likely being that this relatively simple technique survived in the less affluent strata of peasant society or in marginal regions with a poor material culture, such as Scotland or Brittany. The abandonment of cruck construction is also probably connected with the slow diffusion of the two-storey rural house from the end of the medieval period. It is difficult to insert an upper storey into a building constructed in this way. Two-storey houses began to appear earlier in the Mediterranean regions such as Italy or Provence then they did in more northerly lands. Thus in the village of Dracy in the Côte-d'Or (France) the thirteenth- to fourteenth-century buildings had lofts installed rather than upper-storey rooms. The two-storey house was late in appearing in those parts of Britain that have been well studied, such as Worcestershire or Monmouthshire – the only medieval example recorded in documents relating to the former county is from the late fifteenth century, and in the latter changes of this kind do not appear until the mid sixteenth century.

The decline of cruck construction in rural architecture from the thirteenth century onwards is without question attributable to the development of construction techniques that enabled wide spans to be roofed directly from load-bearing walls. Furthermore, the increase in timber prices in the post-medieval period, together with competition from shipbuilding, led to this type of construction becoming rarer in the countryside. Naturally curved timbers were particularly sought after for shipbuilding. Over the whole of Europe, and especially in France, there was a substantial growth in shipbuilding from the end of the seventeenth century, as evidenced by the very restrictive forest ordinances issued by Colbert in France. Similar restrictions with the same objectives were imposed in Tudor England.

3   Load-bearing walls

Examples of houses with load-bearing walls and no independent supporting elements, whether internal or external, are known from as early as the first century AD. They did not, however, become common until the early Middle Ages, between the sixth and tenth centuries: Chalton (see Figure 105), Maxey (cf. Figure 98), West Stow, Thetford etc. in Britain; Husterknupp, Haithabu, Stellerburg and Hamburg in Germany, and Antwerp a little later, in the eleventh century, in Belgium.

Archaeological observations lead to the identification of three groups: walls without supports strong enough to bear a roof and where internal or external posts are required; walls with integral supports that are capable of bearing a roof, but of which there is a large number, all of the same size and closely spaced; and finally walls with both heavy load-bearing uprights and lighter vertical elements, the role of which is essentially to facilitate the fixing of the wall filling – wattle and daub, for example. In this case the vertical load-bearing elements are known as corner posts.

Two additional factors that may also need to be taken into consideration are the more or less straight alignment of the posts and the presence or absence of horizontal cross-members – tie beams or collars.

When walls do not contain strong enough members, the roof structure has to be carried, partially at least, on the tops of the walls; in this case a true wall plate becomes indispensable, and this requires that the elements making up the wall are aligned as precisely as possible (cf. Figure 98). This may even lead to the insertion of sill beams. The example of Büderich in Germany is very characteristic of this type of non-bearing wall construction, which requires the use of the different types of internal upright support discussed earlier. However, when walls are load-bearing it is possible to dispense with a proper wall plate and line up the upright elements of the walls with great care. However, in those cases where corner posts alone or corner posts and secondary supports are used, internal uprights are not needed, since the whole wall can become load-bearing. This results in single-aisled buildings freed from any internal supporting members.

Undifferentiated load-bearing elements

In the case of structures with walls based on relatively closely spaced and undifferentiated corner posts, two types can be distinguished according to whether the posts are aligned on the axis of the walls or not. As in all cases where it is essential to use a wall plate, buildings with unaligned uprights make use of tie beams upon which the wall plates are supported. In a sense this is an inverted version of the early, more traditional structure in which the wall plate is located below the tie beams. In the case under consideration, although the corner posts do not necessarily have to be aligned longitudinally, it is essential that uprights should be aligned transversely in pairs, so as to be able to carry the tie beams. An example of this type of inverted construction (German *Überrähmverzimmerung*) is the reconstruction of the phase 3 buildings of the medieval English village of Goltho (cf. Figure 82).

When, on the other hand, the corner posts are properly aligned, the wall plates are placed directly on top of them. Two types can immediately be distinguished. The first is the structure, fairly common in the Middle Ages, covered with common rafters of the same cross-section. The buildings from the early period of occupation at Goltho and house B1 at Chalton (see Figure 105) belong to this group, quite common in rural architecture. The second type uses a *faux entrait* [there is no accepted term in English for this building element, best described as a false tie beam, since it does not occur in English vernacular buildings], a wooden beam fixed below the tops of the corner posts, to support the upper wall plate (see Figure 106). This type of construction (German *Unterrähmverzimmerung*) first appears around the ninth century, notably at Haithabu (Germany). It later becomes very typical of the large three-aisled buildings of the thirteenth century and later in Frisia and the region of the Lower Saxon house (*Niedersachsenhaus*: cf. Figures 29, 79). In both these types of construction, the roof is made up of closely spaced rafters equal in cross-section. A third and final possibility associated with the use of undifferentiated corner posts is the tie beam inserted between each pair of corner posts. Examples of this type of construction can be found in religious architecture before 1200, with numerous closely spaced tie beams located at the base of all the common rafters (see Figure 107). It is, however, difficult to identify this system of construction, which was very lavish in its use of large-section timbers, from ground-level remains. It is more logical, notwithstanding, to contemplate

303

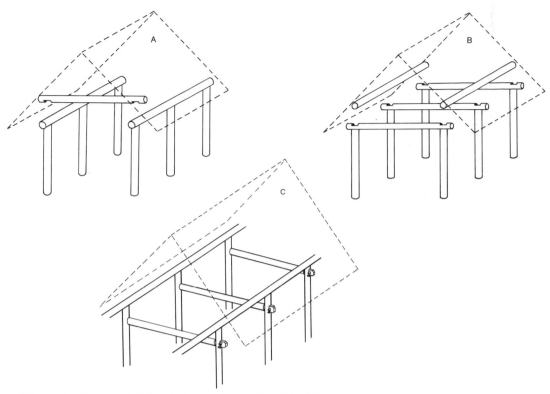

Fig. 106. *True and false tie beams in medieval building*

A   Classic layout at the end of the Middle Ages: the tie beam is carried on the upper wall plates, which are themselves located either on the tops of stone walls or, as here, on upright wall posts, which in this case must be carefully aligned longitudinally, though not necessarily in the transverse direction in pairs.

B   Inverted positioning of tie beam and wall plate. In cases where the wall posts are not aligned longitudinally, they cannot carry the wall plate directly. The posts are therefore arranged in pairs in opposite walls; they then carry the tie beams directly, the two wall plates being then located on the ends of the tie beams. Using this system it is therefore unnecessary to align the wall posts longitudinally. It was often used in the Middle Ages, in both later and developed constructions.

C   Use of false tie beams. In this case, the special constraints of the two previous types are combined: the upright wall posts, which bear the wall plates directly, must be aligned longitudinally, and, since the tie beams join the wall posts in pairs, and are no longer borne by the wall plates, as in the first example, they must also be aligned carefully in pairs in the transverse direction. This system using false tie beams is especially typical of medieval rural buildings in northern Germany (cf. Figure 100, 4). The importance of this type of construction lies in the simplification of the jointing needed, since the three elements – wall posts, tie beams, wall plates – need only to be joined in pairs.

(H. Hinz, Zur Geschichte der niederdeutsche Halle, *Zeitschrift für Volkskunde*, 60 (1964), 4; B. Trier, *Das Haus im Nordwesten der Germania Libera*, IV, Veröffentlichungen der Altertumskommission im Provinzialinstitut für westfälische Landes- und Volkskunde, Aschendorffsche Verlagsbuchhandlung, Münster/Westfalen (1969), Tafel 19, 20)

the general use of tie beams in connection with the third type of construction, which will be dealt with next, in which corner posts and secondary supporting members exist side-by-side in the walls (cf. Figure 105, A and B).

In the latter case, however, even if a bayed form of construction seems obvious, the link is not obvious and its existence cannot be substantiated with certainty on the basis of postholes alone. Nevertheless, logic and constructional history, as shown by surviving monuments, point in this direction.

Differentiated load-bearing elements: the appearance of the bay

The appearance of a distinction in wall construction between corner posts and secondary supporting members marks an important evolutionary stage in the history of rural architecture. This system, linked with changes in roof construction, led to savings in the use of heavy-section timbers, which had already become an important consideration. It also represents a very significant step towards the development from primitive forms of construction of the true timber-framed structure which appears at the end of the medieval period. This bayed form of structure – the *chas de maison*, as it is called in certain medieval documents from the Blésois or Burgundy – is a step towards standardization of timber building. From the documents in which it is described, it is possible to gain an impression of normal house sizes. Thus in thirteenth- to sixteenth-century Worcestershire, the characteristic house type consisted of two, or more often three, bays – only very rarely of a single bay. The largest houses could spread to four bays and measure some 4.8 × 22.5m (16 × 74ft). These were cruck-framed buildings, but they are identical in form. The bayed type of construction seems to have appeared first in one form or other early in the medieval period, to judge from houses such as those from the Anglo-Saxon village of Chalton, but it does not seem to have become widely diffused in the rural world before the twelfth to thirteenth centuries.

The principal rafter system

The transition from the classic and very common roof structure with common rafters and collar beams to one based on principal rafters – i.e. the juxtaposition of elements at relatively wide spacings, corresponding to the widths of the bays (1.5–2.5m [5–8ft]), and thinner timbers disposed between the principals – may have been linked from the start with the origin of walls with corner posts and secondary supporting uprights. This system, which also economizes in the use of heavy-section timbers, cannot be reconstructed with assurance in every case where walls composed of stout corner posts and secondary members are revealed by excavation. However, here once again logic and building history point this way. This system can certainly be postulated for certain of the Chalton houses (sixth to seventh centuries). Its subsequent development depended upon the systematic addition of a tie beam beneath each of the principal rafters and on each pair of corner posts. This led to the development of the classic truss system, which evolved considerably and gave rise in the post-medieval period to many regional variations.

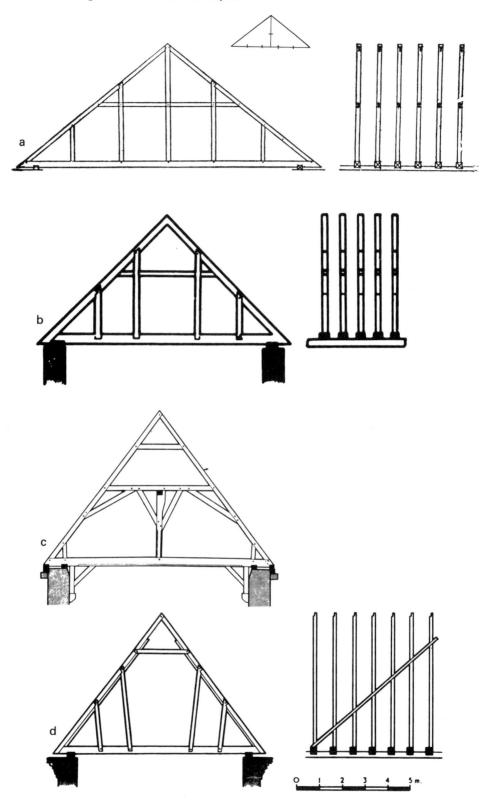

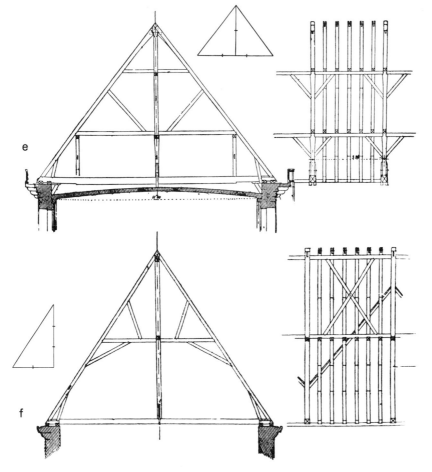

Fig. 107. *Truss constructions from eleventh- to fifteenth-century churches*

a. Saint-Pierre de Montmartre (Seine, France), built in 1147: collar and king post; all internal members vertical or horizontal; closely spaced trusses, not connected longitudinally.

b. Soignes (Hainault, Belgium); eleventh-century nave and mid twelfth-century chancel: same general characteristics as a. (no king post in nave).

c. Harwell (Berkshire, England), nave of c.1220: collar linked by crown post to centre of tie beam. Two developments over a. and b.: oblique connecting members within the truss, and introduction of linkage between trusses – in this case horizontal collar purlins joining the tops of the crown posts beneath each collar. The trusses are still closely spaced (62cm [24in.]).

d. Haguenau (Bas-Rhin, France), late twelfth century: no king post, closely spaced trusses, oblique transverse bracing members, longitudinal element between trusses.

e. Mantes (Yvelines, France), early thirteenth century: king post, collars, multiplication of transverse bracing members, introduction of two purlins connecting the vertical members beneath each collar.

f. Seignelay (Yonne, France), fifteenth to sixteenth centuries: king post, collar, transverse bracing members, through purlins linking trusses, and false ridge beneath rafter joint.

(*a, e, f:* C. Enlart, *Manuel d'archéologie française*, Part 1, vol. II, Paris (1929): figs. 247, 346, 375. *b, c, d:* J. M. Fletcher and P. S. Spokes, The origin and development of the crown post roof, *Medieval Archaeology*, 8 (1964), figs. 43, 46, 54)

To conclude this discussion of walls with corner posts and secondary supports, it should be noted that it is possible to build upon an upper wall plate (which is essential in this form of construction) either a roof of common rafters and collar beams or – which is more likely and more logical – one based on principal rafters and collar beams. In certain cases, indeed – no doubt the most highly evolved cases (not overlooking a possible early appearance before the twelfth century) – it may even have led to the classic, developed truss system.

So far as the wall structures of these timber houses are concerned, the three types described above – no vertical supporting elements, undifferentiated corner posts, corner posts plus secondary uprights – evolved simultaneously in medieval Europe up to the point when two important factors led to considerable changes in the possibilities available to house builders: bayed construction and the general use of tie beams, coupled with the development of the truss. The latter will be considered in more detail.

The introduction of the tie beam (or false tie beam) is certainly connected with the desire to provide house structures with greater spans and better stability (see Figure 106). The use of the single-aisled house certainly does not imply the systematic use of tie beams – far from it. However, the two phenomena are doubtless to some extent connected, in so far as they betoken a wish to free and enlarge the living area. The use of tie beams for houses 5–6m (16–20ft) wide makes it possible to roof the building in a form that other forms of construction do not permit.

The single-aisled house became more and more common between the sixth and the tenth centuries. A study of examples from this period, notably in Germany, shows, as A. Zippelius has pointed out, that these were mainly seigneurial buildings within fortified enclosures (Haithabu, Hamburg), i.e. buildings on sites where space was restricted, but where the standard of living of the inhabitants and the general environment allowed the most highly developed techniques to be used and the best craftsmen to be employed. At the same time, the limitation on available space led not only to the lengthening of buildings, which was possible with all constructional systems, but also, and more especially, to their being made wider. The single-aisled form of construction using tie beams was very appropriate in this respect. Whether or not it was used in these examples is of little importance in the last analysis; what is certain is that they illustrate a long-standing and pronounced trend towards the enlargement of buildings, which explains the subsequent spread of the single-aisled building in the rural world and the perfecting of constructional techniques.

A decisive step forward: the appearance of the truss

The problem of the tie beam is connected with that of the truss. A truss is a triangular member, more or less complex in form, which is set up vertically. As a result of its shape, it can normally not be deformed in the vertical plane.

The development of truss construction plays an important role in the history of medieval building, and indirectly in rural architecture. Three lines of development can be distinguished: the definition of various types of truss on the basis of the disposition of their transverse connecting elements; the appearance of a distinction between two types of structural element – the truss as a main bearing member and simple rafters as secondary members; and finally, the gradual introduction of longitudinal connecting members between the trusses.

The most simple truss consists of a horizontal element or tie beam and two symmetrical oblique members, the rafters. In practice, various secondary members are introduced into the vertical structure defined in this way, which act as braces or stiffeners: the most typical are collars and king posts. From the late twelfth century, deriving from the use of these two types of secondary member, most commonly in the structures of large civil and religious buildings, two different traditions developed, on either side of the English Channel. In Britain, the crown post system was used, based on an upright member linking only tie beam and collar. In France, this construction was unknown; instead, the king post was in use at this time, which joined the ridge beam to the tie beam. It may be observed, however, that the use of the king post, which was very important in ensuring rigidity in the truss, did not become general in France until the thirteenth century. Moreover, the transverse links within the vertical framework of the truss were for a long time few in number and exclusively horizontal or vertical. It was not until the early thirteenth century that these links multiplied and were disposed obliquely, thereby becoming more efficient.

The second main period of truss construction began after 1200, again according to the evidence provided by church architecture. The structure of Saint-Pierre de Montmartre (see Figure 107), from the mid twelfth century, is typical in this respect: there is no difference in thickness between the rafters, which are usually rather slight in section and very closely spaced (60–85cm (24–33in.)). The fundamental difference between heavy-section trusses, usually more than 1.5–2m (5–6ft 6in.) apart, and lighter ones disposed in between the heavy trusses, does not appear until relatively late – before the fifteenth century in certain regions, as shown by the cathedrals at Rheims, Paris and Amiens, but sometimes even later, as in Burgundy and Champagne. This led to the introduction of bayed construction, which resulted in savings in heavy-section timbers.

The third important factor is the very gradual appearance of longitudinal connecting members between trusses. This presented a technical problem: in buildings over 7–8m (23–26ft) long, the introduction of longitudinal members, such as ridge beams, presupposes the butting together of stressed lengths of timber, a delicate problem which was only solved in the more highly evolved constructions of the larger late medieval buildings. Until around 1200 there were no longitudinal joints in church structures: it was not until the first half of the thirteenth century that these began to appear, as in the churches at Haguenau or Mantes, in the form of purlins. It was not until the mid thirteenth

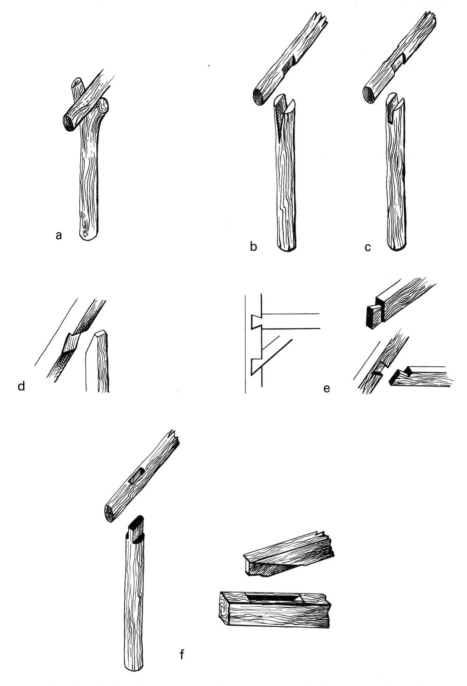

century – in the bishop's palace at Auxerre in 1258, for example – that the first example of a false ridge beam is to be observed. Longitudinal linking members of all kinds multiplied in the fourteenth century, but they only became common in the fifteenth century. Purlins were not in use before the late fifteenth century.

It was in this way that the constructional techniques of the post-medieval period evolved during the twelfth to fifteenth centuries. Although it is difficult to transpose this evolutionary process directly into the rural context, its study can provide an idea of the potential and of the limitations of rural architecture.

Fig. 108. *Joints in medieval carpentry*

a.   Load-bearing fork
b–c. Simple joint
d.   Simple notched joint
e.   Through and halved dovetail joints
f.   Mortise and tenon

The most common joints were between two pieces of timber, either at right angles (e.g. wall plates or sill beams and upright posts) or obliquely (e.g. trusses and wall plates). It was rarer for three timbers to be joined at the same point (joint between a tie beam and a wall plate carried on wall posts and not a stone wall). The simplest way of joining two timbers at right angles or obliquely is to use a natural fork (a). This was doubtless a very common technique in primitive medieval structures. A joint worked in a more developed way, whilst still retaining the features of the simplest system, is also possible (b,c).

Four more developed joints were also in use but at different periods, on the basis of evidence from the larger civil or, in particular, religious buildings, as well as that from archaeological contexts.

The simple notched joint (d) is the most elementary, but it can only be used in oblique joints. Another simple form of joint is the halved joint, known in particular from Büderich, where it was used for joining the sill beams and elements of the internal partition (Figure 90, C and D) of the eleventh- to twelfth-century building. This technique has the advantage over the preceding one of preventing lateral displacement.

Dovetailing was usually combined in the Middle Ages with halving (the dovetail is at least as thick as half the thickness of the timber into which it is to be inserted), and could be used for right-angled (e) or oblique (f) joints. In the latter case, it would be a half-dovetail. As with halved joints, this method has the advantage of not coming apart under pressure or strain on the axis of the two joined timbers, an essential requirement for certain applications. Until at least the mid thirteenth century, dovetailing was the main method used in French churches, along with notched joints. The most evolved jointing method, using mortises and tenons (and eventually pegging of the tenon in the mortise, which ensures complete joint stability), first appears in French churches at the end of the twelfth century. This technique can be used for both right-angled and oblique joints. It was used in some rural or other buildings earlier than the twelfth century, especially in Scandinavia.

Joints in three timbers at the same point are more complex but can all be related to the examples described above. There are some examples of its use in medieval rural architecture, as in building 3 at Husterknupp (Figure 88, 7), but these are exceptional.

At the same time it makes it possible to define the difficulty of making comparisons between the traditional rural architecture of the Ancien Régime and that of the Middle Ages, and one of the main factors in the transition from one to the other.

In this attempt to analyse the history of building construction during the medieval period, certain major technological and chronological trends have been demonstrated. Regional variations are perhaps less clear-cut, especially in relation to certain of the factors involved and given the current state of research. There are major socio-economic implications that are decisive in this respect. However, it would be a mistake to lose sight of more general factors such as the incontrovertible technological progress, especially in the field of jointing techniques, the constraints imposed by the materials available, old local traditions, and divergent developments, sometimes at a very early date, from a common – or apparently common – origin.

Take, for example, technological progress. Joinery provides an excellent example of the factors involved and the consequences.

Medieval constructional techniques, apart from those used in high-grade late medieval buildings, knew nothing of butt joints, except for members jointed under pressure, such as load-bearing uprights, which constituted a significant constraint on the use of longitudinal linking members such as ridge beams, since this involved of necessity the use of butt-jointed timbers.

In the simplest case, that of two members joined at an angle, the most rudimentary system consisted of using natural forks (see Figure 108a). This system was certainly used a great deal in the most common forms of rural building, particularly those built of logs rather than squared-up timbers.

In the latter case, more developed systems were used, as shown by certain rural buildings, the timber components of which have survived, or by higher-quality buildings such as churches. The simple notched joint is one of the most elementary jointing methods. It can only be used for an oblique joint between two timbers (cf. Figures 102, 108d). Three other more or less classic systems have much wider applications for both oblique and perpendicular joints, usually on squared-up timbers. The joints between the sill beams and the uprights in the Büderich house provide a good example of halved jointing (cf. Figure 90). In France in particular, up to the thirteenth century, dovetailing was the most common form of developed jointing in use, even in churches. Classic mortise and tenon joints do not appear in French churches, however, until the end of the twelfth century (see Figure 108f). These are first attested France in the cathedral of Lisieux (Calvados) around 1180. It is therefore likely that this technique did not spread into the French countryside until relatively late and to a restricted extent. By contrast there are rural and other buildings dating to earlier than the twelfth century which bear witness to its use in other regions, such as Scandinavia.

A more complex problem is that of joining three timbers at a single point, an operation that is necessary to ensure the linkage between an upright post, a wall plate, and a tie beam. Various excavated medieval buildings – Huster-knupp, for example – show how this problem was solved (cf. Figure 88). It certainly requires some delicacy in handling, at least in relation to rural architecture, which probably explains why a system such as that of the false tie beam was utilized, which in the case under consideration makes it possible to join wall post, wall plate, and tie beam in joints between two members at a time (cf. Figure 106).

The method of selected jointing, which depends on the tools available, the skill of the craftsmen, regional traditions etc, has direct effects on the resulting building, its size, which was usually restricted, the strength of the structure, and its solidity. This is therefore an important factor that has to be taken into account in evaluating rural architecture.

The properties of the materials used certainly played a part. Where common rafters and collar beams were used for roof structures, the most common structural elements were poles or *perches* – small-diameter pieces of wood used with the bark removed. Certain species that lend themselves well to this technique were used directly. In the case of other species, such as hornbeam, aspen, or ash, which have straight shoots, a measure of preparation was needed.

In order to obtain the curved members needed for cruck buildings, there may have been special cultivation methods; some English scholars believe this may have been the case. It is, furthermore, certain that more complicated or mortised structures would have required the use of heavier timbers and this, given the opportunities available for medieval people to obtain building timber, must automatically imply a clear social differentiation and, in consequence, a measure of technical constraint. One line of development of medieval construction seems to have been towards economies in the use of large-section timbers, particularly in the use of corner posts and secondary uprights or of bayed construction. One aspect of medieval roof construction that is closely linked with this concern to reduce the use of heavy timbers and which also has clear socio-economic implications is the hipped roof. This type of roof obviously reduces the amount of roof timbering: for the same overall building length, a gabled roof would necessitate the use of a ridge beam the same length as the building itself and, where crucks were not available, of principal rafters or trusses in each gable. It is not by chance that ordinary peasant houses, such as those from thirteenth- to nineteenth-century Brittany that have already been discussed, have hipped roofs.

E Roofing materials

In the great majority of cases it is very difficult to know for certain what roofing materials were used on medieval rural buildings. Apart from tiles or certain roofs of stone flags, the materials used have left no traces, save in very exceptional circumstances. Moreover, they are often easy to reuse, which also reduces the chances of identification. Archaeologists are therefore generally reduced to making use of indirect evidence: certain flimsy constructions could not have supported heavy roofing materials or, by contrast, very solid load-bearing elements in certain contexts would have made it possible for any type of roofing to have been utilized. The presence of nails favours the use of slates or tiles, whilst their absence suggests the use of vegetable materials.

In certain rare cases where the building has been exceptionally well preserved, it is possible to assess the pitch of a roof, which is also an important factor, since certain types of roofing cannot be used on steeply pitched roofs or, on the other hand, do not permit a shallow pitch. At the German settlement of Husterknupp, the survival of the halved joint between a rafter and the wall plate on which it rested made it possible to calculate the slope as 51°, a rather steeply pitched roof which would have permitted the use of thatch. Such observations are, however, exceptional.

Most often, lacking any direct or indirect information, archaeologists can only study the regional possibilities, particularly those provided by ethnographic studies, which allow them to say whether a certain material – turf, wooden shingles, limestone or schist flags etc. – is feasible or not in this context. In practice it is possible in this way to assign certain degrees of probability to the use of various materials, rather than to be certain that a specific material was used at any given site.

Although we can thus enumerate and characterize the roofing materials available in the Middle Ages, it is not possible in every case to detail regional variations or historical evolution.

1   *Sheaves of vegetable materials*

Let us begin with the vegetable materials of various kinds used in the form of sheaves or bundles: the best known and most widely used was certainly thatch, made from corn straw (the French word for thatch, *chaume*, is the origin of *chaumière*, which has come to be used for a cottage, whether thatched or roofed in some other material, and the English dialect word 'thack' is often used for any form of roofing). Rye produces the best straw and in certain cases the use of ryestraw for thatching may have had a direct influence on the plants selected for cultivation or on farming practices. In the Limagne, for example, rental agreements under the system of *métayage* during the Ancien Régime required the peasant to supply a certain number of sheaves (*glens*) of rye. At the same time, in the Bigorre, rye was cut with sickles to prevent the straw being damaged. The use of ryestraw for thatching meant that care had to be taken more generally in threshing, often requiring the use of special techniques.

Other types of plant material were also used – reeds in medieval Sologne or Limagne or East Anglia, broom most probably at Saint-Victor-de-Massiac (Puy-de-Dôme) in the later Middle Ages, or heather, to name just a few.

This method of roofing was simple to perform and must still be the most common on earth. It does, however, have a number of disadvantages. Once it becomes soaked from snow or humidity it quickly rots, which means that it cannot be used in certain regions. The life of a thatched roof is estimated to be a few decades, and it requires constant attention. In colder climates its use can often pose another problem: it deprives livestock of part of the small amount of food available to them. This becomes more significant when considerations of heat conservation favour the use of other materials in such regions.

In addition to these special constraints, plant-based roofs (and thatch in particular) have the further more general disadvantages of being combustible, of harbouring undesirable animal life – rodents, wasps, hornets and spiders – and, above all, of requiring a steeply pitched roof, between 40° and 55°, and in consequence greater amounts of roof timbering. Thatching also precludes the use of sharp angles, with the result that attic stories are usually illuminated by dormer windows.

Nevertheless, there is various evidence to confirm the very widespread use of this form of roofing in medieval rural buildings, even though at the end of the Middle Ages it had begun to lose ground for certain types of building to other roofing materials, such as tiles.

2 Turfs

Turfs laid with the grass uppermost were often used in those regions where the soil lent itself to the development of thickly set grass with matted roots. This roofing material has the advantage, in those cold, windy regions where it commonly occurs, of being an excellent heat-insulating medium and of retaining snow on roofs, preventing it from sliding off – a dangerous and regrettable occurrence, since a good coating of snow insulates a roof admirably. However, turf is not to be found everywhere, especially for this purpose, which means that its use is limited.

3 Stone flags

Flat stone has often been used in some regions, either in the luxury form of slate, the use of which is late and very marginal in the medieval period, confined to certain areas and in particular to high-class buildings, or in the more common forms of limestone, schist, or pumice flags.

In view of the weight of this type of material, its use in roofing requires very strong roof structures, capable of supporting some 100 kg per sq. m (220 lb per sq. yd) of roof, which restricts the use of stone flags to wet, wooded areas – Burgundy, the uplands of Quercy or Rouergue, or the Yugoslav Karst for limestone, Galicia, Brittany, or the Massif Central for schist, and the Planèze in Auvergne for large pumice slabs. Slate, which is lighter (20–30kg per sq. m [44–66lb per sq. yd]) was little used in the Middle Ages, and never in rural buildings.

Stone-flagged roofs have the disadvantage of causing snow to slip off, with the results that have just been discussed. The massive roof structures needed, because of the weight of the covering and the steep pitch that is essential in order to distribute this load – usually 50–60° – and the heavy uprights also restrict the use of this type of roof covering; nevertheless, examples are known from as early as the twelfth to thirteenth centuries in Burgundy, for example, or at Saint-Victor-de-Massiac in the Massif Central from a more recent period.

4 Wood: the use of shingles

Metal – essentially lead in this context – was not used as a roofing material in rural architecture in the Middle Ages: it was only used in the later medieval period, and then for roofing ecclesiastical buildings or palaces. However, wood in the form of shingles was undoubtedly widely utilized in many regions. Although it is difficult to prove that wood was used by excavation, its use has been confirmed by certain discoveries, such as those at Winchester from the late eleventh century or at Tours (Indre-et-Loire) from a castle well that was filled in the fourteenth century. A roof of this kind was the best possible to use in colder regions, in default of turfs. It is, moreover, a roofing material that is both light in weight and easy to fix.

The use of shingles in ninth- to eleventh-century English and Scandinavian rural architecture is well attested, from two-dimensional (paintings, tapestries, manuscripts) and three-dimensional (hog-back tombs) representations. The latter, which can be up to 2m (6ft 6in.) long and are very realistic representations, are particularly common in the ancient kingdom of Northumbria and in the Orkneys, regions of the British Isles that were dominated by Scandinavians in the tenth and eleventh centuries. They show that, in this region, houses of the period were usually shingle-roofed. An oaken shingle was discovered during excavations at the Danish fortress of Trelleborg, dated to the early eleventh century.

5 Tiles

The problem of tiles has been reserved to the last because it is difficult to resolve, for the present at least. During the classical period, a standard type of tile was in use in the lands subject to the authority of Rome – *c*.40 cm (16 in.) long, relatively thick, with a flange on each of the long sides (*tegulae*). Another form of tile (*imbrices*), similar to the hollow tiles currently in use in southern France, served to cover the joints between the *tegulae*, which were laid side by side on roofs. This constituted a heavy roof covering, requiring stout timbering; in consequence it was almost always associated with stone buildings.

This method of roofing was very widely used, to judge from the presence of tile fragments on Roman sites all over the Empire. The disappearance of Roman craft and commercial structures dealt a fatal blow to the use of this method of roofing. However, it would be a mistake to assume that it disappeared completely. In the first place, there is evidence of the reuse of Roman materials. There is documentary evidence from the early Middle Ages of tiles of Roman origin being used for roofing major buildings, especially churches. However, it seems possible that manufacture continued to a marginal extent, since there are some documentary references to tileries in the early medieval period. It would be difficult to assume that, over several centuries, the tiled roofs attested by archaeology, and the inevitable repairs to them at intervals, were made other than by recourse to the ruins of Roman buildings. Roofs in this type of material were still in use in the nineteenth century in the Massif Central, in the area between Issoire (Puy-de-Dôme) and Brioude (Haute-Loire), on both churches, such as the famous one at Brioude, and on rural buildings. These were undeniably manufactured in the medieval, or even post-medieval, periods.

Even if there was a measure of continuity in the manufacture of tiles of this type, the production would have been very small and limited in its application, reserved for special types of building or regions. This was not the case, however, with the new types that began to appear in the medieval west in the twelfth to thirteenth centuries.

Typology of medieval tiles

Even though it is reasonable to suppose that tiles of the Roman type continued to be made in certain regions, such as Provence, up to the eleventh to twelfth centuries, these would have been completely supplanted by the new types devised during the Middle Ages, which remained in use until the end of the nineteenth century, when mass-produced flat tiles came into general use. Moreover, one can see that from the twelfth to thirteenth centuries onwards, according to a chronology and to certain processes that are only dimly understood, a clear distinction developed between roofs in northern France (Ile-de-France, Burgundy, Orléanais etc.), using thin flat nibbed tiles nailed on to battens, and the south, where the so-called 'Roman' curved tiles were in use, a distinction that has persisted to the present day. This is an observation of major importance for the history of rural architecture, since it illustrates another aspect of the early divergence between building methods, dating well back into the Middle Ages. It should, however, be borne in mind that the distribution of these two types of tile was not necessarily the same in the Middle Ages as it was in the nineteenth century, nor were the types themselves standard within the two regions. These questions need more detailed consideration.

Curved tiles were in use on sites such as Rougiers, in the late twelfth century, or Saint-Victor-de-Massiac, a little later in date, and these were being manufactured by the tilemakers of the Saintonge in the thirteenth to fourteenth centuries. This was in the region where this type of roofing was no longer in use in the nineteenth century.

In the thirteenth or fourteenth century, on the other hand, flat nibbed tiles were in use at the fortified manor houses of Boiscommun (Loiret), Villy-le-Moutier (Côte-d'Or), and elsewhere, whilst they were being manufactured during the same period by the potters of Argentan (Orne) or the Beauvaisis (Oise), though naturally enough with considerable variations in shape and size.

Distribution in the rural world

The introduction of tiles brought about a rapid and profound change in the roofs of the rural world. Although at first, in the thirteenth to fourteenth centuries, they still largely represented a rare and expensive material reserved for urban buildings or those of higher quality, tiles rapidly conquered the countryside, or at least a part of it. A slow evolution began which, in certain regions of France and Britain, was not complete by the nineteenth century. Gradually tiles pushed out those materials that had dominated the early Middle Ages, principally thatch and wooden shingles.

A specific example, that of the village of Saint-Victor-de-Massiac (Puy-de-Dôme), excavated over several years by Luc Tixier, admirably demonstrates the complexity of this process and its importance for the historian. Human occupation on this basalt plateau in the Middle Ages began in the Merovingian period, and continued more or less uninterrupted until the seventeenth to eighteenth centuries. The earliest Merovingian structure known was probably roofed over with plant material. During the Carolingian period, baked clay in the form of *tegulae* and *imbrices*, the classic Roman materials, was used for the roof of a small seigneurial chapel built a short distance from the village. Since Saint-Victor is situated in a region where this method of roofing seems to have persisted, at least marginally, right up to the nineteenth century, it is difficult to say whether this was a case of reuse of ancient material or contemporary manufacture.

Later, when the village developed in the thirteenth century, this chapel was enlarged to become the parish church. It was completely reroofed, but this time in stone flags, a mixture of basalt and schist, in conformity with the local tradition. The houses in the village of this time began to be roofed with overlapping curved tiles – the first appearance on the site of this material which was to become the classic roofing of the region. The barns alongside the houses were more summarily roofed with vegetable materials, according to a process which used simpler materials for roofing ancillary buildings that could be obtained in the immediate vicinity without expense. Gradually thereafter the houses of the medieval village illustrate the classical development from that period to the present day: the replacement of one roofing material by another. Here roofs of curved tiles replaced roofs of vegetable materials in the seventeenth century, when the village was reoccupied. At this period, as in the later Middle Ages, there was a mixture of curved tiles and thatch.

This process continued its course from the end of the Middle Ages, as shown by Odette Chapelot's work on fourteenth- to fifteenth-century Burgundy and by work in Britain. It was at this time that regional variations, still profoundly visible in French rural architecture (see Figure 109), began to appear, along with evidence of social stratification – distinction between those who retained simpler materials, notably thatch, and those who replaced this with tiles. Once again it was in this key period of the twelfth to thirteenth centuries that the foundations were laid for one of the basic factors that were later to characterize traditional rural architecture.

This distinction was not purely technological: it had consequences for the structure and for the habitability of buildings. The curved tile roofs of the Mediterranean region were easy to install and were suited to a simple roof structure. By contrast, flat tiles require more complicated roof structures, and in particular steeper pitches – generally more than 60° in the post-medieval

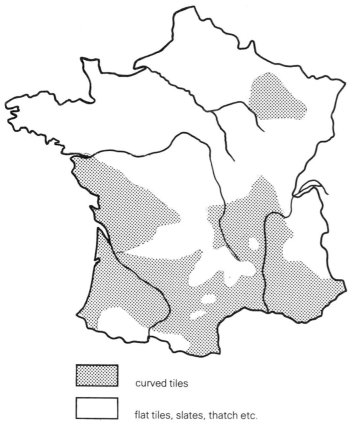

curved tiles

flat tiles, slates, thatch etc.

Fig. 109. *Distribution of various types of tiled roof in France on the basis of ethnographic data* (G. Doyon and R. Hubrecht, *L'architecture rurale et bourgeoise en France*, new ed. (1969), p. 255)

---

period in Alsace or Germany, for example. Once again it is a matter of the links between the roofing technique on the one hand, and the local woodland resources or the personal opportunities for access to constructional timber on the part of the builder on the other.

The existence of these two types of tile, and of the two regions in which they were in use concurrently, doubtless had wider consequences so far as the use of the living area was concerned. With the low-pitched Mediterranean roofs there were only limited opportunities to make use of the attic space, whereas they could be fully exploited with the steeply pitched roofs of the regions of flat tiles.

The origin of this distinction between flat and curved tiles is difficult to comprehend. Nevertheless, it is a phenomenon of great significance which has remained important up to the present day.

F   Conclusion

Whilst it has been shown that important, often decisive, changes were brought about during the twelfth to fifteenth centuries in rural building types – from the unitary house to the mixed house or the farm – there were developments of equal significance in the field of building materials and techniques.

As with building types, the changes in materials and techniques were in the direction of new technological solutions which became not only common, but also very often typical of regional practices in the post-medieval period. Thus the appearance of the farm as a unit in rural architecture, even though it remained restricted in geographical, social and numerical terms, like so much progress in materials and techniques in this period, represented a decisive step towards the establishment of traditional rural architectures and their special technological solutions.

1 *The birth of regional characteristics*

On a broader canvas, one can see during this period the appearance of definitive regional distinctions in terms of the materials and techniques adopted.

The existence of local traditions is indisputable in certain instances, as, for example, in Scandinavia, where wall posts were very early placed on padstones, a technique which does not appear until much later – the thirteenth or fourteenth century – in Yorkshire, in the construction of fortified manor houses. The emergence of regional differences is also very important.

We have already seen that there was an early divergence in truss techniques between France and Britain – the king post in the former and the crown post in the latter. In other fields there were also distinctions, for reasons that remain unclear. In Britain the concept of the large manorial hall, at first with aisles and then aisleless from the thirteenth century onwards, survived for a considerable period, as did the central open fireplace, whereas in France wall chimneys were being installed in comparable buildings. The practice of keeping the roof structures open also persisted much longer in Britain than in France. Both examples are significant in terms of differences in construction and had a considerable influence on rural architecture – on, for example, the early generalized use and spread of the wall chimney.

2 *The concept of progress in medieval rural architecture*

The problem of the concept of progress in the field of rural architecture demands consideration in a wider sense. It affects both the choice of materials as well as constructional techniques. One aspect of the question is immediately apparent: the span that could be roofed without interior supports. Before the seventh to ninth centuries the central aisle of a three-aisled structure was usually less than 4m (13ft) wide; the handful of single-aisled buildings of this period were also less than 4m (13ft) wide. From the ninth to tenth centuries onwards, the central aisle of three-aisled buildings gradually increased in breadth up to 5m (16ft) and more, equal to that achieved in single-aisled buildings. Up to this period only cruck construction could achieve spans of this size, but from then onwards (and especially after the twelfth to thirteenth centuries) cruck construction entered more and more into direct competition with more developed forms of building, especially the use of trusses. As we have seen, this did not mean the end of cruck construction, which continued in use well after the end of the Middle Ages, in particular because of its economic use of timber and its simplicity in assembly by comparison with truss construction. It survived, however, in specific socio-economic contexts, different from those in which it found applications prior to the fifteenth century. The growth of animal husbandry and the consequent need for storage capacity for large quantities of fodder influenced the decline of the cruck and the adoption of truss construction, because the latter, unlike the cruck, lent itself naturally to the insertion of an upper storey for storing reserves for both men and animals.

Another aspect of technological progress was the continual interchange between ancillary buildings and dwelling houses. So far as building materials and techniques were concerned, the former served either as test beds or, in the post-medieval period, as museums, in effect, which explains their contemporary importance in the study of traditional rural architecture.

Finally, independently of larger questions such as building plans, the use of space, or the selection of constructional materials, medieval building methods provide data on technological and economic constraints on the use of raw materials and styles of building, in addition to information on regional differences and the general directions of technological progress. Although we cannot always comprehend everything, what we can derive from this study is still of sufficient importance and interest to demonstrate a major aspect of the overall problem.

3 From 'sub-building' to true medieval rural architecture

The most striking aspect of the later medieval period is the transition from basic constructional materials – what may be termed 'sub-building' – to the more developed materials and techniques that constitute the basis for a true rural architecture, a term which cannot be applied to the different types of rural building to be found in most European regions before the twelfth to thirteenth centuries.

The materials and techniques in use before that period are characterized by their poor resistance to the effects of weather. The materials were essentially perishable – unbaked clay, wood, branches, leaves – and the techniques extremely simple, not using mortise and tenon joints and utilizing timber that was not squared up – thin poles rather than proper timbers. This was a form of building which was based largely on materials that lay readily to hand in the settlement itself or its immediate vicinity and which could be obtained without any expense; the building would be erected by its future occupants, perhaps aided by their neighbours.

These are the characteristics of a 'sub-building' – what the ethnologists call a *maison pour rien*. There is another, very important characteristic to be added: the ease and speed with which such a building can be erected. Experiments have been carried out for some years in the building of houses comparable with those of the early Middle Ages using the appropriate battery of tools, particularly in Britain. In addition, ethnographic observations and discussions with the builders of present-day ancillary buildings, employing materials and techniques very similar to those in use in the early medieval period, have thrown light on this question; an outstanding example is the work done on the barns of Touraine. The great ease and speed with which the required materials can be collected together from a very limited area around the building site and with which the structure itself can be put up become very apparent.

The reconstruction in the summer of 1976 of a large Neolithic house excavated on the settlement site of Cuiry-les-Chaudardes (Aisne), provided an opportunity to carry out experiments relating to the problems of the techniques and working times needed to put up a building made of timber, daub and reeds. Although it dated from a much earlier period, this building was very similar to medieval examples, in terms of both materials and general dimensions (5.5m [18ft] wide by 12m [39ft] long). This is very close to buildings on early medieval sites such as Chalton (sixth to seventh centuries), although the jointing techniques used at Chalton were more complex and evolved than those used in the Cuiry house. This would have had the effect of producing savings in the use of materials, since the 18 internal uprights would not be needed.

The framework of the Cuiry house was made up of unsquared 15–30cm (6–12in.) diameter timber posts spaced c.1m (3ft) apart and sunk 0.7–1.2m (2–4ft) into the ground. Between these uprights the wall was composed of wattle and daub. The roofing material was most likely of vegetable origin – probably reeds in this instance – and the roof was supported on three parallel rows each of six internal posts.

The materials needed to construct this building consisted of tree trunks for the structural members of the wall and roof, poles for the rafters and battens, thin pliable twigs for the wattling, clay for the daub, bundles of reeds for the roofing, and flexible plant ties to join the wooden elements together, in the absence of evidence of the use of nails or pegs, as was normal in early medieval 'sub-buildings'.

The heavy-section timbers were of two types: 26 trunks of 15–30cm (6–12in.) diameter and 2.8m (9ft) long, intended to make up the framework of the walls, and 18 trunks of the same diameter to support the roof, disposed in three parallel rows, those in the centre row being 4.8m (15ft) long and those in the two flanking rows 3.8m (12ft) long; and thinner timbers, 8–15cm (3–6in.) in diameter and 4–6m (13–20ft) long, which were used as main roof timbers.

One important observation must be made: buildings such as those at Chalton and elsewhere show that in medieval rural architecture the internal uprights would not have been needed, thanks to the availability of better jointing techniques. This would represent a saving of approximately half of the total length of 150m (164yd) of heavy-section (15–30cm (6–12in.) diameter) timber needed in the reconstruction of the Cuiry Neolithic house. It will be obvious from this that progress in carpentry techniques is an important economic factor which must be taken into consideration in assessing medieval 'sub-building' and its development.

The roof structure of the Cuiry house required 200 poles of 4–6cm ($1\frac{1}{2}$–$2\frac{1}{2}$in.) diameter (80 4m [13ft] long for the rafters and 120 2.5m [8ft] long for the battens). A total weight of 1.5 tonnes (tons) of reeds (2,500 bundles) was used for the roofing. To join the rafters to the beams and the battens to the rafters, to tie the bundles of reeds, and to secure them to the battens required 5km (3 miles) of vegetable material (in this case hemp).

Building the walls needed in all 6,000 flexible sticks 1.25m (4ft) long and 1–2cm ($\frac{3}{8}$–$\frac{3}{4}$in.) in diameter and 15 tonnes (tons) of clay soil (10 cu.m (13cu.yd)). Excavation had shown that this was derived from pits dug near the buildings. Preparation of the daub required several thousand litres of water and the mixing with the clay of 200kg (441lb) of chopped straw.

The tools required for all these operations comprised an axe for cutting and dressing the main wall and roof structural elements, a sickle for cutting the straw and the reeds, and a spade for digging out the clay and preparing the daub.

It is less easy to assess the difficulties involved in obtaining this material and the minimum distances over which they had to be transported. All that need be said is that none of the materials listed above is in any way exceptional or rare and that the main work involved must have been the search for them and, in particular, their transportation, which is difficult to evaluate. The time taken at Cuiry-les-Chaudardes in the summer of 1976 by a team from the University of Paris I in assembling and preparing materials, and in putting up the building, was about 300 man-days, each of eight to ten hours – i.e. a month and a half of work for a group of six people, and only a month for a team of ten. Bearing in mind that Neolithic peoples, like those of the Middle Ages, were individually very experienced in this type of work, and given the number of buildings, rebuildings, and repairs that they must have been obliged to carry out in the course of a single generation, this estimate of the time required can doubtless be reduced by one-third. This gives some 200 man-days of ten hours, or about one month for a team of six people; this probably gives an acceptable idea of the time needed to build an average house in timber and clay in the medieval period.

Coming nearer to the present day, the building of one of the *hangars* of Touraine – large buildings enclosing a surface area of 50–60 sq. m (60–72 sq. yd) made entirely of thin poles and bundles of vegetable materials – occupied a specialized craftsman, helped by one or two apprentices and, perhaps, the client himself, for one week in bringing together the constructional materials and three weeks in putting it up – i.e. a total of 100 man-days which, since building usually took place in high summer, were long ones. This was a type of building very different from that just described, which was largely built of wattle and daub. However, many early medieval buildings have been

Fig. 110. *Reconstruction of buildings at the Anglo-Saxon village of West Stow (Suffolk)*

The buildings excavated at West Stow, which date to the fifth to seventh centuries, have been reconstructed in an open-air museum. In the background there is a sunken hut of the most common European type (cf. Figure 33). To the left and right in the foreground, two more sunken huts have been reconstructed with floors and above-ground walls on the basis of excavated data (cf. Figure 36). A ground-level building can be seen in the left background in course of reconstruction (cf. Figure 34, d).

(Photograph: Stanley E. West, 1978)

---

excavated in Britain and Germany which are very similar to the Touraine *hangars*. Materials of this kind or walls of vertical planks were used in the recent reconstruction of the Anglo-Saxon village of West Stow (see Figure 110).

The two examples described above, leaving aside differences of technique and period, each enclose a considerable area and were put up in 100–200 working days. These figures can be accepted as an average value for this type of building.

With other constructional techniques – that of the 'log cabin', for example – erection would certainly have been more speedy, as Canadian observations of such methods in the eighteenth and nineteenth centuries confirm. As we have seen, however, such a method of building would only be feasible in special heavily wooded regions.

These are essentially buildings constructed after a relatively easy process of collecting together the materials required and a short erection time. The whole process – acquisition of materials, transportation, erection – cost nothing in monetary terms and required no special tools (in particular metal ones) nor any highly developed craft skills.

By contrast with this 'sub-building' technique, the rural architecture that began in the twelfth to thirteenth centuries was diametrically different in character.

First there is a trend observable – gradual at first and then systematic in its application – towards the use of materials that are highly weather-proof: stone is a typical example, but there are other materials that replace it in regions without stone which were adopted for the same basic reason. This is the case with the transition to high-quality timber-frame construction or the appearance elsewhere of building in brick. Brickmaking began in the mid twelfth century in the northern Netherlands or East Anglia, and around 1200 in Flanders, and gradually spread between 1200 and 1300 in these and comparable regions, such as the Toulousain in France. Although there are no examples of the exclusive use of brick in building in English rural architecture earlier than the fifteenth century, this was not the case in the Low Countries where, from as early as the fourteenth century, rural buildings are known to have been built at least in part in brick. Some notable examples are the barn at Waal Harbour, near Rotterdam (fourteenth century) and the Belgian sites of Lampernisse (West Flanders) and Roeselare (East Flanders).

It is obvious that the replacement of timber and of wattle and daub or *pisé* by stone has the effect of considerably extending the building time. Whilst clay can readily be found close to the building site, which makes transportation relatively unimportant, the same does not hold good for stone. This means that, in addition to the much greater problems associated with extraction (time-consuming by comparison with clay, as a result of the need to remove the overburden, and the use of more complicated tools), stone demands longer and more systematic transport arrangements. Building a stone wall also needs more highly developed tools than 'sub-building' and, in addition to the problem of craft skills on the part of the workers, a considerably longer working time. There is a transition to a method of building which, simply in terms of the time needed for its completion, was incomparably more time-consuming than that of the early Middle Ages, by a factor of two to four. Account must also be taken of the problems posed by greater demands in terms of equipment, transport, and technical expertise.

Alongside this change in materials of construction, new technologies began to be introduced into rural architecture at this period: the use of squared-up timbers and mortise joints, and the appearance of methods of construction which freed the space enclosed by the walls, in particular the use of trusses.

Linked with this development in the field of materials and techniques was the new obligation in respect of the supply of materials, from specialized craftsmen or sources – on the one hand tiles, nails, or bricks, and on the other main structural members, which in the later part of the Middle Ages had to be purchased by peasants, as a result of restrictions imposed on free rights of gathering materials. The problem of access to at least some of the materials required became more complicated and involved both more time and the expenditure of money. Moreover, the services of specialized craftsmen became necessary for the first time, at least for the more highly developed types of rural building, especially in the period of major rebuilding during the second half of the fifteenth century (or earlier in some cases). Documentary sources describe the growing emergence from the twelfth century onwards of rural craftsmen skilled in the art of building. It was this group that was involved in the great rural rebuilding of the later Middle Ages, and it is certainly to the activities of its members that certain architectural constraints, such as the establishment of rural building traditions, from the second half of the fifteenth century at least, can be attributed.

In this context it can be seen that what took place in the twelfth to thirteenth centuries was much more than mere progress in materials and techniques – rather the transition from one form of rural architecture to another (if not from one form of rural society to another), and the replacement of a form of 'sub-building' by an architecture proper. This transition was based on the appearance of higher-quality materials and improvements in their application.

The importance of this phenomenon is much greater, in the last analysis, than the mere replacement of wood as a constructional material by stone in certain parts of twelfth- to thirteenth-century Europe. It represents a major problem of civilization, an upheaval which had profound consequences in the socio-economic field. The earlier appearance of stone-built houses and the use of mortar – in the Mediterranean region, for example – implies an earlier transition, under various influences, from one concept of the house to another and the earlier creation of the forms and techniques of traditional rural architecture. It is justifiable to assert that this transition was undoubtedly the most significant event in the field of medieval rural settlement.

Conclusion

In archaeology just as in history, a long period is needed to allow the major decisive phenomena of cultural history to become apparent and to enable their importance to be evaluated. Similarly, vast areas of land, such as the whole of western Europe, need to be studied in order to reveal the main lines in the history of rural settlement and its heterogeneous nature, within defined limits which, despite dissimilarities and regional variations, highlight the unique nature of this period in the history of rural settlement and the close relationship between the types that originated at that time and those of the present day.

During the millennium spanned by the Middle Ages as traditionally defined, ending around 1500, a number of fundamental phenomena occurred which throw one special event of the tenth to twelfth centuries into high relief: the birth of the village as a unit of settlement, as a socio-economic framework, and as an architectural reality. Regional variations in building form, chronology or materials are of little importance since the phenomenon was a general one, producing similar effects almost everywhere.

Those characteristics that define village settlement have already been set out – concentration of population, organization of land settlement within a confined area, communal buildings such as the church and the castle, permanent settlement based on buildings that continue in use, and socio-economic organization that in particular involves the presence of craftsmen.

The whole of Europe, with the exception of certain peripheral regions such as Ireland and Scandinavia, bears witness to the same phenomenon, albeit with variations in chronology, settlement, building etc. There is an overall comparability in terms of both socio-economic and architectural factors. It is not part of the present study to investigate the causes of these parallel forms of development or their subsequent consequences for the history of western Europe. Three facts must, however, be stressed. First, in the twelfth to thirteenth centuries a phase in the history of rural settlement came to an end which dated back, in western Europe at least, to the metal ages, if not to the beginning of the Neolithic period. Second, in chronological terms at least, the birth of the village was closely linked to the general establishment of the 'feudal system'. Finally, there was a long period of population growth which

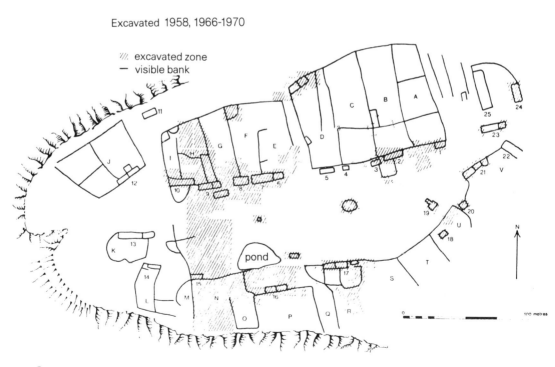

Excavated 1958, 1966-1970

/// excavated zone
— visible bank

Fig. III. *The deserted village of West Whelpington (Northumberland)*

The earliest buildings date to the twelfth to thirteenth centuries. The classic phase of population decline in the later medieval centuries resulted in reorganization of the settlement between 1400 and 1550. The buildings in use at that time were mixed houses, 4.6m (15ft) wide by 11–16m (36–52ft) long, built in stone and thatched. In the sections reserved for humans, there was always a central open hearth, whilst in the part used by animals, which opened on to the living room and was separated from it only by a paved passage linking a door in each of the two longer sides, the floor was paved and contained an axial drain.

These classic mixed houses were rebuilt in the second half of the seventeenth century. The number of farming units declined, and the farm lands were progressively abandoned. The mixed house continued in use, but it shows a development known from elsewhere, especially in the post-medieval period: the byre section was enlarged, a partition was built between the two parts of the house, and the open hearth was moved up against the internal partition wall. Various outbuildings were added, but at no time during the life of the village, which was abandoned around 1720, were animals stabled anywhere but inside the mixed houses.

The development of the West Whelpington houses in the post-medieval period is more interesting by virtue of the fact that few rural sites of this period have been excavated. It is a good example of the late survival of the mixed house in a number of European regions and of its later evolution.

The reasons for the late survival of this form of dwelling may vary from one region to another, but one is probably constant: the relationship between dwelling form and the type of agriculture practised (and in particular the role of stock rearing).

After it was abandoned in the eighteenth century, this medieval village was invaded by grass. As with many comparable English examples, West Whelpington shows up well on oblique air photographs (a), on which it is possible to distinguish the general plan of the site and the stone enclosures with houses on their shorter sides. The working of a quarry, to be seen to the right of the photograph, led to a rescue excavation starting in 1958. The site plan (b) combines excavation data and structures visible on the ground. When compared with the air photograph, it shows how aerial photography can be an indispensable tool in cases of this kind and a priceless aid to historians of the village. The fragile nature of the evidence is also apparent.

(M. G. Jarrett and S. Wrathmell, Sixteenth- and seventeenth-century farmsteads: West Whelpington, Northumberland, *The Agricultural History Review*, 25 (1977), fig. 3, p. 114. Photograph: Cambridge University Collection)

---

undeniably formed the basis of one fundamental aspect of subsequent rural history, and one of the most characteristic features of European history until the Industrial Revolution.

The phenomenon was thus a significant one, by virtue of the discontinuity that it represents and also of its later consequences. Building types as well as their disposition and the materials used in them very clearly illustrate the contrasts between the early Middle Ages, directly linked with the Iron Age or earlier periods, and the eighteenth or nineteenth centuries. Although all historians are in agreement that the peasants, constituting as they did the overwhelming majority of the population, should form the basis of historical researches, they do not always have at their disposal the documentary resources needed to define the main lines of medieval rural history.

It is necessary to reiterate that a history of the Middle Ages based on documentary sources runs up against a major obstacle: the unequal distribution of texts as between one end of the period and the other, and the resulting inaccuracy or inadequacy of those facts needed for a study of the major factors in rural history, such as villages and buildings. It is far from our intention to ignore or to belittle the contribution of written sources: they remain irreplaceable as a data base, even for certain aspects of the early Middle Ages. They are no longer adequate, however, for two reasons. First, medieval archaeology has come of age in most countries of Europe. It has produced results and will yield many more in the years to come, and these results are becoming more and more appropriate for integration into historical studies.

This leads directly on to the second reason why archaeology will henceforth play a major role in understanding many aspects of medieval history. It is no longer merely used to illustrate history as defined by the study of written sources alone – the quick sketch, slight or uncertain in content used by historians in an almost casual way to brighten up their lectures. In the future, medieval archaeology will construct from a growing data base its own structure of problems for solution, designed both to enrich its own documentation and to exploit that documentation. It will throw light on aspects that historians are incapable of recognizing. Finally, it will increasingly have recourse to documentary sources in order to extract original or unrecognized data from them – data which have often been passed over by historians or which they have been unable to make use of without supporting data from archaeology. In return, documentary studies will often invoke archaeological help, reorientating both conclusions and methods of approach as well as the selection of areas for research.

The independence of archaeological reasoning is an elementary factor which is largely explicable in terms of the very nature of the documents available to archaeologists and their processes of research. Archive and record offices ensure that the basic documentation for historians will pass to their successors with a considerable degree of certainty, and probably in its entirety. In these circumstances any piece of work is reproducible. For the archaeologist the situation is altogether different, and this has a profound influence on his documentary practices and on his relationship with his documentation. In practical terms archaeological sites cannot be protected in the same way as archives by being brought together. Nor is legislative protection *in situ* conceivable in economic terms. The very act of investigation archaeologically is one of destruction. It is impossible to ensure that they will be handed down to our successors, in either quantitative or qualitative terms. Moreover the daily life of modern European societies is regularly destroying a non-renewable form of documentation. Account must be taken of these fundamental facts: they strongly condition the work of the archaeologist and, as a consequence, his working methods (see Figure III).

In the pages above we have attempted, at the same time as demonstrating the importance to the history of western Europe of a single phenomenon, the birth of the village, to give an account of the reciprocal contributions of archaeology and documentary sources and their fundamental interconnections. The science of history tends to proceed in leaps, which are often the result of a fresh examination of classic documentary data or of the introduction of new information. Whilst the results contributed individually by archaeology and textual study are of great interest, it is essential to understand how it has recently become possible to synthesize results from original documents and the fresh study of sources. Historical knowledge is a continuous process of interrogation. The picture we have painted of the history of the village and the house in western Europe is heavily dependent upon the current state of disciplines that are in the process of evolution, documentary studies and archaeology, or, in other words, history. It is essential to take account of this fact in order to give due weight to the results and to take account of what is to come.

It is also necessary to understand it in order to grasp the undeniably specific nature of the main documentary orientations. Archaeology is an independent discipline, at least so far as its techniques of data acquisition are concerned – an historical discipline, certainly, but to a considerable extent autonomous in its application. Synthesis is essential in the long run, but both the historian working on archives and the archaeologist excavating the village must to the best of his ability become master of his working methods, work on his data and confirm them – all this before bringing the two sets of data together. This is precisely what we have attempted to do.

Bibliography

This bibliography contains only basic material. The intention is to provide, so far as possible, an overview of the complete bibliography relating to this subject in all the countries covered in the book. For each example given in the main text, the original reference is given in the bibliography so that it may be consulted if required. For volumes of proceedings or essays only the name of the editor and the title of the work is given, without listing the articles in detail. [The present bibliography reproduces that in the original French edition, published in 1980; a number of more recent works have been added, to bring it reasonably up to date, while preserving the authors' intentions as to the function of the bibliography. *Translator*]

The references are subdivided under the following headings:

1 Sources and their use
2 Works of reference relating to economic and social aspects
3 Men, animals, plants and climate
4 General conditions of settlement of the land
5 Land allotment systems
6 Churches and castles
7 The village
8 Excavation reports
9 Rural buildings – types, techniques and materials

1   Sources and their use

Bautier, R. H. & Sornay, J., *Les sources de l'histoire économique et sociale de la France . . .* (1968) [covers Provence, the Comtat, the Dauphiné, and Savoy]

Beresford, M. W. & St Joseph, J. K. S., *Medieval England: an aerial survey*, 2nd ed., Cambridge (1979)

de Bouärd, M., *Manuel de l'archéologie médiévale*, Paris (1975)

Chertier, B., Prospection au sol et prospection aérienne en Champagne, *Annales Fac. Lettres de Toulouse*, Trav. Inst. art préhist., V (1962)

Chevallier, R., Un document fondamental pour l'histoire et la géographie agraires: la photographie aérienne, *Études rurales*, I (1961)

332

Clarke, H., *The archaeology of medieval England*, London (1984)

Crawford, O. G. S., *Archaeology in the field*, 3rd ed., London (1953)

Fossier, R., *Censiers, terriers, et polyptyques* (Typologie des sources du Moyen Age occidental), Paris (1978)

Gille, B., Recherches sur les instruments de labour au Moyen Age, *Bibliothèque de l'École des Chartes* CXX (1962)

Giot, P.-R., La céramique onctueuse de Cornouailles: contribution à l'étude de l'économie médiévale, *Bull. Soc. archéolog. du Finistère* 97 (1971) pp.109–30.

Haudricourt, A. G., & Bruhnes-Delamare, G., *L'homme et la charrue à travers le monde*, Paris (1953)

Jalmain, D., *Archéologie aérienne en Ile-de-France*, Paris (1970)

Leser, P., *Entstehung und Verbreitung des Pfluges*, 2nd ed. (1971)

Platt, C. P. S., *Medieval archaeology in England: a guide to the historical sources*, Salfleet (1969)

Potiers de Saintonge (Catalogue of the exhibition at the Musée des Arts et Traditions populaires, Paris, 1975)

St. Joseph, J. K. S., *The uses of air photography*, London (1966)

Salin, E., *La civilisation mérovingienne*, 4 vols., Paris (1950–59)

Taylor, C. C., *Fieldwork in medieval archaeology*, London (1974)

White jr., L., *Medieval technology and social change*, Oxford (1965)

Wilson D. M. (ed.), *The archaeology of Anglo-Saxon England*, London (1976)

Wilson, D. R., *Air photo interpretation for archaeologists*, London (1982)

2 Works of reference relating to economic and social aspects

Abel, W., *Geschichte der deutschen Landwirtschaft vom frühen Mittelalter bis zum 19. Jahrhundert*, Berlin (1967)

Agricoltura e mondo rurale in Occidente nell'alto Medioevo: Settimane di studio . . . Spoleto, XIII (1965–66)

Bloch, M., *Les caractères originaux de l'histoire rurale française*, Oslo and Paris (1929)

Bonnassie, P., *La Catalogne du milieu du Xe à la fin du XIe siècle* (1975)

Crossley, D. W. (ed.), *Medieval industry*, CBA Research Report 40 (1981)

Deléage, A., *La vie économique et sociale de la Bourgogne dans le haut Moyen Age*, 3 vols., Paris (1941)

Dion, R., *Essai sur la formation du paysage rural français* (1934)

Duby, G., *L'économie rurale et la vie des campagnes dans l'Occident médiéval*, 2 vols., Paris (1962)

Foote, P. G., & Wilson, D. M., *The Viking achievement*, 2nd ed., London (1973)

Fossier, R., *La terre et les hommes en Picardie jusqu'à la fin du XIIIe siècle*, Paris and Louvain (1968)

Fournier, G., *Le peuplement rural en Basse-Auvergne durant le haut Moyen Age*, Paris (1962)

Histoire de la France rurale, 4 vols., Paris (1975–76)

Hodges, R., *Dark Age economics: the origins of towns and trade* AD 600–1000, London (1982)

Hodges, R. and Whitehouse, D., *Mohammed, Charlemagne & the origins of Europe*, London (1983)

Krüger, B. (ed.), *Die Germanen*, 2 vols., Berlin (1983)

Miller, E., La société rurale en Angleterre (Xe-XIIe siècle), *Settimane di studio ... Spoleto*, XIII (1965–66)

Miller, E., & Hatcher, J., *Medieval England: rural society and economic change 1086-1348*, London and New York (1978)

Musset, L., *Les peuples scandinaves au Moyen Age*, Paris (1951)

Roupnel, G., *Histoire de la campagne française*, Paris (1932; reprinted 1973)

TeBrake, W. H., Ecology and economy in medieval Frisia, *Viator*, 9 (1978), pp.1–29

Toubert, P., *Les structures du Latium médiéval*, Paris (1973)

3 Men, animals, plants and climate

Acsadi, G., *History of human life span and mortality*, Budapest (1970)

Daugas, J. P. & Tixier, L., Variations paléoclimatiques de la Limagne de l'Auvergne, *Géologie méditerranéenne* (1977)

Fossier, R., Remarques sur les mouvements du peuplement en Champagne méridionale à la fin du Moyen Age, *Bibl. École des Chartes* (1964)

Fugedi, E., Pour une analyse démographique de la Hongrie, *Annales* (1969)

Hooper, M., Historical ecology, *Landscapes and documents*, London (1974), pp.41–8

Lamb, H. H., *Climate: present, past and future*, London (1977)

Lange, E., *Botanische Beiträge zur mitteleuropäischen Siedlungsgeschichte: Ergebnisse zur Wirtschaft und Kulturlandschaft im frühgeschichtlicher Zeit*, Berlin (1971)

Le Goff, J. & Biraben, N., La peste dans le haut Moyen Age, *Annales* (1969)

Leroy-Ladurie, E., *Histoire du climat depuis l'an mil*, Paris (1967)

de Lumley, H. & Demians-d'Archimbaud, G., Le paysage et le climat en Languedoc méditerranéen à la fin du IVe et au début du Ve siècle de notre ère, *Études quaternaires*, 1 (1972), pp.371–3

Nemeskeri, J., Die archäologischen und anthropologischen Voraussetzungen paläodemographischer Forschungen, *Prähistorische Zeitschrift*, 47 (1972), pp.5 et seq.

Noel, R., *Les dépots de pollens fossiles* (Typologie des sources du Moyen Age occidental), Paris, 1972

Parry, M. L., *Climatic change, agriculture and settlement*, Folkestone (1978)

Piponnier, F., Recherches sur la consommation alimentaire en Bourgogne au XIVe siècle, *Annales de Bourgogne*, 46 (1974)

Russell, J. C., *Late ancient and medieval population*, Philadelphia (1958)

4   General conditions of settlement of the land

Archéologie du village médiéval, Louvain and Ghent (1967)

Beresford, M. W. & St Joseph, J. K. S., *Medieval England: an aerial survey*, 2nd ed., Cambridge (1979)

Boussard, J., Essai sur le peuplement de la Touraine du Ier au VIIIe siècle, *Le Moyen Age*, 40 (1954)

Cagiano de Azevedo, M., Ville rustiche tardoantiche e installazioni agricole altomedioevali, *Settimane di studio . . . Spoleto*, XIII (1965–66)

Cunliffe, B. W., Chalton, Hants: the evolution of a landscape, *Antiquaries Journal*, 53 (1973), pp.173–90

Cunliffe, B. W., Saxon and medieval settlement-pattern in the region of Chalton, Hampshire, *Medieval archaeology*, 16 (1972), 1–12

Dion, R., *Histoire de la vigne et du vin en France des origines au XIXe siècle*, Paris (1959)

Dion, R., *La part de la géographie et celle de l'histoire dans l'explication de l'habitat rural dans le Bassin Parisien*, Publications de la Société de Géographie de Lille (1946)

Donat, P. & Ulrich, H., Einwohnerzählen und Siedlungsgrösse der Merowingerzeit. Ein methodischer Beitrag zur demographischen Rekonstruktion frühgeschichtlicher Bevölkerungen, *Zeitschrift für Archäologie*, 5 (1971), 234–65

Jankuhn, H., *Archäologie und Geschichte. I: Beiträge zur siedlungsarchäologischen Forschung*, Berlin and New York (1976)

Jankuhn, H., *Einführung in die Siedlungsarchäologie*, Berlin and New York (1977)

Platt, C. P. S., *Medieval Britain from the air*, London (1984)

Roberts, B. K., *Rural settlement in Britain*, London (1977)

Rowley, T. (ed.), *The origins of open field agriculture*, London (1981)

5   Land allotment systems

Abel, W., *Die Wüstungen des ausgehenden Mittelalters. Ein Beitrag zur Siedlung- und Agrargeschichte Deutschlands*, Jena (1943)

Ault, W., *Open-field farming in medieval England*, London (1972)

Bowen, H. C., *Ancient fields: a tentative analysis of vanishing earthworks and landscapes*, London (1965)

Bradford, J., *Ancient landscapes: studies in field archaeology*, London (1957)

Brunet, P., Problèmes relatifs aux structures agraires de la basse Normandie, *Annales de Normandie*, 5 (1955)

Cantor, L. (ed.), *The English medieval landscape*, London (1982)

Chapelot, J., L'étude des terroirs fossiles. Orientations méthodiques et résultats récents de l'archéologie médiévale en Europe du Nord-Ouest, *Actes du Colloque Archéologie du Paysage*, Tours (1977), pp.396–419

Chaumeuil, L., L'origine du bocage en Bretagne, *Mélanges . . . Lucien Febvre*, I (1954)

Dodgshon, R. A., *The origin of British field systems: an interpretation*, London and New York (1980)

Flatres, P., Les anciennes structures rurales en Bretagne d'après le cartulaire de Redon, *Etudes rurales*, 10 (1972)

Hewlett, G., Reconstructing a historical landscape from field and documentary evidence, *Agricultural History Review*, 21 (1973), 94–110

Hoskins, W. G., *The making of the English landscape*, London (1955)

Hoskins, W. G., *English landscape*, London (1973)

Janssen, W., *Studien zur Wüstungsfrage im fränkischen Altsiedelland zwischen Rhein, Mosel, und Eifelnordrand*, Cologne (1975)

Juillard, E., Formes et structures parcellaires dans la plaine d'Alsace . . ., *Bulletin de l'Association des géographes français* (1953), pp.72–7

Näsman, U. & Wegraeus, E., *Eketorp – fortification and settlement in Öland, Sweden. 2: The setting*, Stockholm (1979)

Nielsen, V., Iron Age plough-marks in Store Vildmose, North Jutland, *Tools and Tillage*, 1:3 (1970)

Orwin, C. S. & Orwin, C. S., *The open fields*, 3rd ed., Oxford (1967)

de Planhol, X., Essai sur la genèse du paysage rural en champs ouverts, *Annales de l'Est*, 21 (1959)

Proudfoot, V. B., The economy of the Irish rath, *Medieval archaeology*, 5 (1961), 94–122

Rowley, T. (ed.), *Anglo-Saxon settlement and landscape*, Oxford (1974)

Steensberg, A., *Ancient harvesting implements*, Copenhagen (1943)

Steensberg, A., Østergaard Christensen, J. L. & Nielsen, S., *Atlas over en del af middelalderlandsbyen Borups agre i Borupris skov ved Tystrup sø, Sjælland*, Copenhagen (1968)

Taylor, C. C., *Fields in the English landscape*, London (1974)

6 Churches and castles

Barker, P. A. & Higham, R., *Hen Domen, Montgomery. A timber castle on the English-Welsh border, I* (Royal Archaeological Institute Monograph), London (1982)

de Bouärd, M., Quelques données françaises et normandes concernant le problème de l'origine des mottes, *Château-Gaillard*, 2 (1967)

Bur, M., Essai de typologie de l'habitat seigneurial dans l'Argonne aux XIe et XIIe siecles d'après les vestiges relevés sur le terrain, *La construction au Moyen Age* (Congrès des médiévistes 1972), Paris (1973)

Decaens, J., Les enceintes d'Urville et de Bretteville-sur-Laize, *Annales de Normandie*, 18 (1968)

Decaens, J., Un nouveau cimetière du haut Moyen Age en Normandie: Hérouvillette (Calvados), *Archéologie médiévale*, I (1971)

Duparc, P., Le cimetière séjour des vivants (XIe–XIIe siècles), *Bull. philologique et historique* (1964)

Fossier, R., *Chartes de coutume en Picardie (XIe–XIIIe siècles)*, Paris (1975)

Fournier, G., *Châteaux, villages et villes d'Auvergne au XVe siècle, d'après l'Armorial de Guillaume Revel*, Paris (1973)

Martin-Lorber, O., Une communauté d'habitants dans une seigneurie de Cîteaux aux XIIIe et XIVe siècles, *Annales de Bourgogne*, 30 (1958)

Mayes, P. & Butler, L. A. S., *Sandal Castle excavations 1964–73*, Wakefield (1983)

Morris, R. K., *The church in British archaeology*, CBA Research Report 47 (1983)

Pesez, J. M. & Piponnier, F., Les maisons fortes bourguignonnes, *Château-Gaillard*, 5 (1972)

Platt, C. P. S., *The parish churches of medieval England*, London (1981)

Platt, C. P. S., *The castle in medieval England and Wales*, London (1982)

Renn, D. F., *Norman castles in Britain*, London (1968)

Rodwell, W. J., *The archaeology of the English church*, London (1981)

7 The village

Agache, R., *La Somme pré-romaine et romaine*, Amiens (1978)

Beresford, M. W. & Hurst, J. G., *Deserted medieval villages*, London (1971)

Beresford, M. W., *The lost villages of England*, 4th ed., London (1963)

Constantinescu, N., Le stade et les perspectives de la recherche archéologique du village médiéval de Roumanie, *Dacia*, 8 (1964), pp.265–78

Demians-d'Archimbaud, G., *Rougiers, village médiéval de Provence. Approche archéologique d'une société rurale méditerranéenne*, Thèse de doctorat d'Etat, University of Paris I, March 1978

Harmand, J., *Les origines des recherches françaises sur l'habitat rural gallo-romain*, Brussels (1961)

Hilton, R. H., Villages désertés et histoire économique: recherches françaises et anglaises, *Études rurales*, 32 (1968)

Hurst, J. G., The changing medieval village in England, in P. J. Ucko (ed.), *Man, settlement and urbanism*, London (1972), pp.531–40

Janssen, W., Research on medieval settlement sites in the Rhineland, *Report of the Medieval Village Research Group*, 29 (1981), 36–40

Piboule, P., Les souterrains aménagés de la France, *Archáeologie médiévale*, 8 (1978), pp.117–63

Raymon, V., Les villages perchés d'Outre-Siagne, *Bull. philologique et historique* (1966)

Rivet, A. L. F. (ed.), *The Roman villa in Britain*, London (1969)

Roberts, B. K., Village plans in County Durham: a preliminary statement, *Medieval archaeology*, 16 (1972), pp.35–56

Roberts, B. K., *Village plans*, Aylesbury (1982)

Rowley, T., *Villages in the landscape*, London (1978)

Rowley, T. & Wood, J., *Deserted villages*, Aylesbury (1982)

Sawyer, P. H. (ed.), *Medieval settlement: continuity and change*, London (1976)

Villages désertés et histoire économique, Paris (1965)

8 Excavation reports

Addyman, P. V., A Dark Age settlement at Maxey, Northants, *Medieval archaeology*, 8 (1964), pp.20–73

Addyman, P. V., Leigh, D. & Hughes, M. J., Anglo-Saxon houses at Chalton, Hampshire, *ibid.*, 16 (1972), pp.13–31

Addyman, P. V. & Leigh, D., The Anglo-Saxon village at Chalton, Hampshire. Second interim report, *ibid.*, 17 (1973), pp.1–25

Alcock, L., *Dinas Powys: an Iron Age, Dark Age and early medieval settlement in Glamorgan*, Cardiff (1963)

André, P., Bertrand, R. & Clément, M., En Morbihan, permanence d'un type d'habitat: la maison à pignons en abside, *Archéologia*, August 1976, pp.28–36

Andrews, D. D. & Milne, G., *Wharram: a study of settlement in the Yorkshire Wolds. Vol. 1: Domestic settlement. Part 1: Areas 10 and 6*, Society of Medieval Archaeology Monograph 8 (1979)

Archéologie du village déserté, 2 vols, Paris (1970) [study of deserted villages of Condorcet, Dracy, Montaigut, and Saint-Jean-le-Froid]

Atti del Colloquio Internazionale di Archeologia Medievale, Palermo-Erice, 20–22 settembre 1974, 2 vols., Palermo

Beresford, G., *The medieval clay-land village: excavations at Goltho and Barton Blount*, Society for Medieval Archaeology Monograph 6 (1975)

Beresford, G., Three deserted medieval sites on Dartmoor: a report on the late E. Marie Minter's excavations, *Medieval Archaeology*, 23 (1979), 98–158

Beresford, M. W., Wharram Percy: a case study in microtopography, in P. H. Sawyer (ed.), *Medieval settlement*, London (1976), pp.114–44

Bertrand, R. & Lucas, M., Un village côtier du XIIe siècle en Bretagne: Pen er Malo en Guidel (Morbihan), *Archéologie médiévale*, 5 (1975), pp.73–102

Biddle, M., The deserted medieval village of Seacourt, Berks, *Oxoniensia*, 26–27 (1961–62), pp.70–201

Blomqvist, R. & Mårtensson, A., *Thule grävningen*, Lund (1965)

Charmasson, J., L'oppidum bas-rhodanien de Lombren (Gard): l'habitat paléochrétien, *Cahiers rhodaniens*, 9 (1962), pp.64–102

Cunliffe, B. W., Manor Farm, Chalton, Hants, *Post-medieval archaeology*, 7 (1973), pp.31–59

Dannheimer, H., Die frühmittelalterliche Siedlung bei Kirchheim, Lk. München, Oberbayern: Vorbericht über die Untersuchungen im Jahre 1970, *Germania*, 51 (1973), pp.152–69

Davison, B. K., The Late Saxon town of Thetford: an interim report on the 1964–1966 excavations, *Medieval archaeology*, 11 (1967), pp.189–208

Demians-d'Archimbaud, G., Artisanat et échanges en Provence médiévale d'après les fouilles d'habitat rural, *Atti del colloquio internazionale di archeologia medievale ... 1974*, Palermo (1976), pp.3–12

Demians-d'Archimbaud, G., Monnaies, céramiques et chronologie: essai d'analyse des fouilles de Rougiers (Var), *Provence historique*, tome 25, fascicule 100 (1976), pp.227–41

Demolon, P., *Le village mérovingien de Brébières (VIe–VIIe siècles)*, Arras (1972)

van Doordelaer, A. & Verhaeghe, F., *Excavations at the 14th century village of Roeselare (Sint Margriete), East Flanders, Belgium*, Dissertationes Archaeologicae Gandenses 15, Bruges (1974)

Dudley, D. & Minter, E. M., The medieval village at Garrow Tor, Bodmin Moor, Cornwall, *Medieval archaeology*, 6–7 (1962–63), pp.274–94

van Es, W., *Wijster: a native village beyond the imperial frontier 150–425 AD*, Groningen (1967)

van Es, W., Dorestad, *R.O.B. Overdrukken*, 105 (1978)

van Es, W. & Verwers, W. J. H., *Excavations at Dorestad 1. The harbour: Hoogstraat 1*, Amersfoort (1980)

Fehring, G. P., Grabungen in Siedlungsbereichen des 3. bis 13. Jahrhundert sowie am Töpferofen des Wüstung Wülfingen-am-Kocher, *Château-Gaillard*, 3 (1969), pp.48–60

Fox, A., A monastic homestead on Dean Moor, South Devon, *Medieval archaeology*, 2 (1958), pp.141–57

Frere, S. S. & Hartley, D. R., Fouilles de Lezoux (Puy-de-Dôme) en 1963, *Cahiers de civilisation médiévale*, 9 (1966), pp.557–63 [sunken huts with pisé walls]

Gelling, P. S., Medieval shielings on the Isle of Man, *Medieval archaeology*, 6–7 (1962–63), pp.156–72

Grimm, P., *Hohenrode, eine mittelalterliche Siedlung im Südharz*, Berlin (1939)

Grimm, P., *Tilleda, eine Königspfalz am Kyffhäuser. Teil 1: Die Hauptburg*, Berlin (1968)

Grimm, P., The Royal Palace at Tilleda: excavations from 1935–1966, *Medieval archaeology*, 12 (1968), pp.83–100

Grimm, P., Beiträge zu Handwerk und Handel in der Vorburg der Pfalz Tilleda, *Zeitschrift für Archäologie* (1972), pp.107–47

Haarnagel, W., *Die Grabung Feddersen Wierde: Methode, Hausbau, Siedlungs- und Wirtschaftsformen sowie Sozialstruktur*, Wiesbaden (1979)

Hamilton, J. R. C., *Excavations at Jarlshof, Shetland*, London (1956)

Heidinga, H. A., *Verdwenen dorpen in het Kootwijkerzand*, Amsterdam (1976)

Herrmann, J., *Die germanischen und slawischen Siedlungen und das mittelalterliche Dorf von Tornow, Kr. Calau*, Berlin (1973)

Hilton, R. H. & Rahtz, P. A., Upton, Gloucestershire, 1959–1964, *Transactions of the Bristol & Gloucestershire Archaeological Society*, 85 (1966), pp.70–146

Holden, E. W., Excavations at the deserted medieval village of Hangleton, Part I, *Sussex Archaeological Collections*, 101 (1963), pp.54–181

Hugoniot, E., Une aire d'habitation à Bruère-Allichamps (Cher), *Revue archéologique du Centre* (1969), pp.III–132

Hurst, J. G. & Hurst, D. G., Excavations at the deserted medieval village of Hangleton, Part II, *Sussex Archaeological Collections*, 102 (1964), pp.94–142

Hurst, J. G. & Hurst, D. G., Excavations at the medieval village of Wythemail, Northamptonshire, *Medieval archaeology*, 13 (1969), pp.167–203

Jankuhn, H., *Haithabu: ein Handelplatz der Wikingerzeit*, 4th ed., Neumünster (1963)

Janssen, W., *Königshagen: ein archäologisch-historischer Beitrag zur Siedlungsgeschichte des südwestlichen Harzvorlandes*, Hildesheim (1965)

Jones, M. U. & Jones, W. T., The crop-mark sites at Mucking, Essex, in R. L. S. Bruce-Mitford (ed.), *Recent archaeological excavations in Europe*, London (1975), pp.135–86

Jones, W. T. & Jones, M. U., The early Saxon landscape at Mucking, Essex, in R. T. Rowley (ed.), *Anglo-Saxon settlement and landscape*, Oxford (1974), pp.20–35

Jope, E. M. & Threlfall, R. I., Excavation of a medieval settlement at Beere, North Tawton, Devon, *Medieval archaeology*, 2 (1958), pp.112–40

Klingelhofer, E. C., *The deserted medieval village of Broadfield, Herts*, Oxford (1974)

Kramer, W., Frühmittelalterliche Siedlung bei Burgheim, Landkreis Neuburg a.d. Donau, *Germania*, 29 (1951), pp.139 et seq.

Mallett, M. & Whitehouse, D., Castel Porciano: an abandoned medieval village of the Roman Campagna, *Papers of the British School at Rome*, 35 (1967), pp.113–46

Medieval Village Research Group (Deserted M.V.R.G. until 1970), *Annual Reports* from 1953 (No 1)

Müller-Wille, M., Eine Niederungsburg bei Haus Meer, Gemeinde Büderich, Kr. Grevenbroich, *Rheinische Ausgrabungen*, 1 (1968), pp.1056

Nørlund, P. & Stenberger, M., *Brattahlid: Researches into Norse culture in Greenland*, Copenhagen (1934)

Nørlund, P., *Trelleborg*, Copenhagen (1948)

Olsen, O. & Schmidt, A., *Fyrkat: en jysk vikingeborg I*, Copenhagen (1977)

O'Riordain, B., Excavations at High Street and Winetavern Street, Dublin, *Medieval archaeology*, 15 (1971), pp.73–85

Pesez, J. M., Brucato et la civilisation matérielle du village en Sicilie médiévale, *Mélanges de l'École française de Rome, Moyen Age*, 86 (1974)

Pesez, J. M., Une maison villageoise au XIVe siècle: les structures, *Rotterdam Papers*, 2 (1975), pp.139–50

Piponnier, F., Une maison villageoise au XIVc siècle: le mobilier, *ibid.*, pp.151–70

Rahtz, P. A., Upton, Gloucestershire, 1964–1968: Second interim report, *Transactions of the Bristol and Gloucestershire Archaeological Society*, 88 (1969), pp.74–112

Ramskou, T., Lindholm Høje, *Acta Archaeologica*, 18 (1957), pp.193 et seq.

Roesdahl, E., *Fyrkat: en jysk vikingeborg II*, Copenhagen (1977)

Sage, W., *Die frankische Siedlung bei Gladbach, Kr. Neuwied*, Rheinisches Landesmuseum Bonn, Kleine Museumhefte 7 (1969)

Scapula, J., *Un haut lieu archéologique de la Haute Vallée de la Seine: la Butte d'Isle-Aumont en Champagne*, I, Troyes (1975)

Schietzel, K., *Stand der Siedlungsarchäologischen Forschung in Haithabu – Ergebnisse und Probleme*, Neumünster (1981)

Schweitzer, J., Leibersheim, *Bulletin du Musée d'Histoire de Mulhouse*, 83 (1975–76), pp.67–145

Scollar, I., Verhaeghe, F., & Gautier, A., *A medieval site at Lampernisse, West Flanders*, Dissertationes Archaeologicae Gandenses 13 (1970)

Steane, J.M. & Bryant, G.P., Excavations at the deserted medieval settlement at Lyveden, *Journal of the Northampton Museums and Art Gallery*, 12 (1975)

Steensberg, A., *Borup AD 700–1400: a deserted settlement and its fields in South Zealand, Denmark*, 2 vols., Copenhagen (1983)

Stenberger, M., *Vallhagar: a migration period settlement on Gotland, Sweden*, 2 vols., Copenhagen (1955)

Stenberger, M., *Eketorp: eine befestigte eisenzeitliche Siedlung auf Öland*, Göttingen (1970)

Thompson, F. H., The deserted medieval village of Riseholme, near Lincoln, and a description of some trial excavations on the site, *Medieval archaeology*, 4 (1960), pp.95–108

Trimpe-Burger, J.A., Oost-Souburg, Province of Zeeland: a preliminary report on the excavation of the site of an ancient fortress (1969–1971), *Berichten van R.O.B.*, 23 (1973), pp.355–66

van de Walle, A., Excavations in the ancient centre of Antwerp, *Medieval archaeology*, 5 (1961), pp.123–36

Waterbolk, H. T., The Bronze Age settlements of Elp, *Helinium*, 4 (1964), pp.97–131

Waterbolk, H. T., Odoorn im frühen Mittelalter: Bericht der Grabung 1966, *Neue Ausgrabungen und Forschungen in Niedersachsen*, 8 (1973), pp.25–89

West, S. E., The Anglo-Saxon village of West Stow: an interim report of the excavations, 1965–68, *Medieval archaeology*, 13 (1969), pp.1–20

Whitehouse, D., Excavations at Satriano, a deserted medieval village in Basilicata, *Papers of the British School at Rome*, 38 (1970)

Willems, J., Le quartier artisanal gallo-romain et mérovingien de 'Batta' à Huy, *Archaeologica Belgica*, 148 (1973)

Winkelmann, W., Eine westfälische Siedlung des 8. Jahrhunderts bei Warendorf, Kr. Warendorf, *Germania*, 32 (1954), pp.189–213

Winkelmann, W., Die Ausgrabungen in der frühmittelalterlichen Siedlung bei Warendorf, Westfalen, *Neue Ausgrabungen in Deutschland*, Berlin (1958), pp.492–517

Zimmermann, W. H., A Roman Iron Age and Early Migration settlement at Flögeln, Kr. Wesermünde, Lower Saxony, in T. Rowley (ed.), *Anglo-Saxon settlement and landscape*, Oxford (1974), pp.57–73

9 Rural buildings – types, techniques and materials

Addyman, P. V., The Anglo-Saxon house: a new review, *Anglo-Saxon England*, 1 (1972), pp.273–307

Ahrens, C., *Frühe Holzkirchen im nördlichen Europa*, Hamburg (1981)

Alcock, N. W. (ed), *Cruck construction: an introduction and catalogue*, CBA Research Report 42 (1981)

Alcock, N. W. & Laithwaite, M., Medieval houses in Devon and their modernization, *Medieval archaeology*, 17 (1973), pp.100–25

Bans, J.-C., Le granges 'à courbes' de l'Ancien Régime en Limousin, *Revue Félibréenne et Régionaliste Lemouzi*, 72 (1979), pp.3–20

Barker, P. A., Some aspects of the excavations of complex timber buildings, *World archaeology*, 1 (1969), pp.220–35

Barley, M. W., *The English farmhouse and cottage*, London (1961)

de Bouärd, M., Note sur les matériaux de couverture utilisés en Normandie au Moyen Age, *Annales de Normandie*, 15 (1965), pp.415–36

Branigan, K., The origins of cruck construction: a new clue, *Medieval archaeology*, 12 (1968), pp.1–11

Brunskill, R. W., Distribution of building materials and some plan types in the domestic vernacular architecture of England and Wales, *Transactions of the Ancient Monuments Society*, 23 (1979), pp.42–65

Bugge, A., Origin, development, and decline of the Norwegian stave church, *Acta Archaeologica*, 6 (1935)

Capelle, T., 'Schiffsförmige' Hausgrundrisse in frühgeschichtlicher Zeit, *Frühmittelalterliche Studien*, 3 (1969), pp.244–56

Chapelot, O., La construction rurale en Bourgogne, in *La construction au Moyen Age*, Paris (1973), pp.239–57

Chapelot, O., La fourniture de la pierre sur les chantiers bourguignonnes (XIVe–XVe siècles), *Actes du 98e Congrès des Sociétés Savantes: Archéologie*, Paris (1977), pp.209–24

Chapelot, O., *Les matériaux de construction en Bourgogne (1340–1475)*, Thèse de troisième cycle, University of Paris I, June 1975

Charles, F. W. B., *Medieval cruck-building and its derivatives: a study of timber-framed construction based on buildings in Worcestershire*, Society for Medieval Archaeology Monograph 2 (1967)

Davey, N., *A history of building materials*, London (1961)

Decaens, J., Recherches récentes concernant la maison paysanne en bois au Moyen Age en Europe du Nord-Ouest, in *La construction au Moyen Age*, Paris (1973), pp.125–36

Deffontaines, P., *L'homme et sa maison*, Paris (1972)

Delmas, J., *Les matériaux de couverture* (Catalogue de l'exposition de Rouergue, 1975)

Dolling, H., *Haus und Hof in westgermanischen Volksrechten*, Münster (1958)

Donat, P., Zur Nordausbreitung der slawischen Grubenhäuser, *Zeitschrift für Archäologie*, 4 (1970), pp.250–69 van Es, W., Etablissements ruraux de l'époque romaine et du début du Moyen Age aux Pays-Bas, *IXe Congrès de l'Union des Sciences Pré- et Protohistoriques*, Nice 1976: Colloque XXX: Les relations entre l'empire romain tardif, l'empire franc et ses voisins, pp.114–44

Fehring, G., Zur archäologischen Erforschung mittelalterlicher Dorfsiedlungen in Südwestdeutschland, *Zeitschrift für Agrargeschichte und Agrarsoziologie* (1973), pp.1–35

Field, R. K., Worcestershire peasant buildings, household goods and farming equipment in the later Middle Ages, *Medieval archaeology*, 9 (1965), pp.105–45

Fletcher, J. M. & Spokes, P. S., The origin and development of crown-post roofs, *ibid.*, 8 (1964), pp.152–83

Fox, C. & Raglan, L., *Monmouthshire houses: Part I, Medieval* (1951); *Part II, Sub-medieval houses (c.1550–1610)* (1953)

Guyan, W. U., Einige Karten zur Verbreitung des Grubenhauses in Mitteleuropa im ersten nachchristlichen Jahrtausend, *Jahrbuch der Schweizerischen Gesellschaft für Urgeschichte*, 42 (1952), pp.174–97

Harvey, N., *A history of farm building in England and Wales*, 2nd ed., London (1984)

Herrnbrodt, A., *Der Husterknupp, eine niederrheinische Burganlage des frühen Mittelalters*, Cologne (1958)

Hewett, C.A., Structural carpentry in medieval Essex, *Medieval archaeology*, 6–7 (1962–63), pp.240–71

Hewett, C. A. *The development of carpentry 1200–1700*, Newton Abbot (1969)

Hewett, C. A., *English historic carpentry*, Chichester (1980)

Hinz, H., Zur Geschichte der niederdeutschen Halle, *Zeitschrift für Volkskund*, 60 (1964), pp.1–22

Hurst, J. G., The medieval peasant house, in A. Small (ed.), *The Fourth Viking Congress*, Aberdeen (1965), pp.190–6

Meirion-Jones, G. I., The long house in Brittany: a provisional assessment, *Post-Medieval archaeology*, 7 (1973), pp.1–19

Mcirion-Jones, G. I., *The vernacular architecture of Brittany*, Edinburgh (1982)

Mercer, E., *English vernacular houses*, London (1975)

Müller-Wille, M., Zur mittelalterlichen Besiedlungs- und Wirtschaftgeschichte Grönlands, *Jahrbuch des Römisch-Germanischen Zentralmuseum Mainz*, 19 (1972), pp.155–76

Neveux, H., Recherches sur la construction et l'entretien des maisons à Cambrai de la fin du XIVe au début du XVIIIe siècle, in *Le bâtiment: enquête d'histoire économique XIVe-XIXe siècles*, Paris and The Hague (1971), pp.191–312

Oswald, A., Excavation of a thirteenth century wooden building at Weoley Castle, Birmingham, 1960–1961, *Medieval archaeology*, 6–7 (1963), pp.109–34

Le Patourel, H. E. J., *The moated sites of Yorkshire*, Society for Medieval Archaeology Monograph 5 (1973)

Pesez, J. M., L'habitation paysanne en Bourgogne médiévale, in *La construction au Moyen Age*, Paris (1973), pp.219–38

Radford, C. A. R., The Saxon house: a review and some parallels, *Medieval archaeology*, 1 (1957), pp.27–38

Rahtz, P. A., Buildings and rural settlement, in D. M. Wilson (ed.), *The archaeology of Anglo-Saxon England*, London (1976), pp.49–98

Salzman, L. F., *Building in England down to 1540: a documentary history*, Oxford (1952)

Schmidt, H., The Trelleborg house reconsidered, *Medieval archaeology*, 17 (1973), pp.52–77

Schmidt, H., *Trelleborghuset og Fyrkathuset*, Copenhagen (1981)

Smith, J. T., Cruck construction: a survey of the problems, *Medieval archaeology*, 8 (1964), pp.119–51

Smith, J.T., The reliability of typological dating of medieval English roofs, in R. Berger (ed.), *Scientific methods in medieval archaeology*, Berkeley–Los Angeles–London (1970), pp.239–69

Smith, P., *Houses of the Welsh countryside*, London (1975)

Steensberg, A., *Bondehuse og Vandmøller in Danmark gennem 2000 aar*, Copenhagen (1952)

Zimmermann, W., 'Ecclesia lignea' und 'ligneis tabulis fabricata', *Bonner Jahrbücher*, 158 (1958), pp.414–53

Zippelius, A., Das vormittelalterliche dreischiffige Hallehaus in Mitteleuropa, *ibid.*, 153–154 (1953–54), pp.13–45

Zippelius, A., Zur Frage der Dachkonstruktion bei den Holzbauten von Haithabu, *Berichte über die Ausgrabungen in Haithabu*, 1 (1969), pp.61–72

Index

Index

Index

Index

Index